DISCARDED

William Penn
A Topical Biography

WILLIAM PENN THE FOUNDER

WILLIAM PENN
A Topical Biography

By William I. Hull

F
152.2
H936
1971

LAMAR UNIVERSITY LIBRARY

710487

BOOKS FOR LIBRARIES PRESS
FREEPORT, NEW YORK

First Published 1937
Reprinted 1971

INTERNATIONAL STANDARD BOOK NUMBER:
0-8369-6654-6

LIBRARY OF CONGRESS CATALOG CARD NUMBER:
78-179525

PRINTED IN THE UNITED STATES OF AMERICA
BY
NEW WORLD BOOK MANUFACTURING CO., INC.
HALLANDALE, FLORIDA 33009

TO
HANNAH CLOTHIER HULL

PREFACE

The numerous biographers of William Penn, in seven lands, seven languages and seven generations, have written accounts of his life in chronological order. Although this order may seem to be logical, it necessitates an intermingling of the varied threads of his career, and a skipping to and fro in England, Ireland, and Europe, back and forth across the Atlantic, and a repetition of topics only partially treated in any one place. This makes it impossible to maintain a desirable unity either in the narrative itself, or in the reader's mind.

The biography herewith presented endeavours to avoid this confusion by an arrangement of thirty topics in Penn's life and character, each topic treated consecutively from beginning to end. The time and place factors are presented both in each topic and in a chronological review at the end of the book.

Some of the topics may appear to be given a disproportionately large amount of space, at the expense of others which are of equal or greater importance. But the former have been treated somewhat in extenso because of the fact that they have been given scant or no attention by previous biographers; while the latter have been so universally and extensively discussed as to become familiar knowledge—'what every school-boy knows.' Those episodes, too, which have been the subject of prolonged controversy on the part of his biographers and of the general historians have demanded in all fairness extended treatment.

Aside from the new topical arrangement of the book and the many pictures illustrating its text, an earnest effort has been made to include all the salient facts of Penn's life, and to present them impartially, so that his greatness and his weakness may be known, not from panegyric or indiscriminate criticism, but from a knowledge of the actual facts themselves. Not only have the source materials of his life been studied, but the interpretation of them by many biographers and historians has been sympathetically considered.

While candour will compel both author and reader to acknowledge failures in Penn's career and defects in his character, the genuine greatness in both has deservedly brought him enduring fame. As a founder of the Society of Friends, and of a great American commonwealth; as an eloquent and convincing preacher, and a successful champion of religious toleration; as a learned scholar and author of classic litera-

ture, and a law-giver and international statesman of the highest rank: no other personality in American colonial history looms so large or shines so brightly; and but few great men in England in the last quarter of the Seventeenth Century have left a better or more lasting influence upon succeeding generations of the English-speaking peoples on both sides of the Atlantic.

Swarthmore College
December 27, 1936

CONTENTS

PENN'S ENGLAND	1
THE ERA	2
RELIGIOUS ENVIRONMENT	4
PENN'S HOMES	6
PATERNAL ANCESTORS	15
PENN'S FATHER	17
PENN'S MOTHER	25
PENN'S FAMILY	31
GULIELMA SPRINGETT PENN AND HER CHILDREN	32
SPRINGETT PENN	40
LETITIA PENN	44
WILLIAM PENN JUNIOR	48
HANNAH CALLOWHILL PENN AND HER CHILDREN	57
JOHN PENN, 'THE AMERICAN'	61
THOMAS PENN	63
RICHARD AND DENNIS PENN	64
BOYHOOD	65
OXFORD	73

Contents

THE GRAND TOUR	78
WAR, PESTILENCE, AND LAW	83
PENN IN IRELAND	88
PENN BECOMES A QUAKER	106
QUAKER PREACHER AND MISSIONARY	119
THE DEBATER	132
THE CONTROVERSIALIST	137
THE AUTHOR	154
THEOLOGY AND ETHICS	166
QUAKER LEADER AND ORGANIZER	174
IMPRISONMENTS	181
THE PROTAGONIST OF TOLERATION	197
THE COLONIZER	216
THE STATESMAN	224
'JESUIT' AND COURTIER	241
'JACOBITE' AND TRAITOR	265
LAST YEARS	279
PENN'S PERSONAL APPEARANCE	294
PENN'S CHARACTER	309
PENN'S ACHIEVEMENTS	325

Contents

APPENDICES:

PENN'S CHRONOLOGY 341

ALLEGED PORTRAITS OF GULIELMA PENN 344

PENN'S FAMILY (A GENEALOGICAL TABLE) 346

BOOKS AND MANUSCRIPTS CITED IN THIS VOLUME 349

INDEX 353

ILLUSTRATIONS

William Penn the Founder   *Frontispiece*
From the original painting by Henry Inman in the old City Hall,
Chestnut and Fifth Streets, Philadelphia.

London Tower and All Hallows Church, Barking   6
From *The Tower of London* by Arthur Poyser and John Fulleylove

Penn's Home at Rickmansworth   10
From a pencil sketch by George Coventry in the Gibson MSS.

Penn's Philadelphia Home, 1699-1701   14
'The Slate Roof House'; destroyed in 1867.

Pennsbury   16
From a recent photograph

Admiral Sir William Penn   18
From a portrait by Sir Peter Lely in Greenwich Hospital.

Gulielma Maria Springett Penn   32
From an engraving of a painting on glass by an unknown artist
(cf. infra, p. 344).

'The Quaker Wedding'   34
From a painting by Percy Bigland, R.A.

The Graves of the Penn Family at Jordans   38
From a photograph.

The So-called Penn (or Letitia) Cottage   44
From a photograph of the original now standing in Fairmount Park,
Philadelphia.

James Logan   46
From a portrait in the library of the Historical Society of Pennsylvania.

Hannah Callowhill Penn   58
From a portrait in the library of the Historical Society of Pennsylvania
(cf. infra, p. 299).

Thomas Penn, Son of the Founder   64
From a portrait by Peter van Dyck, in the library of the Historical Society of
Pennsylvania.

Chigwell School   68
From a print in the Friends House, London.

Illustrations

Christ Church College Stairway, Oxford University   74

William Penn at the Age of Twenty-two   90
From the painting in the library of the Historical Society of Pennsylvania (cf. infra, pp. 294-297).

The Blue Idol Meeting-house   106
From a recent photograph

George Fox   110
From the original painting by Sir Peter Lely in the Friends Historical Library of Swarthmore College.

Penn's Seat in the Blue Idol Meeting-house   120
From a recent photograph

Penn's 'Travails in Holland and Germany,' 1677   122
From a copy of the first edition in the Friends Historical Library, Swarthmore College.

Penn's Writing-desk   136
A photograph of the original in the library of the Historical Society of Pennsylvania.

Penn's 'No Cross, No Crown,' 1669   156
From a copy of the first edition in the Friends Historical Library, Swarthmore College.

Penn's 'Fruits of Solitude,' 1693   160
From a copy of the second edition in the library of Haverford College.

Penn's 'Essay on the . . . Peace of Europe,' 1693   164
From a copy of the first edition in the Friends' Reference Library, London.

Penn's Copy of the Bible   168
From the original in the library of the Historical Society of Pennsylvania.

'The Quakers' Synod'   174
From a caricature in Friends' Reference Library, London.

London Tower Liberties   184
A survey made in 1597 by W. Haiward and F. Gascoyne; reproduced from The Tower of London by Arthur Poyser and John Fulleylove

Penn's 'The People's . . . Liberties Asserted,' 1670   190
From a copy of the first edition in the Friends Historical Library, Swarthmore College.

Algernon Sidney   212
From an engraving in the library of the Historical Society of Pennsylvania.

Illustrations

Penn's Landing at Chester, 1682 — 218
From a wood-cut in J. F. Watson's *Annals*, Philadelphia, 1845.

Penn's Landing at Philadelphia, 1682 — 220
From a wood-cut in J. F. Watson's *Annals*, Philadelphia, 1845.

Penn's 'Some Account of Pennsylvania,' 1681 — 222
From a copy of the first edition in the library of the Historical Society of Pennsylvania.

Penn's 'Charter of Liberties for Pennsylvania,' 1682 — 228
A facsimile of the original preserved in the State Archives at Harrisburg.

Penn's 'Frame of Government for Pennsylvania,' 1682 — 230
From the original in the library of the Historical Society of Pennsylvania.

Penn's 'Treaty with the Indians' — 232
From the original painting by Benjamin West, 1772, in the State House ('Independence Hall'), Philadelphia.

'The Penn Elm Tree' — 234
From a painting by Brittan, engraved by J. Serz.

King James II — 242
From a copy of the painting by Sir Peter Lely (Dalkeith Palace) in the library of the Historical Society of Pennsylvania.

King William III — 268
From a copy of the painting by Sir Godfrey Kneller (Windsor Castle) in the library of the Historical Society of Pennsylvania.

Jordans Meeting-house — 292
From a water-color sketch by Alfred Rawlins in the Friends Historical Library, Swarthmore College.

Penn's Statue on Philadelphia's City Hall — 298
From a photograph taken before its erection.

Penn at the Age of Fifty-two — 300
The so-called Place Portrait in Blackwell Grange, County Durham; from a copy in the library of the Historical Society of Pennsylvania. The original is said to have been painted from life by Francis Place in 1696; the copy made and brought to Philadelphia in 1875 (cf. p. 299).

Penn in Old Age — 302
An unknown artist's plausible but unauthenticated portrait in oil; in possession of Mr. Morris L. Clothier of Philadelphia.

The Bevan Bust of Penn — 304
A photograph of the ivory medallion by Sylvanus Bevan (cf. infra, p. 300).

Illustrations

Penn's 'Treaty with the Indians'   330
From a copy of West's painting by an unknown English artist

Philadelphia about the Time of Penn's Death   334
From a painting by Peter Cooper (enrolled as a freeman of Philadelphia in 1717)

The Prophecy of Isaiah, XI : 6, II : 2-4   338
From a painting by Edward Hicks in the Friends Historical Library, Swarthmore College.

WILLIAM PENN

WILLIAM PENN
A Topical Biography

PENN'S ENGLAND

THE national background of William Penn's life impresses the modern reader by its smallness and by its startling contrasts. England had then a population of about five million,— less than the present population of London or New York alone,— while London had about a half-million and Bristol, the next largest city, about thirty thousand. Most of the people were scattered in rural districts, but lived chiefly in the south and midlands where their life was still rude, and their lands still overrun by forests, fens, and the wild beasts and fowl of woods, fields, and moorland. The present great industrial districts of the north were frontier lands, whose people lived a rude border-life, terrorized by marauding Scots and bands of footpads, moss-troopers, and highwaymen — there were blood-hounds to protect the villagers and fortified homes for the rich.

In dangers and difficulties of travel, in abundance of wild animals and wild men, England as a whole was still not far in advance of the sylvan life led by the colonists in America. So slow was transit, even in the recent invention of 'flying coaches,' that it required twenty-four hours to make the oft-taken journey between London and Oxford ; and even this speed of two and a half miles per hour was possible only over the dry roads of summer. The upset of coaches was a common experience, and one shared, we are told, on at least one occasion by Penn's mother.

The contrasts in both rural and urban life were extreme, and pitiful at both extremities. In the country, the deep-drinking, large-eating, fox-hunting squires and their dependents, the semi-literate clergy, lived in pretentious barbarism side by side with the desperately poor. The 'cottage homes of England' lacked comfort, cleanliness, and cheer ; and the lives of the mass of urban dwellers formed a sordid, shabby contrast with the luxuriousness of the rich and upper middle class.

The austerity of Puritan lives, with its lack of art, drama, and most of the amenities of life, accused and shrank from the profligacy, obscenity, and luxuriousness of the Cavalier, both before and especially after the Restoration. Indeed, the asceticism of Puritan life was a reaction against the licence of the Cavalier and courtier, as well as an obsession to find the soul's salvation from a future hell. Penn's *Address to Protestants,* written when its author was only thirty-five, contains a stern rebuke (in eleven folio pages) of the 'Vice, Presumption and Violence' which he deplored as being rife among his fellow-Englishmen : 'Drunkenness, Whoredoms and Fornications, Luxury or Excess in Apparel, Furniture and in Living, Profuse Gaming and finally, Oaths, Blasphemy and Prophaneness : These Swarm in our Streets, these are a Scandal to our Profession and cry aloud to Heaven, and provoke Divine Wrath against us.'

And yet, in this as in all other times of striking contrasts — accentuated doubtless because of the contrasts — there were such splendid lives and characters as those of John Milton, George Fox, Richard Baxter, John Locke, Algernon Sidney, John Bunyan, and many others who illuminated their age and gave lustre to all humanity. With such contemporaries as these, as well as with four sovereigns of the House of Stuart, Louis XIV, Czar Peter the Great of Russia, the Viceroy of Ireland, the Princess of the Palatinate, and a host of minor celebrities and obscure men and women, Penn came into living contact. From vital relation with the world of great and little men, and from the spirits of men and women who spoke to him from books in many fields and ages of literature, Penn drew resources for his own development and career.

THE ERA

THE historic events which transpired during his three score years and ten were far beyond the ordinary in themselves and fruitful of much for posterity. His birthday (October 14, 1644) occurred three months after the battle of Marston Moor, which decided the triumph of Oliver Cromwell over Charles I in the Civil War. This was the middle point of the eighty-six years of struggle between parliamentary government and the absolutist rule of the Stuart kings. Penn's life lasted until thirty years after that struggle ended, and included first-hand acquaintance with and considerable participation in many of its stirring events. He was four years old when Charles I's head fell upon the scaffold, and he passed his boyhood in the era of the Commonwealth.

The Thirty Years' War with its manifold horrors was drawing to its close in his infancy, and he must have heard in his boyhood days many of the dark tales of that terrific struggle between Protestants and Catholics on the Continent of Europe. Louis XIV's career began about the same time as Penn's and, with its four wars against England, was to prove almost fatal to Penn's holy experiment in the New World. From across the Atlantic, came tales of Roger Williams and John Eliot, of the four Quakers hanged on Boston Common, of the seizure of Jamaica from the Spaniards by an English fleet under his father's command, and of the acquisition of New Netherland by his father's friend, the Duke of York. The Cromwellian subjugation and settlement of Ireland; the restoration of the Stuart kings, of the Parliament and the Anglican Church; the beginning of England's empire in India; and the German wars against the Turks — all fell within Penn's minority.

While he was in his twenties, he lived through the last great outbreak of the Plague in England, the Great Fire in London, a bitter persecution of the Quakers and other Dissenters under the 'Clarendon Code,' a third war with Holland, the triumphant advance of the Dutch fleet in the Medway, the first war of England with France, and two of Louis XIV's wars of aggression.

In his thirties, there occurred the Popish Plot, the rise of political parties, his own entrance into politics in behalf of toleration and a Whig parliament, the execution of his friend, Algernon Sidney, the forfeiture of the charters of Massachusetts, of London and other towns; while he himself became a proprietor in New Jersey, received the grant of Pennsylvania, spent two years in the founding of his colony and its two pioneer towns, Philadelphia and Germantown.

During his fifth decade, he rode the tide of Stuart absolutism in England and America, striving for universal toleration while the kings at whose court he laboured conspired for the Catholic domination of England, and in the 'Grand and Glorious Revolution' of 1688 shared the Stuart downfall. During the three years of his own public disgrace and private retirement, two of the three great objects of his public activities, namely, religious toleration and parliamentary government, were achieved in the Toleration Act and the Declaration and Bill of Rights; and he himself had his province restored to him after its temporary confiscation. In that same decade, a great impulse to emigration to lands of freedom was given by the Revocation of the Edict of Nantes, the devastation of the Palatinate, and the third of Louis XIV's wars of aggression. Penn's colony was to profit greatly by these troubles on the Continent, and he himself found time to write two of his greatest books, the *Essay on the Peace of Europe* and *Fruits of Solitude*; but at the same time he lost his two great Quaker comrades, Robert Barclay and George Fox, and the beloved wife of his youth ; while the 'Pacification' of Limerick, the Penal Laws against the Irish, and the climax of the witchcraft delusion, added their gloom to the dark years of his fifties.

During his sixth decade, he saw Louis XIV's third war of aggression end, but a fourth one of twelve years begin, and the Great Northern War start on its devastating course. He made a second happy visit to Pennsylvania, but realized what difficulties were entailed upon his Quaker colony from the incessant warfare among the English and Continental rivals.

His final decade brought to him personally a lawsuit, a debtor's prison, and the strokes of paralysis which incapacitated him for a half-dozen years and finally caused his death ; while 'Queen Anne's War' in America, the wars of the Spanish Succession, those between the Austrians and Turks in Europe, and an attack upon England by the Old Pretender, underscored in blood and misery the dire necessity that civilized Christian nations should put into practice the third of the principles most deeply cherished and successfully practised by him, namely, peace and good will among men.

RELIGIOUS ENVIRONMENT

RELIGION or theology in one form or another, was (next to the bare necessities of life and often before even these) the chief preoccupation of men, women, and children, of every class and condition. The varieties of religious experience or profession were probably more numerous than in any other time or land. The old Catholic creed was still cherished by a minority of the people, and two Stuart kings hoped to see its church restored. The Anglicans who had won the victory over it in the spacious days of Queen Elizabeth ruled the national church throughout the century, except during the dozen years of the Commonwealth. The Presbyterians, aided by the Scotch alliance during the Civil War, established their church and tried to crush out all opposition to it, until Oliver Cromwell and his Independents compelled them to grant partial toleration to the Protestant sects.

Beside these three forms of church policy which strove to realize each for itself the establishment of a single church, supported by a single state, and compelling all Englishmen to accept uniformity of faith, ecclesiastical government, and worship, there arose a crowd of 'sects' which rejected the theory of a totalitarian church and demanded the right to survive and flourish. The Independents, or Congregationalists, and Baptists shared with the Presbyterians during the Commonwealth the formal recognition and financial support of the state; but during the rest of the century, they too were driven into the wilderness of 'Dissent.' There they met and wrestled with a horde of rival sects who were lumped all together by their foes, but who rejoiced in such names as Antinomians, Arians and Unitarians, Atheists and Agnostics, Diggers, Erastians, Etheringtonians, Fifth Monarchists, Levellers, Millenarians, Muggletonians, Quakers, Ranters, Sabbatarians, Anti-Sabbatarians, Seekers, Soul-Sleepers, and Traskites. The whirlwind of doctrines these sects professed gave rise to a veritable cyclone of controversial pamphlets, thirty thousand of which are said to have been published during the score of years between 1640 and 1660! Indeed, during the entire period from the accession of James I to the fall of James II, successive waves of religious fervour and ecclesiastical strife submerged the private and public activities of nearly every year; while the continual warfare which raged either in England or on the Continent was largely motivated and carried on in the name of religion.

At the heart of this cyclone of sects and pamphlets, there was the voice of that genuine Puritanism which was to triumph at the end of the century. This voice gave rise to varied appeals; but since these appeals were made primarily to 'the masses'—the poorer classes—they aroused the great silent majority of the people from their lethargy and eventually enabled the *vox Dei* to be heard through the *vox populi*. This was the great opportunity afforded especially to that extreme of Puritan sectarianism known as Quakerism. At the time when George Fox began to preach Quakerism (a few years after the birth of William Penn) the politically, ecclesiastically, and socially aristocratic Anglicans had been overthrown; and the ecclesiastically aristocratic Presbyterians, by proving that 'new Presbyter is but old Priest writ large,' had alienated the plain people. Fox and his comrades utilized this opportunity and gathered many thousands within their fold, until they too lost touch with the common man and left the wide harvest open for John Bunyan and John Wesley.

PENN'S HOMES

LIKE most sea-faring families of today, Penn's mother and her children moved from place to place; and even after he possessed a separate home of his own, Penn lived in at least a dozen different places. His birth-place was in the parish of St. Catherine's, London, on or close to the east side of Great Tower Hill, in a court adjoining London Wall. Here, his parents occupied a simple lodging of two rooms, one above the other. This was a location convenient for his father, a naval officer, being near the river Thames and the centre at that time of London's maritime activity. The near neighbours were also sea-going people, one of them being a Mr. Turner, a clerk in the navy, whose wife appears to have been as malicious a gossip as Samuel Pepys himself. London's ancient Tower, and one of England's most historic spots, dominated the neighbourhood, and must have filled the childish imagination of William Penn with gruesome pictures of the past and gloomy impressions of man's inhumanity to man. It cast a shadow over coming events in his own life, when he too was a prisoner within its walls. On the hill itself stood the scaffold where many a victim of 'fallen greatness and of blighted fame' was publicly beheaded.

Two days before Penn was born, his father had been ordered to sail for Ireland; but the voyage was delayed for a fortnight, and Captain Penn was enabled to attend his son's christening in the near-by church of All Hallows, Barking, on October 23, 1644. This church narrowly escaped destruction by the Great Fire of 1666, and is still standing, one of the very few remaining landmarks of the life of Penn.

When Penn was between three and four years of age, his father chose for his family's residence, while he was himself so much at sea, the pleasant countryside of Essex. About a dozen miles north of London Tower on the borderland between the parishes of Wanstead and Walthamstow, he gave to his son William a second home. This was a favourite suburb of London with retired naval officers and other

LONDON TOWER AND ALL HALLOWS CHURCH, BARKING

official folk; and their young people doubtless appreciated the romantic beauty and opportunities of Epping and Hainault Forests, some of whose wooded heights and dells stretched then almost to the gates of London. Nearby was Wanstead House, with its memories of Queen Mary and Queen Bess, of Elizabeth's faithless lover, the Earl of Leicester, and his second wife, Amy Robsart's successor, the Countess of Essex. Far more important to the boy Penn, was the neighbouring school in the village of Chigwell, where he was to begin the long journey of his formal education. By this time, Captain Penn had been promoted to be rear admiral, and his family led a much more comfortable life in the rural spaciousness of Essex than in the crowded lodgings near London Tower.

But a return of the family to London was necessitated in the autumn or winter of 1654, when a fleet under command of Vice Admiral Penn was fitted out for an attack upon the Spanish West Indies. Great Tower Hill was again the neighbourhood selected, but this time a suite of rooms took the place of their former humble lodgings.[1] The expedition to the West Indies seized Jamaica, which so fascinated its captor that he considered for a time the investment of his life and fortune in that beautiful island. Even hard-headed Cromwell, who had sent Penn forth to drive the Spaniards from the Caribbean, seriously attempted to induce English colonists to desert the stern coasts and forests of New England and take up their abode in the sunny lands of Jamaica and its neighbours. What a strange irony of fate it would have been for the Puritan colonists to have been removed from New England and settled in the luxurious islands of the tropics, and for Pennsylvania, New Jersey, and Delaware to have been prevented from becoming the seat of Quaker commonwealths!

The Penn family's sojourn in London at this time appears to have been a short one, and probably ended soon after the expedition put out to sea. They then returned to their home near Wanstead and Chigwell, in which latter village William had probably been left at school. On the return of the admiral from Jamaica, both he and the commander of the land forces on the expedition, General Venables, were imprisoned in the Tower. The capture of Jamaica was con-

[1] P.Gibson, a subordinate of Admiral Penn, in a letter to William Penn, March, 1711-12 (Quoted by Granville Penn, II, 612-616), gives this locality as the Penns' residence in 1655.

sidered a poor compensation for the failure to capture Hispaniola, or San Domingo, and the Spanish treasure fleet, which the expedition had been especially desired by Cromwell to achieve; moreover, Penn had returned to England with his fleet before he had received orders to do so. Cromwell's second thought, however, prevailed, and he ordered an honourable release of both Penn and Venables from their imprisonment, which had lasted about five weeks in the autumn of 1655. Penn thereupon joined his family at Wanstead.

But having been deprived of his command, the admiral turned his attention to his Irish estates and removed his family in the late autumn of 1655, or the spring of 1656, to Macroom in the county of Cork. Here, about twenty miles west of the town of Cork, Cromwell planned to settle one of the English colonies by means of which he hoped to hold Ireland in subjection. Besides the manor and castle which went to Penn, there was in the town of Macroom a garrison of English troops. Penn devoted himself to the extension and improvement of his estate, and succeeded so well in this task that he increased its value from £300 to £858 a year. With cheap Irish peasant labour, he developed farms and roads upon his own estate, and induced sundry relatives of his wife and himself to settle on neighbouring estates. His son William was now a lad of from twelve to fifteen years and doubtless took an active share in this enterprise, which may have helped him in his own later planting and proprietorship on a far larger scale. Here, too, he had his first contact with that religion which was to make of him a Quaker statesman and thus give him a place almost unique in history.

Stirring public events soon changed the placid country life of the Penn family and brought the admiral back to London, while his son was sent to Oxford University. On the abdication of Richard Cromwell in May, 1659, the elder Penn went over to Charles II, and was appointed to a seat in the new Convention Parliament which was summoned in April, 1660, for the restoration of the Stuarts. As loyal supporter of the restored monarchy, the admiral came into great favour with the new king, was knighted by him on board his ship, and was appointed a Commissioner of the Navy at a salary of £500 a year. But another great favourite with Charles was the faithful royalist, Lord Muskerry, Earl of Clancarty, whose estates at Macroom had been given by Cromwell to Penn; the latter was therefore obliged to surrender them, but received other Irish lands in their stead and, in his new official position, acquired lodgings for his family on the northern side of the London Navy Office Gardens.[2]

For some months, the mother and younger children remained in Ireland, while the father worked at the Navy Office, kept bachelor quarters in his new house and arranged for its enlargement; while his older son went to Christ Church College. When the king was crowned, William came up to London to witness in his father's company the exuberant coronation of the king, and possibly to meet his father's chief and his own great friend of future years, the Duke of York. College vacations too were spent in the fine new London home and were evidently times of great merriment and pleasure. After his expulsion from Oxford and his banishment from home in 1662, William spent only brief periods at his father's house. On his return from a two years' visit to the Continent, he was again at home in the Navy Garden house during his father's absence in England's naval war with Holland. His father's triumph over the Dutch fleet at Lowestoft, on June 3, 1665, was hailed as a great victory by the family and by all of England, and is thought to have been the chief reason why a province in America was granted to the son, fifteen years later, and named in honour of the father who had proved in the battle his courage and discretion. William, defending his father's name after death, gave the details of the victory 'as matter of fact,' although at the same time he deprecated wars as 'arising from lusts,' and concluded that the battle had been 'greatened beyond all common eulogies by the unsuccessfulness of later engagements.'[3]

Meanwhile, the Plague had broken out in London the month before, but Penn's family remained in their London home throughout that dreadful summer when as many as 2,000 victims in the city died in some weeks and four times that number in others. The escape of the family from the contagion was doubtless helped by the frugality of their meals, which their gossipy neighbours, Mrs. Turner and Samuel Pepys, ridiculed as mean and nasty. It was during this year of 1665, also, that William while living at home studied law in Lincoln's Inn.

At the beginning of the next year, his father sent him to try out his legal training and executive ability in defending law-suits against and administering the Irish estates which the king had granted in compensation for the loss of those at Macroom. The new lands were also

---
[2] P.Gibson, l.c. *supra*, p. 7.
[3] *Truth rescued from Imposture*, written in Newgate Prison and printed, 1670.

in County Cork and included eight square miles lying at the southern tip of Ireland, on the shores of Cork harbor and the Atlantic Ocean. The admiral had been made governor and captain of Kinsale, while the lands and castle bestowed upon him were not far away and bore the name of Shangarry.[4] Here, William the younger could enjoy the ocean breezes mingled with the damp warmth of Ireland; here he could gaze out across that ocean of historic adventure and dream perchance of some undefined achievement of his own in the mysterious land of the sunset. A brief visit to his father's home in London, to attend his sister's wedding on St. Valentines Day, 1667, was followed by his return to Ireland, and by his 'convincement' as a Quaker.

Recalled to London by his bitterly disappointed father, Penn adhered to his Quakerism, but continued to live at intervals in his father's home. During his temporary exile from this, before the reconciliation with his father, he was doubtless cared for in the homes of the Friends in and near London, and among these appears to have been that of Isaac Penington, the step-father of his future wife.

Soon after his famous victory at Lowestoft, Admiral Penn yielded to his old enemy the gout and retired permanently from the sea. He continued at his former work of equipping and provisioning the fleets to be used (not so successfully) by other men; but while he did this in the Navy Office, he determined to procure for his family a home in the purer air of Wanstead, where he too could spend his week-ends. Here, near his former home of twenty years before, he leased a large house which proved to be his last earthly home (1667-1670).

The tasks of preaching and writing which were imposed upon William Penn by his acceptance of Quakerism led him to leave his mother and brother, after his father's death, in their home at Wanstead, while he took lodgings in 'Walthamstow in Essex' (as his marriage-certificate described it) so as to be near his mother, and at the same time have a home of his own. But in the winter of 1670-71, we find him occupying lodgings in the County of Buckingham in his distant relatives' parish of Penn. The beautiful county of Bucks, extending its placid length through the valley of the middle Thames, had within it even then numerous comfortable and hospitable Quaker homes.

4 Shangarry and its estates were for a long time after Penn's death in chancery, and were not released until 1800, when they were divided between the Penn-Gaskell family and the heirs-at-law of William Penn Junior. The castle became an ivy-covered ruin in the nineteenth century, but its tall tower continued to afford a distant view and made the ruins themselves impressive and picturesque.

PENN'S HOME AT RICKMANSWORTH

Chief among these, in the eyes of other men than Penn, was that of the great Quaker mystic, Isaac Penington, his wife, the former Lady Mary Springett, and her daughter, the fair Gulielma. Penn had met Gulielma in the house of a London Friend on the day of his banishment from his father's house; and he may have spent some of his exile at the home of her step-father. Now, after three years of sorrow and imprisonments, he could not resist the magnet in Gulielma's home and made frequent pilgrimages thither. The Peningtons' first home was 'The Grange,' in the neighbouring parish of Chalfont St. Giles, a place immortalized by the cottage-home of Milton during the London Plague and Fire and a couple of years afterwards, when he was completing *Paradise Lost* and beginning *Paradise Regained*. Religious persecution drove out the Peningtons and they retired, in 1665, to Lady Penington's estate near Amersham, not far from Chalfont, at a place called Bury House.

But before Guli Springett became his wife, Penn had much labour to do for Quakerism, including a trip to Holland and Germany in 1671. On his return to England, he spent some time in London, but wrote from there at least one letter indicating a design to settle on the Springett estate at Worminghurst in Sussex. He and Gulielma were married in the spring of 1672 at King's or King John's Farm, Chorley Wood, where the Friends held their meetings for worship at the time. They then took up their abode, first in 'Basing House' at Rickmansworth, Hertfordshire, and about three years later at Walthamstow, Essex. Although in a different county from Bucks, their first home was only a half-dozen miles from Chalfont and a half-mile from Chorley Wood, so that the bride and groom were in close touch with the family circle. Their stay at Walthamstow was a brief one, and was near Penn's mother's home at Wanstead, perhaps in the lodgings he had occupied after his father's death. It was here that the fourth child, Springett, was born in January, 1676.

At Rickmansworth, the Penns lived for five years, during which time three children were born to them; two of these were twins, and all three died in infancy. England's third war with Holland, Louis XIV's second war of aggression, and King Philip's War in America marked these years with blood; but Penn enjoyed for the first and almost the last time in his life a period of tranquil ease with his beloved wife amidst the rural peace of his home. The loss of their infant children made the year 1674 a sad one for them both, and it may have stirred them to face the large issues of life before them. New Jersey and America loomed up the next year, and the great struggle for religious toleration came close behind.

Perhaps it was either a desire for the health-giving breezes of the sea for his prospective family, or the too close proximity to the busy Quaker life at London which made Rickmansworth and Walthamstow unduly visited by 'travelling Friends,' that caused the Penns to remove to their next home, namely, Guli's paternal estate about fifty miles due south of London at Worminghurst in Sussex. Here they lived in a house on the South Downs, overlooking the sea a few miles away; the port of Shoreham, and Brighton, the ultra-fashionable seashore resort of the next century, were within a half-dozen miles; their friend Algernon Sidney already had an estate near by; and, as in Ireland, they attracted other friends and relatives to their neighbourhood. During nearly all the score of years from 1677 to 1697, Penn's home in England was at Worminghurst; here his son Springett was brought as an infant and lived during the nineteen years of his life; here two daughters and another son were born; here Gulielma died after twenty-five years of married life; and it was round this home that most of the great and sad events of Penn's career found their centre. The historic mansion exists now only as part of a more recent barn;[5] and the land was absorbed, first in the domains of the Duke of Norfolk, and now forms a part of a splendid estate owned by staunch members of the Society of Friends, Mr. and Mrs. William Hanbury Aggs.

Worminghurst, too, remained the Penns' real home, during their absences in America or London.[6] In the years when Penn was active at the courts of Charles II and James II, he took lodgings in or near the city — for example, at Charing Cross and Teddington; and when he was especially busy with clients and petitioners of varied kinds he rented extensive lodgings in London's suburb of Kensington, in Holland House. This was a baronial mansion owned by the earls of Holland and Warwick, and stood in gardens adjoining those of Kensington Palace, which became a favourite residence of William III and Queens Mary and Anne. During Queen Anne's reign, on his return from his second visit to Pennsylvania, when Penn was once more

---

5 Vestiges of the foundations of the house were to be seen until recent years, and in the stables there are still visible the chimneys of the fireside once graced by its illustrious host and charming hostess.
6 There are extant letters from Penn dated at Worminghurst in June, 1702, 1703, and 1704; and one as late as $X^{br}/29/1708$.

persona grata at the royal court, he and his family again lived in Holland House (1701-1703). When Penn was a prisoner for debt in the Fleet, his family, to be near him, lived in Ludgate Parish, London, where his youngest daughter Hannah was born (September, 1708); and on his release, the family again lived in Kensington lodgings, where Hannah died (January, 1709).[7]

During 1690-93, when Penn was under a cloud of suspicion, he lived in close retirement, somewhere in the heart of London, in places which were known only to his wife and his nearest friends. Gulielma doubtless spent as much time with him as she could leave the children; and he made short but frequent visits to Worminghurst. On his acquittal from the charge of treason in 1693, he hastened to Hoddesdon, in Hertfordshire, where Gulielma died soon afterwards.[8]

The year after his marriage to Hannah Callowhill, the Penns removed from Worminghurst — which soon afterwards became the home of William Penn the younger — and settled in Bristol. This city was the home of the Callowhills, and here the Penns resided from 1697 until they went to Pennsylvania in 1699.[9] On their return, as has been said, they resided first in Kensington and removed thence to Knightsbridge in 1703. This home was on the southern edge of Hyde Park and it too was in close proximity to the royal residences at Kensington and St. James's.[10]

Three years later, the family moved again, this time to a house at Ealing, about one mile from Brentford, eight miles west of London. It may have been the existence of a Friends' meeting at this place that drew them to it. Brentford is the county town of Middlesex and lies on the north bank of the Thames. Its air was probably more salubrious then than in London; but the residence of the family here was interrupted by Penn's confinement in the Fleet.

His financial difficulties had caused him to sell the old home at Worminghurst in 1707; hence after his release from the Fleet and the second residence at Kensington referred to above,[11] he removed his

---

[7] Letters from 'London' are dated from 4/21/1702 until 4/26/1709.
[8] Two of Penn's letters, telling of Gulielma's illness and death, are dated from 'Hodson,' 10/11/1693 (December, 1693) and 12/27/1693 (March, 1694).
[9] Their subsequent visits to, or brief residences in, Bristol are marked by Penn's letters from there in 1704, 1705, and 1706. It was at Bristol, too, that he suffered the first strokes of paralysis in October, 1712.
[10] A letter is dated at 'Orchard,' ½/1705-6 (March, 1706), and one at 'Hyde Park,' 2/30/1705-6 (May, 1706).
[11] Two letters are dated from Reading in March, 1709.

family for the last time, in 1710, to Ruscombe, near Twyford, about six miles east of Reading, in Berkshire. His country mansion here was still in the valley of the Thames, and still near a royal residence, that of Windsor. Twyford became later the temporary home of another celebrated Pennsylvanian, Benjamin Franklin, who wrote part of his Autobiography while living there. Two years after Penn's settlement here, he incurred the final stroke of paralysis which permanently disabled him; and here he lived for the rest of his life with the happy insouciance of a child. Here, too, his faithful helpmeet, Hannah, passed away eight years after him. They were buried together in the same grave at Jordans.[12]

William Penn made two visits to Pennsylvania, and had three homes in his province. On his first visit in 1682-84, he had built for his private and public use a clap-board building which stood in Philadelphia on what was known as Letitia Court, which ran north from Chestnut to Market between Front and Second Streets. On this site, in later years, was built the so-called 'Penn Cottage,' or 'Letitia House,' which is supposed to have been the first brick house in Pennsylvania; it was removed a century and a half later (in 1883), and is still standing in Fairmount Park; but the popular belief that it was the residence of William Penn ('the first State House') and of his daughter Letitia is not based on authentic evidence, or even on probability.

On his second visit to Pennsylvania, Penn brought with him his wife and daughter Letitia and his young secretary, James Logan, so that his former house in Philadelphia was probably too small for their use. On this visit, therefore, he made his residence in the Slate Roof House, on Second Street north of Walnut. In this house was born his son John, 'the American,' the only one of the Founder's children born in his province. It stood until 1867.

On both visits, however, Penn had a country home in Bucks County called Pennsbury. It was an estate of about eight thousand acres lying on the Pennsylvania bank of the Delaware River about twenty-five miles above Philadelphia, and eight miles from the present town of Bristol. The two and a half-story brick mansion (sixty feet on the river front, with a depth of forty) which he built there fell into ruins a century and a half ago; but its site (and foundations), together with eight surrounding acres, have recently been presented to the State of

---

[12] The house at Ruscombe was removed about 1850, to make way for a railroad.

PENN'S PHILADELPHIA HOME

Pennsylvania, which plans to restore it and its out-buildings precisely as the Founder left them. Almost every detail for this restoration is extant; and Penn himself left copious records of the estate and its varied and alluring delights which made it the home that he loved the best of all.

From this sketch of Penn's various homes, it is seen that they numbered seven under his father's roof, and twelve under his own. The cities of London, Bristol, and Philadelphia, the English counties of Essex, Bucks, Herts, Sussex, and Middlesex, the Irish county of Cork, and the Pennsylvania county of Bucks, lent their varied attractions to beautify and dignify his homes and to aid in the development of his own many-sided character and career.

PATERNAL ANCESTORS

THE influence of Penn's heredity upon him is more difficult to trace than is that of his environment and era. The familiar 'ancestor who came over with William the Conqueror' was attributed to him by a Norman French lady of a family of De la Penn who claimed kinship with him. But a much more likely ancestral origin is that of Wales, the name of Pen (head or highland) being a common one in that land. William the Founder related, in jest or earnest, that an ancestor of his was a Welshman called John Pennmunrith, or John On-the-top-of-the-hill; and when Pennsylvania was to receive its name, Penn desired it to be called 'New Wales.' This desire was overridden by the king, who nevertheless gave the new province a combined Welsh and Latin name, the 'land of sylvan hills.'

From Wales, the ancestral line drifted into the neighbouring English county of Gloucestershire, and settled as yeomen at Penn's Lodge and Minety, about eighty-five miles west of London in the vicinity of Bristol. Another member of the family, bearing the same arms as the others, went on to the parish of Penn in Buckinghamshire and became the ancestor of typical country gentry. At Minety, an early William Penn died in 1591, his land was sold, and his grandson Giles (the Founder's grandfather) betook himself as a youth to Bristol and entered on a maritime and trading career. As captain and owner of a ship, Giles traded far and wide, and notably with the Barbary merchant-pirates, from whom he is reputed to have brought African hawks and

Barbary horses as presents to Charles I. There is a romantic story [13] that Captain Giles induced the king to send a fleet under him to recapture the port of Sallee from rebel pirates, release the English prisoners there, and restore it to the Emperor of Morocco; and as reward for this, Giles was appointed consul to Sallee in 1637. To match this story is another [14] that Giles's elder brother had been sent as an envoy to Spain in 1623; and that Giles's elder son, George Penn, married a Catholic lady and Spanish subject in Antwerp, became an opulent merchant in Seville, was imprisoned for three years by the Inquisition ('in a dungeon eight feet square and dark as the grave ... every month being scourged to make him confess his crimes'), was compelled to "confess" after being put twice to the rack, stripped of his property (£12,000), expelled to England, avenged by his younger brother, William, the Founder's father, and appointed envoy to Spain for the express purpose of recovering damages for himself from the government; but dying in 1664 before he could set out upon his mission! [15] It was on this last occasion that Pepys records (August 1, 1664): 'Last night, at 12 o'clock, I was waked with knocking at Sir W. Pen's door; and what was it but peoples running up and down to bring him word that his brother, who hath been a good while, it seems, sicke, is dead.' His claims were bequeathed to his brother and became the basis of very expensive and unsubstantial 'castles in Spain.' [16]

The facts as to Penn's paternal ancestors are meagre, but sufficient to show that his forebears had the Celtic touch (from Wales) and English stock, and were of yeoman, sea-faring, trading, and fighting stock. His parents, too, it will be seen, contributed markedly to the last three (and perhaps the first) of these strains. As for his maternal ancestors, they have been variously assigned to English, Irish, Dutch and even French Huguenot or Walloon origin; but as to their personal history, we have only conjecture.

13 Hepworth Dixon, *A History of William Penn*, New York, 1902, pp. 12-15.
14 Granville Penn, *Memorials of . . . Sir William Penn, Knt.*, London, 1833, I, 550-56.
15 Mynors Bright, in the 1875 edition of Pepys's 'Diary.' Under date of September 30, 1661, Pepys records: 'Then to Sir W.Pen's and there supped, where his brother, a traveller, and one that speaks Spanish very well, and a merry man, supped with us.' To this H.B.Wheatley adds the note: 'George Penn, elder brother of Sir William, was a merchant at San Lucar.'
16 Indicative of the difference between the biography of Penn by the littérateur, Hepworth Dixon, and by the Quaker historian, Samuel M. Janney, is the fact that Dixon devotes eight pages to these romantic tales, while Janney passes them over in silence.

PENNSBURY

PENN'S FATHER

It is evident from the data in regard to Admiral Sir William Penn that he was a remarkable man. There are divergent opinions as to his character, and also as to his influence on the development of his son William. But there is no doubt as to the main facts of his career, and these show him to have been a man far beyond the ordinary in the extraordinary era and company in which he lived.

He was the second son of Giles Penn, born in 1621, a score of years after his elder brother George, with a family of sisters in between. His mother was Joan Gilbert, for whom he had a strong affection during life and beside whose grave he requested on his deathbed that he should be buried. The inscription on his tombstone in the Church of St. Mary Redcliffe at Bristol gives a summary of his career, beginning with his birth and parentage, and the statement: 'Addicted from his Youth to Maritime Affairs.'

At the age of ten he appears to have been taken by his father down to the sea in ships, and there taught the sciences as well as the arts connected with navigation. Seven years later, when his father began his consular duties at Sallee, the youth of seventeen took over the father's ship and trade and plied both of them for a time in the Atlantic and Mediterranean.

But this was the fateful time of 'ship-money,' when Charles I was building up a royal navy with which to checkmate his Puritan enemies on the land. Hence the young and ambitious captain or 'master commandant' of an armoured trading-vessel found it an easy step to secure a commission as lieutenant in the king's navy. This step was taken before he was twenty; and at twenty-one, he became 'second captain' on the flag-ship of one of England's greatest admirals, Robert Blake.

Having advanced thus far, Captain Penn married at twenty-two Margaret Jasper van der Schuren; and the next year, a son and namesake was born. Then followed a score of years of naval warfare, first against the king and for the Parliament—for Penn had followed Blake into the party of the people in the Civil War. Within a year after his marriage, he was appointed Rear-Admiral of Ireland, and cruised in St. George's Channel on guard against the Parliament's enemies from France and Spain. At twenty-five, he was made Vice-

Admiral of Ireland; and, after a month's imprisonment in the Tower on a disproved charge of complicity with the king's Irish friends, he was made by Cromwell 'Admiral to the Streights,' and sent to chase Prince Rupert's raiders along the Atlantic coasts and through the Straits of Gibraltar and the Mediterranean. At thirty-one, he was made Vice-Admiral of England; and the next year, participated in that capacity and as General of Marines in Cromwell's war against Holland. In this war, he fought in nine pitched battles, three of them bloody ones, including the famous battle of the Texel, in 1653, in which Admiral van Tromp was killed.

It was evidently Penn's practical seamanship, admirably supplementing the strategic skill of the English sea-generals Blake and Monk, which caused his rapid promotion and which induced Cromwell to appoint him in 1654 to the command of an expedition against the Spanish West Indies. The purpose of the latter was, as in the days of Drake and Raleigh, to capture the Spanish treasure-fleet and the Spaniards' stronghold in Hispaniola, or Santo Domingo. Penn landed an army under General Venables on this island, but the jungle, tropical diseases, and the wretched recruits and improper supplies and equipment of the English army caused the attack to fail. Then, without waiting for the treasure-fleet, the two commanders decided to return to England. Before doing so, however, Penn decided to capture at least some Spanish possession, and seized and garrisoned the island of Jamaica. This exploit laid the foundation of the British Empire in the West Indies, thus making the admiral an American 'founder,' but of a very different kind from that of his Quaker son.

On his return to England, Cromwell was naturally incensed that Penn should have returned without orders, deserting — as Cromwell put it — 'a company of poor sheep left by their shepherd,' and without having accomplished his chief mission; he therefore ordered Penn and Venables to be imprisoned in the Tower. At this point in the story, the many biographers of the two William Penns part company; most of them follow the lead of Clarendon in his *History of the Rebellion* (1704), and Granville Penn (the admiral's great-grandson) in his *Memorials.... of Sir William Penn* (1833), who portray Penn as a traitor to Cromwell. Their story is that just before or after sailing on the expedition, Penn offered to surrender his fleet to Prince Charles, then in Holland, but that Charles, lacking a harbour and money, was obliged to decline the offer with grateful thanks. They say that Crom-

ADMIRAL SIR WILLIAM PENN

well learned of this treachery, and that this was the real cause of the two leaders' imprisonment.

Miss Brailsford (1930), who has made as much of a hero of William Penn the Admiral as she complains that Quakers have made of William Penn the Quaker, gives a vigorous and plausible defence of Penn against this charge of treason.[17] She points out that both Clarendon and Granville Penn were enthusiastic loyalists, and that the latter's book was written a dozen years before Carlyle had re-established Cromwell in Englishmen's respect; hence, they would both denounce one of Cromwell's most successful admirals. However this may be, it appears obvious that Cromwell's disappointment and high displeasure at the failure of a favourite and highly promising attack upon the Spanish foe, especially in face of a return without orders, would account for the imprisonment; while treason would scarcely have been met with so slight a punishment. Penn was kept in the Tower only five weeks and then released, although shorn of his rank and command in the navy, and deprived of a share in the distribution of lands in Jamaica (whose value soon increased in the mind of Cromwell); but at the same time, he was permitted to retain the lands which Cromwell had granted him in Ireland before setting out on the West Indian expedition. Indeed, one of his son's biographers comments on this failure to secure Jamaica lands that it was the foundation of his son's fortune, because *Pennsylvania* was given to him a quarter-century later in lieu of his claim on *Jamaica!*[18]

Some of the biographers who denounce the admiral as a traitor to his benefactor, Cromwell, say that he was throughout his career 'a Trimmer' and changed his allegiance three times over,— from Charles I to the Parliament, to Cromwell, to Charles II. Others condone him as being not a politician, but a naval man whose duty it was to guard England at sea against the foreign foe, and not to meddle in the contest over the English flag at home on land; moreover, as commander of the fleet, Penn had seized Jamaica, and could not be held directly responsible for the failure of Venables and his army at Hispaniola. The letter he wrote to Cromwell just before his release

---

17 She makes good use of the official Calendar of State Papers as an offset to Clarendon, Granville Penn and Pepys.
18 Sidney George Fisher, 1900. Dixon (1851), Buell (1904), Grant (1907), Graham (1917), Dobrée (1932), and Vulliamy (1934) all accept the Admiral's guilt; Stoughton (1882), leans towards that view; while Clarkson (1814), Janney (1852), and Jenkins (1899) do not raise the question.

from the Tower was certainly not 'a cringing apology,' as some writers describe it, but a dignified explanation of his conduct. 'I returned home without leave,' he wrote, 'for which I have incurred your displeasure, and this is more displeasing to me than any worldly cross. My heart bears me witness that my return was not through refractoriness against superiors, but for the advancement of the service, in giving an account of what would not otherwise be represented.'

It is perhaps significant that no mention of the West Indian expedition appears in the inscription on the admiral's tomb, and especially so if this were written by his son. His son published three years later a forthright defence of him against a charge of dishonesty made by one John Faldo. In this, Penn says:[19] 'What kind of Sea-Captain he was, becomes not me to tell, nor need I; the World knows it;' he then devotes a paragraph to an indignant denial that his father had swelled his estate by taking any mean advantage of his defeated adversaries. The admiral himself had written to his son, the year before his death: 'I challenge all mankind with whom I have had dealing, to charge such a thing [unfair dealing] upon me.'[20] Clarendon's specific charge against him of treason in 1655 was not published until 1704, a half-century after the event and thirty years after the admiral's death.

Released from the Tower, Penn spent a winter in his Wanstead home, then took his family to his estate at Macroom in Ireland, where he led that active planter's life which gave his youthful son and helper a practical knowledge of developing a new country. This estate, as has been said, was assigned him by Cromwell on his departure for the West Indies; but the gift may have been not so much an anticipated reward of victory as it was in lieu of an estate of some £7500 which Penn's wife had lost in Ireland during the troubles of a decade before.[21]

There is some evidence that Penn was reappointed to the navy by Cromwell in March, 1658; but during the next six months before Cromwell's death, he does not appear to have had an active command. Nor is there any evidence that he was active in restoring Ireland to the king's control. But after the death of Oliver Cromwell and the

---

19 *The Invalidity of John Faldo's Vindication*, 1673, *Works*, Vol. II, p. 451. This is one of three pamphlets devoted to Faldo's attack on the Quakers and the two Penns; but among their nearly 250 folio pages occur no other references to his father's naval career.
20 Granville Penn's *Memorials*, II, 570.
21 Brailsford, p. 15, quoting Cal. S.P., 42, 351.

proved inadequacy of his son Richard, the Penns returned to London, and the admiral gave active support to the restoration of the Stuarts to the English throne. He was elected a member for Weymouth in the Convention Parliament, and was sent as one of that parliament's representatives to bring Charles II back from his exile in Holland. In gratitude therefor, and doubtless to aid in binding the navy to his support, the new king conferred knighthood upon Penn and appointed him Commissioner for the Navy, Vice Admiral of Munster, Governor of Kinsale, and proprietor of Shangarry Castle and its lands.

It was just at this time on his restoration to favour, rank, and fortune that the admiral had his first anxious difficulties with his Puritan-minded son; but before the serious break came over his son's Quakerism, the admiral reached the pinnacle of his career. It may be that, as one biographer claims,[22] he was sent with a royal message from Charles to William of Orange, in 1661; but four years later, England was again at war with Holland. During the intervening years, Penn had led the life of a favourite courtier, but also a busy life as commissioner in the restoration and outfitting of the navy. When war was declared, Penn was appointed Great Captain Commander of the flagship of the Duke of York, who had become his friend and pupil as well as his superior officer, the Lord High Admiral of England. In this command, he took part and greatly distinguished himself in the decisive victory over the Dutch fleet off Lowestoft, June 3, 1665.[23]

After this crowning achievement, Penn decided to retire from his naval career. As a reward for his services, the Duke of York desired to have him raised to the peerage with the title of Viscount Weymouth, and he did appoint him Captain-General of the fleet. But Penn's son by this time had cut himself off by his Quakerism from the inheritance of a peerage; and Penn had made up his mind to retire from active life. Repeated attacks of what was called the 'gout' helped in this decision. His declining health was due to the fact, his envious detractor Pepys declares, to immoderate drinking; but a score of exciting and difficult years in the strenuous sea-service of the time, and subjection to the varied climates in which he had lived, had made him feel

---

22 Buell, p. 41, quoting Pepys, Diary, under date of March 12, 1662. If this embassy really did occur, it was repeated by his son a quarter-century later, when he went as envoy to William from James II. The elder Penn's place at court with Charles II was more than duplicated by that of his son at the court of James II.

23 'Y^t Signall and most evidently successful fight against the Dutch fleet,' the inscription on his tomb calls it.

old now, when he was still only forty-five. The Duke of York was desirous that he should take up another command; but the courtiers and the ex-military sea-captains were jealous of him as the leader of the 'tarpaulins,' or old sea-dogs, and they procured his impeachment by the House of Commons on the charge of misappropriating navy funds. He sent a vigorous defence which was accepted by the House of Lords, but the reading of which was delayed in the Commons until after the fleet had gone to sea again to fight the Dutch. Since the impeachment had been designed to keep Penn at home, and had thus been fulfilled, it was quashed and never brought up again. The king and the Duke of York were fully satisfied of Penn's honesty, and their gratitude for his aid in the victories over the Dutch was one of the factors which caused them to grant his son Pennsylvania.[24]

'Thus, He took leave of the Sea, his old Element,' the inscription on his tomb concludes; 'But continued still his other employs [as Commissioner of the Navy] till 1669; at what time, through Bodely Infirmities (contracted by ye Care and fatigue of Publique Affairs), He withdrew, Prepared and made for his End; and with a gentle and Even Gale, in much peace arrived and anchored in his Last and Best Port, at Wanstead in ye County of Essex, ye 16 Sept. 1670, Being then but 49 [years] and 4 months old. To whose Name and merit his surviving Lady hath erected this remembrance.'

During his last days, his son William was undergoing imprisonment and the Penn-Meade Trial; but after a serious break in their relations, they were completely reconciled. William wrote affectionate letters daily to his father, who secretly paid the fines imposed upon the two prisoners eleven days before his death, and thus procured the presence of his son at his death-bed. In *No Cross, No Crown,* William gives an affectionate account of his father's last days and his last words, which were filled with simple piety and courage. An imposing funeral procession, adorned with all the pomp and circumstance of military and naval glory, accompanied his body to its tomb in the architecturally famous church of St. Mary Redcliffe, Bristol.

The career of Admiral Penn shows him to have been an unusual man in an extraordinary era and among exceptionally able contemporaries. It gives evidence of such traits of character as physical courage, financial honesty, and marked ability in his profession. That there were darker traits in keeping with some of the beliefs and prac-

---

24 See *infra*, p. 221.

tices of the times, there can be little doubt. For example, the ruthless treatment of his foes and the brutal usage of the sailors impressed on men-of-war, were shared in or permitted by the 'men higher up' in the navy. That he was ambitious of attaining rank, fortune, and social prestige, was equally true, and this ambition was marred by selfishness or family pride, and not justified by altruistic motives. A royalist and aristocrat, his son made great advance over him at least as far as political and social democracy was concerned.

On the other hand, there are extant letters to show that the admiral had a strain of marked piety which cropped out at various times even before his son exerted so powerful a Quaker influence upon him. What the Quakers call 'that of God within every man,' his son appealed to in his trouble, and with complete success; so that on his death-bed, the 'witness within him' gave testimony to 'the Truth' as his son explained and exemplified it. Indeed, it was no mere death-bed repentance which led him to say : 'This troubles me, that I have offended a gracious God, that has followed me to this day;' nor could it have been merely the echo of his own pious tone and words which the son records in his *No Cross, No Crown*. It is a convincing evidence of his candour and open-mindedness that he was able at the height of his career to acknowledge and approve the sincerity of his son who, at the crucial age of twenty-one, had withstood the dictatorial habit of a naval officer accustomed to implicit obedience; who had dashed all his father's hopes and apparently nullified all the toil and anxieties he had exercised on his behalf; and who had turned his back on the high and useful career of a statesman of the first rank and had apparently doomed himself to an ignominious and ignoble life among the outcasts and reviled of an outlandish religious sect. Forgetting the son's real future, one's sympathies must go out strongly to the disappointed father, and respect and even admiration for his acceptance of his great disappointment cannot be withheld.

As to his influence upon the character and career of his son, there are diverse opinions. The enthusiastic biographers of Penn the Admiral regard him as the greatest factor in the making of Penn the Founder.[25]

---

25 Cf. especially M.R.Brailsford (1930). The envious and hostile Pepys has nearly five hundred references to Sir William Penn in his Diary, the first one dated April 4, 1660, and the last one, May 10, 1669; he mentions Lady Margaret Penn sixty-five times, between August 16, 1664, and September 22, 1668; William Penn the son appears twenty-six times in the Diary, between November 1, 1661, and December 5, 1667; William's younger brother Richard is mentioned only twice, but his sister,

From him, came the son's most influential friendships, including that of three Stuart sovereigns; an example of courage which did not flinch before cannon-balls and which was transmuted by the son into tranquil ignoring of hostile mobs, brutal soldiery, and bullying judges; a scorn of the immoralities which vitiated the characters of most of the courtiers of the Restoration; a deep and abiding affection for a pure family life; an implicit faith in the existence of God, and an unquestioning acknowledgment of, though, alas, not a uniform obedience to, the supremacy of the Divine will.

The striking resemblances and differences between the portraits of father and son are paralleled by those between some parts of their careers. Against the father's strong desire, the first turned his back on trade and went into the navy; the second turned his upon a courtier's career and became a Quaker preacher. Obedience to conscience brought both of them happiness and fame in their respective fields. The attacks of enemies upon them both in the last part of their lives did not permanently tarnish their reputations, which continue to shine brightly, the one as a naval victor, the other as a Quaker statesman. During the first twenty-six years of the son's life, the father contributed to it much of weal and woe, both in his absence and his presence, despite the long time he was obliged to spend at sea. Impossible though it be to measure the father's influence on his son's character and career, it was assuredly a strong factor in both of them, and it helps to supplement in accounting for them that unknown force of 'genius.'

In a material way, Penn's father was of great assistance to his son's career. The income from his Irish estates enabled the son to lead a life of large means, to preach and publish widely, and to contribute generously to the aid of the persecuted Quakers and to the expenses of their travelling ministers; while to his father's several claims upon the Stuart kings was partly due William's opportunity for one of his two greatest achievements, namely, the founding of Pennsylvania.

'Pegg' (Mrs.Anthony Lowther) is referred to nearly a hundred times. Pepys was Clerk of the Acts in the Navy Office and the two families of Pepys and Penns lived side by side in the Navy Yard, and were quite intimate, despite Pepys' suppressed contempt and hatred for the elder Penn.

PENN'S MOTHER

THE greatness of great men has often been attributed to their mothers. This has been the case with William Penn, a few of whose biographers have made his mother play a large part in his character and career. Most certainly it was she who bore him, and who brought to bear upon him the influence of both heredity and environment. Singularly little is known about her. There has even been uncertainty as to her nationality. Penn himself does not enlighten us upon it; and her great-grandson, Granville Penn, dismisses her from his two-volume account of her husband with the statement: 'Sir William Penn married very early in life, Margaret, the daughter of John Jasper, of Rotterdam.'[26] The first two historians of Quakerism, both of them Hollanders and both of them contemporary with Penn and his mother, make no mention of her, but state only that he was the son of the admiral,—although one of them adds the information that Penn 'was not born to him but to his Country, and to the Commonwealth!'[27] Even the first biographer of Penn in English mentions in stating his birth only his father.[28]

The first mention of the mother in print is in the diary of the not always veracious Samuel Pepys, who says under the date of August 19, 1664: 'After dinner my wife and I to Sir W. Pen's, to see his Lady, the first time, who is a well-looked, fat, short, old Dutch woman.' Pepys makes in his diary no amplification of this adjective 'Dutch'; and Lord Braybrooke, in his edition of Pepys' Diary merely adds after John Jasper's name the word *merchant,* although one of Braybrooke's editors calls him 'Sir John.'[29] Successive biographers of William Penn inferred from these statements that Margaret Jasper was born in Rotterdam of good Dutch parents.[30]

Contemporary Rotterdam records give no clue to a 'John Jasper,

---

26 *Memorials of . . . Sir William Penn,* 1833, Vol. II, p. 572.
27 Gerard Croese, *Historia Quakeriana,* 1695, p. 285: 'tanquam natum non sibi, sed patriae ac communi.' Cf. also Willem Sewel, *Histori van de . . . Quakers,* 1717, p. 544: 'zoon van den Ridder en Admiraal Penn.'
28 Joseph Besse, 1726.
29 Braybrooke's editions, 1825-1854. The Calendar of State Papers, 47, 24 cites a John Baptist Jasper, who lived on the Strand in London and bought numerous pictures, between 1649 and 1653, which had belonged to Charles I. It has been suggested that he was Penn's maternal grandfather. Cf. Brailsford, 12.
30 One of his biographers (Buell, 1904), determined to make Penn 'a full-blood, thorough-bred Englishman,' draws on his imagination and states: 'His mother was Margaret, daughter of John Jasper, an English merchant, settled in Rotterdam as correspondent or "resident partner" of an important London trading-house.'

merchant of Rotterdam'; but in 1908, Dr. Albert Cook Myers, of Philadelphia, discovered in the records of the Dutch Reformed Church of Austin Friars, London, that John and Marie Jasper, who resided before 1641 at Ballycase, County Clare, Ireland, had a daughter named Margaret; that this daughter was married before 1641 to Nicasius Vanderscure (or Van der Schuren), of Kilconry and Parish of Kilrush, County Clare, Ireland; and that on June 6, 1643, in St. Martin's Church, Ludgate, London, Captain William Penn was married to Margaret Van der Schuren, widow.[31]

After this, it was assumed that the Jaspers were Irish; that William Penn's 'Celtic touch' came through his mother from Irish, as well as through his father from Welsh ancestry; and that his mother was a 'Dutchwoman' only by virtue of the fact that her first husband had a Dutch name, and that she was known as the Widow Van der Schuren when she married Captain Penn. But since then, Dr. Myers has discovered records in Ireland which show that the Jaspers had been citizens of Holland and had been naturalized in County Clare, Ireland, in 1634-35. Their daughter, Margaret, who was older than her second husband, must have been born some years before her parents' naturalization in Ireland; hence she was herself of Dutch ancestry and citizenship, and was probably born in Rotterdam, where her father had been a merchant.[32] So that after all, the contemporary diarist's 'Dutchwoman' may have been correct.

In view of William Penn's important connexions with Holland in later years, it is of much historic and biographical interest to associate him through his maternal ancestry with that sturdy land of religious toleration and political freedom. In this indirect way, as well as directly through the Dutch colonists who founded Germantown, his colony of Pennsylvania owed much of its virtue and its prosperity to his mother's mother-land. Margaret's mother is said to have been

---

31 *Journal* of the Friends' Historical Society, London, Vol. V (1908), p. 118. Howard M.Jenkins, *Family of William Penn*, 1899, p. 20, note 3, says: 'Mr.Charles P.Keith, of Philadelphia, a distinguished genealogist, has informed me that he has seen in printed records, but precisely where he has not been able to recall, evidence that Margaret Jasper was a widow at the time of her marriage to Captain Penn, Jasper being her maiden name.'

32 The official records which reveal this naturalization have since been destroyed by fire; but Dr. Myers possesses a transcript of them. They give Margaret's first husband's name as Vander Scu*d*en, which means 'of the vagrants' (perhaps 'wanderers' or 'immigrants'), if Scuden be a variant of Schudden. Van der Schuren means 'of the barns.' No Rotterdam records of this family of Jaspers are extant (cf. Monograph No. Two, *William Penn and the Dutch Quaker Migration to Pennsylvania*, pp. 1-2).

named Marie; and this raises the question if she or *her* mother was originally not Dutch, but French (Huguenot), or Anglo-Irish. At all events, through her, or perhaps through Jan Jasper's purchase of lands in Ireland and their subsequent loss in the Irish Rebellion of 1641, Margaret is said to have had a claim on land in County Clare; and this may help to account for the subsequent cession of an Irish estate to her second husband, Captain Penn.

In the absence of authentic information regarding her, her son's biographers have permitted their fancy to play round her appearance, character, and influence on her son. Samuel Pepys appears to have been the only person who wrote a contemporary account of her. According to him, she was 'a well looked, fat, short old Dutch woman, but one that hath been heretofore pretty handsome.' At various other places in his Diary, he gives very picturesque impressions of her gayety and unrestrained manners, and makes her out to be an innocent but unpleasing reflection of the Restoration Court. His longest reference to her is as follows:[33] 'Then we fell to talk of Sir W. Pen, and his family and rise. She [Mrs. Turner] says that he was a pityfull [fellow] when she first knew them; that his lady was one of the sourest, dirty women, that ever she saw; that they took two chambers, one over another, for themselves and child, in Tower Hill; that for many years together they eat more meals at her house than at their own; did call brothers and sisters the husbands and wives; that her husband was godfather to one, and she godmother to another (this Margaret) of their children, by the same token that she was fain to write with her own hand a letter to Captain Twiddy, to stand for a godfather for her; that she brought my Lady, who then was a dirty slattern, with her stockings hanging about her heels, so that afterwards the people of the whole Hill did say that Mrs. Turner had made Mrs. Pen a gentlewoman, first to the knowledge of my Lady Vane, Sir Henry's lady, and him to the knowledge of most of the great people that then he sought to.'

Taking hints from Pepys, sundry biographers have written such descriptions of her as 'a homely, boisterous woman, loud, rompish, untidy if not slatternly, with no pretensions to breeding and elegance.'[34] Another says: 'She was short, plump, good-looking, free-handed, and

---

[33] Under date of May 21, 1667. Mrs. Turner was the wife of Thomas Turner, chief clerk in the Navy Office.
[34] Vulliamy, p. 32.

happy-go-lucky, fond of a frolic and remarkably untidy; she would allow her stockings to draggle about her heels, while her clothes were crushed and toil-stained.'[35] Another, on the contrary, has suggested that Penn's *'Irish* mother brought with her from the wilds of Clare a merry and indomitable spirit and a hand always ready to help the sick and distressed;'[36] while still another opines that she was 'stout and handsome with many of the sprightly ways that she had learned in the *Dutch* city [of Rotterdam].'[37] Taking a median view, one author regards Lady Penn as 'a woman as merry as she was tender-hearted; she was as much at home in a boisterous party at Lady Batten's, where the guests blacked their faces and danced jigs till midnight, as at the bedside of her husband's old captain, Sir John Harman, invalided home from the war.'[38]

Captain Penn's wooing of his bride is equally uncertain and therefore guessed at. One author surmises: 'At Rotterdam, the Bristol boy had fallen in with Margaret, a daughter of Hans [!] Jasper—of that town,—a girl with rosy flesh and nimble wit, and being taken by her comely face, had offered her his heart, and taken up her own in pledge.'[39] Another says: 'When William Penn the elder met her, she was in England as a refugee from the massacre of Protestants [in Ireland?], and already the widow of a Dutchman.'[40] And still another asserts that 'Margaret Jasper was quite as English as Captain Penn, and their son was a full-blood, thoroughbred Englishman.'[41]

There is even some uncertainty as to the time of her marriage with Penn. Most writers give this date as January 6, 1643-44, accepting as authentic the following statement of Pepys: 'January 6th (Twelfth day), [1661-62]: This morning . . . to dinner to Sir W. Pen's, it being a solemn feast day with him, his wedding day, and we had, besides a good chine of beef and other good cheer, eighteen mince pies in a dish, the number of the years that he hath been married.' From this, it seems clear that *January* 6, 1643 (that is, 1644) is the correct date; but the records in St. Martin's Church, Ludgate, London, where the marriage occurred, appear to give the date as *June* 6, 1643.

We catch but very few glimpses of the wife and mother after this.

35 Dobrée, p. 2.
36 Brailsford, p. XVII.
37 Huckel, p. 33.
38 Brailsford, p. 149 (citing Cal. S.P., 296,12).
39 Dixon, p. 15.
40 Dobrée, p. 2.
41 Buell, p. 5.

For some years, the family was poor, and Mrs. Penn's housekeeping was severely criticized as being on a low plane, disregardful of the ordinary rules of polite society, and in keeping with her disregard of dress, even to the extent of allowing her stockings to hang about her heels — 'a piece of carelessness only tolerable in the bogs of Clare.'[42] But this criticism was retailed by the malicious Pepys as related to him by a gossipy neighbour. Pepys himself was a coarse individual, with only the thin veneer of a gentleman; and his bitter envy of Sir William Penn's success and position found expression in persistent malice, which may have been extended to his wife as well. It has even been suggested that Pepys called Lady Penn a *Dutch* woman for the purpose of discrediting her husband at a time when England was at war with Holland and when everything Dutch was denounced and despised as having to do with England's 'enemy.' William Penn the younger found favour in the eyes of the old cynic, who despite his innumerable gibes at the boy's parents and Quakerism, bequeathed to him a ring valued at twenty shillings.[43]

We have a few glimpses of Penn's mother during his boyhood and youth, both in his education and in his troubles with his father. If she were a Dutch woman, then, it is argued, it was from her that he acquired a speaking knowledge of the Dutch language which was to stand him in such good stead on his three missionary and colonizing journeys in Holland. The strong religious bent of the son is attributed to his mother's influence;[44] and it is even claimed that his great championship of religious toleration received its impulse from his freedom-loving ancestors in tolerant Holland.

On his expulsion from Oxford, his mother tried to shield him from his father's chastisement; and on his two expulsions from home, she is credited with sending him secret means of support.[45] His first imprisonment in the Tower should have afforded her a splendid opportunity of showing her affection and assistance; but it is only his ultra-romantic biographers who can seize and make appropriate use

---

42 Brailsford, 14. Cf. Pepys' Diary under date of May 21, 1667 (*supra*, p. 9).
43 Penn was only one of about 140 individuals to whom rings were bequeathed; so that, if they were intended as a kind of post mortem *amende honorable*, the testator must have had many recipients of his apology as well as of his cynicism. Penn was not present at the funeral, which occurred on June 5, 1703, and his ring was sent to him by Pepys' executor; it should be one of much personal interest!
44 Cf. Weems and Marsillac, in Monograph Number Three (*Eight First Biographies of William Penn in Seven Languages and Seven Lands*).
45 Besse, I, 4; Clarkson, I, 233; Webb, p. 189.

of this opportunity.⁴⁶ One of these invents the theory that when his mother visited him in the Tower, hoping to convert him back to a rational religion, he succeeded in persuading her of the truth of Quakerism. But another resourceful biographer suggests that when he was twenty-two, by refusing to attend the christening of his sister Pegg's daughter, he at last offended even his mother: 'She was outraged by a piety which checked her pitiful efforts at merriment and looked askance at the gay young life which she introduced to the house to distract the Admiral from his sorrowful preoccupations.'⁴⁷

With Lady Penn's relations with her husband, even the envious Pepys could find no fault. She is named first among the heirs in the will of the Admiral, who bequeathed to her ('my dear wife, Dame Margaret Penn'), £300, most of her jewels, and one-half of his personal property. He made his son William the sole executor of his will, and directed that if any differences should arise between him and his mother they should be settled by arbitration, although, he said, 'I cannot apprehend that any differences can fall out or happen between my said dear wife and my said son William.'⁴⁸

Lady Penn doubtless spent much of the time after her husband's death in the Yorkshire home of her daughter Margaret, then Mrs. Lowther; but she lived also with her son William, and died in his home at Worminghurst. She was buried at Walthamstow, March, 1681-82;⁴⁹ and thus lived to see her son become a great landed proprietor in the New World, although she died some seven months before his first visit to it, perhaps in the midst of his extensive preparations for the voyage. The strong affection which he cherished for her is indicated by the fact that his grief for her death caused him an illness so severe, it is alleged, that he could not bear the light for many days.⁵⁰ His own comment is preserved in a letter, in which he wrote: 'My sickness upon my mother's death, who was last seventh day interred, permitted me not to answer thee so soon as desired.'⁵¹

Like most of the writers who have endeavoured to trace the greatness of Abraham Lincoln to his almost unknown mother, so some of the biographers of William Penn have declared that he was peculiarly his

---

46 Weems and Marsillac (Monograph Number Three).
47 Brailsford, p. 206.
48 Granville Penn, II, 566.
49 ibid. II, 572.
50 Huckel, p. 140.
51 Clarkson, I, 233.

mother's boy; that during the impressionable years of his childhood he saw his father for only brief periods at long intervals; and that he was wholly unlike his paternal forebears. But since his character and career were unique in his entire family, before and since he lived, it must probably be said of him, as of most other geniuses, that he was born of the Spirit which like the wind bloweth where it listeth, and we hear the sound thereof, but cannot tell whence it cometh, nor whither it goeth.

PENN'S FAMILY

THE parents of William Penn had three children: himself, his sister Margaret, and his brother Richard. Margaret was about eight years younger than he, but was married to Anthony Lowther in February, 1667, at the age of fifteen. She is the lively 'Pegg Pen' who appears so many times in the Diary of Samuel Pepys; and she and her descendants remained in the aristocracy and minor nobility of England, far from Quaker circles.[52]

Richard Penn, or 'Dicke Pen,' was the 'Valentine' of Pepys' wife on St. Valentine's Day, 1665, and was at that time, according to the diarist, 'a notable, stout, witty boy.' He was then, apparently, about ten years old, hence a dozen years William's junior. He was sent to sea in his 'teens, and was probably designed to follow his father's maritime career; but he died, unmarried, in April, 1673, at about the age of eighteen, and was buried at Walthamstow. By his father's will, he was to have received £120 a year until he was twenty-one, and then £4,000; but on his death, his share in the father's estate reverted to his older brother. He lived to attend his brother's wedding and sign his marriage certificate, and died in his brother's home at Rickmansworth. A nephew, one of William Penn's sons, was named for him.

The difference in age between William and his sister and brother, and his absence at Oxford and on the Continent, prevented much companionship between the children in their early years, and William's Quaker activities separated him from them in his early manhood.

---

52 Margaret's home was in Yorkshire at the time of her brother William's marriage, and distance or family affairs may have prevented her from attending his wedding; her name is not signed with those of her mother and brother Richard on his marriage certificate.

GULIELMA PENN AND HER CHILDREN

At the age of twenty-seven, William was married to Gulielma Maria Springett, the daughter of Sir William and Lady Mary Springett. Lady Mary — one of the most interesting of the early Quakers — was the daughter of Sir John and Lady Anne Proud, and was born in Holland, her father being at the time a colonel in the service of the Dutch Republic. Left an orphan at the age of three, she was brought up in the home of her guardian, Sir Edward Partridge, and married at the age of eighteen, William Springett, the elder son of Sir Edward's sister. Educated in a Puritan college, St. Catherine's Hall, in Cambridge, Springett studied law at Lincoln's Inn and, through the influence of his royalist uncle, Sir Thomas Springett, was knighted by Charles I.[53] But in the Civil War, Sir William sided with the Parliament, took part in the battles of Edgehill and Newbury, was made a colonel and placed in command of Arundel Castle, which he had helped to capture. Here, he fell ill of a wound received at Newbury, which resulted in spinal meningitis, and he died in 1644, in his twenty-fourth year. This was three years after his marriage, two years after the birth of his only son (who died in infancy), and a few weeks before the birth of his only daughter and namesake, Gulielma.

Gulielma was born early in 1644, and was thus some months older than William Penn. When she was ten years of age, her mother married the noted Quaker mystic, Isaac Penington, son of Sir Isaac Penington, the Puritan lord mayor of London in 1642-43. When she was fourteen, she and her mother and step-father united with the Friends in London, and soon afterwards removed to the Penington estate at Grange, Chalfont St. Peter's, in Buckinghamshire. Six imprisonments for Quakerism, and the confiscation of most of their property did not dim Penington's mystical faith, or daunt his wife's intrepid spirit.

The marriage of William Penn and Gulielma Springett occurred on the 4th of April, 1672, as stated in the marriage certificate,[54] 'in a godly

---

53 His knighthood appears to have been confirmed by Parliament because of his services in the Puritan cause.
54 A copy of this certificate is preserved in Somerset House, in the close vicinity of which (No.21 Norfolk Street) was one of Penn's London residences. The copy is in the handwriting of Thomas Ellwood, the friend and amanuensis of Milton, the editor of Fox's 'Journal,' author of a valuable autobiography, a tutor for seven years of the Penington children, and a life-long friend and undeclared admirer of Gulielma.

GULIELMA MARIA SPRINGETT PENN

sort & manner (according to the good old Order & practice of the Church of Christ) in a publick Assembly of the People of the Lord At King's, Chorle-wood in the County of Hertford [King's Farm, Chorleywood].'

Thomas Ellwood's autobiography gives us a satisfactory impression of Gulielma's charm and excellence. She was, he says,[55] 'in all respects a very desirable Woman, (whether regard was had to her outward Person, which wanted nothing to render her compleatly Comely, or to the Endowments of her Mind, which were every way Extraordinary, and highly Obliging; or to her outward Fortune, which was fair, and which with some hath not the last, nor the least place in Consideration).' Her habitual kindness was 'expressed in an innocently open, free and familiar Conversation, springing from the abundant Affability, Courtesy and Sweetness of her natural Temper.' But she was not to become Ellwood's wife, being reserved, as he himself quaintly says, for another.

None of the love-letters of Penn to Guli before their marriage are extant; but on the eve of his first visit to Pennsylvania, ten years after their marriage, he gives us glimpses of his regard for her. 'My dear wife!', he writes; 'remember thou wast the love of my youth, and much the joy of my life; the most beloved, as well as the most worthy of all my earthly comforts: and the reason of that love was more thy inward than thy outward excellencies, which yet were many. God knows, and thou knowest it, I can say it was a match of Providence's making.' In the same letter, he says to his children: 'Be obedient to your dear mother, a woman whose virtue and good name are an honour to you. . . . Honour and obey her, my dear children, as your mother and as your father's love and delight; nay, love her too, for she loved your father with a deep and upright love, choosing him before all her many suitors.'

The first meeting between Gulielma and William Penn is said to have occurred in 1667, soon after his return from Ireland, where he had accepted Quakerism and was still under his father's displeasure. This story is as follows:[56] 'coming to London went to a meeting before

55 Life, 1714, pp. 210-14.
56 The MS. containing the story was in the possession of the Huntley family of High Wycombe, from whom Maria Webb borrowed it and utilized it in her *Penns and Peningtons of the Seventeenth Century,* 1867, pp. 189-199. The MS. is dated 1729, and was written by an unknown author, who says that the narrative was related by William Penn himself to Thomas Harvey (also unknown) 'about thirty years since wch Thos: Harvey related me in a brief manner as well as his Memory would serve

he went to see his Father after meeting went up into ye Room where a Friend brought Guly Springett wch was ye first time he saw her who was afterwards his wife; but returning home his Father told him he had heard what work he had been making in the country and after some discourse his Father bid him take his cloaths and be Gon from his house for he should not be there also that he should dispose of his Estate to them that pleased him better.'

During the next four years before their marriage, Penn saw his future wife on his various travels, for her home was conveniently located *en route* from London to Ireland and was in (or made) the centre of his Quaker meeting activities.[57] The marriage was performed in strict accordance with the custom of the Society of Friends. The records of Jordans Monthly Meeting (held at that time in the house of Thomas Ellwood) for the 7th of 12 Month, 1671 (February, 1672) state the preliminary step as follows: 'William Penn, of Walthamstow, in the County of Essex, and Gulielma Maria Springett, of Tiler's End Green, in the County of Bucks, proposed their intention of taking each other in marriage. Whereupon it was referred to Daniel Zachary and Thomas Ellwood to inquire into the clearness of their proceedings and give an account to next meeting.' On the 6th of the next month, the committee reported to the Monthly Meeting that the 'clearness' was satisfactory; the meeting therefore gave 'the consent and approbation of Friends,' and the marriage duly followed on the 2nd of April. The record of the marriage certificate, with the signatures of forty-six witnesses is preserved; and there is extant the following extract from a later contemporary diary: '4th of 2nd Mo. 1672. They took each other in marriage at Charlewood, at a farmhouse called Kings, where Friends meeting [for worship] was yn kept, being in ye parish of Rickmansworth, in ye county of Hertford.'[58]

This crown of Penn's happiness came to him after the ten troubled years of his early manhood, after his imprisonments in Cork, in London Tower, and in Newgate. Nearly twenty-one years of an idyllic married life followed, but these too were marked with many troubles, as well as with Penn's greatest achievements. His many absences from home on religious and political labours were cheerfully endured by his

---

after such a distance of time.' It is now in the possession of the Library at Friends House, London, and has been published in the *Journal* of the Friends' Historical Society, London, Vol. 32 (1935), pp. 22-26.
57 Cf. *infra*, p. 114.
58 Howard M. Jenkins, *The Family of William Penn*, 1899, pp. 60-61.

'THE QUAKER WEDDING'

wife, even though they began almost immediately after the young couple entered upon the building of their home and lasted continuously until the end of her life. 'She would not suffer me to neglect any Publick Meeting,' he says,[59] 'after I had my Liberty [in 1693], upon her Account, saying often, "O go my Dearest! Don't hinder any Good for me. I desire thee go : I have cast my Care upon the Lord : I shall see thee again!"' Indeed, in the early years of their married life, she rode with her husband upon many of his religious travels in England. She could not accompany him, because of family cares, on his journey to Holland in 1677, or on his first visit to Pennsylvania in 1682. During the time of this latter visit, she suffered a severe illness, and in the course of it called upon her old friend Thomas Ellwood to advise with her on business affairs. Ellwood had just published, at the time of the 'Rye-House Plot' against the king, a tract [60] which gave offence to the magistrates of Rickmansworth, and they summoned him to appear before them; but when he told them of the call from 'Madam Penn,' they readily excused him out of respect for her, and indeed dropped the persecution.

Gulielma's strength and health had been depleted by the arduous and perilous journey of her mother before her father's death and before her own birth a few weeks afterwards. The many vicissitudes of her mother's and step-father's life, which she shared, and a severe attack of the small-pox which she experienced a few years before her marriage, did not conduce to a rugged physique.[61] The hard horseback travel over rough roads on preaching journeys with her husband when she was about to become a mother, also helps to account for the death of three of their children in infancy, the physical decline and death at twenty of their son Springett, the weakness in body and morals of their son William, and her own premature death at the age of forty-nine.

There are very few references to Gulielma — except for the birth and death of her children — during her married life. It was probably the illness and death of her own mother, which occurred at the Penn's

---

59 His *Account of the Blessed End of Gulielma Maria Springett,* 1694 (*Works,* 1726, Vol. I, p. 231).
60 It was entitled *A Caution to Constables . . . concerned in the Execution of the Conventicle Act.* Cf. Ellwood's *Autobiography,* 1714, pp. 323-338.
61 The casual way in which small-pox infection was treated at that time is illustrated by Thomas Ellwood in an account of a visit which he made to the family when Gulielma was recovering from her attack but came down stairs to see him 'with the Marks of the Distemper fresh upon her' (*Autobiography,* 1714, pp. 42-43). Ellwood himself soon afterwards developed the disease, and suffered an impairment of his sight therefrom (ibid. pp. 129-130).

home at Worminghurst, that prevented her from accompanying her husband to Pennsylvania in 1682. Lady Mary Springett Penington died on the 18th of 7th Month (September), 1682, about a fortnight after Penn sailed in *The Welcome;* and earlier in that same year (about March 1), Penn's own mother had died in his home, having doubtless been lovingly nursed in her last illness by her daughter-in-law.

The next year, Gulielma herself had an alarming illness,[62] but recovered from it before her husband's return from America. During his absence she wrote at least two letters which have been preserved, and which show that she had planned to join him in Pennsylvania. In the first of these, she says:[63] 'There have been great reports of my husband coming with J. Purvis, A. Parker's brother-in-law; but he has returned without him, and brought letters. My husband was then very well on the 8th of the Fourth-month, and has some thoughts of coming, but when he did not mention. This puts a stop at present to my going; but with the Lord I desire to leave it, and commit him and myself to His holy ordering.'

Two months later, Penn arrived from America, and soon afterwards wrote to Margaret Fell Fox, who had been his wife's affectionate correspondent during his absence. 'My dear wife relates,' he says,[64] 'thy great love to her in my absence, and so she also wrote me word, which affected my heart and soul. I return thee my tender acknowledgment. . . . It is now a few days above three weeks since I arrived well in my native land. It was within seven miles of my own house that we landed. I found my dear wife and her children well, to the overcoming of my heart because of the mercies of the Lord to us.'

The other letter attributed to Gulielma is endorsed 1690, but it must have been written in 1684. It is also addressed to Margaret Fox, and after telling of a dream which she had had about Margaret and George Fox, it contains the following interesting paragraphs:[65] 'Dear Margaret, I received thy acceptable letter long since, but have delayed writing to thee, in the hope to give a fuller account of my husband and of our going [to Pennsylvania]. But the winter and spring have

---

62 *Supra*, p. 35.
63 It was writen to Margaret Fell Fox, under date of Worminghurst, 2nd 6th mo. 1684, and is preserved in the Thirnbeck MSS. of Bristol, now in Friends House, London; it is quoted *in toto* by Webb, pp. 370-372 (Phila., 1868), pp. 354-355 (London, 1867).
64 ibid. p. 372 (356).
65 This letter is printed in Webb, pp. 373-5 (London, 1867), 389-91 (Philadelphia, 1868); it is in the Sylvanus Thompson collection of MSS., in Friends House, London.

been so severe that letters have been hindered; and now that many are come, none of them of late dates are for me, because my husband has been in daily expectation of seeing us there, and I am sorry for his disappointment. I should have been truly glad to have seen him before [our] going, as thou sayest, but am contented, and desire not his coming merely to fetch us, as I know he has a great deal of business to attend to; and also know it is not for want of true love or the desire to see us that keeps him, but it is that he must first mind the duties of the place in which he now stands, and do that which is right, and in which he has peace. If the Lord gives clearness and drawings to come, I would be glad, but see no likelihood at present.

'We have been much hindered, and are still, by reason of the Friend who does our business here being under some trouble; having many years ago been bound for a man who is lately dead, and whose creditors are now coming on him; so that I cannot depend on his remaining here, and know not where to get another that is fit to leave things to at present, which is a great strait to my mind; my husband writing every letter for us.'

Press of business affairs evidently prevented Gulielma from going to Pennsylvania during her husband's first visit; and before he went a second time, she had died. The memory of her gracious presence in Philadelphia would have added much interest to the history of the beginnings of the City of Brotherly (and Sisterly) Love. As it is, there are very few memorials of her in her husband's colony.[66]

During the stormy years of Penn's life as a courtier at the court of King James, and as a suspected traitor under King William, we get almost no glimpses of Gulielma. There is a legend recorded in Agnes Strickland's *Lives of the Queens of England*[67] that 'every year,' after the fall of James II, 'Mrs. Pen, the wife of James's former protégé, the

---

66 One of these is a fine elm tree, the 'grandchild' of the historic Elm of Shackamaxon, which stands beside another scion of the same tree on the campus of Swarthmore College; the trees shade the Friends Historical Library of the college. The original tree was blown down in 1810, aged 283 years.

67 Philadelphia, 1846, Vol. IX (Mary Beatrice of Modena), p. 272, footnote No. 2. In this footnote, Miss Strickland refers to 'Kennersley's Life of Pen, 1740,' and makes the statement: 'Mrs. Pen was the daughter of a cavalier of good family.' 'Kennersley's Life of Pen' is entirely unknown. Janney, in his *Life of Penn*, 1852, p. 376, quotes this legend, with the footnote: 'The author [Miss Strickland] refers to Carstairs State papers.' William Carstares (1649-1715) was a private secretary of William III, and his State Papers and letters addressed to him were edited by J. M. M'Cormick and published in Edinburgh, 1774; but Miss Strickland's reference to these is in her footnote No. 3, and relates to a Jacobite spy, a Mrs. Ogilvie of Scotland, and not to Mrs. Penn.

founder of Pennsylvania, paid a visit to the court of St. Germains, carrying with her a collection of all the little presents which the numerous friends and well-wishers of James II. and his queen could muster. Mrs. Pen was always affectionately received by the king and queen, although she maintained the fact that the revolution was necessary, and what she did was from the inviolable affection and gratitude she personally felt towards their majesties.'

This legend appears as improbable as it is unauthenticated. Very soon after the Revolution had driven the Stuarts from the throne, Penn went into seclusion and semi-parole in London for three years, during which time Gulielma had her hands quite full with care of her children and occasional visits to her husband. He was acquitted in December, 1693, and went immediately to his 'poor wife and children.' Of the former, he wrote: 'My wife is yet weakly; but I am not without hopes of her recovery, who is of the best of wives and women.'[68] This letter was written from Hoddesdon, in Hertfordshire, where the family were united after Penn's release from surveillance in London, and it was here that Gulielma died two months later, February 23, 1694, in her fiftieth year. Four days later, Penn wrote to Robert Turner as follows:[69] 'My extreme great affliction for the Decease of my dear wife, makes me unfit to write much, whom the great God took to himself from the troubles of this exercising world the 23d inst. In great peace and Sweetness She departed, and to her Gain, but our incomparable Loss, being one of *ten thousand*, wise, chaste, humble, plain, modest, industrious, constant and undaunted. But God is God, and good— and so I hope tho afflicted, not forsaken.'

'In the 12th Month, 1693,' Penn's first biographer says, 'departed this Life his Beloved Wife, Gulielma Maria, with whom he had liv'd in all the Endearments of that nearest Relation about Twenty One Years. The Loss of Her was a very great Exercise, such, himself said, As all his other Troubles were nothing in Comparison of. Her Character, Dying Expressions, and Pious End, were related by himself in an Account he published.' This *Account of the Blessed End of Gulielma Maria Penn, and of Springet Penn, the Beloved Wife, and Eldest Son of William Penn*, was printed, without date, 'for the Benefit

---

68 Letter to Thomas Lloyd and others in Philadelphia, dated at Hodson (Hoddesden), 11th of 10th Month (December), 1693; MSS. collection of Pennsylvania Historical Society, IV, I.
69 *Memoirs* of the Pennsylvania Historical Society, IV, I, 200-1.

THE GRAVES OF THE PENN FAMILY AT JORDANS

of his Family, Relations, and particular Friends in Memory of them, and the Lord's Goodness to them.'[70] Of Gulielma's illness, this Account says that it had lasted eight months, 'though she never perfectly recovered her Weakness the Year before, which held her about Six Months.' This steady break-down of her health is a reflection of the sorrow and anxiety she suffered for her husband's troubles, and his imprisonment was heavily burdened by the realization of her failing health. With her departure, he felt that the sun of his life was sinking rapidly towards its setting; but the chief work of his life had been achieved in the sunshine of her love.

'She quietly expired in my Arms,' he says, 'her Head upon my Bosom, with a sensible and devout Resignation of her Soul to Almighty God;' and she was buried beside her mother in the Friends' graveyard at Jordans, near the beautiful scenes of their youthful courtship and marriage a score of years before. After another quarter-century of sad, laborious years, her husband was to take his place beside her.

GULIELMA'S CHILDREN

SEVEN children were born to William Penn and Gulielma, between 1673 and 1685, but four of these died in infancy.[71] The first three were a daughter, Gulielma Maria, and the twins, William and Mary, who were born in 1673 and 1674, respectively. The eldest daughter lived about two months; and the twins were born about ten months later. The twin son and daughter lived only four months and thirteen months, respectively.[72] In 1685 Gulielma's youngest child was born and was named, like the eldest, Gulielma Maria; but she too died in early childhood, at the age of four. Three of these infants were born and died at Rickmansworth; the last was born at Worminghurst, and died at Hammersmith, near London; all four were buried at Jordans.

[70] It was probably written soon after the wife's and son's deaths in 1694 and 1696, respectively, but its printed version is grouped under his writings in 1699 (in Joseph Smith's *Catalogue of Friends' Books*, 1867, Vol. II, p. 318); it appears in Besse, op.cit., I, 231-4.
[71] Howard M.Jenkins, op.cit., p. 64, citing the records of the Friends' Meetings for the Upper Side of Bucks and for Surrey and Sussex.
[72] It was of the twin daughter, Mary (or Margaret, as she was also called after both her grandmothers), to whom Penn referred in a letter to George Fox, December 10, 1674, as follows: 'My wife is well, and child; only teeth, she has one cut.' (Sylvanus Thompson MSS.).

SPRINGETT PENN

THE three children of Gulielma who reached maturity were Springett, Letitia, and William the Younger. Springett was born at Walthamstow, in Essex, 11th Month 25, 1675 (that is, February, 1676). It may have been the fear lest Rickmansworth's unhealthful location had caused the death of their first three infants, that caused the Penns to remove to Walthamstow for the birth of their fourth. Proximity to the home of Lady Penn at Wanstead and Penn's earlier residence in Walthamstow may have been additional reasons for this removal. The next year, however, the family removed to Worminghurst, in Sussex, and it was here that Springett spent most of the twenty years of his life. Many pages have been written by Penn's biographers, and by Penn himself, on Springett's death, but very few facts are known about his life.

Penn begins the narrative of his journey to Holland and Germany in 1677, when Springett (his only child at the time) was a year and a half old, with the words: '22d. 5. Month, being the First Day of the Week, I left my Dear Wife and Family at Worminghurst in Sussex, in the Fear and Love of God, and came well to London that Night.' At the end of this narrative, he writes: 'The first day of the next week [November 5, 1677, after his return from Holland], I went to Worminghurst, my house in Sussex, where I found my dear Wife, Child and Family all well, blessed be the name of the Lord God of all the families of the Earth. I had that Evening a sweet meeting [for worship] amongst them, in which God's blessed Power made us truly glad together.'[73]

Five years later, Penn set sail for Pensylvania and before his ship, the *Welcome,* left the Downs, he wrote to Springett, then six and a half years old, the following note:[74] 'My dear Springett. Be good, learn to fear God, avoide evil, love thy book, be kind to thy Brother and Sister & God will bless thee & I will exceedingly love thee. farewell dear child

thy dear Father

Wm Penn.'

---

73 *Travails, 1677,* 1694, pp. 1 and 281-2.
74 It was dated 19th 6 mo (August) 82, and superscribed: 'For Springett Penn, at Worminghurst, Sussex.— By Arundell Bagg.' It was one of three notes — the others addressed to his daughter and younger son — all written on a single sheet of paper which is preserved among the MSS. of the Pennsylvania Historical Society. Cf. Jenkins. op.cit., p. 66.

A Topical Biography 41

The brother and sister mentioned in this note were William Junior, then two and a half, and Letitia, then four and a half years old. The long letter which Penn had written before leaving home, addressed to his Dear Wife and Children, was evidently intended to be kept for the latter and given them in their later years, perhaps in case of their father's death; for it was far above even their possibly precocious heads when it was written.[75]

Besides the tutors whom Springett doubtless had in England, it is interesting to find that he lived and studied for a time in the home and under the tutelage of his father's friend and translator, Willem Sewel of Amsterdam. Penn visited Sewel in 1686 and arranged for the latter's Dutch translation of *No Cross, No Crown*. In Sewel's letters which followed, he sends his greetings from time to time to Springett, and in the summer of 1693, before Penn was released from his internment, Springett went to Amsterdam to Sewel's home. Writing of this visit to Penn, Sewel says: 'It grieves me sorely that he himself [i.e. Springett] was not permitted to partake longer of our comradeship (*contubernio*); for although I am not at all accustomed to making great promises about myself, nevertheless I perceived such talents in him, that I am more than sufficiently persuaded that within a few weeks I would have rendered him useful assistance. The opportunity for this was lacking; otherwise it would not have been owing to me that he did not carry back with him some knowledge of the Italian language.'

Springett took one of Robert Barclay's books to Sewel, as a gift from Penn, and after his return to England, wrote him a letter to which Sewel replied in a Latin letter dated October 27, 1693, which reads in part as follows:[76] 'To Springett Penn,

'Zealous in the Liberal Arts

'Your letter in which you state that you had returned to your own country, I received, honoured youth, and gladly learned of your safe return; but not so the news of the illness of your mother, for whose better health I earnestly pray, and whom I esteem highly although she is personally unknown to me, for I am more than convinced from things which I have heard here and there, that she is a woman of unusual type. But does any love of the Italian and Dutch tongues still linger with you now? And have you made any progress in them?

75 *Infra*, pp. 172f.
76 Cf. Monograph Number One (*Willem Sewel of Amsterdam*), 1933, pp. 109-111.

Or do you still give more attention to Latin eloquence? If the last named is especially dear to your heart, good luck to your courage; for by the testimony of Curtius, "Nothing is so highly placed by nature that it cannot be striven for by courage"; the same thought which is expressed in this very brief saying by Ovid, "No path is impassable to courage."

'Since these things are true, why not bend your efforts seriously to your studies to acquire an understanding of those who have written not only brilliantly, but also in a style somewhat more abstruse. For since you have already built firmly enough the first foundations, do not despair, but strive vigorously, especially while you are young, your memory is fresh, and your health is good; in order that you may ultimately obtain a pure and firm knowledge of the Latin language. But this cannot be acquired without frequent — nay, almost constant, reading of the most excellent authors, even though for this reason the task seems to hold something almost exasperating (*molestiam*). But what does it matter? You are young, you are strong, and

"He deserves not the sweet who has not tasted the bitter."

'Therefore, scorn all labour, and then you will discover that the end is far more pleasing than the beginning... But why do I say these things to you, whose father is truly pious and prudent, a man who has not failed to sow in you good seeds of virtue, walking before you with his own illustrious example. Continue, therefore, as you have begun and apply yourself to the reading of the best Latin authors, so that you can finally report a harvest of your work not to be despised. Farewell.

'I pray you to deliver this letter enclosed, to him whom you know. I forgot when you were here to ask of you how a letter can be sent to you directly. If at any time you wish to write to me, and there is no chance of enclosing your letter in another's wrapping, use an inscription of this sort.'

The letter contains an eloquent passage on the desirability of reading good literature in its original language; and its concluding paragraph gives evidence of the caution which was still used in connexion with Penn's correspondence. Springett appears to have spent much time with his father during the latter's semi-imprisonment, and it may be that the confinement and anxiety had undermined his health and developed latent germs of tuberculosis. He was seventeen during his visit in Amsterdam, and he had only three years more of life. His mother's death occurred when he was eighteen; and this grievous blow could be only partly softened by his father's second marriage, which occurred two years later. By this time, it was evident that he was declining rapidly, and his father took him down to Lewes, near the seashore, where they spent the last sad month together, and where he died, April 10, 1696. He was buried at Jordans, in a grave just behind that of his grandmother, Lady Mary Springett Penington, whose great favourite he had been, and for whose behoof she had written before her death in 1682 a memoir of her early life.

Penn had devoted himself untiringly to the care of Springett during the last few years of his life, and his death was a hard cross indeed. He tried to console himself by writing a pathetic memorial, entitled *Sorrow and Joy, in the Loss and End of Springett Penn*. This was printed together with that which Penn wrote for Gulielma, and together they reveal the pious abandon and religious resignation to death which was so characteristic of both young and old in Seventeenth Century England.[77]

The place which the eldest surviving son held in his father's heart is poignantly stated: 'So ended the Life of my Dear Child [lying as his mother had done before him, with his head on his father's breast] ... in whom I lost all that any Father can lose in a Child,— my Friend and Companion, as well as most Affectionate and Dutiful Child.' His virtues are fervently recorded in this memorial and illustrated, according to perennial custom, by incidents which occurred at his death-bed. Friends, household servants, sister and brother were all exhorted to lead a moral and religious life. Gratitude for his stepmother's and father's solicitude for his comfort was expressed in touching words: 'Being ever almost near him, and doing any Thing for him he wanted or desired, he broke out with much Sense and Love, My dear Father, if I live I will make thee amends— When he, at one Time, more than ordinarily, expressed a Desire to live, and entreated me to pray for him, he added, And, Dear Father, if the Lord should raise me and enable me to serve him and his People, then I might travel with thee sometimes, and we might ease one another (meaning in the Ministry): He spoke it with great Modesty.' Hoping until within an hour or two of his death that he might be able to travel in a coach the twenty miles drive to his home— thereafter to become strong again and live to employ his strength "in the Lord's service"— he never-

77 Cf. *supra*, p. 38; Besse's edition of Penn's *Works*, 1726, Vol. I, pp. 232-234.

theless became fully resigned before the end, and almost his last words were : "Come Life, come Death, I am resigned : O the Love of God overcomes my Soul !" '

Messages of consolation poured in upon the bereaved father, among them a letter from the Dutch friend of both parent and son, Willem Sewel, who wrote :[78] 'As to what Thou writest of the Death of thy very good Son Springett & of thy second Marriage — As I heartily congratulate Thee on the latter so not without sensible Grief I learned the former some Weeks ago. But it needs must be a very great Comfort to Thee in thy sorrow that though his Death might seem premature it was accompanied with a safe & glorious departure. For such an end I long & pray for thee & me when we have to leave behind this earthly house.'

LETITIA PENN

THE eldest surviving daughter of William and Gulielma was born at Worminghurst, March 6, 1678, and was named Letitia ('Joy'). When her father was sailing for Pennsylvania in 1682, he wrote to his four year old daughter as follows : 'Dear Letitia : I dearly love y^e & would have thee sober, learn thy book & love thy Brothers. I will send thee a pretty Book to learn in. ye Lord bless thee & make a good woman of thee. farewell.

Thy Dear Father Wm Penn.'

At the age of sixteen she lost her mother, and two years later her older brother. Of and animated and determined disposition — resembling therein her Grandmother Penn — her stepmother made a none too successful effort to supply her own mother's place and training during the difficult years of her early womanhood.

At the age of twenty-one, she accompanied her father to Pennsylvania, where he presented her with the manor of 'Mount Joy,' including about 7,800 acres of land, with a yearly quit-rent of one beaver skin. It was located near Philadelphia ;[79] while in the city itself, Penn presented her with a lot of land on which was later built a house afterwards called Letitia Cottage.[80] She probably did not have a house

78 A Latin letter dated, Amsterdam, 2nd 6 mon. 1696 ; cf. Monograph No. One, pp. 149-151.
79 In what is now Upper Merion Township, Montgomery County.
80 Cf. *supra*, p. 14.

THE SO-CALLED PENN (OR LETITIA) COTTAGE

built here for herself, but lived with her father's family at the 'Slate Roof House' in Philadelphia and at the Pennsbury estate.

A few incidents are related of her in Pennsylvania which illustrate her vivacious and adventurous notions. Among these, it is related that on a visit to a farm at Gwynned, she witnessed the operation of threshing wheat — doubtless for the first time — and 'desired to try her hand at the use of the flail, which, to her great surprise, brought such a racket about her head and shoulders that she was obliged to run into the house in tears and expose her playful freak to her father.'[81]

During her stay in Pennsylvania, in 1699-1701, Letitia was claimed as his fiancée by a young Quaker of good family and fortune, named William Masters, who pursued her on her return to England and tried to prevent her marriage with a more successful suitor, a well-to-do Englishman, named William Aubrey. The Philadelphia Monthly Meeting of Women Friends had been importuned by her unsuccessful suitor; for it adopted the following minute, dated 27 : 7th mo 1701 : 'Our worthy and much esteemed ffriend Hannah Penn having acquainted this Meeting with her Intended return to Great Brittain in Company with her dear Husband the Governour hath requested three certificates in behalf of herself Daughter and Nurse. This meeting is sorrowfully affected in Consideration of Parting with them and appoints Sarah Goodson, Hannah Carpenter Hannah Hill and Rachel Preston to write them.'

It was doubtless by this committee of four that the following certificate was drafted :[82]

'To our worthy and well beloved sisters in London, Bristol, or wherever these may come, grace, mercy, and peace, from God the Father be greatly multiplied among you all. Amen.

'These may certify you that our worthy and well beloved Friend, Laetitia Penn, intending to cross the seas with her honourable parents, hath for good order sake desired a certificate from us, and we can freely certify to all whom it may concern that she hath well behaved herself here, very soberly and according to the good instructions which she hath received in the way of truth, being well inclined, courteously carriaged, and sweetly tempered in her conversation

---

81 John F. Watson, *Annals of Philadelphia and Pennsylvania,* 1844, I, 117.
82 A search through the minutes and extant MSS. of this Monthly Meeting has not revealed a copy of the certificate ; but the original was sent to Friends in England and entered upon one of their minute-books, from which it was copied about 1825 and published in *The Friend,* Philadelphia, Vol. III (1830), p. 5.

amongst us, and also a diligent comer to Meetings, and [we] hope hath plentifully received of the dew which hath fallen upon God's people to her settlement and establishment in the same.

'She is free from any engagement on the account of marriage, as far as we know, and our desires are earnestly for her preservation, that she may faithfully serve the God of her fathers, that her green years being seasoned with grace, may bud and blossom, and bring forth ripe fruits to the praise of God, and the comfort of his people, which is the true desire of your friends and sisters in the near relationship of the unchangeable truth.

'Signed on behalf of and by appointment of the meeting.'

Letitia's father desired to leave her and his wife and infant son in Philadelphia while he returned to London for what he thought would be a brief stay in order to prevent the passage of a bill in Parliament for converting his proprietary colony into a royal one; but, as Penn wrote to his Pennsylvania secretary, James Logan:[83] 'I cannot prevail on my wife to stay, and still less with Tishe [his diminutive for Letitia]. I know not what to do. Samuel Carpenter seems to excuse her in it; but, to all that speak of it, say I shall have no need to stay [long in England], and a great interest to return.' Evidently, Letitia did not care to play the part of the Puritan maiden, Priscilla, even though Masters would have gladly been John Alden and kept her in America.

From two of Logan's letters to Penn and his daughter, it might seem that Logan himself may have been among Letitia's suitors.[84] To the latter, he writes: 'We exceedingly long, dear mistress, to hear of you, and especially to be put out of doubt about thy marriage, which is commonly reported here, if so, I wish thee happiness, and shall say no more. Jos. Shippen is married at Boston— Since thy departure, I cannot inform thee of one wedding.—J.S. has taken a journey to New England, having once more received a denial. As for my own part, I must vow celibacy. But perhaps thou art married, and then all this is flat and dull, shall therefore leave it and conclude. Thy most faithful and affectionate friend and servant, J.L.'

83 Letter to James Logan, 8th 7 br. (September), 1701 : (*Penn-Logan Correspondence*), Philadelphia, 1870, Vol. I, p. 55 (An error is made on this page in giving *Fisher,* instead of *Tishe*). This Correspondence was published in the *Memoirs of the Historical Society of Pennsylvania,* Vols. IX and X (1870, 1872).
84 ibid. I, pp. 105-6, 128-130 (28th of 3rd mo., and 14th of 6th mo., 1702).

That this was only social gossip, however, retailed by Logan for Letitia's benefit, and not an evidence of his own misplaced affections, is made plain by a letter from William Penn Junior to Logan, of about the same date as the above (Worminghurst, August 18, 1702). In this, Letitia's brother says : 'I am sorry you are like to be unsuccessful in your amours. I assure you you have my good wishes, and should have my assistance were I there. Pray give her and her brothers my respects, and tell Joe I hope he will be your friend, for the friendship's sake he promised me when here, as well as for your own. I will write to him by the next ship that sails.'

The obdurate young lady referred to in the above paragraph was a beautiful young Quakeress named Ann Shippen, daughter of Edward Shippen, a leading merchant and mayor of Philadelphia. Ann preferred another suitor, Thomas Story ; and the rivalry between the two men reached an open quarrel when Logan 'spoke to' her father. Logan wrote to Penn about it, in September, 1703,[85] and Penn reproved his young secretary for having permitted the affair to develop into a public quarrel.[86] Ann Shippen married Story, during the course of this correspondence, but died six years later, without children. Logan became reconciled to his successful rival,[87] but it was not until eight years later—two years after Ann's death—that Logan was married. His wife, Sarah Read, bore him five children, and his family became prominent Philadelphians.[88]

Letitia sailed for England with her father, November 4, 1701 ; and in London, a marriage was arranged for her with William Aubrey. Writing to Logan from London, 6th 7th mo. (September, 1702), Penn says :[89] 'Tishe.—My daughter is married next Fifth day . . . inst.

---

85 This part of the letter is omitted from the *Penn-Logan Correspondence,* I, p. 231.
86 ibid. I, 358 (16th of January, 1705 ; cf. also Logan's reply, I, 367).
87 Cf. ibid. II, 158 (Logan's letter to Wm. Penn Jr., August 12, 1706 : 'Thomas Story carries very well since his marriage. He and I are very great friends, for I think the whole business is not now worth a quarrel.'
88 The following paragraph in a letter from Isaac Norris to James Logan, dated April, 1711 (when Logan was in London), appears to show that Logan had married before that date Norris's daughter Rachael : 'I only add our affliction in the loss of thy spouse, Rachael. She was taken ill this day three weeks in the night, and died before day the next [Probably of yellow fever]. My poor wife has been in continual tears, and I must acknowledge it almost unmanned me, but I hope we both patiently submit to the will of God.' ibid. II, 434-5. Rachael was a child of eleven years when she died ; and Dr.A.C.Myers explains the words 'thy spouse' as simply a playful allusion to Logan's fondness for her.
89 ibid. I, p. 134.

will be three weeks [i.e. August 20, 1702]. We have brought her home, where I write, a noble house for the city, and other things, I hope, well. But S. Penington's, if not S. Harwood's striving for William Masters against faith, truth, righteousness will not be easily forgiven, though things came honorably off to his and the old envy's [sic] confusion, his father's friends nobly testifying against the actions of both.'

William Masters, thus circumvented by Penn's determination and his daughter's caprice, returned to Pennsylvania, married a fair Quakeress there, and got even with the Penns by having one of his descendants marry Penn's grandson, Governor Richard Penn! Letitia, on the other hand, had no children, and her cantankerous husband gave his father-in-law infinite vexation by his exacting demands for his wife's income from Pennsylvania lands.[90] He would have carried his pursuit to Pennsylvania itself in 1709, had it not been for her opposition to going over; 'my poor child's regards for the country,' Penn wrote, 'are at a low ebb, which is my trouble.'

Penn's illness of 1712 finally shielded him against the annoyance of Aubrey, who lived until 1731. Letitia survived until 1746, and bequeathed her Pennsylvania estates to William Penn 3rd, son of her brother William. She had broken entirely with Quakerism soon after her marriage; but she left in her will the sum of £50 for the poor women members of the Friend's meeting at Devonshire House, London, and was buried in the Quaker graveyard at Jordans, in a grave behind her mother and beside her brother Springett.

WILLIAM PENN JUNIOR

THE third of William and Gulielma's children who reached maturity was named, like his older brother who died in infancy, after his father. He was the only one of Gulielma's children who had issue; but he

90 ibid. II, 354. One of Penn's numerous complaints to Logan about Aubrey's demands, says: 'My son-in-law Aubrey grows very troublesome, because he gets nothing thence [from Pennsylvania] almost to an open break, did I not bear extremely. . . . I desire thee to hasten all the relief thou canst, both to me and son Aubrey, of whom I would be clear, of all men. He has a bitter tongue, and I wish I had nothing to do with him in money matters.' (ibid. II, 228-9 : 10th June, 1707). In another letter, Penn writes: 'All our loves are to thee, but W.A. a tiger against thee for returns. Come not to him empty as thou valuest thy credit and comfort.' (ibid. II, 236 : July 8, 1707). Cf. also ibid. II, 354: 26th 4th mo., 1709.

died about two years after his father, and although one of his sons married and had issue, none of his (or of Gulielma's) descendants became proprietors or governors of Pennsylvania.

He was born at Worminghurst, March 14, 1681, ten days after his father received the grant of Pennsylvania. It became evident in his boyhood that he would not attain the high standard of his father's ability and character. When Penn was sailing for America on his first visit in August, 1682, he wrote the following note to 'Dear Bille : I love thee much, therefore be sober & quiet, & learn his book, I will send him one, so ye Lord bless ye. Amen. Thy dear father
Wm Penn.'

Billy was only thirteen when his mother died; and he did not become the 'sober & quiet' boy his father desired. By the time he was fifteen, impulsiveness and unreliability were developed in him to such a degree that his brother Springett, only five years older, calling for him to his death-bed, solemnly assured him that 'there is a God, a Great and Mighty God, who is a Rewarder of the Righteous, and so he is of the Wicked, but their Rewards are not the same. Have a Care of idle People and idle Company, and love good Company and good Friends, and the Lord will bless thee : I have seen good Things for thee since my Sickness, if thou dost but fear the Lord.'[91]

Two months before he was eighteen, Billy married the daughter of a Quaker merchant of Bristol, named Mary Jones, who was four years his senior, but, according to her father-in-law, 'a good and pretty woman.'[92] The marriage was performed under the care of the Friends' meeting in Bristol, and the marriage-certificate is extant. On this certificate, are the signatures (as witnesses) of William Penn's sister, Margaret Lowther, his daughter, Letitia, and his wife, Hannah; these are all together in the relatives' column, while in the next column, separated from the groom's and bride's families, is the name of William Penn.

His mother's estate at Worminghurst was conveyed to William Junior after his marriage, and his father hoped that the double responsibility would serve as an anchor to the youthful bridegroom. Eight months later, when Penn and his wife and daughter Letitia sailed for Pennsylvania, the young couple were left behind; and it was chiefly

---

91 William Penn's *Sorrow and Joy in the Loss and End of Springett Penn.*
92 *Penn-Logan Correspondence,* I, 74 : January 4, 1701.

for the son's behoof that the father wrote his treatise entitled *Fruits of a Father's Love: being the Advice of William Penn to his Children, Relating to their Civil and Religious Conduct*.[93] This was a long discourse replete with excellent moral and educational counsel, and repeated injunctions to practise Christianity as interpreted by the Friends.

That William Junior read or profited greatly by this advice is not evidenced by his conduct; and the father afterwards bitterly regretted the separation from his son which his two years' absence in Pennsylvania had caused. Although two children (Gulielma Maria and Springett) were born to the youthful parents during these two years, the father continued his irresponsible course, frequenting 'top company,' as Penn called it, incurring heavy debts, and indulging in luxurious equipment and pastimes. For a short time after Penn's return to England, he appears from his correspondence to have been hopeful of amendment on the part of William Junior. 'My son has been very serviceable [in opposing the annulment of Penn's charter],' he writes, 'but costly, and half given away *soy memes* for the country.'[94] 'I hope my son in some way answers my expectation, and those he gave at parting more especially. Do thy endeavor, I desire thee, that he may be my comfort and honor while I live.'[95]

Penn never ceased to regret that he had not taken William Junior with him to Pennsylvania, for he attributed the culmination of his waywardness to that omission. In one letter to Logan, he says:[96] 'Pennsylvania has cost me dearer in my poor child than all other considerations.' And in another, in anticipation of his son's return to England in disgrace, he exclaims:[97] 'I am sorry to have ... ventured my poor child so far from his wife and pretty children and my own oversight. O Pennsylvania! what hast thou cost me? above £30,000 more than I ever got by it, two hazardous and most fatiguing voyages, my straits and slavery here, and my child's soul almost, as I have formerly expressed myself.'

The son's bad reputation had already spread to Pennsylvania, and

---

93 This was not published until 1726, under the caption: 'Written occasionally many years ago [in 1699], and now made Publick for a General Good.— He being Dead yet speaketh.' It was printed in 1726, in his *Works* (Vol. I, pp. 893-911), reprinted a dozen times in English, and in two French editions.
94 *Penn-Logan Correspondence*, 4th 11th mo., 1701 (January, 1702), I, 69.
95 ibid. 11th 5th mo. (July), 1704, I, 298.
96 ibid. ——— 1702, I, 172.
97 ibid. ——— 1704, I, 280.

Logan had duly informed him of it. 'I am most infinitely obliged to you,' he writes to Logan,[98] 'for letting me know the base and scandalous reports some people have given of me to you, that I might have an opportunity of vindicating myself, both to you and all my friends with you, wherefore I hope you will be assured I am far different from what I am represented to be; I love my friends, keep company that is not inferior to myself, and never am anything to excess. My dress is all they can complain of, and that but decently genteel, without extravagancy; and as for the poking-iron, I never had courage enough to wear one by my side. You will oblige me if you give this character of me till I make my personal appearance among you, (which shall not be long, God willing) and I will show you I have been villainously treated.'

Penn, too, hoped much from the visit to Pennsylvania, both for the vindication and for the stabilizing of his son's character. Writing to Logan before he set sail, Penn gave minute instructions for the care he desired to be given him. 'My son shall hasten; possess him, go with him to Pennsbury, advise him, contract, and recommend his acquaintance. No rambling to New York, nor mongrel correspondence. He has promised fair; I know he will regard thee; but thou wilt see that I have purchased the mighty supplies at a dear rate. . . . Be discreet; he has wit, kept the top company, and must be handled with much love and wisdom; and urging the weakness or folly of some behaviors, and the necessity of another conduct from interest and reputation, will go far; and get Samuel Carpenter, Edward Shippen, Isaac Norris, Phineas Pemberton, Thomas Masters, and such persons, to be soft, and kind, and teaching. It will do wonders with him; he is conquered that way, pretends much to honor, and is but over-generous by half, and yet sharp enough to get to spend. . . . Immediately take him away to Pennsbury, and there give him the true state of things, and weigh down his levities, as well as temper his resentments, and inform his understanding, since all depends upon it, as well for his future happiness, as in measure your poor country's. . . . Watch him, out-wit him, and honestly overreach him, for his good; fishing, little journeys, (as to see the Indians,) &c., will divert him; and pray Friends to bear all they can, and melt towards him, at least civilly if not religiously.'[99]

98 August, 18, 1702 : ibid. I, 130.
99 ibid. I, 75 (January 4, 1701), 171-2 (———, 1702).

Again he writes: [100] 'My son comes to see how he likes, and to stay, or return to fetch his wife, or settle here. I refer thee to my former letters for what concerns him, and thy respect and care of him every way. He aims to improve his study this winter with thee, as well as to know the country, the laws and people thereof, and his interest and mine therein. Use thy utmost influence upon him to make him happy in himself and me in him; watch over him for good, qualify his heats, inform his judgment, increase his knowledge; he has a more than ordinary opinion of thee: advise him to proper company, give him fitting hints how far to go, he being naturally but too open; and prevent his quarrelling with our enemies, an advantage they may improve to our common prejudice. In short, keep him inoffensively employed, at those times that he is not profitably concerned. ... If my son sends hounds, as he has provided two or three couple of choice ones for deer, foxes, and wolves, pray let care be taken of them, and J. Sotcher quarter them about, as with young Biles, &c.'

Although Penn had written in June, 1702,[101] 'my son comes as fast as may be, after his sister's affair is over,' it was not until February, 1704, that William Junior arrived in Philadelphia. Logan then wrote of him: [102] 'Thy son's voyage hither I hope will prove to the satisfaction of all, and to his, and therefore thy happiness. It is his stock of excellent good nature that in a great measure has led him out into his youthful sallies when too easily prevailed on; and the same, I hope, when seasoned with the influence of his prevailingly better judgment, with which he is well stored, will happily conduct him into the channel of his duty to God, himself, and thee. He is very well received, and seldom fails of drawing love where he comes, and hope it will be increased; 'tis his good fortune here to be withdrawn from those temptations that have been too successful over his natural sweetness and yielding temper with his associates.'

This kindly reception in Philadelphia was the natural one to be extended to the only surviving son of Penn by his first wife, and the prospective proprietor of the province. But, alas, kindliness, good company, the comparative seclusion of Pennsbury, hunting and fishing, an opportunity to keep in touch with public affairs and the development of his father's estate — both of which were designed to become his own

100 ibid. I, 208-9, 214 (August, 1703).
101 ibid. I, 116.
102 ibid. I, 266-7.

— did not suffice to keep the wayward young man steady. Unfortunately the lieutenant-governor of Pennsylvania, John Evans, whom Penn sent out with his son, was not a Quaker and was only twenty-six years of age; and despite Penn's encomiums of him, it soon became evident that he was not a wholesome companion for the proprietor's son.[103] Their voyage was a long and tedious one, lasting from November or December, 1703, until February, 1704, and was probably a bad preparation for a sober sojourn in the Quaker colony. Disillusionment on both sides soon occurred, and the breaking-point came over a quarrel about militia service. Queen Anne's War was in progress, and the Church party in the colony desired to recruit militia for defence against the French and Indians. Evans and Penn Junior supported the desire, and were implicated in two tavern brawls which occurred between the new recruits and the regular constables of the Quaker party.[104] In these brawls, the young men were roughly treated, and the Quaker authorities of the city added insult to injury by indicting young Penn for disorderly conduct. This legal proceeding was quashed; but the offended youth, using it as a pretext for quitting the dull life in the wilderness, sold his manor of 'Williamstadt,'[105] paid off some of his debts, and returned to England.

His seven months' stay in the New World did not cure, but confirmed, his bibulous and unreliable habits, and he arrived in England in January, 1705, to become an added burden upon his much harassed father. Illustrative of one cause of offence which he took against his father is a remark of Logan to Penn after the son's departure. ' 'Tis a pity his wife came not with him,' Logan writes;[106] 'there is scarce any thing has a worse effect upon his mind than the belief thou hast a greater regard to thy second children than thy first, and an emulation between his own and thy younger seems too much to rivet him in it, which, were it obviated by the best methods, might be of service, for he is and must be thy son, and thou either happy or unhappy in him. The tie is indissoluble. What I write will, I hope, be taken as designed, and as the result only of an affectionate concern, knowing I write only to thyself.'

As to his reception in England, his father's forecast proved cor-

103 ibid. I, 206.
104 ibid. I, 317-320, 322 : September and October, 1704.
105 7,400 acres on the Schuylkill, where Norristown now stands; it was sold by Penn for £850. (*Penn-Logan Correspondence,* I, 326.)
106 ibid. I, 346 : November, 1704.

rect:[107] 'If he brings not wherewith to pay his debts here, his creditors will fall foul upon him most certainly.' Nor did old debts prevent new extravagances. Just after his return to London, we find him writing to Logan as follows:[108] 'You must believe I cannot live here about a court without expenses which my attendance occasion, and I must own to you I never was so pinched in my life, wherefore must beg you to endeavor all you can to send over my effects, with all the speed you possibly can. . . . I hear the prosecution against me still continues, and that they have outlawed me upon it: I have complained to my father, who tells me he has, and will now write about it, and that I shall have right done me in it, which I do expect at your hands, I mean at the Quakers', who are the people who have given me this affront; or else I shall make use of a shorter cut to do myself justice, and will lay my complaint before the Queen and council, which if they force me to, be assured I shall make them dearly repent they ever made use of their charter in such a manner as to use those people so ill that endeavored to settle a militia according to law—that was partly the ground of their quarrel with me, added to my not being of their opinion.' And as a characteristic postscript to this letter, he adds: 'Pray put Isaac Norris and William Trent [the purchasers of his manor] in mind of their promise to send me over a pipe of old Madeira, which I shall take kindly.'

To escape from his ills, he proposed to go into the army or navy, but stood instead for election to Parliament.[109] This last venture was a failure, because of bribery on the part of his opponent, his father thought.[110] During the chancery suit of the Fords against the latter, when his financial and political affairs were at their blackest, and when a debtor's prison loomed up before him, he wrote to Logan with unusual petulance, as follows:[111] 'Depend upon it, if God favours me and my son with life, one, if not both will come [to Pennsbury] as soon as possible. Worminghurst he has at last resigned for sale; so that having conquered himself and wife too, who has cost me more money than she brought, by her unreasonable and for that reason imprudent obstinacy for dwelling there, to which she could have no pretence either by family or portion, but by being my son's impetuous

107 ibid. I, 341: November, 1704.
108 ibid. I, 368: (1705-6).
109 ibid. II, 14: May, 1705.
110 ibid. II, 16: May, 1705.
111 ibid. II, 235-6: July, 1707.

inclination; and I wish she had brought more wisdom, since she brought so little money, to help the family. Worminghurst, with some land to be sold in Ireland, about £45 per annum, will lighten his load, as well as mine; for his marriage, and my daughter's too, have not helped me—his, to be sure, more especially. We are entering, or it seems likely we should, into nearer friendship than before, he knowing the world and duty to a father better; for he has been of no use, but much expense and grief to me many ways and years too, losing him before I found him, being not of that service and benefit to me that some sons are, and 'tis well known I was to my father before I married. But oh! if yet he will recommend himself, and show himself a good child and a true Friend, I shall be pleased, and leave the world with less concern for him and the rest also.'

Worminghurst, fortunately for his creditors, was sold in the autumn of 1707, with a net profit of some £2500 or £3000.[112] After Penn's attack of apoplexy in 1712, Hannah Penn was kind to her stepson's family, and advanced them £300 within the five subsequent years.[113] As for William Junior, he spent his time (and what money he could get) in a dissipated life on the Continent, chiefly in France, until his father's death in 1718. He then returned to England, claimed the proprietorship of Pennsylvania, and sent over instructions to the governor to have his claim published and acknowledged. His father, however, had made a will in 1712, bequeathing Pennsylvania's proprietorship in trust to the Earl of Oxford and Mortimer and Earl Powlett. This will superseded that of 1701, which had bequeathed Pennsylvania to William Junior.[114] The latter's effort to secure the proprietorship was overruled by the Royal Board of Trade and Plantations and by the Assembly and Council of Pennsylvania. Two years after his father's death, his son's life came to its sad end (June 23, 1720), in Northern France, or perhaps in Brussels.[115]

The widow of William Penn Junior, Mary Jones Penn, survived until December, 1733, and left three children. The eldest of these was Gulielma Maria who was born at Worminghurst in November, 1699, while her grandfather was on his second visit to Pennsylvania. On the latter's return, he wrote of her as being 'a sweet girl' and 'a

---

[112] Dixon, p. 297.
[113] Jenkins, p. 133.
[114] *Memoirs of the Historical Society of Pennsylvania*, Vol. I, 219 and 222, gives the two wills in full.
[115] Jenkins, p. 140.

beauty.'[116] She married first, Aubrey Thomas, a native of Pennsylvania, and a nephew of William Aubrey, the husband of Letitia Penn. They had one son, but no other descendants. Her second husband was Charles Fell, a great-grandson of Judge Thomas and Margaret Fell, by whom she had one son, who died unmarried, and two daughters, whose descendants are now extinct.[117]

William Penn Junior's second child was a son, named Springett, who was also born at Worminghurst, in February, 1701, while his grandfather was still in Pennsylvania. Writing of him, his father says :[118] 'Yesterday, at half hour past eight in the morning to a minute, my wife was brought to bed of a brave boy. If thee [James Logan] will calculate his nativity, thee will much oblige.' Again, he writes of Springett : 'The boy is a jolly fellow, able to make two of his uncle already.'[119] His grandfather calls him 'a Saracen of a boy' and 'my grandson Springett a mere Saracen.'[120] Springett did not come to Pennnsylvania, but lived at Stoke, England, and in Ireland ; he did not marry, and died at the age of thirty.

William Junior's third child was a son, named William. He was born at Worminghurst, in March, 1704. His grandfather, writing of him, says : 'My son has another boy — mine and his name ;'[121] again, he says of him :[122] 'a fine boy,— which he has called William ; so that now we are major, minus and minimus.' William the Third inherited, after the death of his older brother, the estate of 'Shangarry' in Ireland, and spent much of his life there. He married, first, Christian Forbes, a young Quakeress of London (a granddaughter of Robert Barclay, the Quaker 'Apologist'), and was himself for a time thereafter 'a plain Friend.' Before his marriage, he had been compelled to pay to a young Irish lady £1,000 for a breach of promise ;[123] and a second marriage resulted in unhappiness, the wife's elopement, and a long divorce suit. From this marriage, a son (another Springett) was born ; but he died, unmarried, in 1766, at the age of twenty-eight.

It was from William 3rd's first wife, that all William Penn the

116 *Penn-Logan Correspondence,* I, 74 and 213.
117 Jenkins, p. 142. Gulielma left the Society of Friends, and was 'publicly baptized,' in St. Paul's, London, at the age of twenty-four.
118 *Penn-Logan Correspondence,* I, 23.
119 ibid. I, 131. Springett's 'uncle' was the Founder's son John (born in Pennsylvania a fortnight earlier).
120 ibid. I, 74 and 213.
121 ibid. I, 188.
122 ibid. I. 213.
123 Beck & Ball's *London Friends' Meetings,* 1869, p. 323.

A Topical Biography

Founder's and Gulielma's descendants came. Christian Forbes Penn died of child-birth within a year after her marriage, and at the early age of eighteen; but her daughter, Christiana Gulielma, survived, and married Peter Gaskell, of Bath, England. Their children took the name of Penn-Gaskell. One of these, Peter Junior, inherited the Irish estate of Shangarry, but came to Pennsylvania about 1785, married a Pennsylvania girl, and lived for the rest of his life (until 1831) on his Delaware County estates.[124]

Thus, it is seen, William Penn's daughter and son by his first wife, namely, Letitia and William Junior, were not a solace in his old age. His three grandchildren were a source of satisfaction to him during the ten or twelve years of their childhood, before his paralytic stroke; but he appears to have been but little conscious of them during his eight remaining years. Nor did any of his first wife's descendants participate in the government of their great ancestor's province. This honour was left to his children by his second wife.

HANNAH CALLOWHILL PENN AND HER CHILDREN

Two years after Gulielma's death, Penn was married a second time. He had long been acquainted with and had greatly esteemed a Quaker lady of Bristol, the daughter of a well-to-do linen-draper, Thomas Callowhill. She was thirty-one when he began to court her in the latter half of 1695, and he was twenty years her senior. On his preaching tour of that year, he proposed to her, and they were married after a delay against which he mildly protested.

There are extant ten letters which he wrote to her during the five months of his courtship; and these show that the first and chief 'reason' for his desiring to marry her was that he was in love with her.[125] But the marriage of great men have to be accounted for — like all their actions — by a variety of reasons; and it has accordingly been suggested that Penn took this step because he was lonely after Gulielma's death, and depressed by his varied other troubles and losses; because he planned to live in Pennsylvania, and needed a home-

---

[124] His mother lived until 1803, but never came to Pennsylvania.
[125] In the Penn-Forbes collection of MSS. in the library of the Historical Society of Pennsylvania; published in the *Pennsylvania Magazine*, XXVII (1903), pp. 296-304.

maker for himself and a mother for his three children, who were still under the age of twenty-one; and because he himself was frequently absent from home on public business and religious duties.

His love-letters are very simple and homely, with frequent mention of his son Springett's illness, and allusions to his daughter Tishe's desires in regard to her maid and her bed in the new household.[126] The more intimate passages may be judged by the following: 'And Lett me Say, that the loveliness yt the tendring & blessed Truth hath beutified thee with, hath made thee amiable in my eyes, above many, & for yt it is my heart, from the very first, has cleaved to thee. Did I say above many, ay, above all, & yt is my confidence in this thing at all times, to my Selfe and others. o let us meet here, most Dear H! the comfort is unspeakable, and the fellowship undesolvable. I would perswade my self thou art of the same minde, tho it is hard to make thee say so. yet yt must come in time, I hope & beleive; for why should I love so well & so much where I am not wellbeloved? . . . ffor myselfe, since thou art not worse, I must be better; for thou mayst Judge of me by thyselfs. No Clock or weatherglass goes so true; such is ye power of simpathy above Art. . . . It is hard for me to tell when & where to make an end, when I am writeing to thee, and how can I, when y^t wch excites it has none. . . . I cannot forbeare to Write where I cannot forbeare to Love as I love my dearest Hannah, and if yt be a fault, till she ceases to be so lovely, I need no Apology for it.' One present at least is known to have been given by him to his prospective bride, namely, a copy of his *Travails in Holland and Germany in 1677*.[127]

The marriage rules of the Society of Friends were strictly observed. First, to the men's Monthly Meeting at Bristol, in November, 1695, they jointly 'manifested their intentions of marriage'; then, in Penn's own Monthly Meeting at Horsham, Sussex, in December, 1695, 'Did the first time Declare his Jntentions of taking Hannah Callowhill of the City of Bristol, to be his wife.' The next month, a committee of six men Friends appointed for the purpose of 'Enquiring Concerning

---

126 For example: 'Tishe desires thee to excuse her sending her white curtains, unwasht, she had not time, I pressing her, & promessing to excuse it. overlook her outside. It was a gift of her mothers, & she never made it up before. ye curtains are to come no lower then ye bedsteed at bottom of counterpan reaching the Ground, serves for lower vallens. . . Tishe prays if her bed be set up before we come yt y^e vallens be turn'd in 3 or 4 inches.'

127 This copy was long in the possession of his great-great-granddaughter, Lady Elizabeth Knox, from whom it went to Northland House, Dungannon, Ireland. (Grant, p. 192).

HANNAH CALLOWHILL PENN

his Clearness on the Account of Marriage' reported that he was 'very Cleare in that matter.' A certificate to this effect was accordingly sent to the men's Monthly Meeting in Bristol,[128] where 'such their intentions were on the ffoure and twentieth day of the eleventh month in the yeare aforesaid [January-February, 1696] published in the publique meeting house of the said People (called Quakers) in the psence of many people there congregated.' Finally, on the fifth day of March, 1696, the ceremony was performed in the manner of the Friends in their meeting-house in Bristol.[129]

Among the sixty-six signatures of the witnesses to the marriage, were those of the bride's parents and of the groom's three children. So that, Springett's desire to attend the wedding was fulfilled; but only two weeks later, his death brought deep sorrow to the new home. The first year after his marriage Penn spent for the most part at home, writing of his son's character and dying words, and a treatise entitled *Primitive Christianity Revived*, which was reprinted a half-drozen times and translated into Welsh and German. The next year, the family of four removed from Worminghurst to their new home in Bristol, where four of Penn's six other children were born. The first child was not born until the family's visit to Pennsylvania, in 1700; but the other five were born within seven years thereafter.

The biographers of Penn pay but scant attention to his second wife, until after he was incapacitated by illness; but they characterize her by such terms as excellent, capable, broad-minded, a hard-fibred English woman, with a superior understanding, great prudence, energy, talent and remarkable business ability, very popular in Pennsylvania, and dominating Penn himself — much to his satisfaction. From her portrait, and from what little is known of her, she was evidently a stalwart helpmeet and support to her husband during his declining years. One sole letter of hers to Penn is extant, dating from January, 1704, which is replete with specific details of household needs and financial straits which were then as usually pressing. Penn was in London at the time, negotiating with the government in regard to Pennsylvania, and

---

128 From the Minute Books of Horsham Monthly Meeting; published in the *Journal of the Friends' Historical Society* (London), VIII (1911), p. 32.
129 Extract from the Register or Record of Marriages of the Society of Friends (No. 116); copied in the General Register Office, Somerset House, London, July 4, 1896 (Jenkins, pp. 78-9). The meeting-house is known as The Friars, and stands on the site of an ancient monastic foundation; one of its extant halls (Cutler's Hall) is about seven centuries old.

his wife sent him 'the best Doe we have—doubting 't will not answer thy expectations if for any extraordinary occasion [i.e. for the entertainment of his aristocratic, official guests?].[130] Indicative of Penn's long absences from home at this and other times, is his statement: 'I have not been with them [his family] but seventeen days these five months.'[131]

The economy which she introduced into his affairs brought notable results. It is probable that she disbursed with greater wisdom the pensions or gifts which he made to sundry impecunious Quaker preachers and others. On his visit to Ireland in 1698, despite the lure of missionary work, he complied with her advice to bring his Irish estate into more profitable condition. And although she preferred England to Pennsylvania as a home, she went with him to his province in 1699-1701 to watch over him and his daughter Letitia, and to become acquainted first hand with colonial men and affairs. She returned with him to England, and there rendered valiant aid in defeating the attempts of the Fords to acquire a large part of his fortune, and in retaining the proprietorship of Pennsylvania in the family's possession.

Her father and mother died in 1712, and from her father's estate she received an annual income of about £3,000 which was of large assistance in meeting Penn's varied obligations.[132] It was while writing to James Logan the news of the death of Hannah's parents that Penn himself suffered the stroke of paralysis that incapacitated him. Thereafter, his affairs in both England and America fell entirely into the hands of his wife and his faithful American secretary, James Logan. Within two years, she was able to repay to the government the £1,200 advanced on the sale of the proprietorship; and she succeeded also in stopping all further proceedings for annulling Penn's charter. On her husband's death in 1718, she became by his will the sole executrix of his estate, and exercised his proprietary powers also until her own death in 1727.

130 This letter is said to be in the possession of the Earl of Ranfurly, at Northland House, Dungannon, Ireland. It is published *in toto* by Grant, pp. 215-218.
131 *Penn-Logan Correspondence*, I, 116 (June, 1702).
132 Her grandfather was a prominent early Quaker of Bristol, named Dennis Hollister, who made a modest fortune in the grocery business. One of Penn's biographers—ever hostile to the Quakers—has stated without evidence or probability that her father (who was a linen-draper) 'had amassed a snug fortune in the West India trade,' and that when he was unable to exchange English goods for sugar, molasses and rum, he would send a cargo of African slaves, 'the Gaboons,' for sale to the Caribbean planters. (Buell, pp. 231-232).

At the time her husband died she received many testimonials of regret and sympathy, one of these being a message from the Pennsylvania Indians, together with a present of splendid skins out of which to make a cloak. This, they said, was to protect her 'while passing through the thorny wilderness without her guide.'[133] A wilderness of care—of briers and thorns—as she expressed it, she continued to traverse; and four years after her husband's death, she herself suffered a stroke of paralysis. This incapacitated her left limbs and side, but not her intellect; a second stroke five years later caused her death. She was buried at Jordans, in her husband's grave.

It was due to her efforts chiefly that for her children had been preserved the most magnificent of private estates and the proprietorship of a great American province. The children born to her were seven in number, four sons and three daughters. The oldest daughter, Hannah Margarita, was born in 1703 and died at the age of four, while her father was in a debtor's prison at London. Penn refers to her as 'an excellent child, the admiration of all that knew her.'[134] Hannah, the youngest daughter and child, was born in the parish of Ludgate, London, in September, 1708, while her father was still in prison, and died in Kensington at the age of five months. Margaret, the second daughter, and fourth child, was born in 1704 and died at the age of forty-six; she married Thomas Freame, had children (one of whom was born in Philadelphia, but returned to England and married Viscount Cremorne), and was buried with her husband at Jordans in a grave beside her brother John.

JOHN PENN, 'The American'

THE eldest child was John, usually called 'the American' because he alone of Penn's children was a native of Philadelphia. He was born in February, 1700, or 'Third-day, 31st 11th mo., 1699,' as a contemporary correspondent wrote: 'Our governor has a son, born last First-day night, and all like to do well.'[135] Another Philadelphia correspondent, writing when John was a year old, says: 'The Governor, wife and daughter well. . . . Their little son is a comely, lovely babe, and has

---

133 Stoughton, pp. 357-8.
134 *Penn-Logan Correspondence*, II, 296-7 (29th 7th mo.— September — 1708).
135 ibid. I, 11 (note).

much of his father's grace and air, and hope he will not want a good portion of his mother's sweetness, who is a woman extremely well beloved here, exemplary in her station and of excellent spirit, which adds lustre to her character, and has a great place in the hearts of good people.'[136]

John's father, writing of the return voyage to England in 1701, says: 'Tishe and Johnne, after the first five days, hearty and well, and Johnne exceeding cheerful all the way.'[137] Five months later, Penn writes: 'Johnnie perpetually busy in building [perhaps in building colonial block houses!] or play otherways, but when he eats or sleeps.'[138] Again (August, 1703): 'Johnne lively;'[139] and about the same time, Penn's wife wrote to him in London:[140] 'I hope Johnes briches at least are done, and that thou wilt bring y^r coat body for Hanna [Hannah Margarita], both wch are very much wanted.'

That John recalled or was reminded of the city of his birth, even as a small boy, is evident from his father's letter of December, 1703, which says: 'My wife, Johnny (who is still going to Philadelphia in Pennsylvania), Tommy and Hannah, were also pretty well last post.'[141] Penn made sure of John's Pennsylvania lands, also; in one of his letters, he wrote:[142] 'Remember por Johnnee, the little American, according to what I writ, both of his grandfather's [Thomas Callowhill's] lot and land, and what I gave him in my former letters.'

John was twelve years old when his father was stricken, and eighteen at the time of the latter's death. The intervening years he spent with his grandparents, the Callowhills, in Bristol, and was brought up with a cousin in the linen trade.[143] On his mother's death in 1727, he inherited one-half of Penn's lands in Pennsylvania, Delaware and 'elsewhere in America.' Seven years later, he went to Pennsylvania in company with his sister Margaret and her husband, Thomas Freame, and remained there a year. The Philadelphians and other colonists received him with much cordial ceremony, and among the gifts he presented them in return was a service of silver plate, which he gave to the church at Lewistown, Pennsylvania. On October 25, 1746,

136 ibid. I, 40 (Isaac Norris to Jeffry Pinnell).
137 ibid. I, 76.
138 ibid. I, 116.
139 ibid. I, 213.
140 *Supra*, p. 59.
141 *Penn-Logan Corespondence*, I, 252.
142 ibid. I, 277.
143 Watson, *Annals*, 1844, I, 116.

he died, unmarried, and was buried at Jordans, in a grave behind that of Isaac Penington.

THOMAS PENN

THE second son of William and Hannah Penn was named Thomas, after his grandfather Callowhill, in whose house he was born in March, 1702. Penn refers to him when an infant of three months, as 'thriving much';[144] and, at the age of a year and a half, as 'a lovely, large child.'[145] He was ten years old when his father was stricken, and a few years later was sent to London to learn the mercer's trade. It is natural that, as a boy in his 'teens in the large city, his health, clothing, and morals should have been a source of grave anxiety to his mother, a number of whose letters to him have been preserved.[146] But, on the other hand, he was evidently a steady, reliable youth, on whose aid in her pressing financial difficulties his mother leaned heavily.

This was more than ever the case after his father's death, when he established himself in business in London, and when his mother was carrying on a six years' suit in the Court of Exchequer to establish her own and his children's rights under the Founder's will. Soon after the mother's death, the court sustained the rights of her children, and her three surviving sons (John, Thomas, and Richard) became joint proprietors of Pennsylvania and heirs to their father's landed estates. After John's death in 1746, Thomas possessed three-fourths of these, and became a very wealthy man, and for nearly thirty years (until his death in 1775) the head of his family and of the government of Pennsylvania. Between the age of thirty-two and forty-one, Thomas resided in Pennsylvania and participated in formal fashion in its public affairs.[147]

Ten years after his return to England, he married Lady Juliana Fermor, a daughter of the Earl of Pomfret. This young lady was twenty-seven years younger than her half-century old bridegroom; and it was doubtless through her influence that Thomas never carried out

---

144 *Penn-Logan Correspondence*, I, 116.
145 ibid. I, 213.
146 Jenkins, 101-112: they are preserved in the library of the Historical Society of Pennsylvania.
147 There is a large mass of his MS. writings in the library of the Historical Society of Pennsylvania.

his intention of returning to Pennsylvania. He bought the beautiful estate of Stoke Park at Stoke Poges, Buckinghamshire, in 1760, which remained for more than eighty years the seat of the Penn family. The park, village, and parish church have been immortalized in Gray's 'Elegy in a Country Churchyard.' Here, in the graveyard, lies the poet himself; and in the church, were buried Thomas, in 1775, Lady Juliana, in 1801, and many of their descendants.

Thomas and Lady Juliana had eight children. Four of these died in early life, two sons and two daughters lived to maturity. The elder son, John, never married, and the American Revolution deprived him of the proprietorship of Pennsylvania and lands worth (according to his own statement) £1,536,545 4s. 3d.;[148] but he took his losses philosophically, endowed a society for the promotion of matrimony, and made a visit of five years in Philadelphia. Here, he had a city home on Market Street at Sixth, and a small country residence, 'The Solitude,' which still stands in the Zoological Garden in Fairmount Park.

The younger son of Thomas and Juliana, named Granville, had children, but no other descendants; one of their two daughters had a daughter, who died without issue; and from their other daughter, descended the Earls of Ranfurly and the families of Stuart and Dugald.

RICHARD AND DENNIS PENN

OF the two other sons of William and Hannah Penn, namely, Richard and Dennis, the latter (a namesake of his mother's grandfather, Dennis Hollister) died, unmarried, at the age of sixteen and was buried in the family lot at Jordans. Richard was the namesake of the Founder's younger brother, who had died in his youth thirty years before the younger Richard's birth. Writing in March, 1706, Penn says:[149] 'We are all through mercy well, and a Richard Penn fills up my brother Richard Penn's vacancy, a stout boy, and about 6 weeks old, so that now our stock speaks five.'

Born in January, 1706, Richard was a child of six at the time of his father's stroke, and was one of that little group of three children (Margaret, Richard, and Dennis) and three grandchildren (Gulielma

---

148 The Pennsylvania Committee on Claims allowed the Penn heirs £500,000 and left Parliament to consider the balance of their claims (Janney, 535, note); in 1790, the House of Commons voted them an annuity of £4,000.

149 *Penn-Logan Correspondence,* II, 110.

THOMAS PENN, SON OF THE FOUNDER

Maria, Springett, and William 3rd) in whom Penn in his last years took such a pathetic interest. After his father's death, Richard was sent to school for a time and was then apprenticed to some business in London. Soon after he was twenty-one, he was married to Hannah Lardner, the daughter of a London physician, and his first child was named after his brother John 'the American.' A daughter, Hannah, and two sons, Richard and William, followed; but all of these except Richard died without issue, while the last-named married Mary Masters and had four children, but no grandchildren.

Richard, the Founder's son, was one of the co-proprietors of Pennsylvania and owned one-fourth of the family's land there; but, unlike his brothers, he never went to the province. He died in 1771, and was buried at Stoke Poges. His son John was appointed by the two proprietors, Thomas and Richard, their lieutenant-governor in Pennsylvania. This was in 1763, when the American Revolution was looming up, and John was destined to be the last proprietary governor of the province. During the war, John was deposed, along with the proprietors, but was treated kindly by the American patriots, and dwelt among them until his death in 1795. He lived in his estate of 'Lansdowne,' now a part of Fairmount Park, and was buried in Christ Church, Philadelphia.

John's younger brother Richard acted as lieutenant-governor of Pennsylvania from October, 1771, until August, 1773, during John's absence in England. When the war began, Richard returned with his family to England, where he became a member of Parliament for a dozen years, and died at Richmond, Surrey, in 1811.[150]

BOYHOOD, 1644–1660

WILLIAM PENN was born in his parents' lodgings on Great Tower Hill, London, on October 14, 1644, and was baptized nine days later in the neighbouring church of All Hallows, Barking. The dial and part of the porch of this church were burned, and the rest of it had a very narrow escape, in the Great Fire of 1666, being saved 'by the workmen out of the King's [Navy] yards sent up by Sir W. Pen.'[151] It is still standing at the foot of Great Tower Street. Its parish register devotes

---

150 For a table of the Penn family, cf. *infra*, pp. 346f.
151 Cf. Pepys' Diary under date of September 5, 1666.

one line to the infant's baptism as follows : '23 william sonn of william pen & margaret his wife of the Tower Liberty.' The name given to him was that of his father, his great-grandfather, and his great-great-grandfather ; and it was handed on to numerous generations of his own descendants.

We know not what other ills of infancy he experienced, but are told that at the age of three he suffered a severe attack of smallpox. This information comes to us from the following letter which George Fox wrote to a Friend (Henry Sidon) thirty years afterward :[152]

'Dr. Friend   'London ye 25th of ye 3rd moth, 1677.

'To whom is my love & all the rest of Friends in ye Truth of god, & my desire is, that thou & all the rest may be preserved in gods peacable Truth & in ye love of it.

'Now Concerning the thing thou speakst to me of, that Sarah Harris should say to the that Wm Mead & Wm Penn did ware Perrywiggs & Call them Periwigg men ; first concerning Wm Mead, he bid me putt my hand vpon his head, & feel, & said he never weare Perriwig in his life, & wonder'd at it ; & as for Wm Penn he did say that he did ware a little civil border because his hair was Come of his head, & since J have seen & speak wth Wm Penn, his border is so thin, plain and short, y^t one Cannot well know it from his own hair. W. Penn when but 3 years ould so lost his hair by ye small Pox y^t he woar them then, long & about 6 years before his Convincem^t, he woar one, & after y^t he endeaverd to goe in his own hair, but when kept a close Prisoner in ye Towr next the leade, 9 monthe & no bar ber suffer'd to come at him, his hair shed away : & since he has worn a very short civil thing, & he has been in danger of his life after violent heats in meetings & rideing after y^m, & he wares them to keep his head & ears warm & not for pride; wch is manifest in that his perriwigs Cost him many Pounds apiece, formerly when of ye world, & now his Border, but a five shillings ; & he has lay'd of more for Truth than her & her Relations and J am sorry the should speak such things, & the did not do well to discours of such things, J desire the may be wiser for the time to come.

'And so wth my love to thee & thy wife & father & N. Newton.

G. ff

---

152 *Journal* of the Friends' Historical Society, Vol. VI (1909), p. 187. This letter is stated to have been taken from a MS. in the handwriting of *William Penn*.

'And hees more willing to fling it off if a little hair come, then ever he was to putt it on.'

Penn was to have much trouble in later years with his wig or 'border'; but he doubtless was, and we should be, duly grateful that he did not succumb at the early age of three to that disease which was so fatal among his contemporaries. The attack of smallpox thus happily survived may have brought its compensation in the form of immunity from the Great Plague in London, in 1665, and the epidemic of smallpox on board *The Welcome* in 1682, through both of which he passed unscathed. Its immediate result was to send his parents with their son from the dangers of the city to the more salubrious air of Wanstead and Chigwell.

Chigwell had another attraction for the parents, namely, a Free Grammar School which, although only a quarter-century old at the time, was already famous. To this school, William was sent for a half-dozen years between the ages of six or seven and twelve. It was one of the many free schools which sprang up in the post-Elizabethan, Puritan age, its founder being Dr. Samuel Harsnett, for eight years vicar of Chigwell and later Archbishop of York.

The school comprised a lower, English, school and a higher, Latin, one, designed to carry its pupils on to the age of sixteen and to prepare them for a university training. Penn ended his schooling in it at the age of twelve, when his father was imprisoned in the Tower and the family returned to London; but he is believed even at that age to have exhausted the school's curriculum. The school's programme was a strenuous one, consisting of eight hours work in winter and ten hours in summer. One hour each on Thursdays and Saturdays was dedicated to play, and three holidays were given each year. These opportunities were used by the boys for sports in the fields and woods of Hainault Forest, where young William doubtless became familiar with the giant Oak of Fairlop, which boasted a girth of forty-eight feet at its foot and shaded an area of three hundred. Far more celebrated in later years became his own giant Elm of Shackamaxon, beneath whose branches legend has placed his 'Treaty with the Indians,' and his competition with the Indians in sports which he had learned at Chigwell School.

In the English school, were taught writing ('fair secretary and

Roman hands') ; [153] cyphering and accounting ; [154] and such reading as would improve the pupils' manners and morals. 'I charge my schoolmasters respectively [in both schools],' wrote the founder, 'as they will answer it to God and good men, that they bring up their scholars in the fear of God and reverence toward all men : and that they teach them obedience to their parents, observance to their betters, gentleness and ingenuity in all their carriages ; and above all that they chastise them severely for three vices — lying, swearing and filthy speaking.'

In the Latin school were taught the usual Greek, Latin, and mathematics, with William Lily's ('The King's') Latin Grammar and Nicolas Cleynaerts's (Clénard's) Greek Grammar. The writing of Latin was to be modelled on the styles of 'no other than Tully and Terence' ; and 'no novelties, nor conceited modern writers' were to be tolerated. With William Shakespeare so lately dead and John Milton's 'L'Allegro,' 'Il Penseroso,' 'Comus,' 'Lycidas,' and 'Areopagitica' so recently published, this last rule seems strange and was certainly unfortunate. One of Penn's defects was his apparent ignorance of England's great native literature : apparent, because it might have been concealment of his knowledge in deference to Quakerism's rejection of the artistic, and especially their disdain of the literature of the Restoration. Chaucer and Cowley alone among England's poets seem to have been quoted by Penn ; but his knowledge of the writers of Greece and Rome was profound and far-reaching and was used in notable fashion in some of his own writings. The foundation of this classical learning he laid at Chigwell school.

The masters who taught these subjects were to be, in accordance with the founder's instructions, 'good poets' ; of sound religion, neither Papal nor Puritan ; of grave behavior, 'no tipler nor haunter of alehouses, no puffer of tobacco' ; and 'above all, apt to teach and severe

---

[153] Probably from John de Beau Chesne's book on penmanship, which was the first book on that art published in English (London, 1570), went through many editions, became the standard textbook in schools and taught not only Shakespeare and his contemporaries, but also Penn and his, the variety of 'secretary hands' which their manuscripts have made familiar.

[154] The most popular English textbook on arithmetic from the date of its publication in 1542 for a century and a half was Dr. Robert Recorde's *The Ground of the Artes*. It is in dialogue form, full of practical facts and illustrations, and with many touches of humour which must have charmed the schoolboys on their thorny path to learning. Recorde wrote a geometry, also, entitled *The pathewaie to knowledge*, 1551 ; and his only rivals in arithmetic were Humfrey Baker's *The Well spring of sciences*, 1580, and in geometry H.Billingsley's *The Elements of Geometrie*, 1570. (These notes 153 and 154 are based on Dr. George A.Plimpton's fascinating book, *The Education of Shakespeare*, Oxford University Press, 1933).

CHIGWELL SCHOOL

in government.'[155] The provisions of the founder for both masters and studies were designed to 'stir up the buds of virtue in the pupils' youth'; and that they succeeded in doing so in the case of Penn is evident at many points in his life and writings. His Letter to his Wife and Children, written before sailing to Pennsylvania in 1682, is replete with the matured teaching of his childhood; and his aversion, not only from the grave vices common in his time, but from such minor habits as the use of tobacco, are reminiscent of the Puritanism of his school-days.

For, although Chigwell school was founded by an archbishop of the Anglican Church, it was surrounded and penetrated by strong Puritan influences. In the time of Penn's school-days, Marston Moor, Naseby, the capture of Bristol, the execution of the King, Dunbar and Worcester were all very fresh and potent in the minds of Chigwell's citizens, and Cromwell and the Puritan Commonwealth were in the ascendant. Despite the natural loyalist leanings of Penn's father, due to his affection for Charles I, Charles II, and James of York, and despite his own friendship for Charles II, James II, and Queen Anne, the Puritan struggle for civil liberty and parliamentary supremacy appealed strongly to their sense of right. Perhaps the fact that in Chigwell school there were twelve boys selected for their poverty and lower social standing, but supported by a special fund on an equal footing with the other pupils, may have given Penn the opportunity of practising that social democracy which was to characterize him both as a Quaker and as a colonial governor. In church as well as state, Puritanism was triumphant in Penn's school-days. The residents of neighbouring Wanstead had made a successful protest against all 'popish innovations' and in favour of 'the true reformed protestant religion'; and Chigwell's own citizens had ejected their vicar because he had 'erected an altar,' had used 'offensive bowing and cringing,' had 'kissed the altar twice in one day,' and read prayers with his back to the people.[156] The anti-ecclesiastical Puritanism which was soon to cause Penn's expulsion from Oxford University must have been strengthened, perhaps originated, in the Puritan stories and religious discussions which he heard in his school and its neighbouring homes.

Among his schoolmates and friends in the neighbourhood were prob-

---

155 Cf. Stoughton, Jenkins and Brailsford, quoting from Rev. Daniel Lysons, *Environs of London*, 1796, IV, 128; *Victoria History of the Counties of England*, II, 544; and Wright's *History of Essex*, II, 385.
156 Quoted by Stoughton from David's *Annals of Nonconformity in Essex*, 220-223.

ably boys of a Jasper family, and the daughters of his father's great friend, Admiral Batten, who lived in a mansion near Wanstead. It has even been surmised that he became acquainted in these early years with his future wife, Guli Springett, whose stepfather, Isaac Penington, had lost his estate at Walthamstow because of his Quakerism, but who still had family and other interests in the neighbourhood. When Penn was a schoolboy at Chigwell, his sister Margaret or Pegg and his brother Richard or Dick were born. His father was absent most of the time at sea, pursuing French, Dutch, and Genoese vessels through the Mediterranean; but he made occasional visits to his family, wrote them frequent letters and brought home from his forays prize ships and chests full of gold and silver for his government, all of which must have been of thrilling interest to a boy who was becoming absorbed at school in the story of the Mediterranean adventures of another, classic Odysseus.

When William was nine years old, his father participated prominently, as has been seen, in the first Dutch War which brought to the English the decisive battle of the Texel, in August, 1653. For his part in the war, Cromwell bestowed upon Vice-Admiral Penn that 'gold chain & medall' which were bequeathed to William in his father's will. Despite their warlike origin, these must have been treasured by William, even as a Quaker, in memory of his father's triumph and perhaps as a souvenir of his own boyhood's hero-worship of a gallant naval commander, the sound of whose guns may often have been heard by his son in the Essex school.

But there was one event in the schoolboy's inner life which eclipsed even the exciting stories of his father's career and all other external happenings. This was an event which is described as follows : 'While here [at Chigwell school] and alone in his chamber, being then eleven years old, he was suddenly surprised with an inward comfort and as he thought an external glory in the room, which gave rise to religious emotions, during which he had the strongest conviction of the being of a God, and that the soul of man was capable of enjoying communication with him. He believed also that the seal of Divinity had been put upon him at this moment, or that he had been awakened or called upon to a holy life.'[157]

---

[157] Clarkson, I, 5-6. Penn himself alluded to this incident on his visit to the Labadists at Wieuwerd, in September, 1677, when, he says (*Travails*, 1694, p. 181) : 'Here I began to let them know how and when the Lord first appeared unto me,

The various biographers of Penn have attempted to rationalize this spiritual experience and account for its occurrence by referring to the sombre influences exerted upon the sensitive mind of the boy by the civil and foreign wars and their carnage and suffering; by the startling eclipse of March 29, 1652, that terrifying 'Black Monday,' when, at nine A.M the sun was blotted out in the heavens and all England was in darkness; by the sombre impressions of Hainault Forest, as impressive perhaps as Joan of Arc's visions in the forest round Domrémy; by the gloom of the family at the fall and imprisonment of the Admiral on his return from Jamaica, the anxiety of the mother lest a stop had been put to his career, and the shame of the son at the jeers of his schoolmates for the family disgrace; by 'a low and feverish state of mind,' or perhaps by the joyous reaction and gratitude to God for the sudden release and return of the beloved earthly father. Three of Penn's biographers [158] suggest that the boy, young though he was, had heard of and read that mystical book entitled *Sparkles of Glory,* whose author was John Saltmarsh, a native of Wanstead. Saltmarsh is said to have died insane when Penn was three years old; and since this was two years before George Fox began to preach Quakerism, it is assumed that it was Saltmarsh's eloquent rhapsodies, and not Quakerism, which gave the first religious impulse to Penn's development. Indeed, one of these biographers goes so far as to attribute to Saltmarsh's book the vagaries of Fox and Quakerism, which were to act like a cancer in Penn's character and cause all the defects and failures of his public career!

These varied influences may have played their part; but without them, it is probable that such a mind as the sensitive boy possessed — like wax to receive and marble to retain — surrounded by a devout Puritan faith in the immanence of God, should have felt keenly the reality and nearness of the spiritual world and the very presence of the father of spirits in the midst of everyday life. His experience was by no means uncommon among youths of his age and period. Even a quarter-century later, in the midst of the Restoration era, the children in a Quaker school at Edmonton had similar vivid experiences.[159] In

---

which was about the 12th year of my Age, *Anno* 1656.' (Cf. Monograph Number Two: *William Penn and the Dutch Quaker Migration to Pennsylvania,* pp. 12-13). One of Penn's romantic biographers, Mason L.Weems, makes great use of this incident; cf. Monograph Number Three *Eight First Biographies of William Penn*).
158 Stoughton, 1882, pp. 4, 8; Buell, 1904, pp. 13-23; Grant, 1907, pp. 11-12.
159 Cf. Monograph No. One (*Willem Sewel of Amsterdam*), pp. 52-55.

Penn's case, whatever its origin and exact character, it played its part in making 'the life of the spirit' an enduring reality, and in causing him to dedicate himself to working for what he believed to be God's will in God's kingdom on earth.

The schooling which Penn received at Chigwell, in preparation for a university course, was supplemented by private tutoring at the several homes of his boyhood and youth. Returning with his family to London, he attended a private school on Great Tower Hill, and had also a tutor in his home near by. Going with his family to Ireland, the next year (1656), he had the benefit of tutors in his home at Macroom for about three successive years. Who these men were is not known; but they must have aided the lad's native industry and ability to acquire a very considerable knowledge of the classics.

These critical years in his life, between the ages of twelve and sixteen, were filled not merely with book-learning; he gained much also from participating in his father's active pioneering on his Irish estates, and he must have been deeply grieved by the manifold misery which Cromwell's 'Settlement' and man's inhumanity to man had inflicted upon the Irish peasants. Three-quarters of the land in the island were given over to English landlords; one-third of the people were destroyed by war, pestilence, and famine, and the rest were left to see their class destroyed, their race enslaved, and their religion proscribed.[160]

The tales of suffering which the lad must have heard, and some of its dire results which he must have seen, impressed upon him the virtues of benevolence and beneficence which distinguished him in the days of his wealth and power, when he advocated in his writings and exemplified in his acts a tender care for the afflicted. He kept in spiritual touch with God, during these years also: 'At times,' he said,[161] 'betwixt that [Anno 1656] and 15, the Lord visited me, and gave me divine Impressions of himself.' It was during these years, too, as will be seen, that he came into his first contact with Quakerism.

160 Trevelyan, *England under the Stuarts*, p. 320.
161 Discourse to the Labadists, 1677 (*Travails*, 1694, p. 182).

OXFORD

PENN's father was eager that he should enter upon the career of a statesman, and the door to that career led through one of the two universities. Oxford was chosen; and as soon as Admiral Penn had helped to restore Charles II to the Stuart throne, he sent William to that famous institution of learning and entered him as a gentleman-commoner in Christ Church, where he was matriculated as the son of a knight. Now, his father might be assured, he was taking rank as an aristocrat among other aristocrats in a very aristocratic environment.

But the Stuart régime was bent on making the college High Church Anglican, as well as aristocratic, and ordered the chapel organ to be returned, the surplice to be worn again by dons and students at chapel-services, and the Prayer Book to be restored in place of extemporaneous sermons.[162] These formalistic measures went against the grain of youths who had accepted whole-heartedly the ideals of the Puritan régime, and even seemed to them to be evidence of a determination to restore England to the Church of Rome. Penn was one of the nonconformist students who absented themselves from chapel exercises, held meetings of their own for prayer and exhortation, and rode out into the suburbs to listen to the eloquent Dr. Owen, the former dean of Christ Church and vice-chancellor of the university, who had just been dismissed for his dissenting views.

Besides this divergence on religion, the contrast exemplified at the university between the cavalier manners and morals and those of roundhead students like Penn, widened the gulf which was separating him from the career which his father designed for him. In his discourse at Wieuwerd in 1677, he referred to his persecution at Oxford, and how the Lord had sustained him 'in the midst of that Hellish Darkness and Debauchery'; and in the first pamphlet that he published, he denounced the English universities as 'Signal Places for Idleness, Looseness, Prophaneness, Prodigality, and gross Ignorance.'[163] The denunciation was no doubt extravagant; but there must have been much truth in his condemnation of a type of character and mode of

---

162 Anthony Wood, *Life and Times, 1632-1695*, Ed. of 1891 (Quoted by Fisher, 62-66).
163 *Truth Exalted*, 1668.

life which was illustrated by one of his fellow-students, John Wilmot, later the notorious Earl of Rochester.

On the other hand, the university afforded Penn opportunity for much wholesome life of mingled sport and study. He pursued eagerly his reading of the classics, and, to judge from his later writings, must have read widely in metaphysics and theology; but he entered also within the doorway of the physical sciences through the study of anatomy. His proficiency in Latin as a newly arrived freshman is illustrated by an elegy which he wrote on the death of the young Duke of Gloucester, Charles II's younger brother.[164] Although the sentiment expressed in this elegy may appear rather extreme for a non-conformist in religion, Penn was a loyalist in politics throughout his life; and the deep love of royalty cherished, even in democratic England, has received many striking illustrations within this twentieth century. The Duke had died of smallpox (a disease which Penn had survived) one month before Penn's arrival at Oxford, and a few months after the royal family's return to London, when 'England still made her show of public joy' over the Restoration.

In the following spring (April 22, 1661), Penn went up to London and became a participant in some of this show. Pepys tells the story of how he and a party including the two William Penns viewed the royal procession through the decorated streets of the city on the day preceding Charles II's coronation. 'It is impossible,' Pepys writes, 'to relate the glory of this day, expressed in the clothes of them that rid, and their horses and horses-clothes. Embroidery and diamonds were ordinary among them. . . . So glorious was the show with gold and silver, that we were not able to look at it, our eyes at last being so much overcome with it.' The enthusiastic Pepys gives an account, also, of the coronation the next day which he witnessed in Westminster

[164] Part of this elegy and its translation into English are given by Clarkson (I, 7-8) as follows:

> Publica te, Dux magne, dabant jejunia genti.
> Sed facta est, nato principe, festa dies.
> Te moriente, licèt celebraret laeta triumphos
> Anglia, solennes solvitur in lachrymas.
> Solus ad arbitrium moderaris pectora; solus
> Tu dolor accedis, deliciaeque tuis.

> Though 'twas a fast-day when thou cam'st, thy birth
> Turn'd it at once to one of festive mirth.
> Though England, at thy death, still made her show
> Of public joy, she pass'd to public woe.
> Thou dost, alone, the public breast control,
> Alone, delight and sorrow to the soul.

CHRIST CHURCH COLLEGE STAIRWAY

Abbey; but he does not mention the presence of the two Penns on that occasion. He does record, the day before, the very merry dinner which his party—'pleased beyond imagination at what we have seen'—enjoyed after the show; and he states also that young Will and his own boy 'staid and saw the show on Tower Hill.' The royal procession had been viewed by the party from a room overlooking Cornhill—well supplied with wine and cake, and when the king and his brother, the Duke of York, passed by, Pepys declares, 'they took notice of us at the window.' This was probably the first time that Penn saw the royal brothers who were to mean so much to him for weal and woe.

Returning from this glimpse of high society to Oxford, we find Penn buckling down to his studies, which included, as has been said, some natural science, particularly anatomy. A King's Professor of Physics delivered the lectures on anatomy, and illustrated them by the dissection of the bodies of criminals, executed in those days for a multiplicity of crimes large and small, and even by vivisection of animals. John Locke was studying medicine at Oxford at the time, and it is possible that Penn made his first acquaintance with him then. Since Locke was twelve years older, however, this acquaintance would have been only superficial; and it was not until a score of years later that plans of colonial government, the advocacy of religious toleration, and experiences of royal disfavour and exile brought them close together.

Penn's study of anatomy is reflected persistently in his controversial writing against the Muggletonians, in which he particularly states:[165] 'If Soul and Body were intermixedly and inseparably generated by Man, then in all Anatomies it were no more difficult to find out the Soul than any other Part: and in Case of Opening or dissecting of Living Men, as I have at the University seen living Beasts by Anatomists, it would not be impossible, but rational, that one should behold the very Thoughts, Purposes, and Intents of such Men's Hearts and Souls.' John Locke, a youthful don at the time, may have been one of the 'Anatomists' over whose shoulder Penn looked at these operations; but neither he nor his instructor had yet risen to the psychological heights of the 'Essay on the Human Understanding.'

In contrast with his inclination towards the physical sciences, Penn's distaste for the logic and metaphysics of the pre-renaissance era is shown by his aversion from what he later called 'the vain Quiddities, idle and gross Terms, and most sophistical Ways of Syllogizing, with

165 *The New Witnesses prov'd Old Hereticks,* 1672 (*Works,* 1726, Vol. II, p. 158).

the rest of that useless and injurious Pedantry (to Mankind, brought into the Christian Religion by Popish School-Men, and so eminently in vogue in Oxford and Cambridge, and which above all things fame their students).'[166]

Although the Royal Society was founded during his college days for the promotion of science, and he was afterwards elected one of its fellows, Penn's interests then and always were preëminently religious, and it was what he deemed to be irreligion at Oxford that resulted in his premature departure from the university. When his non-conformity was carried to its extreme by the acceptance of Quakerism, he wrote of the things which offended him as follows: 'Whence came your Forms of Prayers, and Church-Government, from the Scriptures of Truth, and the Practice of the Primitive Christians, or the Mass-Book and Popish Canons? Whence is it that Mass-Houses are called Churches? And what President [precedent] do you find for Litanies, Responses, Singing, Quiristers [choristers], Organs, Altars, Bowing, Surplices, Square Caps, Hoods, Rochets, Fonts, Baby-Baptism, Holy Days (as you call them) with much more such like dirty Trash, and foul Superstition?'[167]

The heat generated in these denunciations was due not so much to his dissatisfaction with the affairs of religion at Oxford as it was to his resentment at the persecution of his fellow-nonconformists which began under the Act of Uniformity just as he left the university. At this latter period, Quakerism does not appear to have made a decisive impression upon him. It is possible that he attended a Quaker meeting and heard a sermon preached by Thomas Loe, a Quaker tradesman of Oxford, formerly connected in some way with the university. Loe had been imprisoned in Oxford gaol for his Quakerism during six months preceding Penn's arrival, but had gone thence to Ireland and did not return to Oxford until the beginning of the winter of 1660-61. He was again imprisoned in Oxford, January 13, 1661 and, together with some forty other Quakers accused of complicity in the Fifth Monarchy plot, was kept in gaol for months and perhaps until after Penn had left Oxford for good. Penn may have heard him in December or January, 1660-61, before he was imprisoned; but there is a sur-

---

[166] *A Serious Apology for the Principles and Practices of the . . . Quakers*, 1671 (*Works*, 1726, II, 56). Penn must have studied some logic and rhetoric, either at Oxford or earlier (perhaps under a tutor, in Thomas Wilson's popular text-books entitled *The Rule of Reason*, 1552 and *The Arte of Rhetorique*, 1553).

[167] *Truth Exalted*, 1668 (*Works*, 1726, II, 243).

prising lack of information regarding Penn's contact with Quakerism, if any really occurred during his student days, in Oxford. At intervals during the half-dozen years before his arrival, the students and townspeople had treated the Quaker missionaries in most brutal fashion; and surely Penn must have heard the tragic stories of William Simpson, Elizabeth Fletcher, Richard Hubberthorne, John Camm, and other 'first publishers of Truth' in the city. These had harangued the congregations in the city churches and the college chapels, had distributed Quaker literature, and had converted a few citizens (Thomas Loe among them) who had set up their meetings for worship. The usual reaction of the mob and of 'the black tribe of scholars' met them in the form of ducking, beating, and barbarities of cruel and obscene kinds;[168] and it seems strange indeed if William Penn heard nothing of the story, or made no reference to it.

His own non-conformity brought about his expulsion or suspension from the university. First, at the beginning of his second year, came a fine imposed for absenting himself from college chapel; and finally, in the following March, he was 'sent down' home, or was 'banisht the College,' as he himself phrased it,[169] and never returned as a student. The immediate cause of the break is not definitely stated. It is not probable that he wrote and published a pamphlet 'which the priests and masters of the college did not like';[170] nor is it proved that he led some students in tearing the obnoxious surplices 'over the heads' of the others; still less, is it probable that he began at this time to defend the doctrines of Quakerism. Doubtless, it was his continued refusal to attend chapel and to conform with other 'papist' requirements which led to the termination of his university career. Thus, at the age of eighteen, began his struggle of a quarter-century for religious liberty and the right of every one to worship God in accordance with the dictates of his own conscience. At that time and place, also, this youthful dreamer of dreams which came true, dreamed a dream of a fair Utopia where this precious right could receive full exercise.[171]

---

168 Cf. *First Publishers of Truth*, 1654, pp. 209-214; Joseph Besse, *Sufferings*, 1753, I, 562 ff.: William C. Braithwaite, *The Beginnings of Quakerism*, 1912, pp. 158-9, 297-9. Very nearly the same experiences were suffered at the same time by the Quakers who went to convert the university and town of Cambridge.
169 *Travails*, 1694, p. 182.
170 This is the reason given by his later friend Thomas Harvey, as stated in the 'Harvey MS.' of 1727 (see *supra*, p. 33).
171 Cf. *infra*, p. 218.

THE GRAND TOUR, 1662-1664

RETURNING from Oxford to his father's home in London, Penn was received with coldness, then with arguments and blows, and finally with expulsion from the parental roof-tree. He had spent the preceding Christmas holidays with his father and sister, his mother being still at their home in Ireland; and from the pages of Pepys, it appears that the two Pepys and three Penns had been 'very merry.' The day after Christmas they 'eat some cakes and ale' in an ale-house in Moorfield, where 'a washeall-bowle [wassail-bowl] woman and girl' sang to them; this was followed by a supper at the Pepys' with a good turkey, merriment, and cards. Four days later, the three Penns and Mrs. Pepys went to the theatre to see Chapman's 'Bussy D'Ambois,' and Pepys joined them at the Penns' for a late supper and cards. On New Year's Day, Penn went with Pepys to buy some pictures and maps; and in the evening, he and his sister ate 'a barrel of oysters' with the Pepys and went with them to the theatre to see Beaumont and Fletcher's 'Spanish Curate.' From the play, the two Penns went to the Pepys' and were very merry playing cards till late at night, after having jested with William because he had left his sword in the coach and got it again only after a chase as far as the Exchange. Finally, on January 6, 1662, the three Penns played cards and ate supper at the Pepys', in a farewell visit before William returned to Oxford.

But these merry days were soon followed by the storm. On January 25, 1662, Pepys records that he and Admiral Penn were walking together in the Navy Yard garden when 'Sir William did break a business to me about removing his son from Oxford to Cambridge to some private college, and I proposed Magdalene [Pepys' own college], but cannot name a tutor at present.' Pepys promised to think about the matter; and one week later, he proposed to write to Dr. Fairbrother of Cambridge University to ask for a statement in regard to a tutor, Mr. Hezekiah Burton of Magdalene College. This statement appears not to have been received before Penn's return home; for, on March 16, Pepys writes, he and his wife went to the Admiral's for supper, where they found William 'at home not well.' To this, he adds: 'All things, I fear, do not go well with them; they look discontentedly, but I know not what ails them.' Six weeks later, April 28, 1662, Pepys records: 'Sir W. Pen much troubled upon letters came last night. Showed me one of Dr. Owen's to his son, whereby it appears his son is much perverted in his opinion by him; which I now perceive is one thing that hath put Sir W. so long off the hooks.'

Precisely what occurred between father and son between March 16, when the latter returned from Oxford and April 28, when the father received Dr. Owen's letter, can only be conjectured. The son himself, in his talk to the Labadists in 1677, referred to 'the bitter Usage I underwent when I returned [from Oxford] to my Father; whipping, beating, and turning out of doors in 1662.'[172] This drastic treatment may have been resorted to in May, during which month the Conventicle Act and the Act of Uniformity were passed by Parliament against the non-conforming sects, especially the Quakers. Some of Penn's biographers surmise that he had already become a Quaker, or 'half a Quaker'; but it seems certain that his formal Quakerism did not begin until 1667, when he was in Ireland, and that his first stormy controversy with his father in 1662 was due to his refusal to conform to the Anglican Church, to which the Admiral had given his cordial adhesion. To have his son turn his back upon the court-life for which he designed him and consort with non-conformist sectarians was too much for his father's pride and ambition. His mother, that 'excellent woman,' 'an amiable woman,' an 'amiable Dutch wife,' as she is variously called by his biographers, is said by them to have sent to him from Ireland money and the necessaries of life, and to have written letters to her husband interceding for tolerance and harmony.

The hot-headed but warm-hearted admiral evidently soon relented; for we find William restored to his father's home and favour, and the father himself planning to divest his son of his whims and megrims and of continuing his interrupted education by sending him forth upon the Grand Tour. This was the usual 'finish' of education for young English aristocrats after their university studies were ended, and it included a journey through France, Switzerland, Italy, and home by way of Germany. Those who went only to France or Germany, made a simple Tour. Penn had completed only a part of the Grand Tour before his father recalled him to London. He went first to France, then through Switzerland into Italy, and thence back to England, either by way of France and possibly Holland, or directly by sea.

The two-fold motive of improving his manners and continuing the education of his mind was fulfilled chiefly in France. He went first

---

[172] *Travails*, 1694, p. 182.

to Paris in company with 'certain persons of rank and quality,' who were perhaps one or more of his Oxford friends and the Earl of Crawford. The latter was a leader of the Presbyterian party in Scotland, had played an important part in the Civil Wars, been imprisoned in London Tower in 1655, and may have become acquainted there with his fellow-prisoner, Admiral Penn. Restored to high office at the Restoration, he retired from public life a couple of years later and at the age of sixty-five took his son and the latter's young friends on the Grand Tour which he had himself enjoyed in his youth.

At Paris, the young English aristocrats were introduced at the court of Louis XIV, then a gallant young sovereign a half-dozen years Penn's senior, who had but recently taken over the reins of personal government on the death of Mazarin. Here, Penn may have met and doubtless heard much of that great French statesman, Jean Colbert, the finance and colonial minister, whose splendid work for New France was undone by Louis XIV's wars, and who died broken-hearted in 1683, just as Penn was getting his own colonies well started. Indeed, as Sir Walter Raleigh had been inspired with ideals of American colonization by that great Huguenot leader, Admiral Coligny, so may Penn have owed much to the example of Colbert; and like Colbert, Penn's colonial difficulties were greatly increased by the aggressive wars waged by Louis.

Meanwhile, Louis's brilliant court and the social life that revolved round it provided an unprecedented environment for the development of Penn's own courtly nature. Parisian gaiety gradually overcame his non-conformist gravity, and his costume and demeanour reflected that polish which shone so lustrously in the land of *le grand monarque,* and was so eagerly imitated among all the princelings and nobility of Europe.[173] Either at Oxford, or in Paris itself, Penn learned the art of duelling; and he relates in his *No Cross, No Crown* [174] a duel which was forced upon him. 'I was once myself in France (which was before I professed the [Quaker] communion I am now of) set upon about eleven at night, as I was walking to my lodging, by a person that waylaid me, with his naked sword in his hand, who demanded satisfaction of me for taking no notice of him at a time when he civilly saluted me with his hat; though the truth was, I saw him not when

---

173 Penn, in his *No Cross, No Crown,* 1669 (Part I, 9:33), says of ancient Rome: 'Her fashions, as those of France now, were as laws to the world.'
174 ibid. Part I, 9:2.

he did it. I will suppose he had killed me, for he made several passes at me, or I in my defence had killed him, when I disarmed him (as the Earl of Crawford's servant saw, that was by) : I ask any man of understanding or conscience if the whole ceremony were worth the life of a man, considering the dignity of the nature and the importance of the life of man, both with respect to God his Creator, himself, and the benefit of civil society ?'[175]

After four months of this polishing process in Paris, Penn went to Saumur to fulfil the second purpose of his coming abroad, namely, to supply the deficiencies in his formal education which his premature departure from Oxford had caused. At this artistic medieval town in Anjou, lying on the banks of the historic Loire, Penn spent nearly two years of intense study which must have far more than made up for the lost two years on the banks of the Isis. Saumur was then the centre of Huguenot learning, and possessed a Protestant college or seminar which had been for a generation and more the mecca of both Protestant and Catholic scholars throughout Europe, and especially popular with English students during the period of the Commonwealth. When Penn went there, it was during the palmy days of Huguenotism, before the Revocation of the Edict of Nantes had crushed it nearly out of existence ; and the seminar was presided over by one of the most eminent Protestant divines, Moïse, or Moses, Amyraut. An author of wide influence and renown, Amyraut had been a professor at the college for thirty-three years, and was now, at the age of sixty-six, at the height of his powers and career. He championed a modified form of Calvinism, insisting on freedom of the will and a predestination qualified by universal grace. Under his guidance Penn made an earnest study of the Bible and of the Fathers of the Church in Greek and Latin, the fruits of which were harvested in many later books. His gift for languages was cultivated in both classic and modern tongues, and he appears to have made a particularly close study of the language, literature, and history of France.

It would seem at first sight that it was a dangerous experiment for Sir William Penn to send his son from England to escape non-conformist Puritanism and place him in the very centre of French

---

[175] Another Pennsylvanian, Benjamin Franklin, was once challenged to a duel by an ill-smelling man who thrust a paper into his hand and was admonished to stand farther off. Franklin's *reductio ad absurdum* of the duel, in declining the challenge, was put tersely thus : 'If you should kill me, I should soon smell as ill as you do ; and if I should kill you, you would soon stink even worse than you do now.'

Puritanism — almost, in fact, like throwing him out of the frying-pan into the fire. But he probably considered that in France there were only Protestants and Catholics, and that in the absence of a great cloud of Puritan sectarians, his son would develop only a rational Protestantism consistent with the urbane and seemly manners for which the French were famous. Penn's biographers have differed as to the influence on him of this course in Calvinism, the Quaker writers suggesting that it helped him to react strongly, as did the rest of his fellow-Quakers, against the whole Calvinistic system; but the non-Quakers believing that such a modified system of Calvinism acted as a bridge over into a saner theology than that of Fox and Barclay.

Whatever may have been the case with theology, Amyraut's influence upon Penn may have been strong in other particulars, including especially a simplicity as well as refinement of manners, the profuse use of literary citations in his writings,[176] a passionate devotion to religious liberty and international peace, the doctrine of the Light Within, and a solution of the Seventeenth Century's religious problem by means of 'Comprehension.' Even Richelieu dallied with this last ideal as a means of settling the dispute between French Catholics and Protestants; while Penn in later years gave serious consideration to it as a means of uniting at least all Protestants into a single church.[177]

Leaving France when Amyraut died on the 8th of January, 1664, Penn went through Switzerland into Italy. Of his Swiss journey we have no details except that his companion was Robert Spencer, that Earl of Sunderland who played such a brilliant but renegade part in the later reign of Charles II and under James II and William III. Travellers find strange bed-fellows; but the potentially evil influence of Spencer upon Penn may have been blunted by the sublimity of the scenery through which they passed — but of which they *apparently* took no notice. The two men remained good friends for the rest of their lives, were in close touch with one another at the Stuart court, and despite the disparity in their character and career, co-operated at various times.

Going on into Italy as far as Turin, Penn was halted by a letter from

---

[176] The six-volume work of Amyraut, entitled *Morale chrétienne,* was published in Saumur in 1652-1660; it was one of the first systematic French treatises on ethics based upon a historic plan, and must have inspired in various ways Penn's *No Cross, No Crown.*

[177] Cf. Monograph No. Two (*William Penn and the Dutch Quaker Migration to Pennsylvania,* 1935, pp. 129-132).

his father summoning him to return to England. Spencer may have continued on to Rome; but Penn never saw that city from whose depravity Robert Barclay's father called him back home, and against whose church Penn was to publish burning denunciations. By some biographers, it is believed that Penn was introduced in Italy to Algernon Sidney by Robert Spencer, who was Sidney's nephew.[178] Others think that Penn returned to England by way of France and Rotterdam, and that while waiting for a boat to Harwich met Sidney in the Rotterdam home of the Anglo-Dutch Quaker merchant, Benjamin Furly. Furly was a friend and host of both Sidney and John Locke, and may have been the host of Penn also at this date, although there is no evidence that Penn was in Holland before 1671.[179] Wherever Penn and Sidney met, there can be little doubt that the staunch republican made a deep impression on Penn's mind, as was shown in the election of 1679, when Penn did his best to elect Sidney to Parliament, and in the ideals of civil and political liberty which Penn embodied in his government of Pennsylvania.

WAR, PESTILENCE, AND LAW

AT the end of his fruitful stay abroad, Penn returned to England, and was welcomed with seeming cordiality and expressed admiration by his family's friends and neighbours, the Pepys. Under date of August 26, 1664, Pepys records: 'This day my wife tells me Mr. Pen, Sir William's son, is come back from France, and come to visit her. A most modish person, grown, she says, a fine gentleman.' One of the Admiral's subordinates, P. Gibson, adds his testimony to Penn's stylish appearance as follows:[180] 'I remember your honour well, when you newly came out of France and wore pantaloon breeches.' A few days after his visit to Mrs. Pepys, Penn called on her husband, who records:[181] 'He staid an houre talking with me. I perceive something

---

178 Spencer's mother, Dorothy Sidney, Lady Spencer, appears to have been in Paris during Penn's stay there; hence, the two youths may have planned the Swiss and Italian journey together, and gone to Dorothy's lodgings in Turin, where they found her exiled brother Algernon.
179 There is a possibility, also, that Penn and Spencer met Sidney at Vevey, on the Lake of Geneva, where Sidney sometimes visited in the home of another 'regicide' exile, General Edmund Ludlow, 'the last of the English Republicans.'
180 The letter to William Penn, dated March, 1711-12; cf. *supra*, p. 7.
181 August 30, 1664.

of learning he hath got, but a great deale, if not too much, of the vanity of the French garbe and affected manner of speech and gait. I fear all real profit he hath made of his travel will signify little.'[182]

A year later, Pepys was still leading Penn on to talk of his travels. For example, September 5, 1665 : 'Home pretty betimes and there found W. Pen and he staid supper with us and mighty merry talking of his travels and the French humours, etc., and so parted.' But the topic was becoming stale, and Penn's superiority in the knowledge of French was beginning to irk; for we find Pepys writing, eight days later : 'Landing at Greenwich I saw Mr. Pen walking my way, so we walked together, and for discourse I put him into talk of France, when he took delight to tell me of his observations, some good, some impertinent, and all ill told but it served for want of better.' That same evening the Pepys' supped at the Penns', and after supper, Pepys says : 'Mr. Pen and I fell to discourse about some words in a French song my wife was saying [singing ?], "D'un air tout interdict," wherein I laid twenty to one against him which he would not agree with me, though I know myself in the right as to the sense of the word, and almost angry we were, and were an houre and more upon the dispute, till at last broke up not satisfied, and so home in their coach and so to bed.'

Although such social occasions gave opportunity for the development of Penn's natural gift for conversation and controversy, which was later to serve him in such good stead, the months after his return from the Continent were filled with far sterner realities of life. His admiring parents were doubtless well pleased with the improvement which they noted in his demeanour and mental development ; and his father pursued his ambition to prepare his son for taking high public office.

But meanwhile, the Admiral himself was called upon to play an important rôle in England's history. The letter which he had written his son calling him home from Italy was due to the approach of England's second naval war with Holland and the high command assigned to him in it.[183] Through the summer, autumn and winter of 1664-65, the Admiral was deeply absorbed in preparing the depleted English fleet for battle ; and in the spring (March 24), he sailed in practical

---

[182] September 5 and 14, 1664.
[183] According to Pepys (August 27, 1664), 'the Dutch are, with twenty-two sayle of ships of warr, crewsing up and down about Ostend ; at which we are alarmed,'— and by which Penn may have but just escaped capture on his return from the Continent.

command of it, and his son accompanied him for about a month before the first great battle. Pepys, writing under date of April 25, 1665, says : 'This afternoon W. Pen, lately come from his father in the fleete, did give me an account how the fleete did sayle, about 103 in all. . . .'

Penn was among the many young courtiers who went on board seeking excitement, fame, and fortune. His father and the Duke of York singled him out to carry personal dispatches for the king and official letters for the Secretary of State. He landed at Harwich, and wrote from there to his father on the 23rd of April the following affectionate letter :[184] 'Honoured Father, We could not arrive here sooner than this day, about twelve of the clock, by reason of the continued cross winds and (as I thought) foul weather. I pray God, after all the foul weather and dangers you are exposed to, and shall be, that you come home as secure. And, I bless God, my heart does not in any way fail; but firmly believes, that if God has called you out to battle, he will cover your head in that smoky day. And, as I never knew what a father was till I had wisdom enough to prize him, so can I safely say, that now, of all times, your concerns are most dear to me. It's hard, meantime, to lose both a father and a friend. &c. W. P.'

Returning to the fleet, doubtless with dispatches from the king, William again landed at Harwich, and on his arrival the next morning in London, wrote to his father the following letter :[185]

'Navy Office, 6th May, 1665.
'At my arrival at Harwich, (which was about one of the clock on the Sabbath day, and where I staid till three), I took post for London, and was at London the next morning by almost daylight. I hasted to Whitehall, where, not finding the king up, I presented myself to my Lord of Arlington and Colonel Ashburnham. At his majesty's knocking, he was informed there was an express from the duke : at which, earnestly skipping out of his bed, he came only in his gown and slippers; who, when he saw me, said, "Oh! is't you? how is Sir William?" He asked how you did at three several times. He was glad to hear your message about *Ka*. After interrogating me above half an hour, he bid me go now about your business, and mine too. As to the duchess, he was pleased to ask several questions, and so dismissed me. I delivered all the letters given me. My mother was to

---
184 Granville Penn, *Memorials*, 1833, II, 317.
185 ibid. II, 318.

see my Lady Lawson,[186] and she was here. I pray God be with you, and be your armour in the day of controversy! May that power be your salvation, for his name's sake! and so will he wish and pray, that is, with all true veneration,

Honoured father,
Your obedient son and servant,
William Penn.'

One month later, occurred the 'Battle of the 3rd of June,' off Lowestoft, about 120 miles northeast of London: probably too far away for the Admiral's family to hear the firing of guns on his flagship, *The Royal Charles*. His son, however, heard the details of the battle many times over, and five years later wrote a detailed account of it in defence of his father against an attack made upon his memory.[187] Pepys recorded in his Diary five days after the battle the news and details of the English victory, congratulated the Admiral's family and gave faint praise to him for it.[188] The praise which the public bestowed upon him was far greater and more genuine, and the family participated whole-heartedly in it, while the father became more than ever a hero to his son.

But the slight 'service' which the latter saw in the navy, by no means attracted him to emulate his father's naval career. He had neither the taste nor the training for it; and indeed he had already enrolled as a law student in Lincoln's Inn. On February 7, 1665, he was entered in that famous institution, and spent a full year in a regular course of legal training. This move is sometimes explained as simply a means of keeping his time employed and his mind off the dangerous rocks of religion; also, that his father was planning to vacate his seat in parliament and to have his son trained to take his place as representative of the 'rotten borough' of Weymouth. But the law was probably adopted because it was a customary preparation for a career in civilian office.

Although Penn did not enter parliament, or as 'Viscount Weymouth' fill high public office, the knowledge which he acquired of England's constitutional history and legal theory and practice stood him in excellent stead. His father's lawsuits in Ireland and his own in con-

---

186 Wife of Vice-Admiral Sir John Lawson, who was fatally wounded in the battle.
187 *Truth rescued from Imposture*, 1670, Part III: *A Vindication of my deceased Father's Reputation, Works*, 1726, Vol. I, p. 498.
188 *Supra*, pp. 9, 21.

nexion with Pennsylvania were to give him ample opportunity to exercise his legal knowledge; while in the Penn-Meade Trial and in many another clash of the Quakers with their private and public persecutors and prosecutors, Penn drew with telling effect upon his knowledge of the historic rights and privileges of Englishmen. This legal training in the sad year of 1665-66 was to play an even more important rôle in developing the constitution and laws of New Jersey and Pennsylvania.

The Dutch War, like most other wars in history, was accompanied by pestilence, which was called this time in England 'the Great Plague.' It loomed up in London's suburbs in December, 1664, and was so threatening by the next spring that Admiral Penn hurried the warships which were being out-fitted against the Dutch away from the threatened capital and prematurely out to sea. In June, the month of 'the great victory,' the plague started in earnest upon its devastating career, and its victims in London mounted from 267 per week in June, to 7,000 in September, taking a total toll altogether, it is estimated, of about 70,000, or one in every seven of London's citizens. This huge mortality was centred chiefly in the densely crowded suburbs of the City, but its gruesome sights and sounds must have become terribly familiar to Penn as he walked to Lincoln's Inn or escorted his mother and sister to church.

The contrast between this pestilence that walked in the darkness, this destruction that wasted at noonday, and the gay life of careless and frivolous pleasure which Pepys depicts in his Diary, made a deep and painful impression upon Penn's sensitive spirit. In his discourse at Wieuwerd, a dozen years later,[189] he speaks feelingly, 'and that with great reverence and brokenness of Spirit,' of the Lord's dealings with him 'in the time of the great Plague in London'; of 'the deep sense he gave me of the Vanity of this World, of the Irreligiousness of the Religions of it; of my Mournful and Bitter Cries to him that he would show me his own way of Life and Salvation, and my Resolutions to follow him whatever Reproaches or Sufferings should attend me.'

These thoughts would appear to be the shadow of his approaching Quakerism; but if so, they were not consciously associated with it. He might, indeed, have heard much of the Quakers in London during that dread summer. With the exodus of the fashionable world from the plague-stricken city, the Anglican pulpits were left vacant, and

189 *Travails*, 1694, p. 182.

the non-conformist preachers returned to preach in them and thunder denunciations against the persecuting government. The Quakers were especially active in holding their meetings; and despite the widespread nursing and charity they undertook among the victims of the pestilence — which won them the name of 'the Angels of the Plague'— the Conventicle Act was sternly enforced against them. A thousand of them died of the plague, and two thousand were at one time in London's prisons; while their transportation to Jamaica was demanded by the populace because their blasphemies had brought on the plague from an offended God!

The return of Penn's grave and sober bearing may have been indirectly aided by rumours of the heroism of the Quakers; but it must have been due directly to his reaction against the frivolities and irreligion which formed so violent a contrast with the miseries of the human life around him, a contrast which reawakened all his youthful belief in the necessity of regulating the life of men by the will of God.

PENN IN IRELAND

But Penn at this time was only twenty-one; and to a youth of his age, position and opportunities, life held out many pleasures which he must have considered permissible, while turning his back upon others. When his father proposed that he go to Ireland for the two-fold purpose of applying his legal training to regaining the exclusive ownership of the Shangarry estate and of renovating and developing it, he willingly obeyed. It does not appear that his father was afraid of his 'relapsing into Quakerism,' for he had not yet been in it; but he evidently did desire that active practical tasks should be given a chance to dispel the sombre 'Puritanical' thoughts and demeanour which beset his son's tender conscience in plague-stricken London. In Ireland, too, the Admiral's old friend, the Duke of Ormond, presided over a vice-regal court which had much of the splendour, but with little of the sordid immorality which prevailed in the Stuart court at Whitehall; and to him he wrote a letter commending his son.[190]

In Dublin, Penn was received with much cordiality by the Lord Lieutenant and his son, the Earl of Arran. With the latter, who was eight years his senior, he seems to have formed a warm friendship

190 Granville Penn, *Memorials*, II, 429 (July 19, 1666).

and to have participated with him in the sports and gaieties of the vice-regal court. When a mutiny of soldiers occurred in Carrickfergus and the rebels seized the castle, Arran was sent to suppress them, and Penn volunteered to accompany him. The rebel stronghold was captured by an assault in which Penn participated with a skill and courage much praised by his comrades. His cousin, Sir Richard Rooth, captain of a frigate which was present at the recapture of the castle, wrote to Admiral Penn that 'my cousin William was pleased to accompany his lordship in that action, to his no small reputation.'[191] The Duke was so much pleased with William's prowess that he wrote to the Admiral proposing that he should resign the captaincy of the company of infantry stationed in the fort at Kinsale, and that it be bestowed upon William.[192] A letter from the latter to his father shows that he was willing and perhaps eager to receive this opportunity of entering upon a soldier's career; although in it he stressed not so much his own desire as 'my lord lieutenant's and Lord of Arran's great and daily kindness.'[193]

The Admiral accordingly wrote to the Duke a letter of grateful thanks for his kindness to his son, but asked him to 'be pleased to respite your thought of that favour (towards my son) for the present'; and he hinted as his excuse for not relinquishing his own captaincy of the company that, 'God sending an end to this present war (which I hope will not long continue), I shall endeavour to follow the great inclination which I have to fix in Ireland.'[194] To his son, the Admiral wrote: 'As to the tender made by his grace my lord lieutenant, concerning the fort of Kinsale, I wish your youthful desires mayn't outrun your discretion.'[195]

From these letters it would appear that the father vetoed the son's desire, either because of his own disinclination to be superseded on the eve of retiring to his governorship of Kinsale, or because he deemed his son to be too young for the post. But since he had himself been captain of a warship at his son's own age of twenty-one, the latter reason does not appear to be adequate. A more probable reason is that he was as much opposed to his son entering upon a soldier's career as upon a sailor's, and adhered to his determination of launching him

---

191 ibid. II, 430 (July 4, 1666).
192 ibid. II, 431 (May 29, 1666).
193 ibid. II, 430-31 (July 4, 1666).
194 ibid. II, 432-33 (August 7, 1666).
195 ibid. II, 432 (July 17, 1666).

upon that of a civilian and a statesman. As for the strength of William's desire to become a soldier, about the only evidence we have concerning it is his portrait in armour, which was painted in Dublin by an unknown artist, either before or after his military exploit at Carrickfergus.[196] There is a brief reference to this temptation to become a soldier, in his discourse at Wieuwerd in 1677, in which he said: 'After all this [his grief over the plague and the irreligion accompanying it], the glory of the world overtook me, and I was even ready to give up my self unto it, seeing no such thing as the Primitive Spirit and Church on the Earth, and being ready to faint concerning my hope of the restitution of all things.'[197]

In view of Penn's great career as a Quaker statesman and foremost champion of religious toleration and international peace, there is small wonder that his biographers accentuate the fortunate and providential failure of his military ambition. Even though he had made as great a reputation as a general as his father made as an admiral, his achievements would not have been recorded by so many biographers, and humanity would not have been made so much the better because of them.

Some of Penn's biographers assume that his father procured for him in lieu of the captaincy, the office of Clerk of the Cheque at Kinsale harbour; but it was another William Penn, his Uncle George's son, who held this office,[198] while he himself was appointed Victualler of the Fleet at Kinsale. Since his father was filling this latter office at London, their correspondence concerning its duties must have been of great advantage to him. One of the Admiral's letters on this subject is extant, and it reveals his practical grasp of details.[199]

The Admiral's increasing ill health, his restlessness due to retirement from active service at sea, and his disgust at the petty jealousies and rivalries by which he was surrounded in the Navy Office, impelled him to withdraw from London and settle with his family on the great estate conferred upon him by Charles II in Ireland. But there was a claimant to part of this estate, an old Cromwellian soldier, named Colonel Wallis, and it was the chief purpose of William Penn's mission to liquidate

---

196 *Infra*, pp. 294 ff.
197 *Travails*, 1694, pp. 182-3.
198 It was probably this other William Penn, also, who was commissioned by the Duke of Ormond's eldest son, then Earl of Orrery and President of Munster, an 'ensign in the cavalry' for the protection of Kinsale against the Dutch.
199 Granville Penn, *Memorials*, II, 434.

WILLIAM PENN AT THE AGE OF TWENTY-TWO

this claim, take full possession of the estate, and reconstruct and develop it. Once more, therefore, as in his boyhood ten years before, Penn found himself in County Cork, this time at Shangarry instead of at Macroom, and once more, on his own initiative, he engaged in the congenial tasks of a planter's life. At the same time he pursued with Colonel Wallis negotiations which find an echo in one of his father's letters, dated October 2 [1666], reading in part as follows :[200] 'I have yours, with your answers to Wallis's reasons, and know not how to say more about that business; but must leave you to the direction and blessing of God Almighty, who I am sure will be just, whatever men are. I am as much concerned for your honour (it being the first of your appearance in the world) as for the bone that's contended for; and yet, I judge it to be a bone very full of marrow.'

A few months later, Penn thought that he had persuaded the colonel to come to an agreement. A letter from his father, dated February 2, 1667,[201] reads : 'I have yours of the 26th ultimo, and am glad you are well returned to Dublin. I wish you [may] find that agreement with W. prove according to your relation, and so I shall be satisfied; my frame of mind being for "peace with all men, so far as in me lieth."' But this first attempt of Penn to arbitrate disputes was a failure, and the law-suit was taken over to the Land Commissioners' Court in London. This step was taken on the advice of the Admiral, who wrote : [202] 'Inform yourself rightly of it by particulars; which is, how, and how much, it will really advance our estate there. When you have done this, which I think will take up no long time, and do find that you can settle your business so as no damage may befall us there in your absence, I think you were best make a step over to me (the commissioners being here) to consult upon the whole. Yet let me give you this caution; contrive your passage so as to make it most safe, with reliance upon Him who alone is able to make it so.'

The last caution in this letter was due to the fact that England had not yet finished its war with the Dutch who, in June, 1667, were to send their victorious fleet under De Ruyter into the Medway River, thirty-four miles from London, and burn or capture a part of the English fleet. But Penn's voyage was performed in safety; and the law-suit was ended by the Land Commissioners after his arrival in favour of his

200 ibid. II, 433.
201 ibid. II, 379. The date given is 'February 2d,' and Granville Penn adds the year (66); but it should be 1667.
202 ibid. II, 434.

father, the royalist favourite, and against Colonel Wallis, the roundhead veteran.

While Penn was in London, his sister Pegg was married, and he attended the wedding which Pepys described as a private one, 'no friends, but two or three relations of his [the groom, Anthony Lowther] and hers. Borrowed many things of my kitchen for dressing their dinner. This wedding, being private, is imputed to its being just before Lent, and so in vain to make new clothes till Easter, that they might see the fashions as they are like to be this summer; which is reason good enough. Mrs. Turner tells me she hears Sir W. Pen gives 4500 l. or 4000 l. with her.'[203]

William Penn was doubtless better pleased with the simplicity of his sister's wedding than was the envious Pepys. But his stay in London must have been overcast by the tragic evidences of the Great Fire, and by the desperate poverty and sufferings of the people during an unusually cold winter. At all events, when he returned to Ireland soon afterwards, his mind had again become a fertile soil for the seeds of Quakerism which were soon to be sown within it.

Two years after becoming a Quaker, Penn was again in Ireland, this time for the purpose of looking after his father's estate and of aiding his fellow-Quakers who were then suffering persecution and imprisonment. He had himself been recently released from an eight months' imprisonment in London Tower, and had been only partially reconciled with his father. But the latter, who had been chiefly instrumental in securing his son's release, evidently had a secret admiration for his sturdy independence and endurance, and was probably persuaded by his wife to recognize William to the extent of sending him on another mission to Ireland. He did this, however, with doubt and anxiety, for he sent word to his son : 'If you are ordained to be another cross to me, God's will be done; and I shall arm myself the best I can against it.'[204]

Leaving London on the 15th of September, 1668,[205] accompanied by two Friends, he made a visit in the home of Gulielma Springett, attending Quaker meetings as well as wooing his future Quaker bride;

---

[203] *Diary*, February, 15, 20, 24, 27, 1667.
[204] '*No Cross, No Crown* is a serious cross to me,' he is quoted as saying (Dobrée, 66).
[205] The details of this journey to Ireland are given in Penn's *My Irish journal*, the original MS. of which is in the Granville Penn Collection, Manuscript Division of the Historical Society of Pennsylvania; it was published in the *Pennsylvania Magazine*, Vol. 40 (1916), pp. 46-84.

thence by way of Reading, where he visited the Quaker prison in the famous gaol; and finally, on October 24, after sundry more Quaker meetings which 'grew fresh,' he sailed from Bristol. En route to Cork, he found a fellow passenger, an older Friend, who had encouraged him on his last voyage from Ireland just after his 'convincement,' but who now felt in the presence of Penn's zeal that he himself had not been sufficiently faithful and loyal to the Truth. Perhaps it was this meeting and the older Friend's repentant tears which caused Penn to write when in Ireland his *Letter to the Young Convinced*.

Arriving at Cork, he was not at all disturbed by a return of any of the military and worldly ambitions which had marked his course at Carrickfergus three years before, but went the very day of his arrival to visit the Quaker prisoners, and the next day applied to the mayor of Cork for their release. That evening he held a meeting and dined in the prison, and wrote to the rulers at Dublin that he would visit them as soon as possible in the prisoners' behalf. The next day, he left Cork for Dublin, noting en route the town of 'holy-Cross (so call'd) from a superstitious conceit y^t a peece of X^{ts} cross was brought theither from Jerusalem,' and the town, 'clas town : were ye English were murder'd by the ffitz Pat;' spent one night at 'Thurles, ye Ancient manner hous off the D. of Ormonde'; saw, ye Iron-works' at Montroth; attended 'ye Generall meeting [of the Friends] for Linster ... & heavenly it was'; and arrived in Dublin, November 2.

Here, three days later, 'all friends mett' at Penn's lodging, considered the sufferings of the persecuted Quakers in all of Ireland, and drew up an address which was presented by Penn and another Friend [William Morris?] to the mayor of Dublin, who abused the petitioners, 'but did not relieve ye Prisoners of ye Citty.' The next day, Penn and the 'Nationall meeting' drew up a list of the Quaker 'sufferings' in Leinster and Munster, 'by way of Address to ye Ld. Lt.' While awaiting the Lord Lieutenant's reply to this Address, Penn spent four busy weeks in Dublin, engaged in the varied affairs, secular and religious, of the Society of Friends, and mingling much also in the society of baronets, the Earls of Drogheda, Kingston, Arran and Roscommon, the Countesses of Mount Alexander and Cloncarty, Lady Horny and several others whose initials alone Penn mentions. Sundry religious disputations are mentioned, but 'the Professors of all souls declin'd a meeting' with him. Large meetings were held in the old and new

Quaker meeting-houses, their size being due apparently to a curiosity to see Penn. 'Many people came,' he writes, 'amongst the rest severall off ye Ruder Boisterous Gallants to gaiz on me, which they did for allmost an hour. meeting being done, we went out where I spoak to them very sharply, and so we parted.' His friends of the nobility, or seuerall great ones,' as he calls them, attended at least one of his meetings, where 'gods powr was over them all & they reach'd.'

The Lord Lieutenant's illness prevented consideration of the Quaker prisoners' release at this time; but on the 29th of November, Penn records, 'ffriends were releas'd In this Citty wth great love & Civility from ye Judges.' His influence with the leading men of Dublin, many of whom he entertained at dinner in his lodgings, bore good fruit by bringing the mayor to reason. His father's business with Colonel Wallis and 'ye Inhabitants of Corke' was also ended temporarily by procuring 'Articles of agreement betwixt C. Wallis and I,' and by 'stuling [suing in court?] the purchases of ye Corke Inhabitants.' For his lodging, he paid his Quaker hosts '2 siluer candlesticks & suffers [sic]'; while his lawyer he 'feed wth 6 Cobbs [Spanish dollars, or 'pieces of eight.'].'

Returning from Dublin to Cork by way of Clonmell ('famous for oliuers seige'), he and his companions were nearly drowned in 'ye Blackwater, a riuer of great note, rapidity, & depth.' Their horses were very unruly, and the one ridden by Joseph Pike knocked him overboard, but Penn and the boatman 'by mighty mercy caught & Sau'd him'; and, Penn continues, 'whilest I & ye ferry man were saueing J.P. my horse & his had well neigh flung us both vpon him [Philip Ford] & they vpon us, which ye god of mercy for his name sake preuented.'

Arriving in Cork on the 6th of December, after a week of strenuous travel, Penn went immediately to visit the Quaker prisoners, and visited them again on both succeeding days of his stay. Going on to Kinsale, Penn applied himself to his legal business for the estate, but found time to dine at his father's fort and to give the company of soldiers who might have been his three years before, '2 cobs or plate peeces.' The survey of his father's lands and negotiations with their tenants took him to many small places near Kinsale and Shangarry; but visits to the prisoners in Cork and attendance at numerous Quaker Meetings occupied some of his time, and he read a book by the Jesuits, entitled *An Explanation of the Roman Catholic Belief,* to which he wrote a reply entitled *A Seasonable Caveat against Popery*. He appears to have read the Jesuits' book in two days, and written his reply, in the midst of much pressure of the land business, within a month.[206]

During the intervals of his writing, he had several disputes with neighbouring priests; and made a journey of '29 Irish miles, neer 50 English,' to Cloheen, on which he and his three companions lost their way by six miles and then, though taking a guide, he says: 'we were lost on ye mountain, fain to groape our way. at last gott Ouer by many wonderful prescipisces, & came to cloheen by an other guid from ye foot of the mountain.'

On the 19th of March, he 'sett about a book against persecution call'd y^e *Great Case of L. of C.* [*Liberty of Conscience*] *Debated & defended*'; and the next day 'writt much of ye said discours.' On the 22nd, 23rd and 24th, he 'proceeded much' with his discourse, and 'allmost finish'd it'; but on the 30th of March, and April 1, 24, and 26, he still 'followed his book.' It was probably finished on the last date, and the first edition of both it and his *Seasonable Caveat* were published in Dublin in 1670.[207]

Penn revised his book on liberty of conscience when he was himself a prisoner in Newgate in February, 1671, just after the Penn-Meade trial;[208] but its first edition was written and published in Ireland, as has been seen, and was inspired by the persecution and imprisonment of the Irish Quakers. In his *Irish journall,* he mentions his first visit to the Quaker prisoners at Cork on the day of his arrival there, October 26, 1669; and the last item in the journal, dated 4th Month 31 (that is, July 10), 1670, is a reference to an order in council obtained through him by a Quaker preacher, Solomon Eccles. At many times during these eight and a half months, Penn visited the prisoners in Cork, held meetings for worship with them, ate with them, and several times remained with them over night.

He himself escaped imprisonment, doubtless because of his in-

---

206 December 29 and 30 (read the book: January 2: 'was about ye Ans. to ye Jesuits. January 3: I was very busy about ye Answear all day allmost. J.Hull transcrib'd it. January 4: J.hul went to Corke & carry'd ye first sheet to ye press. January 7: I writt much off my answear to ye Jesuits. & J.P. [Joseph Pike] transcrib'd It. January 9: I writt some of my answear. January 19: I writt more of my Answear. January 26: much was added to my answear. February 12: did something About my book.'

207 March 25, he records: 'sent one sheet of ye G.C. to Dub. Jo: Gay'; the last named was probably the Dublin Friend who printed it or had it printed — without place. June 24 (in Dublin): 'receiu'd my B. off L.C.'

208 *Infra,* p. 195 f.

fluential position and aristocratic friends; but he had several clashes with the mayors of towns outside of Cork and their officials. On one such occasion (February 18), he writes: 'we had A meeting at Bandon. S.E. [Solomon Eccles] spoak. I also spoak. we were at ye end disturb'd for ye Prouost & Priest wth 3 Conestables Came to us. I satisfy'd the Prouest, nonplus'd the Priest. writt him a challenge [to a debate], & gott the victory.' Ten days later, he and three other Friends returned to Bandon, where, he writes: 'we went to meeting I was call'd out by ye Prouests man; I had 3 hours discours wth the Prouests very neere, & Praying wth many of the Dirtyst people of the town. my staying preuented the breaking up of the meeting. I endurd much In spirit, In reproaches, slanders, & ye wickedness of the multitude: yet, in ye end they were trampl'd vpon In ye dominion of ye truth.' Penn continued the 'trampling' a few days later by 'writing a sheet or two against Priest more.' He repeated his visit to Bandon several times, without disturbance; but the controversy with Priest More (or O'More) was continued by the written word, Penn stating that on May 14 he 'writt by Capt more to ye Provost & Burgesses of Bandon. In answear to the Priest.' Again, at Tallow, Penn held a meeting which, he says, was 'disturb'd by a busy Connestable. we refused to goe vnlesse he produc'd his Commission, I spoak much to him, at last ye man was smitt, & departed, Sol. [Solomon Eccles] pray'd & spoak, so did I.'

On the other hand, at Youghall, Penn records: 'we had an exceeding great meeting & ye people sober, & seuerall reach'd, all peaceable, & ye Mayor himselfe said had he not been mayor he would have Come.' But waves of persecution were likely to bear down upon the Quakers at any time and place. In Cork, for example, on the 11th of March, 1670, a persecuting judge arrived and stirred up the mayor against them. During the next two months, 'ffriends were barberously dealt with.' An economic as well as a religious reason caused this persecution. On one occasion when Penn visited the prisoners, he found that their tools had been taken from them. No prison labour was to be permitted to enter into competition with the craftsmen of Cork, who had discovered that the skilled and thrifty Quakers were successful rivals both within and outside of prison.

The distribution of Quaker literature was another grievance, and in this too Penn participated. On one occasion he says: 'I was with the Mayor about my books, he abus'd me with names as, Cokscome,

Jackanapes, fellow, foole, &c.' But one week later, when the mayor received a letter of remonstrance, apparently from Penn's friend, Lord Bryan, he returned the books. The mayor evidently shied off from putting Penn in jail. As Penn states it: 'we had A good meeting we were disturb'd In It & 3 more [preachers] were stop'd they mist me, though they saw me, & came for me. I come home, I spoak twice.'

To the persecuting judge, also, Penn carried his demand for religious toleration. 'I went to the Judge,' he writes, 'Could not speak to him in ye morning;' but in the afternoon of the same day, he went to the judge accompanied by Lord Shannon, Sir St. John Broderick and others who 'lived highly as to ye outward.' This time, the judge was accessible, and Penn 'discoars'd with him. effected but little. but cleer'd truth, & came ouer ye Judge.' The next morning, Penn sent a letter to the judge, who 'seem'd Civil, but dealt wickedly.' His wickedness consisted in insulting the Quakers through Jonathan Demsey; he refused to hear their numerous witnesses in the City Hall and removed the trials to the County Hall, where presumably the witnesses could not go; refused to release the Quaker prisoners, but agreed on pressure from Penn and Lord Shannon, to leave them their tools; and finally left Cork and its 'prisons full, & friends were fin'd 195 pounds besides fees.' One Friend was beaten in the court, Penn concludes, 'but was not regarded by judge nor Jury, a wickeder mayor nor judge had not been in ye Citty of Cork, since truth Came.'

Not having succeeded with the local authorities, Penn immediately carried the matter to the men higher up. The very next day, he began his book on Liberty of Conscience; and, after having prepared the way by correspondence and by visits to the homes of Lords Broghill, Shannon, and Barrymore, and sundry military and civil officials, he set out for Dublin carrying with him 'A Paper of ffriends sufferings,' which he had drawn up in conference with the Quaker prisoners. Riding by post both day and night, he arrived in Dublin 'by Break of day' on the 30th of May, and obtained the same day an order for the release of the prisoners. But this order was not satisfactory, since it was conditioned on 'boyle' (bail); so he took the matter up personally with the Lord Lieutenant and the Chancellor, and was accompanied by his old friend Lord Arran before the Council. His aristocratic friends at the Council meeting 'spoake merely to me,' he records,— and not to his Quaker companions?—'but I urg'd a release of poore ffriends upon them 3 of y^m being Privy Councellors.' The

Council characteristically appointed a commission to 'enquire about ffriends sufferings.' But the Lord Lieutenant cut all further red tape, and on June 6th promised Penn 'to release our friends & did so by order of Councill in ye afternoone.'

This victory was celebrated by Penn during the next three weeks of his stay in Dublin by an odd mixture of preaching in Quaker meetings — some of them 'good ones,' or 'precious & power full,' one 'large and hard'— and by much dining and visiting with numerous noble and aristocratic friends. One of these, Lord Arran, and probably others, he took with him to some of the Quaker meetings; and in acknowledgment of Arran's aid and friendship, he presented him with a horse.

In that age and land of horseback riding, Penn had much to do with horse transactions. He records in his journal several such incidents as 'exchanging horses'; 'I went to C.Gales, put out ye gray gelder to grass. he gave me a stone Coult;' 'at Corabby I chaing'd my dun Nag for a flea bit mare;' 'I have bought his ["my Cos. Rooth's"] stone-hors for 15^lb y^t is my black hors of J ffen. & 9 pounds ster.;' 'I bought his sons hors. gaue one ginny of earnest for 11 [eleven].' On his visit to Ireland twenty-eight years later, he went on a preaching tour with his son and two other Friends and bought for the party four fine saddle-horses. An Irish law forbade Catholics to own a horse worth more than £5, its object being to break up the Irish light cavalry which had given William III so much trouble in conquering the island; it also enabled Protestant English officers to acquire excellent mounts for themselves by confiscating the Catholics' horses, on payment of five guineas. On their way into Waterford, Penn and his companions were mistaken, because of a similarity in costume, for Catholic priests, and their horses confiscated by an English sergeant as being worth far more than £5. But on Penn's appeal to the officer higher up — after a detour of eight miles — his horses were restored to him with ample apologies and an offer — which was not accepted — to have the sergeant flogged and demoted for his stupidity.[209]

Among those whom Penn visited in Ireland in 1670 were some Dutch 'adventurers' who had advanced money to the English Commonwealth for the conquest of Ireland, and had been repaid in confiscated lands. Abraham Fuller and Gershon Boate (son of Charles I's Dutch physician, Gerard Boate) were among these adventurers

---

[209] Thomas Story's *Journal*, 1747, pp. 131-2.

and had become Quakers before Penn's visit.[210] Perhaps they were associated with the Jasper family, and if so, they formed connecting links between Penn and his maternal ancestors. It is significant, also, that soon after this visit, Penn went on his first journey to Holland, and may have taken letters of introduction from his Dutch Irish Friends. Some of the other Irish Quakers were to take an active and helpful part in the colonization of Pennsylvania. Among these were Robert Turner, Anthony Sharp, and Samuel Clarridge of Dublin (the last-named being one of the Friends whom Penn had released from prison in 1670), Thomas Holme of Limerick, John White of Carlow, and members of the Hollingsworth, Childs, Lightfoot, and Harlan families, who either aided in various ways the migration of others, or who themselves became colonists in Pennsylvania. Directly and indirectly, Penn must have influenced many of the hundreds of Irish Quaker families who settled in his province between the years 1682 and 1750.[211] How appealing must have been the Quaker refuge beyond the Atlantic to the Irish Quakers can be judged from the fact that their persecution between 1685 and 1750 — largely because of refusing to pay tithes — resulted in the imprisonment of ninety-one and the imposition of fines to the amount of £92,745.[212]

During his Irish visit, Penn took a zealous part in the activities of the Quaker meetings. The day after his arrival, he attended a meeting for worship in the prison — where he had himself been a prisoner two years before — and this was frequently repeated. Within the week after his arrival, he attended the General Meeting for Leinster and the National Meeting for Ireland; the latter was held at his lodgings in Dublin, and it sent down the advice to all the men's meetings of the Provinces to keep a punctual record of the sufferings of Friends and to transmit them to the National Meeting. In Cork, also, he attended 'ye 6 weeks meeting' in which 'things were well ordered as to truths affairs'; and another men's meeting, where 'we order'd seuerall businesses.'

---

210 Isabel Grubb, *Quakers in Ireland*, 1927, p. 42. Abraham Fuller and Thomas Holme compiled 'A Brief Relation of some of the Sufferings of the . . . Quakers in Ireland, for these last 21 years, viz., from 1650 until 1671;' it was printed (without place) in 1672, and may have been undertaken on William Penn's advice.
211 Cf. Albert Cook Myers, *Immigration of the Irish Quakers into Pennsylvania*, 1902, *passim*; a chart opposite p. 82 cites 167 adult Friends who emigrated from Ireland to Pennsylvania before Penn's death in 1718, and 273 between that year and 1750.
212 John Rutty, *History of the Rise and Progress of the Quakers in Ireland*, 1751, pp. 367-8.

Besides these 'meetings for business,' Penn attended numerous regular and 'appointed' 'meetings for worship,' some of which he described as 'great,' 'very heavenly,' 'fresh and quiet,' 'as precious a meeting as I was ever in'; 'an exceeding great meeting, & ye people sober & seuerall reach'd.' One of them, however, 'disgusted ffds,'— apparently because of one of the speakers. He himself evidently took an active part in the ministry. On one occasion, he records, he 'declar'd 1^h & ½ — pr: twice [i.e. preached one hour and a half, and prayed twice]'; on another occasion, he 'spoak a fwe words to Backsliders,' 'spoak 2 & once call'd vpon ye lord god of life'; in prison, he 'spoak a fwe words In ye pure life'; 'a good meeting in ye powr of ye allmighty . . . I spoak twice' [he 'spoak 2' on several other occasions].

Aside from these meetings with the Quakers, he had sundry disputes with the Roman Catholic clergy and laity; for example, a week before his departure, he records: 'I disputed with the Papists, manifested their great folly.' Sir William Petty, the eminent economist and opponent of the Mercantile Theory, paid him a three hours' visit, and afterwards dined with him; but 'the Professors of all souls declin'd a meeting.'

Among the Quaker preachers with whom Penn consorted in Ireland, was that unique individual named Solomon Eccles. Solomon Eccles, or Eagles, was about twenty-five or thirty years Penn's senior, and had been converted to Quakerism — by way of Anglicanism, Presbyterianism, Independency, and Baptism — when Penn was a boy. Of a family of musicians, he became a music-teacher, and said of himself:[213] 'I could teach men's Sons and Daughters on the Virginals and on the Viol, and I got the two last years more than £130 a year with my own hands.' When he became a Quaker, he gave up his 'worldly' profession, sold his musical instruments, and supported his family thereafter as a tailor. Not satisfied that his conscience had been cleared, he bought back his instruments and made a bonfire of them on Tower Hill.[214]

It has been hinted that Eccles lost his wits, when his beloved music

---

213 *A Musick-Lector*, London, 1667. This is a dialogue on the justifiability of music, between an Anglican musician, 'who calls Musick the Gift of God,' a Baptist, 'who did affirm it to be a decent and harmless practice,' and 'a Quaker (so-called) being formerly of that Art, [who] doth give his Judgment and sentence against it, but yet approves of the Musick that pleaseth God.'
214 Penn may have seen or heard of this holocaust, when a boy. Eccles says that he 'burnt and brake many good Instruments of Musick, and burnt Books of great price and value at Tower Hill' (ibid).

went up in flames; but excessive religious zeal is assigned by his contemporary Quakers as responsible for his aberrations. In 1663, for example, he seized the opportunity of St. Bartholomew's Fair by walking through Smithfield, half-naked, and with a pan of 'fire and brimstone' burning on his head, as a warning against frivolities.[215] During the Great Plague of 1665, he took possession of a church — probably forsaken by its pastor — and plied his shoemaking in its pulpit and on its communion-table.

Of some of his activities in Ireland in 1669 and 1670 (when Penn had joint meetings with him), Willem Sewel writes as follows:[216] 'Solomon Eccles (*Salomon Ekkles*), whom I also knew very well, was this year 1669 in prison at Gallaway in Ireland, where he was put by a strange incident. He was an extraordinary zealous man, and what he judged evil he warmly opposed, even to the hazard of his life. This zeal led him to perform a strange action in a chapel of the Papists without the town; for he went naked above his waist, with a chafing-dish of coals and burning brimstone (*zwavel*) on his head, and entered the chapel when all the people were on their knees to pray to their idol (*misgód*), and spoke as followeth: "Woe to these idolatrous worshippers! God hath sent me this day to warn you, and to show you what will be your portion except you repent." Which when he had done, he went away to the town, where he was presently made a prisoner. What the benefit of this conduct might be I deem it best to leave . . . (*daar gelaaten*).

'About this time [October, 1670] it happened that Solomon Eccles came to Cork in Ireland, and went into the cathedral, where the priest, Benjamin Cross, preached in a surplice (*witte koorkleed*); and having formerly been a Presbyterian preacher in Dorsetshire in England, had there said, that he had rather go to a stake and be burned, than to put on a surplice. This priest (now become a turn-coat for gain) having finished his sermon and concluded with a prayer, Solomon Eccles said that "the prayer of the wicked was an abomination to the Lord." And knowing the deceitfulness of the said priest, and his being an apostate, he added, "What shall be done to the man that makes shipwreck of a good conscience?" For this he was taken, and by

---

215 He wrote and distributed also at this time a broadside entitled *Signes are from the Lord to a People or Nation, to forewarn them of some eminent Judgment near at hand.*
216 *History of the Quakers*, Amsterdam, 1717, pp. 559, 578; New York, 1844, II, 169-70, 196-97. (The two versions are slightly different.)

the mayor committed to prison, where being kept ten days, he was accused as a vagabond, and without any examination, severely whipped along the streets of Cork, from North-Gate to South-Gate, receiving about ninety stripes, and was then expelled.'

Penn gives no hint of such conduct on Eccles's part, but pictures him in his Irish Journal as an active, normal, and helpful Quaker preacher.[217]

On the 6th of June, 1670, Penn was able to record both the success of his efforts for the release of the Irish Quaker prisoners and the fact that his 'ffa. businesse is also done.' He had by no means neglected his father's business, in the midst of his Quakerly activities, and his Journal contains many references to it. His father's former opponent, Colonel Wallis, reappeared on the scene; but most of Penn's transactions were with numerous tenants and prospective purchasers. Correspondence, interviews, measurements of land, civil processes, rentals, arrears, bargainings, sureties, draining and ditching, the use of windmills, burying-grounds, and the disposition of cattle were the varied things that claimed his care; and his management of them elicited expressions of satisfaction from his father. To fulfil both his business and religious duties was a difficult, two-fold task and gave him a strenuous life. On Pye Day [December 25] at Cork, for example, he complained that 'none could be gott to worke'; and sometimes he began his own work an hour before day, or continued it until midnight, and occasionally rode all night.

At times, he would 'abate' his terms to tenants and purchasers; but at others, 'could not be moued from my Commission & judgment.' To one, he 'writt a letter (very smart),; to another (Lieut. Edward Clark), he granted 'a great Bargain in consideration of old friendship & seruice done my ffa.' Another tenant was 'rude & surly'; one 'boyl'd,' Penn 'fell out with him,' but a few days later the tenant 'submitted & leaft himselfe at my mercy,' whereupon Penn granted him a generous bargain ('6lb & 20sh ouer & aboue'), '& finish'd our difference. he acknowledg'd his fault.'

His home correspondence was by no means neglected. His Journal contains frequent lists of the initials of those in England to whom he wrote letters. At first, Gulielma Springett appears in the list under the guise of *G.S.* or *Gul;* but later, *my o.d. ff.* or *o.b. ff.* were made to stand for my own dear (or best) Friend. On one day, he wrote

[217] *The Pennsylvania Magazine,* vol. 40 (1916), pp. 61, 64-67, 84 (*passim*).

her twice; and occasionally he notes the receipt of a letter from *my o.b. ff.* One of these latter entries occurs five days before he left Ireland, and probably contained an invitation from Guli to stop to see her en route to London. Among his purchases or presents in Ireland was doubtless one for her; and it is not difficult to distinguish it among those which he mentioned as follows : basketts ; a Greek Psalter ; 7 & 3 gallens of vsquebough, bespoak at ye widdow goulds ; and frize for fds in England.

Twenty-eight years after this visit, Penn went for the last time to Ireland, this time on the three-fold mission of proselyting members for the Society of Friends, recruiting colonists for Pennsylvania, and looking after his Irish estates. He was accompanied by his son William, and by two other Quaker preachers, one of whom was Thomas Story, of England and Pennsylvania, whose account of the journey takes the place of Penn's own journal of his earlier visit as our source of information.[218] It may be that Story exaggerates the predominance of Penn's religious mission over his business affairs; but from his account of the journey, Penn's own personal interests had but scant attention in the midst of the old familiar 'circuit-riding,' preaching, theological controversies, pleas for toleration, and the overawing of would-be disturbers of Quaker meetings.

Arriving in Dublin Bay, the Quaker missionaries found a ship full of friars exiled to France, and the rumour spread that this time Penn had converted some of them to Quakerism, instead of being himself converted to Jesuitism. In Dublin, they attended the sessions of the Friends' Half-year Meeting, which was attended by large numbers of people of all ranks and conditions. Among the clergy who came several times, was the Dean of Derry, of whom Thomas Story reports : 'He, being asked by his Bishop, Whether he had heard any Thing but Blasphemy and Nonsense; and whether he took off his Hat in time of Prayer, to join with us? He answered, "That he heard no Blasphemy nor Nonsense, but the everlasting Truth; and did not only take off his Hat at Prayer, but his Heart said Amen to what he heard :" Yet he proved like the stony Ground, and brought forth no Fruit. He said, "Though he could die for the Principles of Religion the Quakers prefess'd; yet, to lose his Living and Character for some Incidents they are tenacious of, as plain Language, plain Habits, and

---

[218] *A Journal of the Life of Thomas Story,* Newcastle upon Tyne, 1747 (folio, 780 pp.) ; cf. pp. 127-146.

other distinguishing Particularities, he did not think these of sufficient Weight, or reasonable :" And so came no further in the Way of Truth, but proved unfaithful in the Day of small Things.'

Many crowded meetings in the south-eastern counties followed, the throngs being drawn to them as much by curiosity to see the famous Quaker colonizer as to hear the Quaker preacher. Story records many particulars of these meetings, giving high praise to William Penn's sermons and their effects, but taking the largest space for accounts of his own theological controversies, especially with his brother, George, then Dean of Limerick,[219] and the latter's priest. Of Penn's influence with the authorities in Ireland at that time, Story relates that at Cashel a meeting was held and attended by 'a great Multitude of People of all Notions and Ranks thereaway; that the mayor arrived with his officers to disperse the meeting, but could not seize the preachers because of the dense crowd; that Penn persuaded the mayor to leave the meeting in peace, and after it was ended went to see the bishop who offered the following explanation : "That he went that Morning to Church, to perform his Office (of Preaching) as usual; and, when there, he had no Body to preach to but the Mayor, Church-Wardens, some of the Constables, and the Walls, the People being all gone to your Meeting; which I confess, said the Bishop, made me a little angry, and I sent the Mayor and Constables with that Message, in hope, by that Means, to have a greater Auditory; though I have no Ill-will to you, or those of your Profession." And so, after some Tokens of mutual Respect, they parted in seeming Friendship . . .

'But the Bishop recollecting, when the hot Fit was over, what Noise such an Action might make in the Nation, that such a Meeting should be so disturbed by his Command or Instigation; and which could not be justified, unless the Meeting had been attended with some extraordinary and unlawful Circumstances; he therefore wrote to the Earl of *Galloway,* and the other Lord Justice of *Ireland,* and informed them, though unduly, "That Mr. *Penn* and the Quakers had gathered together in that Place, that Day, such a vast Multitude of People, and so many armed Papists, that it struck a Terror into him and the Town; and, not knowing what might be the Consequence of such an Appearance, he had sent the Mayor and other Magistrates to disperse them; but, seeing they had taken no Notice of him, or the Civil

---

[219] 'He had been sent to France for Education,' Story says, 'and there had embraced the *Romish* Religion.'

Powers there, he thought it his Duty to lay the Matter before their Lordships, that such Remedy might be applied, as in their Wisdom they might think proper, to obviate the Danger and ill Consequences of such Assemblies."' When Penn arrived in Cork, he went to visit his old friend, the Earl of Galloway, who gave him the bishop's letter to read, with the remark: 'The old Dotard! why should he make all this to do on such a Common Occasion?'

The bishops of Waterford and Cork were also stirred to defend their flocks against the Quaker missionaries, or, as Story states it: 'William Penn's Travels through the Nation at that Time made the Envy of the Priests to boil against the Truth and us.' Edward Wetenhall, Bishop of Cork and Ross, wrote a 'Testimony' against Penn's theology, as stated in his leaflet entitled *Gospel Truths;* and in reply Penn wrote a *Defence,* which demanded considerable time after his return to his home in Bristol, Story staying with him some weeks, 'transcribing his Sheets, searching the Scriptures, &c.' But the *Defence* was both published and reprinted before the end of 1698.

It was doubtless at the request of thrifty Hannah Penn that her husband went to his two estates in Ireland, for at least a five days' visit out of a three months' journey; and it may have been due to the rigid supervision which she afterwards gave them that they later yielded large returns to his estate.

On this visit to Ireland also, Penn was far from unmindful of Pennsylvania's need of colonists. He and his family were themselves to sail for his province the next year, perhaps to make their permanent residence there. Meanwhile, Thomas Story left the Penn home in Bristol, in the autumn of 1698, to enter upon a long and useful career in the public and private service of Penn in the New World colony. The stream of Irish Quaker emigration to Pennsylvania continued slowly but steadily after Penn's visit, although it did not reach its height until the severe famine of 1729.[220]

220 Albert Cook Myers, op.cit., p. 83.

PENN BECOMES A QUAKER

EVERY biographer of Penn has given much space to his conversion to, or acceptance of, Quakerism. There are several references to this event of prime importance in his own writings. The first of these occurs in his *Letter to Mary Pennyman,* which was written in 1673, a few years after his adoption of the Quaker faith and practice. One paragraph of this letter is as follows:[221] 'The Knowledge of God, from the Living Witness from Thirteen Years of Age, hath been dear to me : From Sixteen I have been a great Sufferer for it : At the University, by that *Inward Work* alone, I withstood many : I never addicted my self to *School-Learning* to understand *Religion* by, but always, even to their Faces, rejected and disputed against it : I never had any other Religion than what I felt, excepting a *Little Profession* that came with *Education :* I had no Relations that inclined to so Solitary and Spiritual a Way : I was as a Child alone ; yet by the *Heavenly Opening of the Scriptures to my Understanding,* and more *immediate Inspirations,* was I confirm'd, and abundantly comforted. I was a Secret Mourner by the Waters of *Babylon,* and underwent heavy Stripes from my Relations, (afterwards by them repented of) and that frequently, only for my *Inward Persuasion's* Sake, which was too strong for all Opposition or Allurements in the End. And though I was a While in the Midst of this World's Glories, both in this and other countries, yet it was rather to know, that I might the better condemn them with a *Vanity of Vanities; All is Vanity and Vexation of Spirit,* than to sit down and to be married with them. At last my Soul meeting with TRUTH, that is, the Knowledge of that *Inward Tender Principle,* that ever inclined me to Righteousness, Mercy, and Peace, to be the *Truth in the Inward Parts,* that I was to have my Regard to, I embrac'd it with Gladness of Heart, though it was as sharp to me as a well-pointed dart, because of Iniquity.'

Again, in his *Travails* of 1677, he records a long religious conversation he had with the Labadists of Wieuwerd in that year, in the course of which he told them of his youthful trials and tribulations. Referring

---
[221] Dated, 'Rickmersworth, 22d of the 9th Month, 1673' (*Works,* 1726, I, pp. 158-160). Mary Pennyman, to whom this letter was written in reply to one from her, was the wife of John Pennyman of London, who had adopted Quakerism in the 1650's, but had afterwards denounced it, and had been 'disowned' in 1670. Mary wrote Penn in criticism of his *Judas and the Jews,* 1673 (ibid. II, pp. 196-227).

THE BLUE IDOL MEETING-HOUSE

in this to his visit to Ireland in 1667, he says:[222] 'It was at this time that the Lord visited me with a certain sound and testimony of his eternal Word, through one of those the World calls a *Quaker*. I related to them the bitter Mockings and Scornings that fell upon me, the Displeasure of my Parents, the Invectiveness and Cruelty of the Priests, the strangeness of all my Companions, what a Sign and Wonder they made of me; but, above all, that great Cross of resisting and watching against my own Inward vain Affections and Thoughts.'

There is a third account of Penn's conversion to Quakerism which is also ascribed to him by a Friend named Thomas Harvey. A manuscript bearing the date of 1729 tells the story which its author says he received about 1700 from Thomas Harvey, who received it directly from William Penn himself. The narrative is as follows:[223]

'While he [William Penn] was but a child living at Cork with his Father Thos. Low [Loe] coming thither, his Father proposed to some others (when it was rumour'd A Quaker was come from England) to be like ye Noble Berean's to hear them before they Judg'd 'em and sent to T.L. to come to his House where he had a meeting in ye family, and tho' W.P. was very young yet observed what effect T.L.'s Doctrine had on ye Hearers so that a Black of his Fathers could not contain himself from weeping aloud & he looking on his Father saw ye Tears Runing down his Cheeks also; he thought in himself wt If they should all be Quakers [illegible] opportunity he never forgot at times.'

It will be observed that Penn refers in the first edition of his *Travails* (1694) merely to 'one of those the World calls a Quaker'; but in the 'second impression' (also 1694: p. 171) the name of Thomas Loe is given in large type, and the manuscript account just quoted mentions specifically Thomas 'Low' as the minister through whom Penn was convinced of Quakerism. The meeting which Loe held with the Penn family near Cork occurred when William was in his early 'teens, and it did not result, of course, in his immediate acceptance

---

222 *Travails in Holland and Germany, Anno 1677*, 1694, p. 183; cf. *supra*, p. 70.
223 The MS. was used by Maria Webb in her *Penns and Peningtons of the Seventeenth Century*, 1867 (pp. 173-180); in 1935, it was purchased by the Friends Reference Library, London, and published *in toto* in the *Journal of the Friends' Historical Society*, Vol. 32 (1935), pp. 22-26. Thomas Harvey has not yet been identified; nor is the name of the author of the MS. known. (Buell, 1904, gives alleged information—entirely unsupported by evidence—of Thomas Harvey).

of Quakerism, but may have had some influence in predisposing him towards it.[224]

It is possible that this meeting was responsible for an experience which occurred, Penn says, 'when the Lord first appeared unto me, which was about the 12th Year of my Age, Anno 1656'; during the next three years, he adds, the Lord visited him and gave him divine impressions of Himself.[225]

By the time that Penn went up to Oxford, Quakerism had made a great, but very unfavourable impression upon the university and town. Elizabeth Williams had carried the Quaker message thither a half dozen years before, and had been ducked for her pains. Two young Quaker girls, Elizabeth Fletcher and Elizabeth Leavens, had soon followed in her footsteps, and had been brutally whipped by the town authorities and maltreated by 'the black tribe of scholars.' But the Quaker missionaries persisted in holding meetings and distributing literature and had converted a few townspeople. Among these was the Oxford tradesman, Thomas Loe, who participated at once in the missionary activity and in the sufferings of the Quakers, including destruction of their meeting-place, the explosion of gunpowder in their meetings, and the jailing of their leaders.

Loe went from a six months' imprisonment in Oxford, in 1660, to defy the persecution of the Quakers in Ireland; and returning to Oxford towards the end of that year, he was again sent to prison on the 13th of January, 1661. By this time, and since October 26, 1660, Penn had been matriculated at Oxford, and it is possible that in company with other students he heard Loe preach in a street-meeting, as so many of his biographers assert. But there is no evidence of this; and the probability is that Penn did not see or hear Loe between the meeting at his father's house in Ireland, in 1655-56, and the meeting at Cork in 1667 at which he responded to Loe's appeal to accept Quakerism.

In Oxford, while he must have heard of the strange new sect and the stories told of its members by both gownsmen and townsmen, it was the Puritanism of Dr. John Owen, who was the vice-chancellor of the university, that influenced Penn, rather than the words or

---

224 One biographer opines that Penn heard Loe preaching in the market-place in Cork and invited him to his father's house (Buell, 1904); while another implies that Loe was introduced to the admiral by the same shop-keeper Quakeress, who sent Penn to a meeting addressed by Loe in Cork a dozen years later when he was converted to Quakerism (Brailsford, 1923).
225 *Travails*, 1694, p. 181; cf. *supra*, p. 70.

remembrance of Thomas Loe, then a Quaker prisoner in a jail close by Penn's own college of Christ Church.[226]

After the tribulations of the five years following his expulsion from Oxford, Penn was in Ireland and attended a meeting of the Quakers in Cork, where he again heard Thomas Loe. The story as told in the 'Harvey MS.' is as follows:[227] 'He [Penn] wanting some Cloaths went to a woman Friend Shop he had knowledge of about ye time of that Meeting —

'She not knowing him, told her who he was and also of ye Meeting at his Fathers she admired at his remembering that he told her he should never forget it also if he knew where ye person was if 'tware an Hundred Miles he would go to here him again.

'She told he need not go far for ye Friend was lately come thither and would be at meeting ye next day to wch he went another appearing first he was not Effected with his Testimony but when T. L. stood up was exceedingly reach'd so that he wept much and it seemed to him as if a Voice sayd stand on thy feet How dost know but somebody may be reach'd by thy tears so he stood up that he might be seen. After ye Meeting some friends took notice of him and he went to a friend house with T. L. in discourse T. L. was saying he should want a horse either being without one or his own being not fit to travell, W. P. offer'd him his Sumture horse he had brought from France but T. L. said he was not willing to take his, wch made W. P. think he was not friend enough to have his horse accepted. However he went to meetings there till they was disturb [ed] once a soldier came up into ye Meeting making a Great disturbance, W. P. Go's to him takes him by ye collar and would have throw'd him down stairs but a friend or two come to him desireing to let him alone for they was a peaceable people and would not have [him] make a disturbance there then he was very much concern'd he had caused friends to be uneasy by his roughness — The soldier went to ye Magistrates and brought ye Officers wch broke up ye Meeting and made several of them prisoners, and him among ye Rest.'

Penn's first biographer adds the detail that Loe 'began his Declaration with these Words, *There is a Faith that overcomes the World, and there is a Faith that is overcome by the World*; upon which Subject he enlarged with much Clearness and Energy. By the Living

226 But cf. Clarkson (?), Janney, Dixon et al.
227 *Journal of the Friends' Historical Society*, Vol. 32 (1935), pp. 22-23.

and powerful Testimony of this Man, which had made some Impression upon his Spirit Ten Years before, he was now throughly and effectually Convinced, and afterward constantly attended the Meetings of that People, even through the Heat of Persecution.'[228] In a letter which he wrote ten years later to the Princess Elizabeth, Penn himself said: 'Faith in Adam was a righteous act of obedience in his soul; therefore God imputed righteousness unto him; and blessed are his spiritual offspring for ever whose faith overcomes, and is not overcome of, the world.'

It may well be imagined that the experiences of Penn's early life, causing him to hesitate as they did between a world of fashion, ambition, and pleasure, and a spiritual realm of religious piety and devotion, had prepared him to be deeply impressed by a sermon preached on such a text. The hour of his final decision struck in that little Quaker meeting in Cork, and henceforth he grappled to his soul 'a Faith that overcometh the world.' It was of course no sudden or miraculous 'conversion' which he experienced; but it was rather the 'convincement' to which the Friends have always preferred to ascribe the transformation or growth of their minds and lives in the things of the spirit by the conscious visitation of God within their souls.

Among the foremost human agencies other than Loe who helped Penn upon his pilgrimage towards Quakerism were George Fox, the Peningtons and Josiah Coale. For Fox, Penn had a deep reverence as the founder of Quakerism and as an extraordinary personality; but he had never heard him preach. Although he may have read some of the many writings Fox had already published, and possibly heard of his organizing activities among the London Friends in the spring and summer of 1668, the first recorded meeting between them was in August, 1671, when Penn accompanied Fox from London to Gravesend on the latter's journey to America.[229] Their common interest in Quakerism and in America was the strongest and almost the only tie between them; and it is a singular fact that these two chief pillars of early Quakerism had so few contacts. Fox's references to Penn in his writings are few and impersonal, and give no indication of the esteem in which he must have held him.

In view of this fact, and many others, it is laughable to find one of

---

[228] Besse, 1726, Vol. I, p. 2.
[229] Fox's *Journal*, II, 176 f.

GEORGE FOX

A Topical Biography

Penn's biographers, with his usual lack of genuine evidence,[230] charging Fox with having marked the wealthy young aristocrat as desirable game for the Quaker hunters, and as having deliberately set Thomas Loe on to make a convert and conquest of him. At Shangarry Castle (when Penn was twelve), at Oxford, in London at the time of the Plague, and finally with success at Cork, this biographer pictures Loe in eager pursuit of his prey!

Penn's veneration for Fox finds ample and enthusiastic expression in his Preface to Fox's *Journal,* which was written soon after the latter's death;[231] and his efforts in behalf of Fox's liberation from prison he tells in the following passage of his 'Apology':[232] 'The third time I came to court was in '73, having not frequented it for five years. The business that drew me thither, was the imprisonment of that servant of God, my worthy friend George Fox, in Worcester Castle; the cause, worshipping God after another manner than that of the Church of England, and lest it should prove too feeble a tie to hold him, the Justices of the Peace that had laid his commitment, officiously tendered him the oaths of allegiance and supremacy, not that he should take them, but because they were pretty sure he would not take them, as a supplemental snare to gratify their humour, and accomplish their design against him. This ending in a Praemunire, and finding no applications in the country were likely to succeed for his deliverance out of the hands of some very angry, obstinate persons, it was resolved amongst us at London to remove him by habeas corpus to the King's bench, and try what we could do at the court to procure his discharge. It fell to my lot to go on this errand, in which solicitation William Mead accompanied me.'

Penn's efforts were successful in procuring a writ of *habeas corpus* which brought Fox up from his Worcester prison to London, before the Court of King's Bench, where its presiding judge, Sir Matthew Hale, found so many errors in the indictment that he ordered Fox's

---

230 Buell, 68-70. Buell admits that his only evidence for this accusation against Fox is the 'evidences of appearances' and an anti-Quaker pamphlet—'an old tract printed during the reign of William and Mary'—the author and title of which he does not state.

231 Published separately under the title, *The Rise and Progress of the People call'd Quakers,* 1694. Chapter V of this work is devoted to a biographical sketch and appreciation of Fox (Penn's *Works,* 1726, I, pp. 878-884).

232 Probably written during his internment, about 1690; published from his MS. in the *Memoirs* of the Pennsylvania Historical Society, Vol. III (1836), p. 240; cf. *infra,* p. 243.

discharge.[233] This imprisonment had lasted more than a year, but it was the last which Fox was called upon to endure; and it was probably Penn's influence with the last two Stuart kings which brought him this immunity.[234]

The inspiring stories of the youthful Quaker martyrs, James Parnel and Edward Burrough (that 'son of Thunder'), and Penn's intimacy with Josiah Coale, one of the most successful Quaker missionaries in England and in the American colonies, helped greatly to strengthen, perhaps to initiate, his Quakerism. The friendship of the Quaker mystic, Isaac Penington, and his charming wife; and above all, perhaps, his growing love for their daughter, Gulielma, probably made the task of Thomas Loe the easier.

Not much time was left, however, for Loe and Penn to cement their new religious comradeship. In the autumn of 1668, they went with Josiah Coale and George Whitehead to the court of Charles II to appeal for liberation and toleration of the persecuted Quakers; and within a few weeks thereafter, Penn was summoned to Loe's deathbed. Among the *Papers of Isaac Penington*,[235] a letter is extant from Penn to Isaac, dated London, 17th of 8th Month (October), 1668, which gives an account of Loe's last days. 'About four days before he died,' Penn says, 'I fell sick myself: but hearing at what point it was with dear Thomas, I could not long keep my bed, but got up, and though in a sweat, yet I hastened to him, whom I found in a great readiness to be gone. Friends stood, much affected, round his bed. When I came in, and had set myself upon the bedside, severall heavenly expressions fell from his mouth. . . . Then taking me by the hand, he spoke thus: Dear heart, bear thy cross; stand faithful for God, and bear thy testimony in thy day and generation: and God

---

233 Fox's *Journal*, II, 285.
234 Penn's mother, Lady Penn, also wrote to Lord Windsor (Lord Lieutenant of Worcestershire) on behalf of Fox and the other Quaker prisoners in Worcester (Swarthmore MSS., I, 58); and Margaret Fell Fox also appealed to the king for Fox's release, but declined to accept a pardon for him. This last statement is made in Thomas Ellwood's edition of Fox's *Journal*, 1694, but does not appear in the verbatim et literatim edition of Norman Penney, 1911. Indeed, it is a noteworthy fact that no mention of Penn in connexion with Fox's release occurs in Ellwood's edition, and the only reference in Penney's is in a letter of Thomas Moore to Fox, dated 3d 7/m (September), 1674, in which is the single sentence: 'I shall as the Lord shall make my way to London speake with Will: Pen as thou desirest, but I thinke the remedie [another oath of allegiance] will be worse than the desease . . .' (Vol. II, p. 304). The reasons for this strange omission may be found later *infra*, p. 180).
235 IV, 6; quoted by Brailsford.

A Topical Biography 113

will give thee an eternal crown of glory that none shall ever take from thee.' Thus, from his religious guide, philosopher and friend, Penn received a title for his own great work, *No Cross, No Crown,* which he was soon to write in London Tower, as well as a strong and abiding impulse to bear the cross of a persecuted Quaker's life. 'At last he went away with great stillness,' Penn continues, 'having fought like a valiant Souldier the good Fight and overcome, whose works follow him. Whom my soul loved whilst living, and bemoans now dead; and yet have pure fellowship with that which lives for ever. The day following we laid the vessell in the ground, as having done its master's work and will.'

Josiah Coale died soon after Loe, and Penn in his double bereavement wrote a long, sad elegy on his departed friend.[236] Coale and Fox, both missionaries to America, fired Penn's imagination with the ideal of a Quaker commonwealth and refuge beyond the seas; while Loe stirred the soil and sowed the seed which made of Penn a *Quaker* colonizer and statesman. Back of these Quaker leaders, there loom large in the imaginations of Penn's biographers who were not Quakers themselves and who regarded Quakerism as the only, but fatal defect in Penn's statesmanship, religious fanatics like Valdes, the mystic of Spain, and John Saltmarsh of England.

Saltmarsh was buried at Chigwell a few years before Penn went to its school; and one of Penn's biographers,[237] taking a hint from a predecessor of a score of years before him,[238] devotes eight pages to an attempt to prove that not only Penn, but also George Fox, derived their cracked-brain religious theories from Saltmarsh's *Sparkles of Glory, or Some Beams of the Morning Star.* This book was published in London, in 1647, the year in which its author died, and was very widely read and admired or denounced by contemporary theologians and sectarians. The biographer cited asserts that it was 'among the first works — perhaps the very first — that young William Penn read, aside from text-books;' and he ascribes to it the boyhood visions of Penn and the central doctrine of the Inner Light upon which Fox founded the Society of Friends.

Even though this assertion is a baseless assumption, it is indicative of the way in which Quakerism was confused with one or another of

---

236 See Monograph Number Three (*Eight First Biographies of William Penn*).
237 Augustus C. Buell, 1904; cf. pp. 12-20.
238 John Stoughton, 1882.

the innumerable Seventeenth Century religious sects, and of the contempt in which it was held. Penn's father naturally shared this contempt; and when reports came to him from Ireland that his son had become a Quaker, he commanded his immediate return to the paternal admonitions. This summons was evidently received with reluctance by Penn in Ireland; and it was repeated in a second letter from his father, who may have anticipated that he would linger near Bristol, when he arrived in England, either on religious affairs or in his courtship of Gulielma Springett. The two letters have been preserved in the Granville Penn Manuscripts, and are as follows: [239]
'Sonne William
'I have writt several ters to yo since I recd any fr you. By this I agayne charge yo & strictly comand that yo come to mee with all posable speede in expectation of yo complyance. I remayne
yor aff^t father
W. Penn.'

Navy Office October 12 67.

'Sonne William.
'I hope this will find yo^u in health. The cause of this Writing is to charge yo^u to repair to mee with all posable speede p^rsently after yor recept of it & not to make any stay there [Bristol] or any place upon ye roade untill it please God you see mee (unless for necessary rest & refreshm^t.)
Y^r very aff^t father

October 22, 67.

W. Penn.'

Landing at Bristol, the Harvey Manuscript relates, 'he staid some meetings to strengthen himself know[ing] his Father would not be very pleasant upon him.

'J. Coal went with him to London also to his Father's house to see how he was likely to be entertain'd but his Father kept his temper while J. C. was there but at night observing him use thee or thou was very angry W^m told him 'twas in obeydiance to God and not in any disrespect to him however then his Father told him he might thee & thou who he pleas'd except ye King ye Duke of York and himself

---

[239] Published in the *Pennsylvania Magazine*, Vol. 40 (1916), p. 46.

A Topical Biography 115

but them he should not (thee or thou) but he answer'd he must speak in ye singular number both to ye King ye Duke & himself wch made his Father very angry, but as he was Going up stairs to bed his Father bid him rise in ye Morning for he should go out in his coach with him wch caused Wm. to be so uneasy that he could not sleep that night fearing he was to be had to court;

'in ye Morning they went in ye Coach together but Wm. did not know Where they was Going However ye Coach man was order'd to Drive into ye Park then he found his Fathers intent was to have private discourse with him his Father beginning with him told he could not tell what he could think of himself after he had train'd him up in Learning and other accomplishments for a courtier — as for an Ambassador or other Minister that he should become a Quaker he Answer'd 'twas in Obediance to ye Manifestation of God in his own Conscience but a cross to his own Nature also told him of that Former meeting which was of his own promoting also how he observed his Father in tears at that time and that he believe[d] him to be convinced of the truth of ye Doctrine of ye Quakers as well as himself only ye Grandure of ye World was to Great for him to Give up therefore had got over ye Reaches he had received

'after more discourse they return'd and at a tavern his Father proposed taking of a Glass of wine when they came into ye Room his Father lock'd ye Door then Wm. expected he was to be caned but instead of that his Father laying his hands on ye table told him he would kneel down and pray to God that he might not be a Quaker nor go to any more of there meetings; Wm. open'd ye Casement and sayd before he would hear his Father pray after that manner he would leep o[ut a]t winder; A Nobleman was Going by ye Door in his Coach [seeing] Sr Wm's Coach stand there st[opt] his coach to speak wt [Sr] Wm came and knockt at ye [door] which stopt his Father's prayer the door being open'd he came in first came up to Wm and saluted him then turn'd to his Father told him he might think himself happy in a son that could Dispise ye Grandure of ye world & refrain from ye many vices they were running after which very much encouraged Wm : after more discourse they parted then Wm and his Father went to another Noblemans house wch Nobleman also spoke much in favour of Wm to his father; they returned home:

'after some time Wm went to bear a friend company to [place name omitted] — when he came to [place name omitted] they had a meeting where Wm's Mouth was first open'd then went to several other places at one place ye Magistrate knowing who Wm was sent to one of ye Secratarys how Wm with other were causeing tumults by preaching the Quakers Doctrine at that his Father finding where to send to him sent him orders to return home the friend he was with advised him to obey his Fathers order which after some little time he did,

'coming to London went to a meeting before he went to see his Father ; — but returning home his Father told him he had heard what work he had been making in the country and after some discourse his Father bid him take his cloaths and be Gon from his house for he should not be there also that he should dispose of his Estate to them that pleased him better. Wm Gave his Father to understand how great a cross 'twas to him to disoblige his Father not in regard to his Estate but from the Filial affection be bore him but as he was convinced of ye Truth he must be failfull so Go's up stairs and packt up a small bundle comes down again first Salutes his Mother and Sisters then tells his Father how unpleasen[t] his Displeasure was to him but should always think himself obliged to pray for his Father so left his father's house only with his small bundle as he went out of ye house heard Great cry's by his mother & sisters but was not Got far before a servant was sent for him to return when he return'd his Father was gon out of ye way so he soon got to his Room till his Fathers displeasure was something a bated.'

Pepys' characteristic version of the prodigal son's return is given in his Diary under date of December 29, 1667, and is as follows : 'At night comes Mrs. Turner to see us ; and there, among other talk, she tells me that Mr. William Pen, who is lately come over from Ireland, is a Quaker again, or some very melancholy thing ; that he cares for no company, nor comes to any : which is a pleasant thing after his being abroad so long, and his father such a hypocritical rogue, and at this time an Atheist.'

Penn, in his own account of his parents' reaction to his 'convincement,' merely refers to their displeasure but does not mention banishment from his home, as he did in speaking of his expulsion from Oxford. His first biographer [240] is far less reticent, and not only states that he was turned out of doors this second time, but seizes the opportunity — which has been neglected by no subsequent biographer —

240 Joseph Besse, *The Works of William Penn*, 1726, I, 3-4.

to stress the dramatic character of the crisis which had been reached between father and son.[241]

'His Father,' says Besse, 'being informed by Letter from a Nobleman of his Acquaintance, what Danger his Son was in, of being proselyted to Quakerism, remanded him Home, and he readily obeyed. Upon his Return, although there was no great Alteration in his Dress, yet his manner of Deportment, and the Solid Concern of Mind he appeared to be under, were manifest Indications of the Truth of the Information his Father had received, who thereupon attackt him afresh : And here my Pen is diffident of her Abilities to describe that most pathetick and moving Contest which was betwixt his Father and him. His Father acted by Natural Love, principally aiming at his Son's Temporal Honour. He, guided by a Divine Impulse, having chiefly in View his own Eternal Welfare : His Father griev'd to see the well-accomplished Son of his Hopes, now ripe for Worldly Promotion, voluntarily turn his Back on it; He, no less afflicted, to think that a Compliance with his Earthly Father's Pleasure, was inconsistent with an Obedience to his Heavenly One: His Father pressing his Conformity to the Customs and Fashions of the Times : He, modestly craving Leave to refrain from what would hurt his Conscience : His Father earnestly intreating him, and almost on his Knees beseeching him to yield to his Desire ; He, of a loving and tender Disposition, in an extream Agony of Spirit, to behold his Father's Concern and Trouble ; His Father threatning to disinherit him ; He, humbly submitting to his Father's Will therein. His Father turning his Back on him in Anger ; He, lifting up his Heart to God, for Strength to support him in that Time of Trial.

'And here we may not omit to give our Reader a particular and observable Instance of his Sincerity. His Father finding him too fixt to be brought to a General Compliance with the Customary Complements of the Times, seem'd inclinable to have born with him in other Respects, provided he would be uncover'd in the Presence of the King, the Duke, and Himself : This being propos'd, he desired

---

[241] Illustrative of the expansive fashion in which they have treated it, is Hepworth Dixon's account, pp. 53-59. Buell pictures the admiral as telling his son that 'he could tolerate all the Quaker beliefs except that which denied the right of physical self-defense, and at the same time refused the obligation of manliness that necessarily pertained to it' ; nor could he tolerate 'boorishness of manner and rudeness of personal behavior, such as the silly hat worship and the coarse vulgarity of "thee" and "thou," which George Fox considered the pillar of faith and the heart's core of his creed, the central dogma of his alleged "direct revelation from God."' (p. 75).

Time to confider of, which his Father supposing to be with an Intention of consulting his Friends, the Quakers, about it; he assured him that he would see the Face of none of them, but retire to his Chamber till he should return him an Answer. Accordingly he withdrew, and having humbled himself before God, with Fasting and Supplication, to know his Heavenly Mind and Will, he became so strengthened in his Resolution, that returning to his Father, he humbly signified, that he could not comply with his Desire therein.

'When all Endeavours prov'd ineffectual to shake his Constancy, and his Father saw himself utterly disappointed of his Hopes, he could no longer endure him in his Sight, but turn'd him out of Doors the second Time. Thus exposed to the Charity of his Friends, having no other Subsistence (except what his Mother privately sent him) he endured the Cross with a Christian Patience and Magnanimity, comforting himself with the Promise of Christ, Luke xviii, 29, 30.

'After a considerable Time, his steady Perseverance evincing his Integrity, his Father's Wrath became somewhat mollified, so that he winked at his Return to, and Continuance in his Family; and tho' he did not publickly seem to countenance him, yet when imprisoned for being at Meetings, he would privately use his Interest to get him released.'

It may appear, in this twentieth century, that both Penn and his father grossly exaggerated a relatively unimportant point in Quakerism by stressing the use of 'thee' and 'thou' and the custom of doffing the hat to one's social superiors. But in seventeenth century England, these were crucial tests of the profession of Quakerism, and they were symbols not only of a social theory based upon democracy, but of a religion which strove to apply literally the injunction of Paul to the Corinthians: 'Whether therefore ye eat or ye drink, or whatsoever ye do, do all to the glory of *God.*'

QUAKER PREACHER AND MISSIONARY

THE "First Publishers of Truth" had started on their task of preaching Quakerism about fifteen years before Penn's 'convincement,' while he was still a school-boy; but it was only a few months after he professed the new religion that he began to preach it. According to the Harvey Manuscript, as has been seen above, 'Wm's Mouth was first open'd' at a Quaker meeting which he attended after his first interviews with his father on his return from Ireland; and from this it would appear also that his expulsion from home occurred after he had begun to preach and because of the 'tumults' his preaching had incited and the 'work he had been making in the country.'

At all events, his career of preaching by the spoken word began in the summer of 1668, which was soon after he had sent a sermon in the written word to 'A Young Person of his Acquaintance, by Way of Caution against the Follies and Vanities of the World.' This letter was dated 'Navy-Office, 10th of the 5th Month [July], 1668,' and was in part as follows : [242]

'Friend, It was a True Word spoke by *Jesus Christ,* to undeceive all those Careless Wanton Jews, among whom he manifested his Glorious Truth, through That Body prepared of God for that very End, That the Way which leads to Everlasting Life and Rest, was very Strait and Narrow. My Friend, How much it may import the Welfare of thy Immortal Soul, to reflect upon that Course of Life, and Way thou now art walking in, before an Evident Stroke from Heaven call thee hence, and send thy so much indulged Flesh and Blood into the Grave; an Entertainment for no better than Noisome Worms. I beg thee, as ever thou wouldst be saved from that unspeakable Anguish, which is reserved for Worldlings, and from whence there is no Redemption, to keep thy self from those Vanities, Follies, and Pollutions, which unavoidably bring that Miserable State. Alas! How incongruous, or unsuitable is thy Life and Practice, with those Holy Women of Old whose Time was mostly spent in Heavenly Retirements, out of that Rattle, Noise, and Conversation thou art in: And canst thou imagine that those Holy Men recorded in Scripture, spent their Days, as do the Gallants of these Times: Where is the Self-Denying Life of Jesus, the Cross, the Reproach, the Persecution, and Loss of All, which

---
[242] *Works,* 1726, I, 5.

He and His suffered, and most willingly supported, having their Eyes all fixt upon a More Enduring Substance. Well, my Friend, this know, and by these shalt thou be judged, and in it I am clear, That as without Holiness none can see God, so without Subjection to that Spirit, Light, or Grace in the Heart, which God in Love hath made to appear to all, That teacheth to deny all Ungodliness and Worldly Lusts, and to live Soberly, Righteously, and Godly in this present World ; I say, without Subjection hereunto, there is no attaining to that Holiness which will give thee an Entrance into His Presence, in which is Joy and Pleasure for ever. And examine with thy self, how remote thou art from the Guidings and Instructions of this Spirit of Grace, who canst countenance this Age in frequenting their wicked and vain Sports, Plays and Entertainments, conforming thy self to ridiculous Customs, and making One at idle Talking and vain Jesting, wheresoever thou comest, not considering thou shalt account with the Dreadful God for every Idle Word. . . . I have not sought Fine Words, or Chiming Expressions ; the Gravity, the Concernment and Nature of my Subject, admits no such Butter-Flies. In short, be advised, my Friend, to be Serious, and to ponder that which belongs to thy Eternal Peace. Retire from the Noise and Clatter of Tempting Visibles, to the beholding HIM who is Invisible, that He may reign in thy Soul, GOD over All, Exalted and Blessed for ever : Farewel.

I am thy Well-wishing, Real Friend,

W.P.'

It was natural that, having just definitely turned his back upon the frivolities of his time and social station, Penn should have struck this note in his letter ; and it was probably the same note which he continued to strike in many of his early sermons. As a 'convinced' Friend, also, he pointed to the Light Within as the guide to salvation, and insisted that religious profession must be applied in an ethical mode of life.

Thomas Loe or Josiah Coale was probably the companion of Penn on his first appearance in the ministry ; and this may have occurred at Reading, in the home of Thomas and Ann Yeamans Curtis, leaders of the Quakers of Reading and intimate friends of the Peningtons.[243] George Whitehead, a later pillar of the Society of Friends, was the companion with whom Penn associated in his preaching tours in

243 Gulielma Springett, who often visited in the Curtis' hospitable home, may have been one of the auditors of Penn's first sermon.

PENN'S SEAT IN THE BLUE IDOL MEETING-HOUSE

A Topical Biography

southern England during the next few years; and in 1671, occurred his first religious journey outside of England.

It was doubtless due to the encouragement of George Fox, that great missionary leader of the Quakers, that Penn undertook a missionary journey to Holland and Germany. Having gone with Mary Penington and her daughter Guli to see Fox and his companions off from Gravesend on their journey to America, in August, 1671,[244] Penn and his companion, Thomas Rudyard (Penn's fellow-prisoner in Newgate in 1670), went thence to Rotterdam, where they were joined by Benjamin Furly, an Anglo-Dutch Quaker merchant of that city.[245] These three men were in subsequent years to be closely associated in the work of Quaker colonization in America;[246] but on this journey they were concerned only with the religious welfare of the Quakers in Holland, the conversion to Quakerism of the Labadists at Herford, Germany, and the warning of the Dutch and German magistrates against religious persecution. In Amsterdam, on this visit, Penn wrote a broadside entitled *A Trumpet Blown in the Ears of the Inhabitants of High and Low Germany* . . . , which was translated into Dutch by Furly; and on his return to England, he wrote a *Missive or Warning to the Netherlands Nation,* which was also translated by Furly and sent to 'the heads of the Netherlands nation.' These messages were replete with gloomy forebodings as to the miseries which Louis XIV's wars and their own worldliness were to bring upon the people, and with religious and moral admonitions to hearken to the Word of the Lord which they could plainly hear within their own souls.[247]

One of the very few references to this journey of 1671 comes to us from Silas Taylor, the antiquary of Essex, who wrote to Secretary Williamson from Harwich, October 26, 1671, as follows:[247] 'Sʳ On Tuesday out of one of our packet boats from Holland arrived here Sʳ Wᵐ Pen's eldest sonne, the great opinionist, he went presently & associated himselfe with the Quakers of this Towne. I can heare of no more.'

Two more visits were made by Penn to Holland and Germany, in

---

244 Fox's *Journal,* II, 176.
245 See Monograph Number Five (*Benjamin Furly and Quakerism in Rotterdam*).
246 Rudyard was said by a contemporary to be 'skilful in the Law of the Land, and zealous for the Liberties of the People, (Besse's *Sufferings,* I, 426); he became one of the New Jersey proprietors, and was deputy governor of East Jersey between 1682 and 1685.
247 Calendar of State Papers, 1671, p. 541. See Monograph Number Two (*William Penn and the Dutch Quaker Migration to Pennsylvania*).

1677 and 1686; and these were not only journeys in behalf of Quakerism and of religious toleration, but were also devoted to appeals for colonization in New Jersey and Pennsylvania. He visited at least nineteen towns and cities in the Netherlands, addressing public meetings in ten of them, and eighteen towns and cities in western Germany (as far east as Bremen and Herford, but mostly in the Rhineland), addressing meetings in seven of them, and holding unnumbered interviews with people of high class and low, of urban and rural occupations. The fruits of these visits were not many converts to Quakerism, but many thousands of colonists in America, where the Dutch Quakers founded Germantown in 1683, and the German religious exiles settled far and wide in Pennsylvania.[248]

The great migration of the Germans to Pennsylvania began in the year 1709; hence Penn had no opportunity of proselyting them there, while the Dutch who settled in Germantown between 1683 and 1709 were already Quakers when they arrived.[249] On his two visits to his colony, Penn was very active, amidst the pressing cares of founding a commonwealth, in preaching in Quaker meetings, which many non-Quakers frequented to see and hear him; and he was by no means neglectful of the religious welfare of the Indians. Quaker doctrines crept into his numerous interviews and land-negotiations with the Red Men of the forests; and he not only wrote detailed accounts of their beliefs and customs, but also sent them by his commissioners a direct appeal to their religious impulses.[250]

Influenced, perhaps, by a belief that the North American Indians were descendants of 'the lost tribes of Israel,' but even more by his veneration for the tragic history of the Jews and the prophecies of the Messiah in their Scriptures, he addressed to the latter a pamphlet entitled *A Visitation to the Jews*.[251] In this he deplored their 'dispersal over the Face of the Whole Earth' and their consequent captivity among other peoples, and appealed to them to make an end to their sufferings by accepting Christianity. Jews, he argued, might just as well accept the New Testament and its miracles as fully as Christians accept the Old Testament and its miracles; and he pleaded with them to hasten the day when they 'who were the natural Branches broken off through Unbelief, by Faith may come again to be engrafted.' He did

248 ibid.
249 ibid.
250 *Works*, 1726, I, 121.
251 ibid. II, 848.

AN ACCOUNT OF W. Penn's TRAVAILS IN HOLLAND and GERMANY.

Anno MDCLXXVII.

For the Service of the Gospel of Christ, by way of Journal. Containing also Divers Letters and Epistles writ to several Great and Eminent Persons whilst there.

London, Printed and Sold by *T. Sowle,* near the *Meeting-House* in *White-Hart-Court* in *Grace-Church-Street,* and at the *Croked-Billet* in *Holy-well-lane* near *Shoreditch,* 1694.

A Topical Biography 123

not fail to point them to the Light Within, which would reveal the true Messiah to them; nor did he fail to add a postscript addressed to *All Christians* to let their Light so shine before 'Jews, Turks and Infidels' that their faith might be justified by their good works.

When he was in Amsterdam, in 1677, he wrote four pamphlets and had them published in Dutch and German, as follows: [252] *A Summons or Call to Christendom: In an earnest Expostulation with Her, to prepare for the Great and Notable Day of the Lord that is at the door; Tender Counsel and Advice . . . to all those who are sensible of the Day of Visitation; To all those Professors of Christianity, that are externally separate from the Visible Sects and Fellowships in the Christian World (so called) where-ever Hidden or Scattered;* and *A Tender Visitation, in the Love of God.*

Penn's missionary appeals were of the broad catholicity and universality characteristic of all the early Quaker publicists, and he shared their hope, if not their expectation, that all the world would turn to Christianity as the Quakers interpreted it. In particular, he hoped for church unity, based on toleration, throughout Christendom, and participated in the efforts of Robert Barclay, John Durie, and others to bring about a 'Comprehension' at least of all Christians; [253] and he wrote, in 1672, a tract on *The Proposed Comprehension,* which repudiated a partial, prejudiced church-unity and advocated a genuine Christian unity bulwarked by complete religious liberty.[254] Meanwhile, he continued with ardour the preaching of Quakerism, the acceptance of which would be the immediate practical method of solving both the religious and the ecclesiastical problem for all time.

In England, his marriage in 1672 was followed by a preaching tour, in which his bride accompanied him despite long, hard riding on horseback, the prevalence of marauding 'moss-troopers,' and the holding of meetings in twenty-one different places within as many days. An echo of this tour comes to us from the Calendar of State Papers, 1672, (page 450), which includes a report from Major A. Darrell to Secretary Williamson. This is dated 'Sheernesse Aug. 6. 1672,' and reads as follows: 'This place affoordes none (news) but that sr William Penns sonn a Renowned quaker and Two or three Brethren moore are very busy in the wilde of Kent In Planting their Gospell

---

252 *Works*, 1726, I, 187, 198, 209, 216 (see Monograph Number Two, pp. 86, 309).
253 Monograph Number Two, pp. 129-132, 136.
254 *Works*, 1726, II, 186.

and elightening that dark Country wch is the recptacle of all sisme and Rebellion a gentleman of this Country told me this newes yesterday and that these Impostures have numerous Companies following them...'

On Fox's return from America in 1673, Penn and Gulielma went to meet him at Bristol, where Fox and Penn preached to large crowds at the 'Great Fair' and 'ye Lords Infinite power and life was over all & glorious powerful meetinges wee had there.'[255] In the autumn of that year, also, Fox and his wife and two of her family visited the Penns at Rickmansworth, and may have taken the young couple with them to participate in their missionary activities in Oxfordshire.[256]

In 1677, immediately after his return from his second visit on the Continent, Penn travelled on a preaching tour through nine of England's counties. A decade filled with efforts at the Court in behalf of toleration and with the colonization of Pennsylvania prevented many more preaching tours; but in 1687, we find him again traversing nine English counties, and again speaking at the 'Great Fair' in Bristol. By this time, he was famous and his meetings were 'mighty,' one of his hearers records,[257] 'notwithstanding the late Persecution in that City. I never knew greater,' this writer continues, 'though I had been acquainted with them [that is, the Quaker meetings held at the time of the Fair], and frequented them at Times when at Liberty [from gaol] for about Sixteen Years ; ... People flock'd to them like Doves to the Windows : which I note to shew the Ineffectualness of Persecution, and that it never attains its End.'

By the other writer we are told : 'I understand ye Land [which the writer owned in Pennsylvania] is good, William Penn tould me soe, & showed it me in a mapp lately at my owne house, where he Lay as he went down to Bristoll, at ye faire, & as he came upp also. I went down to Bristoll wth him ; he is as well as ever I knew him, & very Large & pretious in his testimony for ye Lord and his Truth ; wonderfull meetings att Bristoll while he was there, of friends & others, ye great meeting House would not neare hould ye people that

---

255 Fox's *Journal*, II, 259.
256 ibid. II, 264. Penn and Guli did not follow Fox into Worcestershire, where he was imprisoned ; see *supra*, p. 39.
257 John Whiting's *Memoirs*, 1715, p. 172 ; and a letter from a Friend in England to two Friends in Pennsylvania, dated 'Marlbrough, ye 28th day of ye 7th month, 1687 (*Journal* of the Friends Historical Society, Vol. IV (1907), p. 73).

came to heare him. His visset was well excepted, & of great servise in that place. As he came upp, he had a meeting at ye Devizes, in ye great market house, where many thousands of people were to heare him; wonderfull sober ye people wer, of all sortes & greatly satisfied. From thence he came to Marlbrough, had a Large meeting here at my House, hundreds of people stood to heare him in ye street; ye rooms being full, ye glass of ye windowes being taken downe, friends stood in ye Penthouse & spoke to ye people to their great satisfaction. Samuel Waldenfeild & francis Stamper came upp from Bristoll with him; he had a meeting at Newbery & Reading. Great is his Labour for ye Lord, his truth & people, & of wonderfull servize his being here has binn & is. Under ye Lord he has binn a great instrument of our Liberty, being very Conversant with ye King, whose eare is open to him.'

A few weeks before this tour, Penn had presented to James II on behalf of the Quakers an address commending his Declaration for liberty of conscience; and during the royal progress which James made during the summer, he came several times into contact with Penn and his companions and attended several Quaker meetings to hear Penn preach. They arrived at Oxford at the same time, when James made his attack on the fellows of Magdalen College, who appealed to Penn to use his influence with the king in their defence. Penn promptly wrote him a frank letter deprecating his attack and telling him that it was 'an act which could not in justice be defended, since the general liberty of conscience did not allow the confiscation of the property of any who did what they ought to do, as the fellows (*de Léden*) of the said college appeared to have done.'[258] He followed this letter with further efforts in behalf of the Oxford fellows, but without avail.[259]

With the fall of James, Penn entered upon four years of retirement from public life: but at the end of it, he again took up with renewed vigour his ministerial work. John Whiting, who had talked with him at London Yearly Meeting in 1694, records[260] that in November of that year Penn went to the western counties and held 'large meetings in most of the great Towns.... I met him at Wells, and went with him to Somerton, where it was some time before we could get a Place large enough for the Meeting (the Market-House where the Meeting

---

258 Sewel, *History of the Quakers,* Dutch edition, 1717, p. 658; cf. Clarkson's *Penn,* 1814, II, 385-393.
259 *Infra,* p. 249.
260 *Memoirs,* 1715, p. 237.

began though large, not being big enough to hold it) and at last was glad to go out into the Field, and a great Gathering there was. I met him again at Bridgwater, where he had a great Meeting in the Town-Hall, as he had in most Places, which the Mayors generally consented to, for the Respect they had to him (except at Wells, of which hereafter) few Places else being sufficient to hold the Meetings.'

Penn went again to Wells in the spring of 1695, and Whiting gives a detailed account of the large meeting which he addressed from the balcony of an inn, his auditors, numbering two or three thousand, standing in the market-place, and of the trouble which ensued with the town authorities. Penn was interrupted in his sermon and haled to the town-hall for investigation; but times had changed since the days of the Conventicle Act; Penn had won his struggle for toleration, and bishop, mayor, magistrates, and constables were obliged to release and exonerate him.[261] His Quaker contemporaries regarded this incident as one of the last outbursts of the spirit of persecution against them, his first biographer remarking:[262] 'Finding that they [the magistrates], by disturbing a lawful for an unlawful Assembly, had overshot themselves, they excus'd the Matter as well as they could and presently dismist him; having done just enough to manifest the Keenness of their Stomachs for the old Work of Devouring, in that they could not refrain from whetting their Teeth again, after the Act of Toleration had blunted them.'

That Penn 'labored in the ministry' in London as well as in the counties in the autumn and winter of 1694-95, is evidenced by a volume of his sermons which he preached there at that time. These were eight in number, and were 'taken in short-hand as delivered, and now Faithfully Transcribed and Published for the Information of those who by reason of Ignorance may have received a Prejudice against them [the Quakers].'[263] They were delivered in the Friends' Meeting-houses on Grace-Church and Wheeler Streets and in Devonshire House at regular meetings for worship, and were doubtless spoken spontaneously; but in the printed version they are attributed by the transcriber or editor to *Mr*. William Penn and are given the following picturesque titles: 'Salvation from Sin by Christ Alone: or, The Arm of the Lord Revealed;' 'The Sure Foundation;' 'God's Call

261 ibid. pp. 240-243.
262 Besse, 1726, I, pp. 142-3.
263 London, 1696.

to the Careless World;' 'The Promise of God for the Latter Days;' 'The Heavenly Race;' 'The Dying Counsel of the Wonderful Counsellor;' 'The Great Design of Christianity;' and [to one preached at a wedding in Devonshire House] 'Two Made One: or, The Happiness of Marrying in the Lord.' It would have been difficult indeed for any of Penn's recent enemies and accusers to find in these sermons any remotest evidence of Jacobitism and Jesuitism!

One more of his sermons was 'taken down' and printed. This was a farewell-sermon preached in the Friends' Meeting-house, Westminister, in August, 1699, one month before he sailed on his second visit to Pennsylvania.[264] Its text was: 'Friends, Take heed that ye observe good Councel, and let not the Light depart from ye: Yea, let the Wonderful Counsellor be your Guide.'

After his return from America in 1701, affairs of government, a lawsuit, a debtor's prison, and serious illness made his preaching tours few and far between; but we find him again touring the western counties in 1705 and 1709. By this time, his first biographer (who was then about twenty-six years of age, and must have often seen and heard his great leader) says:[265] 'Although the Infirmities of old Age began to visit him, and to lessen his Abilities of continuing his Service in the Work of the Ministry with his wonted Alacrity; yet he travelled, as his Strength and Health would admit, into the West of England, as also the Counties of Berks, Buckingham, Surry and other places.'

In 1712, came the three strokes, 'supposed to be Apoplectick,' by which 'his Understanding and Memory were so impaired as to render him incapable of Publick Action for the future.' The ruling passion was strong in death, however; and in 1714, he was driven in his 'Chariot' to the Friends' meeting in Reading, where 'he spake several Sensible Sentences.' The next year, also, he frequently attended the meeting in Reading and 'sometimes uttered short, but very Sound and Savoury Expressions.'[266] This was the end of his ministry by the word spoken in public, which had persisted four years after his last printed exhortations. These, his last printed words, striking the

---

264 London, 1699. It is entitled: 'A Farewell Sermon, preached by Mr. William Penn: on *Sunday*, being the 6th instant, at the Quakers' Meeting-House, at Westminster.' It was reprinted (from the original print in the Westminster Monthly Meeting collection) in *The Friend*, London, Vol. 7 (1849), p. 23.
265 Joseph Besse, 1726, I, 148.
266 ibid. I, 150.

key-note of his own ministry of nearly a half century before, were as follows : [267]

'Now, Reader, before I take my Leave of thee, let me advise thee to hold thy Religion, in the Spirit, whether thou prayest, praisest, or ministrest to others; Go forth in the Ability God giveth thee, presume not to awaken thy Beloved before his Time; Be not thy own in thy Performances, but the Lord's; and thou shalt not hold the Truth in Unrighteousness, as too many do, but according to the Oracle of God, that will never Leave nor forsake them, who will take Counsel at it, which, that all God's People may do, is and hath long been the earnest Desire, and fervent Supplication of theirs and thy faithful Friend in the Lord Jesus Christ.

London 23d of the 12th   W. Penn.'
Month 1711.

As to the character of Penn's preaching, we have but few contemporary evidences. Dr. John Northleigh of London heard him preach (through an interpreter) what he called 'a good Ingenious English Sermon' to a Dutch audience in Rotterdam, in 1686.[268] Thomas Story, who accompanied him on a preaching tour in Ireland in 1698, said of him : [269] 'He was ever furnished by the Truth with Matter fully to answer the expectations of People of all Ranks, Qualities and Professions.' Story was eighteen years Penn's junior and was greatly encouraged by him in his own ministry. His testimony as to this helpful trait of Penn, is as follows : [270] 'That which added much to my Encouragement was, the Fatherly Care and Behaviour of the Ministers in general, but especially of that great Minister of the Gospel, and faithful Servant of CHRIST, William Penn; who abounded in Wisdom, Discretion, Prudence, Love, and tenderness of Affection, with all Sincerity, above most in this Generation; and indeed I never knew his Equal.'

Joseph Besse, who was born in 1680, but who probably heard Penn preach before Thomas Story did, says of him rather epigrammatically and as if *a priori* : [271] 'About the year 1668, being the 24th of his Age,

---

267 Penn's Preface to John Banks's *Journal*, 23rd of the 12th Month 1711 (February, 1712) : *Works*, 1726, I, 149.
268 Monograph Number Two, p. 117.
269 *Journal*, 1747, p. 128.
270 ibid. p. 84.
271 Penn's *Works*, 1726, p. 4.

he first came forth in the Work of the Ministry, rightly called to, and qualified for that Office; being sent of God to Teach others what himself had learnt of him : Commissioned from on High, to Preach to others that Holy Self-Denial himself had practised : To recommend to all that Serenity and Peace of Conscience himself had felt : Walking in the LIGHT, to call others out of Darkness : Having drank of the Water of Life, to direct others to the same Fountain : Having tasted of the Heavenly Bread, to invite all Men to partake of the same Banquet : Being redeemed by the Power of CHRIST, he was sent to call others from under the Dominion of Satan, into the Glorious Liberty of the Sons of GOD, that they might receive Remission of Sins, and an Inheritance among them that are Sanctified, through Faith in Jesus Christ. One Workman thus qualified, is able to do His Master's Business far more effectually, then Ten Bold intruders, who undertake to Teach a Science themselves never Learned.'

Later biographers, basing their judgment apparently on the representation of his countenance made by Sylvanus Bevan years after his death, give a very unattractive impression of his style of preaching. 'Of his preaching little can be said that would be either instructive, or even interesting to those who read by the electric lights of this material age. Of his printing even less.'[272] 'The crowds came to see a famous figure, for it cannot, certainly, have been the quality of the sermons that attracted them, if his discourses were at all like the extremely tedious ones that he uttered in London at this time, in which prosy exhortation connects pious platitude with pious platitude. Not so did Fox preach, nor Wesley, to reduce multitudes to tears, weak men to hysterical prostrations. . . . It must have been his personality that drew the crowds to listen to his honeyed, drawling voice, to get a glimpse of the candid, and at this time sometimes rather puzzled being, that dwelt behind the now corpulent figure, of which something was revealed by the nose that had grown questingly tip-tilted amid the ample folds of his cheeks, and the dreamy blue eyes floating out from under the well-smoothed wig, enlarged to fifty-shilling size.'[273]

[272] Buell, 1904, p. 83.
[273] Dobrée, 1932, p. 329. But this author says of Penn's preaching in 1668 : 'We can be pretty sure that when he was at Meeting, the spirit would single him out for its mouthpiece with regular frequency : no doubt it chooses those who are apt to talk, and Penn had a gift of words which he liked to use. The words were abundant, they flowed with a large generosity he had no desire to quench or refine upon ; he was no castigator of prose. He was popular as a preacher, expounding with a pleasant voice, a little too plangent for a room, perhaps, but excellent for a

'Penn,' writes another recent biographer,[274] 'though he had made a youthful essay in that direction, was not a travelling evangelist, riding or trudging in all weathers along the roads and over the hills, so that he might bring the message to common people; he was not a field-preacher like Vavasor Powell, or Fox himself, or George Whitefield and John Wesley in later times. His public speaking most usually took the form of lecture or debate, and when he travelled to Holland and Germany with Fox, we observe that Keith and Barclay, subtle theologians, were of the same party and more closely associated with Penn. . . . It is not safe to judge a man's preaching on the evidence of his published work (if we did so, we should wonder how John Wesley ever made a single convert), but there is not reason for supposing that Penn was anything but dull, when he opened his mouth. In writing of religion, at any rate, he is duller than most theologians; if any personal impression does emerge clearly, it is that of a little round mouth softly releasing innumerable ohs! and ahs! and a gentle podgy hand perpetually uplifted.'

Thus speak the hasty critics of our electric age; but not so the leisurely readers and writers of candle days. Clarkson, for example, cites one of Penn's contemporaries as follows:[275] 'Sir John Rhodes, who was very intimate with him, and who wrote the preface to his posthumous work, called "Fruits of a Father's Love," . . . says that he was qualified for a high station in life by very bright and excellent parts, and these cultivated and improved by the advantage of a liberal education, and also polished by travelling abroad, and by conversation with some of the greatest men the age produced.'

Clarkson's own tribute is as follows:[276] 'He became eminent as a minister of the Gospel [1675]. In his own neighbourhood indeed he had converted many; and from this cause, as well as from a desire which others of his own society had to live near him, the country about Rickmansworth began to abound with Quakers. . . . Though he was a learned man, he used, while preaching, language the most simple and easy to be understood, and he had a happy way of explaining himself by images the most familiar. He was of such humility,

---

Meeting-House. He was not torn by the vehemence of Fox, who used to have to retire from the room shattered by his own outbursts.' Dobrée refers here to Sewell [sic], II, 277.
274 Vulliamy, 1934, pp. 103, 241.
275 *Life of Penn*, 1814, II, 270.
276 ibid. I, 124, II, 271.

that he used generally to sit at the lowest end of the space allotted to ministers, always taking care to place above himself poor ministers, and those who appeared to him to be peculiarly gifted.'

A quaker biographer of the mid-nineteenth century says that 'as a minister of the Gospel, he was highly esteemed';[277] and a non-Quaker writer of a generation later—himself an eminent English clergyman—adds his praise.[278] It does not appear, however, that Penn himself was enthusiastic over his ability as a preacher, and would seem indeed to have persisted steadily in preaching rather from a strong sense of duty than from any special *élan*. His modest estimate of his success crops out in a letter he wrote to a friend in 1694, in which he said:[279] 'It is my prayer [to remain in a 'low, poor and self-independent condition'] and much of my ministry to God's people. Some are convinced, but not converted; and many that are converted do not persevere; wherefore their oil dries up; and Self, in Truth's form, gets up under specious pretences.'

The length of his extant sermons range from fourteen to twenty-six pages (16mo), and average about twenty-one. A public prayer, uttered at the end of one of his sermons, exists in print, and it fills eight pages.[280] Among seventeenth century preachers, this length is quite moderate and absolves Penn from undue prolixity, besides substantiating Story's and Clarkson's testimony as to his consideration for others who might feel moved to speak in meeting. Although he was 'recommended' as a minister near the beginning of his ministry,[281] he was not, of course, ordained; and instead of receiving any salary or travelling expenses, he contributed largely to the fund which supplied the varied necessities of other and poorer 'travelling ministers.' His views on theology and ethics will be discussed in later pages.[282]

277 Janney, 1852, p. 553.
278 Stoughton, 1882, p. 340.
279 Clarkson, 1814, II, 108-110.
280 Following his sermon on 'The Sure Foundation,' preached in Grace-Church-Street Meeting-House, London, December, 1694: printed in the Collection of 1696: see *supra*, p. 126.
281 Probably by the London 'Morning Meeting of Ministers and Elders.'
282 *Infra*, p. 166.

THE DEBATER

PENN's preaching and missionary labours naturally led him into innumerable private and public debates. In Holland and Germany, as well as in England and Ireland, the necessity of these oral encounters drove him into them despite the handicap of foreign languages. The best known of these was with Galenus Abrahamsz of Amsterdam, the distinguished leader of the Collegiant Mennonites, who, having listened to the sermons of Penn and Fox in the Quaker meetings in Amsterdam, in 1677, challenged them to a public debate. Two meetings were held, each of them lasting five hours, Penn being given the palm of victory by a Dutch historian, who says:[283] 'Penn, after the manner of his Nation, usually spoke nothing but in a premeditated and set form of speech, but shew'd upon this occasion that when he had a mind to it, he was not wanting in the faculty of answering Extempore to the sudden and large Discourses of others.'

In the tolerant circles of Amsterdam, Penn's debates led to no serious consequences to himself; but in his native England, they brought him into prison. The first of these occurred in 1668, just after his acceptance of Quakerism. It was nominally on the Trinity, the Presbyterian view of which was defended by a Presbyterian minister, or one 'who goes under the notion of a presbyter,' as Penn says in his account of the debate given in his *Sandy Foundation Shaken*.[284] The minister, named Thomas Vincent, had been a student in Christ Church College, Oxford — Penn's college — and had been expelled from the Anglican Church, but had been privileged to give 'lectures' to a congregation in Spitalfields.[285] Two members of his congregation, a mother and daughter, withdrew and joined the Quakers; whereupon Vincent preached a violent sermon against Quakerism, and persuaded the husband and father to forbid the two delinquents to attend the Quaker meetings.[286] Penn and Whitehead demanded a public debate, which Vincent granted, but filled the house with his congregation an hour

---

283 Gerard Croese's *Historia Quakeriana*, Amsterdam, 1696. Cf. Monograph Number Two (*William Penn and the Dutch Quaker Migration to Pennsylvania*), pp. 88-94.
284 *Works*, 1726, I, 249.
285 Perhaps because he had stuck manfully to his work in London during the Plague.
286 Penn quotes him as declaring 'that he had as lieve they should go to a bawdy-house as to frequent the Quakers' meetings, because of erroneous and damnable doctrines. And pointing to the window said, "If there should stand a cup of poison, I would rather drink it than suck in their damnable doctrines."'

before the appointed time, and called in three other speakers to his aid. The debate which ensued lasted from two p.m. until nearly midnight, and was but little more than a wrangle between the speakers and an uproar of heckling and abuse of Penn and Whitehead on the part of the auditors. Long after dark, Vincent tried to stop the dispute and gain the victory by falling on his knees to pray against his opponents as Jesuits and blasphemers. He then ordered the candles extinguished, and dismissed the congregation; but many lingered, and the noisy discussion went on in the dark, until Vincent reappeared with a candle and promised the Quakers another opportunity. As this promise was not kept, Penn and Whitehead attended his next church service and at its end demanded a hearing; but when Vincent 'slunk most shamefully away,' Penn resorted to the press and published his view of the Trinity in his *Sandy Foundation Shaken*. Vincent then denounced this pamphlet and its author, who was sent to imprisonment in the Tower.

The Calendar of State Papers for 1671-2 (page 40) tells us that Vincent and his friends as well as the Quakers were in trouble at this time with the government. Sir John Robinson, Lieutenant of the Tower, in a letter to Secretary Williamson, December 23, 1670, writes of them as follows:

'Deare Brother

'You were yesterday very busy, and I was in greate hast. These 14 dayes past I haue euery day imployed myselfe in military & Ciuill affaires in & aboute the Citty, to see them in order before I goe out of Towne. the Militia is in good hands and well setl'd in ye Hamletts; The publique meeting Howses that were [? closed] the preachers haue submitted and promis'd to giue noe further offence; I haue spoake with 2 of the Justices of the peace of Southworke who haue promis'd to take care of that part, and aduertise them that are preachers to desist. My Ld Mayo^r tells me that he sent for Vincent & seu^{r}all others and hath discours'd them He promiseth faire, that if they will not leaue of, he will execute the Lawes vpon them; He is at a stand what to doe with the Quakers. I acquainted him what I did with two Meetinge howses of the Quakers. In my Quart^{rs} I keepe them out of their howses, and if any of them preache take them vpp, and send them to Newgate for six months. Penn I serv'd soe. Own^{rs} of their howses, there's none to be found. They are a besotted people of two sorts fooles and knaues, of knaues some of them are rich men and there's noe other way to proceed ag^t them but to Indict them vpon the Statute of Premunire & seize their Estates & imprison them during the Kings pleasure; If this rule was generally followed & kept close to, it would breake them without any noise or tumult. . .

Yo^r affecconate brother & seru^t
J. Robinson.'

Two years later, Penn debated 'the Universality of the Divine Light' before an audience in West Wycomb, Bucks. A Baptist clergyman named — Ives attacked in a sermon the Quakers' doctrine, and was challenged by Penn to a public discussion. The clergyman's brother, Jeremy, accepted the challenge and brought with him a statement of the clergyman's arguments; but after he had read the statement, he departed without awaiting Penn's reply. Seventeenth century Englishmen, especially during the Puritan ascendancy when other pastimes were largely forbidden, were as keen over public debates on theology as they are now on horse-races and football games, or as Americans of today are over ball-games, or Spaniards over bull-fights, and were apparently quite as noisy and vituperative; many of the audience accordingly remained to hear Penn, and when Ives returned to rebuke them for doing so, they denounced him as a spoil-sport. Thomas Ellwood, who accompanied Penn to the debate, wrote a couplet in Latin which gives the Quakers' view of its result as follows:

'TRUTH hath prevailed; the Enemies did fly:
We are in Safety; Praise to God on high.'[287]

Ives appears to have discontinued his attacks for a few years; but the war was taken up by another Baptist preacher, Thomas Hicks, whose pamphlet-battle of 1673-74 with Penn was a virulent one.[288] Ives joined in this with a broadside, entitled *A Sober Request . . . to the Quakers* (1674), which Penn replied to in another broadside, *Jeremy Ives' Sober request proved in the matter of it to be false, impertinent and impudent.* Ives replied to this in an *Answer to a late Libel, or William Penn's Confutation of a Quaker* [? *an Anabaptist* ?]. Hicks was first exonerated by his congregation from Penn's charge of

---

287 Prævaluit VERITAS : Inimici Terga dedêre : Nos sumus in tuto; Laus tribuenda Deo. (Ellwood's *Autobiography*, 1714, p. 131).
288 *Infra*, pp. 147 f.

A Topical Biography 135

unfairness — in Penn's absence from London; on Penn's return, he responded to the popular interest in the dispute by distributing a broadside offering to meet Hicks 'with the Bible in one Hand and his [Hicks's] Dialogue in the other.' This offer was accepted, and then, on the 9th and 16th of October, 1674, the Baptist and Quaker champions had a debate on the divinity of Christ, in the Baptist meeting-house, the Barbican, in London. Hicks, Ives, Kiffin, Plant, and Ferguson (a Presbyterian) represented the Baptists, while Penn, Whitehead, Crisp, and Keith represented the Quakers, Thomas Ellwood reading the charges against Hicks. The first meeting was replete with theology and metaphysics, each speaker putting in his oar *ad lib.,* very much in the manner of a modern 'panel-debate.' It lasted until dark; and its successor a week later was equally unsuccessful in bringing the disputants to a common recognition of the Light, although the danger of the gallery collapsing with the weight of the audience caused them to agree to a further adjournment and to another meeting, which seems not to have been held.[289]

A Friend, writing of this debate to George Fox, who was then in prison in Worcester, says:[290] 'Wm Pen has laboured hard, and spent himselfe very much in these ... they strik ... him and ... good spirit which doth give him great advantage against them; and his manner and way of managment much takeinge and acceptable to most people; I hope God will keep him humble, & y^t will be his ...'[291]

William Penn also wrote to Fox of this debate, and especially of his answer to the question as to the manhood of Christ. This answer will be given later;[292] but on the debate itself Penn's comment is as follows: 'We have been as poor tossed sheep up and down, much abused, vilified and belied; ... but Truth has manifestly gotten ground, and in no one thing more than our plain confessions of Christ: so much had the Devil roosted and nestled himself in them under their misapprehensions of our words in that particular.'[293]

No sooner had Penn finished with the leader of the London Baptists than he was engaged in a debate with the leader of the Presbyterians, the venerable Richard Baxter. Twenty years before, after the publica-

---

289 Penn, writing of the meeting to George Fox, says that six thousand persons attended it! (Clarkson, I, 99; cf. George Fox's *Journal*, II, 306).
290 Fox's *Journal*, II, 306.
291 The MS. is torn at these places.
292 *Infra*, pp. 168 f.
293 Clarkson, I, 98-102.

tion of his *Saint's Everlasting Rest,* Baxter had had a pamphlet war with Fox, Nayler, Burrough, Whitehead, Fisher, and other early Quaker leaders ; and now in 1674 at the age of sixty, he crossed polemic swords with Penn, thirty years his junior. In this year he was one of the twenty-one divines who attacked the Quakers and called forth Penn's *Just Rebuke*.[294] The next year, he became aware of the increasing number of Quakers who were infesting the neighbourhood of his own and Penn's homes near Rickmansworth. This was because, he said, 'Mr. W Pen, their captain, dwelleth there and keepeth them continually stirred up.' He accordingly challenged Penn to a debate which lasted from ten a.m. to five p.m., without any intermission for dinner, the large audience, including 'one lord, two knights and four Anglican clergymen,' being more hungry for argument than for food. The argument, which was continued in a second meeting, was not satisfactory, of course, to either side, and Penn continued the debate in five letters which he wrote to Baxter.[295] Baxter's letters to Penn are not extant ; but there is a reference in his *Life* to the debate itself, the success of which, he says, 'gave him cause to believe that it was not labour lost.'[296] From the tone of Penn's letters to him, however, it is evident that his labour was lost on his Quaker opponent. For example : 'Thy Fling at my Attempt to prove Man enlightened from John 1 : 4, 9 hits me not in the least.' Despite Penn's rejection of Baxter's 'Senseless, Headless, Tailless Talk,' he signs himself a Sincere Friend, and 'In very much Love, Thy Assured Friend' ; and in his last letter, he forgives him and wishes him 'Good and Felicity in the dear Love of God.'

Penn now became too deeply engaged in statesmanship to continue his oral debates ; but a score of years later, we find him once more participating in a debate at Melksham, in Wilts, between a Quaker, John Clark, and John Plimpton, another Baptist preacher. A contemporary Quaker author,[297] who was present at the debate, says that after Clark had fully answered all of Plimpton's points, but had not satisfied or silenced him, 'towards Night, W. Penn (being there) broke out over his Head in Testimony to the People, which were many, in Thomas Beavon's Court, and so ended the Dispute, concluding in Prayer to God.' Thus, in his last encounter with the Baptists, Penn

294 *Works,* II, 604-618.
295 *Works,* I, 170-176.
296 *Reliquiae Baxterianae,* M. Sylvester, Ed., 1696.
297 John Whiting, *Persecution Expos'd,* 1715, pp. 239-240.

PENN'S WRITING-DESK

reversed upon them the stratagem of Vincent, the Presbyterian, against him in his first debate, a quarter-century before.

THE CONTROVERSIALIST

CONTROVERSY was the native element of seventeenth century Englishmen. Their political disputes they fought out by Civil War and Revolution. Their religious disputes added fervour and bitterness to their political controversies, and were themselves fought out by wars of pamphlets and oral debates. The Quakers, although they abjured hard blows on fields of military combats, were no whit behind their contemporaries in hurling hard words and heavy literature at the heads of their adversaries. This fervent warfare was due, of course, to no peculiar contentiousness of Englishmen; but in that century of ultra-serious religiosity, they devoutly believed that their souls' salvation and that of every other human being depended upon the triumph of their own religious views over those of others. They believed, too, that the survival of their religious or ecclesiastical organizations was at stake, and that the ability to give and return hard knocks in theological logic constituted one of the chief characteristics of the fittest in their struggle to survive.

William Penn, in his youthful ardour and with the zeal of a new convert, performed his first service for Quakerism by plunging eagerly into this war of controversy. During the first seven years after his 'convincement,' he published at least forty-two books and pamphlets! The quality of many of these was as striking as their quantity and their titles. Among them are found such titles as *Truth Exalted; The Guide Mistaken, and Temporizing Rebuked; The Sandy Foundation Shaken; Innocency with her Open Face; Truth rescued from Imposture; A Seasonable Caveat against Popery; The Malicious Aspertions, Erroneous Doctrines and Horrid Blasphemies of Thomas Jenner and Timothy Taylor; The Spirit of Truth vindicated against . . . a late Malicious Libel; The New Witnesses proved Old Hereticks; Plain-Dealing with a traducing Anabaptist; A Winding-Sheet for Controversie Ended; The Devil's Champions Defeated; The Ignorance and Calumny of H. Hallywell; Reason against Railing, and Truth against Fiction; The Counterfeit Christian Detected; Naked Truth needs no Shift; Libels no Proofs; Saul smitten to the Ground.*

There is no murmuring in the text of these writings; they live up to the thunder of their titles. Indeed, the controversialist aspect of Penn's life has been a source of embarrassment to most of his biographers, whether Quaker or non-Quaker, and they have touched but lightly upon the character of his polemical writings and debates. From the time of his first biographer — who said of him that 'he never turned his back in the day of battle'—,[298] down to Clarkson, Dixon, and Janney, in the middle of the nineteenth century, they ignore or condone their bitterness. Janney, for example, gently comments:[299] 'Many of his publications were of a controversial nature, a species of writing which, though needful at times for the correction of errors and the advancement of truth, is seldom interesting or edifying to succeeding generations, especially when tinctured with party zeal, or imbued with the prejudices of the age. He was, perhaps, as clear of these faults as any writer of his day; and if the impartial reader of his works shall find, in his controversial writings, some expressions more harsh than should be expected from his enlarged views and liberal feelings, it must be remembered that all men are liable to be influenced by the spirit of the age in which they live.'

Not so with our twentieth century critics. They have fallen blithely upon this defect, this Achilles Heel, in the great man's character, and have assailed it with vituperations that nearly match his own.[300] A vigorous fighter was Penn; no gently ambling polemist like Isaac Penington; he denounced and affirmed with intemperate violence; with frenetic activity, he sailed over a choppy sea of interminable wranglings, ruffled by the perverse winds of doctrine; he was garrulous, arrogant, bluntly positive, tart, virulent, truculent, abusive, maledictory, even scurrilous; he descended to the low and muddy level of popular controversy, to the worst kind of religious journalism; he had heated, vulgar debates with common ranters, with little dignity and a surprising disregard of good manners; disregarding Quakerly gentleness, he made bitter and malicious attacks upon his enemies; he talked frothily about false prophets, impostors, gross perversions, black slanders, vile forgeries, plain contradictions; he wrote with no imagination, no humour, no courtesy, no subtlety, no artistry or grace

---

298 Besse, *Works*, 1726, I, 44.
299 *Life of William Penn*, 1852, p. 44.
300 Cf. especially: Vulliamy, 1934; Dobrée, 1932; Fisher, 1900. Buell, 1904, although intent on proving the pusillanimity of Penn's Quaker pacifism, does not set down his controversial militancy to his credit.

of utterance! Such is the modern indictment; and there is much in Penn's printed words to substantiate at least some of its items.

His *Seasonable Caveat against Popery* [301]—written when he was only twenty-six, but after long meditation following his residence in France —was decidedly 'severe,' as his apologists call it. Attacking the Papacy as 'the ancient enemy,' he accuses it of promulgating the doctrines of the Devil, which were as false and immoral as their infernal parent. The fundamental doctrine of transubstantiation he denounced as contrary to both the Bible and to reason : 'If this Doctrine were true, their Lord would be made by their Priest ; for till he says the Words, there is no Real Presence ; and so the Creature (and sometimes a sad one too) makes his Creator, which is nothing short of wretched Blasphemy. The Lord they Adore and Reverence, they Eat.' The other cardinal doctrines of the papacy—including its subordination of the Bible, its practical repudiation of the trinity, its justification by merits, its communion in one kind for the laity and in both kinds for the clergy, its prayers in Latin for the dead and to the saints, and its ecclesiastical hierarchy—are disputed as being contrary to the Bible and to primitive Christianity. To support his arguments, Penn cites a learned array of quotations from the Fathers of the Church, leading schoolmen and obscure Roman Catholic apologists, and from the popes themselves. But his most severe denunciation of popery is because of its contravention of the moral law in its worship of images ; its subordination of children's obedience to parents, to their obedience to the church ; its massacre of 'heretics' ; its theft of enormous wealth ; and its 'Dispensations of public Stews, especially at Rome, where the Pope's Revenue is not a little greatened by those ungodly Licenses.' In short, that 'by reason of its Latitude in Point of Indulgence, the Popish Religion is an open Sanctuary for refuge to all loose and debauch'd Livers.'

After quoting such a denunciation, it is right that Penn's specific and emphatic distinction between popery and papists, between Catholicism and Catholics, should be stressed. While he attacked without quarter what he believed to be false and pernicious doctrines, he insisted that 'the great number of Romanists [who] may be abused Zealots' should be tolerated. Accordingly, in his preface, addressed 'To the English Protestant Reader,' he declares : 'I design nothing less than incensing of the Civil Magistrate against them (were such a

---

[301] 1670 : *Works*, 1726, I, 467-486.

Thing possible), for I profess my self a Friend to an Universal Toleration of Faith and Worship.' But in this same preface, he expresses the fear lest the 'Romanish Emissaries' should even then desire to restore the Inquisition; and in his 'Questionary Postscript,' he demands an assurance that the Catholics of England 'would allow a Toleration, were they powerful,' and questions whether or not they could be believed, 'since it's one of their most sacred Maxims, Not to keep Faith with Hereticks.' Nevertheless, despite these questionings, he remained true to his inmost principle of toleration for the Catholics (which was a very rare virtue in his century, and not too well ingrained in ours) both in England and in his colony over seas.

As a typical Protestant of the Quaker 'left wing,' Penn had no soft, condoning words for his fellow-Protestants of the right wing. His first book, *Truth Exalted*,[302] written while a prisoner in Newgate, bears upon its title-page the provocative and imperious words: 'A short but Sure Testimony against all those Religions, Faiths, and Worships, that have been formed and followed in the *Darkness of Apostacy* . . . Presented to Princes, Priests and People, that they may Repent, Believe, and Obey. By William Penn, whom Divine Love constrains in an Holy Contempt, to trample on *Egypt's Glory,* not fearing the *King's Wrath,* having beheld the MAJESTY OF HIM Who is Invisible.' This is a vigorous attack upon all religions based upon 'Rites, Duties and Ceremonies,' and was doubly offensive to partisans of the church and the monarchy because it not only scorned them, but also exalted Quakerism as 'that Glorious Light which is now Risen, and Shines forth in the Life and Doctrine of the Despised Quakers, as the Alone Good Old Way of Life and Salvation.' Papists, Episcopalians, 'Separatists of divers Names' he takes severely to task for their rites and practices of many kinds, which he enumerates and condemns as coming not from the Bible, but from 'the Devil (that subtil Serpent);' and in a 'Cautionary Postscript,' warns the People of England of the 'Calamity, Pining and Distress' which are about to descend upon them for their sins of commission and omission, and specifically for the cruel and wholesale persecution of the Quakers. With a final reference to the salvation of those 'who have forsaken either Father, Mother, Sister, Brother, House, Land [his own recent experience] Husband or Wife' for the blessed testimony of the Light, he signs himself: 'I am not of

---

302 1668: *Works,* 1726, I, pp. 239-248.

this World, but seek a Country Eternal in the Heavens. William Penn.'

This book was read by Penn's friend Pepys, who states in his Diary:[303] 'So to supper, and after supper to read a ridiculous nonsensical book set out by Will Pen for the Quakers; but so full of nothing but nonsense, that I was ashamed to read in it.' And after two and three-quarter centuries, a recent critic condemns it as the 'noisy taunting . . . of a bawling fanatical Puritan, distressingly uncouth.'[304] It was probably not a best seller, even at first, unless among the Quakers; but it was speedily followed by another which demolished a book called *A Guide to the True Religion*. This book was written by an Anglican rector, named Jonathan Clapham, and it stated the essential articles of the true Christian creed as held by the Church of England and denounced all others, especially those of the Papists, Socinians, and Quakers, the doctrines of the last of whom he called 'wicked and damnable.' Penn was stung by its severity towards the Quakers, and he replied to it in a fierce attack called *The Guide Mistaken*.[305] The falsity of the Guide's religion, his uncharitable accusations, his hypocrisy, and his contradictions are 'confuted, reprehended, detested, and compared.'

Some Presbyterians enjoyed Penn's attack on the Anglicans and attended a Quaker meeting to hear more of it; there, they were 'convinced' of the Truth as the Quakers saw it and desired to unite with their society. But their pastor, Thomas Vincent, denounced the Quakers' doctrines in unmeasured terms. This denunciation led to a hot debate between him and Penn, and to Penn's next pamphlet, *The Sandy Foundation Shaken*.[306] In the latter, Penn took up the refutation of the doctrines of the trinity, of eternal damnation without a plenary satisfaction, and of the justification of sinners by imputed righteousness. His reasoning was so cogent that the minister demanded Penn's punishment, which led to his imprisonment in the Tower; and even Pepys declared:[307] 'So home, and there Pelling

303 October 12, 1668 (VIII, 114). Pepys may have read and contrasted it with John Fox's *Book of Martyrs*, a copy of which he received the same evening.
304 Vulliamy, 1934.
305 1668: *Works*, 1726, II, 1-31.
306 *Works*, 1726, I, 249; cf. *supra*, p. 132.
307 February 12, 1669 (VIII, 213). On August 4, 1669, after Penn's release from the Tower, Pepys wrote: 'Young Pen who wrote the blasphemous book is delivered to his father to be transported.'

[his apothecary, book-providing friend] hath got me W. Pen's book against the Trinity. I got my wife to read it to me, and I find it so well writ as, I think, it is too good for him ever to have writ it; and it is a serious sort of book, and not fit for every body to read. So to supper and to bed.' Pepys' contemporary diarist, Evelyn, was more severe and denounced it as 'a blasphemous book against the Deity of our Blessed Lord.' [308]

The Sandy Foundation Shaken having caused Penn's imprisonment, his next pamphlet helped to cause his release. This was entitled — appropriately for its imprisoned author — *Innocency with her Open Face*. This was not a retraction of the views stated in the former book, but an amplification of them clothed in much of the orthodox theological phraseology of the time.

Besides his controversial books and pamphlets, Penn wrote numerous letters which were also distributed in print. Some of these were quite as full of heat as the former. In a letter from Newgate in 1671, addressed to 'My ingenious Friend,' a Roman Catholic who had written him a resentful letter, he begins by saying: [309] 'I am perswaded I was cooler when I read thy Letter than thou wast when thou writ'st it . . .; scolding I utterly abhor, and have been ever bred a Step above so great Rudeness.' But he proceeds to condemn his correspondent's letter as 'an Earnest of a Romish Smithfield Bargain,' and expresses amazement that 'so ingenious Person as thyself should ever play the Bigot for a Religion that never yet dare stand the Test of being read in known, I mean in Vulgar Languages.' A few years later (1675), he wrote another letter to a Roman Catholic, in which he denounced the Church of Rome for having lost its chastity, and become 'the Great Whore that look'd like the Lamb's Bride, Christ's Church, but was not.' [310]

To doctors of divinity, noblemen, persecuting justices of the peace and those with whom he had oral debates, Penn's scathing letters went. The Vice Chancellor of Oxford University incurred his resentment when on a visit to the Quakers in his old college town, a few weeks after his own imprisonment (due chiefly to the persecution of university-trained men) about eight years after his own expulsion from the Oxford world of learning. This university head had set up a system of espionage, blackmail, 'ragging' by the students and cruel imprison-

308 *Diary,* January 3, 1669 (II, 41).
309 *Works,* 1726, I, 42-43.
310 ibid. I, 48-49.

ment, against the Quakers, whose chief offence in his eyes was their rejection of human learning and ordination as a necessary qualification for gospel ministry. The letter which Penn wrote to the Vice Chancellor was couched in 'terms unworthy of a Christian gentleman today,' as one friendly biographer characterized it;[311] or in 'the downright and somewhat unaccountable language of the time,' as another equally friendly one describes it.[312] Possibly thinking of him as clothed in a little brief authority, Penn addressed him as 'Poor Mushroom, Wilt thou war against the Lord ? . . . Dost thou think to escape His fierce Wrath and dreadful Vengeance for thy ungodly and illegal Persecution of his poor Children ? . . . He hath decreed to exalt Himself by *us,* and to propagate His Gospel to the Ends of the Earth. . . . Repent of thy proud, peevish, and Bitter Actings.'[313]

Other, anonymous authors fared severely at his hands. One published what Penn called 'A pretended Answer to the Tryal of W. Penn and W. Mead, &c. writ and subscrib'd S.S.;' and he wrote from Newgate prison a reply to it entitled *Truth rescued from Imposture, or A Brief Reply to a meer Rhapsody of Lies, Folly and Slander.*[314] On the title-page of this, he placed the provocative texts : 'A Fools Lips enter into Contention, and his Mouth calleth for Strokes (Prov. 18. 6) ; A Whip for the Horse, a Bridle for the Ass, and a Rod for the Fool's Back (Prov. 26.3).' One of the most infamous of all Men ; his Fardle of Impostures and Abuse ; scurrilous, false, ridiculous, peevish : such are the harsh words with which Penn opens his thirty-five folio pages of indignant affirmations and bitter personalities.

Of *A Brief Answer* [ten folio pages] *to a False and Foolish Libel,*[315] Penn says : 'Reader, the Petulancy of some Adversary or other has given occasion for this little Treatise.' He then answers one by one the accusations of the anonymous author against the Quakers, which he denounces as 'the Mistakes of his Ignorance and the Reflections of his Malice.'

To an anonymous author who wrote an attack upon the Quakers,

---

311 Stoughton, 1882, p. 76.
312 Grant, 1907, p. 72.
313 1670 : *Works,* 1726, I, 154-155.
314 1670 : *Works,* I, 486-521. Penn's bitter enemy, Samuel Starling, Lord Mayor of London, may have been the author of the pamphlet to which he replied so severely (Cf. *infra,* p. 185); or, more probably, it may have been Rev. Samuel Smith of Hereford, one of the 'Twenty-One Divines' who aided John Faldo in his controversy with Penn (*infra,* p. 146).
315 1678 : *Works,* II, 668-677.

entitled *The Spirit of the Quakers Tried,* Penn wrote a reply entitled *The Spirit of Truth Vindicated,*[316] in which he condemned the attack as full of 'error and envy,' 'a late malicious libel,' and its author as 'filled with nothing but disingenious [sic] Reflection, empty Stories, and unprofitable Cavils about a few Scriptures.' Although he said he 'designed not to be long,' Penn wrote sixty-one folio pages of refutation and confutation !

Other anonymous authors of attacks on the Quakers in several issues of a London magazine called *The Athenian Mercury,* Penn answered in a pamphlet entitled *The New Athenians no noble Bereans.*[317] This was written a score of years after his first controversial works ; and there is pathos in the fact that the new Athenians [Londoners], like those of old, could not be convinced of the truth, no matter how plainly and frequently he might state it. Unlike the nobler Bereans, they continued to charge all the old familiar falsehoods upon the Quakers ; and Penn, who was then experiencing his own persecution upon false charges, wrote more sorrowfully than bitterly in reply. Seven years later still, a pamphlet entitled *A brief Discovery* was published by Norfolkshire clergymen (Dr. Edward Beckham and others), repeating and even exaggerating the old charges which had been denied and disproved so often, but which they denounced as 'the Blasphemous and Seditious Principles and Practices of the People called Quakers : taken out of their Most Noted and Approved Authors.' In reply to this, Penn deemed it wise, in spite of his many previous answers, to circulate among the members of Parliament a brief document denying the charges ; for the obvious intention of the clergy was to procure the repeal of the Toleration Act so far as the Quakers were concerned.[318]

The Anglican clergy received most of Penn's controversial attention, because they had naturally been the most numerous opponents of the Quakers. Besides those already mentioned, Rev. Samul Grevill, whom Penn styles 'a pretended Minister of the Gospel,' wrote a 'Discourse' — against a Quaker book by Alexander Parker, entitled *A Testimony of the Light Within.* Penn called this discourse 'Un-Gospel-like,' and replied to it in *Urim and Thummim*[319] maintaining the doctrine of salvation from sin by the Christ Within. A Lincolnshire rector, John

316 1672 : ibid. II, 91-151.
317 1692 : ibid. II, 792-807.
318 1699 : ibid. I, 145.
319 1673 : ibid. II, 619-634.

Stillingfleet, wrote *Seasonable Advice* as to the methods by which the 'Unlearned Members of the Church of England' could get rid of Quakers in their parishes. A Quaker physician, Daniel Phillips, replied to this book in *Vindiciae Veritatis,* for which Penn wrote a preface. Two Anglican ministers, named Thomas Jenner and Timothy Taylor, attacked 'the Manifold Damnable Errors—, Vain Principles, pernicious Practises, and Blasphemies of the Quakers (denying the Lord that bought them'; to this 'Rapsody of Slander and imposture,' Penn replied in *A Serious Apology for the* . . . *Quakers, against the Malicious Aspertions, Erronious Doctrines, and Horrid Blasphemies* of the two authors.[320] The Quaker authors, Penn and George Whitehead, wrote this *Serious Apology,* which fact Penn explains by saying : 'Nor would I have the Man conceit it was his Strength of Argument that necessitated Two to answer it ; since the Meanest had been more than enough. I am asham'd and troubl'd,' he continues, 'that any Man should live so long, and to so little Purpose. He recommends his Discourse with Sixty Six Years of Age, as if we ought to infer Verity from his Antiquity ; not considering, *Bis pueri senes,* and that his Age gives but a more just Reflection upon his Folly, whose best Apology will be his Doting. Certainly he must have been very envious in his Youth, in whom the Flames of Wrath are so unquenchable in old Age.'

Penn himself records the fate of his rival's (Jenner's) book as follows :[321] 'T. Jenner, a Presbyter-Independent Priest of Ireland, writ a Book against us for Gain ; for he went from House to House of many sufficient, and some great Men, to present them ; some gave him a Crown, some two Crowns, some a Piece ; Among others, he had the Confidence and Avarice to go to the Lord Lievt. of that Kingdom [to present one] : His Secretary carried it to him ; he turning it over, observed many black Charges of foulest and most pernicious Errors to Religion and Civil Government [as laid down] : The Parson still stayed [for an Alms] the Secr. thought he had favoured him sufficiently [in delivering his Book] : but not understanding the Priest's Aim, that is Lucre (the Old Priest's Sin) was prest to tell his Lord, that he waited for His Excellencies Answer : The Secretary was so civil as to answer his Desire ; but when the Lord-Lievt. understood his

320 1671 : ibid. II, 32-90. This is the second part of the 'Serious Apology', and was written in Newgate ; the first part was written by George Whitehead.
321 *The Invalidity of John Faldo's Vindication ; Works,* II, 372 (note). Besse, in his biography (I, 40-41) does not quote this note quite *verbatim ;* the [ ] are his.

Drift, he returned the Book to the Parson, with this Account, That he was sorry to hear that the Quakers held such ill Principles [if what he writ of them was True]. but the Tares and the Wheat must grow together, till the Day of Judgment [or the Time of Harvest]. So the Parson was corrected for his Baseness, and disappointed of the Great Bone he crept thither for.' Besse adds in his biography the information that 'the Answer our Author gave to these Men, met with a General Acceptation, and it was reported, that Jenner vext himself to Death at it in a little Time after.'[322] Reverend Jeremiah Ives, another Presbyterian, made of the Quakers 'A Sober Request' about the same time, which Penn 'proved in the Matter of it to be False, Impertinent and Impudent.'[323]

The Anglican clergy often joined hands with the Presbyterians in attacks upon the Quakers. Among the Presbyterian writers, John Faldo, a chaplain in Cromwell's army and pastor of a congregation in London, was especially successful in procuring Anglican and Independent assistance in his attacks upon them. These included *Quakerism no Christianity*, which Penn answered in *Quakerism a New Nick-Name for Old Christianity*;[324] Faldo replied in *A Vindication of Quakerism no Christianity*, and Penn rejoined in *The Invalidity of John Faldo's Vindication*;[324] this brought forth *A Challenge*, which Penn answered,[325] and *A Curb for William Penn's Confidence*, which Penn also answered.[326] Faldo then called to his aid twenty-one clergymen of several faiths, who endorsed by their Epistolary Preface a new edition of *Quakerism no Christianity*, and Penn levelled *A Just Rebuke* against these 'One and Twenty Learned and Reverend Divines (so called)'.[327] The debate had now lasted four years, and Penn evidently decided it was useless to continue it; but Faldo replied to *A Just Rebuke* by another pamphlet entitled *XXI Divines Cleared of the Unjust Criminations of Will. Penn* (1675), which was brought out in a second edition twenty-three years later (a half-dozen years after Faldo's death).

Meanwhile (in 1676), John Cheyney, an Anglican minister in Lancashire, took up the cudgels against Penn's *Quakerism a Nick-*

---
322 *Works*, I, 41.
323 A broadside, without place or date [1674]. Jeremy was the Ives brother with whom Penn had a debate in 1671 (Cf. *supra*, p. 134).
324 The first two of these writings of Penn are included in his *Works*, II, 227-462.
325 ibid. I, 45-46: *William Penn's Answer to John Faldo's Printed Challenge*.
326 ibid. II, 639-649: *William Penn's Return to John Faldo's Reply*.
327 ibid. II, 604-618.

A Topical Biography 147

Name for Old Christianity, and wrote *A Skirmish made upon Quakerism;* to this Penn did reply, in *The Skirmisher Defeated.*[328] Cheyney published eight more attacks upon the Quakers within the next year; but Penn left these to be answered by sundry other Quakers, who entered valiantly into the lists.

The animus of John Faldo in this long controversy is described by Penn's first biographer as follows:[329] 'He perceiving some of his Hearers drawing off to the Quakers, and being sensible that every Sheep he lost carried away Wool on his Back, was grievously incensed: At length he gave his Fury Vent in a Book.' Faldo's books give evidence of his 'Fury' in such phrases as: 'A Thorow Quaker no Christian;' 'their many Usurped and Unintelligible Words and Phrases;' 'their near approach to Popery and their bold Blasphemy;' 'William Penn's false insinuations and jugglings;' 'the Snake in the Grass . . . or the Quakers no Christians.' Penn on his side did not lack for such hard verbal missiles as: 'the Synagogue of Satan;' 'Enemies to the Cross of Christ, and are at best but Carnal, Historical and meerly Outside-Christians;' 'all the Hideous, Devilish Falsities Satan's utmost Interest can furnish them withal;' 'the Foulest Charges of one of our greatest Enemies;' 'Forgery is his own beloved Crime;' 'Froth, Railing, Barks of Malice: Curs yelping at the Moon.' Penn was in such deadly earnest that he did not see the humour of declaring, in the very midst of such taunts of his own: 'My Rejoynder [shall be] without those insolent Checks, frequent Abuses and very vain and gingling Taunts he has cramb'd his Pamphlet with. . . . My Religion will not allow of a like Return in Vindication.'[330]

An even sharper thorn in the side of Penn the Controversialist, than Faldo the Presbyterian, was a Baptist preacher named Thomas Hicks. This opponent published *A Dialogue between a Christian and a Quaker,* in 1673; and in the same year, a second edition and a *Continuation of the Dialogue.* Penn, while wrestling at the same time with Faldo, immediately replied to Hicks's attacks upon the 'Quakers' perilous and pernitious errors concerning The Person of Christ, etc.' He entitled his reply to the two pamphlets *Reason against Railing, and Truth against Fiction,*[331] in which he roundly rebuked (through sixty-two folio pages) the 'Dis-ingenuity, Prophaneness and Forgeries' of

---
328 1676: ibid. II, 650-667.
329 Besse, Penn's *Works,* 1726, I, 45; Cf. also ibid. II, 315 (Penn's own statement).
330 ibid. II, 317.
331 ibid. II, 498-560.

the accuser. Hicks replied in *The Quaker Condemned out of his own Mouth;* and Penn rejoined in *The Counterfeit Christian Detected and the Real Quaker Justified,*[332] in which he denounced and disproved, by an appeal to 'God and Scripture, Reason and Antiquity', the 'Vile Forgeries, Gross Perversions, Black Slanders, Plain Contradictions, and Scurrilous Language of T. Hicks an Anabaptist Preacher.' Five of Hicks's partisans came to his aid in answering Penn's rejoinder in a pamphlet entitled *The Quakers Appeal Answered;* and Penn called to his aid George Whitehead in writing *The Christian Quaker,*[333] while a half-dozen other Quakers replied independently to Hicks's various pamphlets.

The most important of these writings of Penn was his part of *The Christian Quaker,* which was devoted chiefly to his view of the divinity of Christ, and which will be noticed under a subsequent topic.[334] His pamphlet controversy with Hicks led to a debate with the London Baptists in general,[335] and with several other Baptists leaders. Among these, were John Morse of Watford, who wrote Penn a letter in January, 1673, which Penn included in his reply, entitled *Plain Dealing with a Traducing Anabaptist;*[336] Henry Hedworth, whose *Spirit of the Quakers Tried* and *Controversy Ended* were answered by Penn in *The Spirit of Truth Vindicated*[337] and *A Winding-Sheet for Controversie Ended;* Henry Hallywell, whose *Account of Familism as it is Revived and Propagated by the Quakers* was answered by Penn in *Wisdom Justified of her Children;*[338] and finally, twenty-five years later, John Plimpton of Dublin, whose *A Quaker no Christian* was replied to by Penn and his two travelling companions, Thomas Story and John Everet, in a pamphlet entitled *The Quaker a Christian.*

In these charges and counter-charges, familiar epithets were used by the contestants, the accusation of Familism being chiefly resented by Penn, who charged ignorance and calumny, slanderous reflections, invective spirit, ungodly sly way of defaming, etc., etc., upon his equally tart opponents.

Amidst the wrangle and jangle of controversial contradictions, there occur from time to time, like oases in a desert, really splendid passages

332 ibid. II, 560-603.
333 ibid. I, 521-590.
334 *Infra,* p. 169.
335 *Supra,* p. 135.
336 *Works,* II, 179-186.
337 ibid. II, 91-151.
338 ibid. II, 462-497.

such as the following from Penn's *Wisdon Justified of her Children*. Since Hallywell, whose attack Penn is answering, addressed his book to a knight and baronet, Penn addressed his to the justice of the peace in the County of Sussex, to whom he says: 'I come not to you for Protection (a Thing he and his Cause wanted), but for Impartiality and Justice: Truth is sufficient to patronize and defend her own Cause from the Lash of Envy, without the weak Auxiliaries of Human Force; She gives Sanctuary to all that take to her for Refuge, but is all-sufficient to her own Relief from the deepest Pressure and most inveterate Prosecutions of her implacable Enemies.' Here is a passage worthy of Milton and his *Areopagitica!*

Two of Penn's literary opponents were not the 'inconsiderable wranglers' whom he had mostly to deal with, namely, Roger Williams, the founder of the Baptists in New England, and Richard Baxter, a leading Presbyterian divine. Williams was aroused by the invasion of his realm by George Fox and three other Quaker missionaries, and after a four days' debate with Fox's companions at Newport and Providence, Rhode Island, in 1676, wrote a book against Fox (who had 'slily' escaped from the debate), entitled *George Fox Digged out of his Burrowes*. After Fox returned to England, he and John Burnyeat visited Penn and wrote at his house at Worminghurst a reply to Williams, entitled *A New-England Fire-Brand Quenched,* Penn himself participating in the quenching. The relative importance of the founders of Rhode Island and Pennsylvania in the eyes of Penn's biographers, may be estimated by Clarkson's reference to the great Rhode Islander as 'a person of the name of Williams, then a settler in New England.'

In a preface to his book, Williams told Richard Baxter that 'through your sides, the Devil by the Clawes of this wily Fox hath tore at the heart of the Son of God.' This was the same year in which Faldo had called to his aid against Penn twenty-one clergymen, of whom Baxter was one. Incited, therefore, by Williams and Faldo, or perhaps because of the inroads which Quakerism was making among his own parishioners in Penn's neighbourhood, Baxter not only challenged Penn to a debate, but wrote him several denunciatory letters and signed a letter in support of Faldo's attack upon Penn, which called forth Penn's *Just Rebuke*.[339] After the debate, Penn's five letters to Baxter appear to have closed the controversy between them, although they both continued — Baxter until his death in 1691, and Penn until his

---

[339] *Supra,* p. 146.

paralysis in 1712 — to expound their respective doctrines in numerous publications.

Baxter, in common with many other learned men of the time, stressed the alleged resemblance of the Quakers to the Papists, while others confused them with extreme Protestant sectarians like the Familists and Muggletonians. The leaders of the last named were John Reeve and Ludovic Muggleton, who claimed to be reincarnated Moses and Aaron, respectively, and to be the last two witnesses foretold in Revelation, XI : 3, who would prophesy in sackcloth clothes twelve hundred and sixty days. Reeve 'prophesied' through his pamphlets for nearly twice the appointed time, between 1652 and 1658, while Muggleton continued to pour forth his 'prophecies' until his death in 1698; and their followers reprinted their fulminations for another century.

The Quakers came within the range of the Muggletonians' fire as early as 1656, when *A Divine Looking Glass* was published; and this was followed by sundry other pamphlets, including *The Neck of the Quakers Broken : or, Cut in Sunder by the two-edged Sword of the Spirit which is put into my* [Muggleton's] *Mouth.* Thirty-five Quakers replied, among them William Penn, who wrote *The New Witnesses proved Old Hereticks.*[340] In this, Penn proves the Muggletonian 'mysteries' to be 'mostly ancient Whimsies, Blasphemies and Heresies'; and he regarded them as the most 'compleat Monster on the Stage of Controversie . . . the blackest Work that ever fallen Men or Angels could probably have set themselves upon.' Penn paid Muggleton two visits and records, in several pages towards the end of the treatise, the very extraordinary conversation which ensued between them. Muggleton and his followers are finally dismissed by Penn as having no part in the peace possessed by genuine believers in it, who will 'possess the Habitations of true Peace when Muggleton and his obstinate Brats shall howl in the Lake that burns with Brimstone and Fire for ever and evermore. W. P.'

Muggleton wrote an Answer to Penn's *New Witnesses* (1673), in which he proved Penn to be 'an ignorant Spater-brained Quaker, who knows no more what the true God is, nor his secret decrees than one of his Coach-horses doth, nor so much;' and he had already, in their conversation, declared : 'W.P. I say thou art a Damned Devil; remember Thomas Loe, who was the wickedest Devil that ever I knew, who never went out of his Bed after I Curst him.' This was Muggle-

340 1672 : *Works,* II, 152-178.

A Topical Biography

ton's farewell and benediction to Penn; and it may have been due to his excessive scurrility that Penn became increasingly courteous in his later controversies, so that he was able to say to a denunciatory justice of the peace: 'However differing I am from other Men . . ., I know no Religion that destroys Courtesie, Civility and Kindness.'[341]

In fact, Penn's days of religious controversy through the press were nearly over. In 1675, at the age of thirty-one, he began his great work as colonizer and governor; and almost at the same time, entered upon his outstanding political championship of religious toleration. In the midst of these large and exacting tasks, he had only a minor interest in, and but little leisure for, the hot controversies of his youth.[342]

The student of Penn's character and career, after reading of and through the bitter controversial pamphlets which were hurled from his pen, naturally seeks an explanation of this apparent inconsistency; and for it, various explanations are offered and varied excuses are advanced. Some of these accusing explanations are as follows:

Penn was rude and uncouth by nature, rough in speech as well as in writing. His treatment of so eminent a man as Baxter—thirty years his senior—is illustrative of this obnoxious trait, which crops out in much of his later writings. He was in fact only a skirmisher, a scribbler, a propagandist, giving no sign of any real greatness in his eccentric, noisy early manhood before his spirit had been tempered by the Tower and Newgate to a softer wisdom.[343] Against this is placed his appeal to Baxter to believe that the Quakers wait upon God that they may have their hearts replenished with his Divine love and life in which to forgive their opposers and those that despitefully use them.

One biographer opines that he had inherited from his middle-class ancestors certain qualities which are not associated with good breeding![344] Another thinks that the example of George Fox, George

---

341 To Justice Fleming: *Works*, I, 157.
342 It was only occasionally that he reverted to them in his later years. In 1678, for example, he wrote *A Brief Answer* [anonymous] *to a False and Foolish Libell, called The Quakers Opinions*; in 1692, he replied to the *Athenian Mercury's* attack (*Works*, II, 793-807); in 1695, he wrote *A Reply to a Pretended Answer* (ibid. II, 807-838); and in 1698, he had a theological discussion, rather than a controversy with the Bishop of Cork (*infra*, p. 280). His later attitude towards them he expressed in *A Reply to a Pretended Answer* as follows: 'I submit to Controversies as my Drudgery, not my Pleasure, otherwise than as it is my Duty. . . . It is not in my Nature to remember Injuries Twenty Years ago [from J.Faldo and T.Hicks], tho' this Man commits them unprovoked: Nor had I any Temptation to it, since I had all the Satisfaction I could desire but their Conversion.'
343 Vulliamy; Dixon.
344 Vulliamy.

Whitehead (who at the age of thirty had written twenty-nine Quaker polemics), and other vehement champions of Quakerism was responsible for Penn's extravagances![345] The lime-light of leadership accounts for his kaleidoscopic style, his breathlessly accumulating periods.[346] The love of battle, especially in one who had so recently laid aside the sword and assumed the pen, showed itself in his worldly passion for controversy and caused him to use spontaneously the metaphors of war in his Bible Battles.[347] He was in fact still Ensign Penn and not yet entirely Quaker Penn.[348]

A feeling of personal revenge, a sense of wrong for the undeserved contempt and ostracism from the respect due to his ability, integrity, and social rank, made him virulent in his attacks on his own and his Quaker comrades' enemies. Penn's defenders would naturally reply to this, that if revenge entered into his writings at all it was for his persecuted comrades of the Quaker faith. In his *Truth Exalted* (1668), for example, he cites 'the many Thousands now of late that have been club'd, bruised, imprisoned, exiled, poisoned to Death by stinking Dungeons, and ruined in their outward Estates, contrary to Law, Christian or Humane : Therefore well may I take up the Lamentation and Reproof that was of old [Isaiah, 29:21, etc.].'

The spirit of the age of controversy is relied upon by others to account for Penn's severe polemics. Contentiousness was the common infirmity of his contemporaries.[349] Frankness of expression was also a characteristic of the century. A spade was not only called a spade, but a damned old shovel ; and 'damnation' had very positive meaning then. 'Fool,' 'blasphemous wretch,' 'Son of Belial' were verbal coins in universal exchange. Theological opinions were held in such deadly earnest that thunderous epithets naturally accompanied the whirlwind of controversy. It was marred by spiteful personalities, as the drama was stained by indecency, the most exalted literature (that of Milton, for example) was spotted by the crudest taunts, and even sermons were filled with sarcastic slurs and tremendous personal denunciations.[350] Penn therefore entered unquestioningly into this battle of

345 Brailsford.
346 Dobrée.
347 Fisher.
348 Dixon.
349 Stoughton.
350 Dixon.

A Topical Biography 153

give and take, and proved himself quite equal to forging and hurling weapons as deadly as those of his opponents.

His unquestioning conviction of the validity of the Quaker interpretation of 'the Truth' made him absolutely certain that his opponents not only erred, but were the agents of the Devil in spreading false and pernicious doctrines.[351] This, too, was characteristic of the age; but in Penn's case it was accompanied by an ardent desire both to confute false doctrine and to convert its victims (even the most uncompromising of them, like Ludovic Muggleton) to the true way of life and death. The sects contemporary with the Quakers, even those most extreme like the Familists and Muggletonians, Roman Catholics and Jesuits, were so often and so maliciously confused with them that their champion struck hard blows to shatter this harmful illusion. Throughout all the din of controversy, his supreme desire endured, not for victory over opponents, but for their conversion to the beneficent influences of the Light. He sincerely believed that he was engaged in a battle of reason against railing, and his method of attack was shaped by his defence of truth against rant.[352]

That Penn was divinely commissioned to defend his young and bitterly persecuted sect, he had no doubt; for he regarded Quakerism as a genuine movement to restore primitive Christianity and the true interpretation of the New Testament.[353] His was a struggle not only to prove that Quakerism was the fittest, but to enable it to survive in the bitter struggle for existence. When every man's hand was against it, and its principles were assailed from *every* quarter, an Ishmaelitish policy was the most promising one; hence Penn became 'the sword of the Quakers,' sharpened, unsheathed, and perpetually ready to do battle against their implacable foes. The Quakers, too, regarded him as a champion, endowed with many advantages and raised up by the Lord to wield sword and shield in their defence at a time when so many of their older leaders had been cut off by persecution.[354]

It was not only against hostile sectarians that Penn turned his weapons; he was equally forward to denounce persecutors in the seats of power. Numerous magistrates became the object of his denunciation; and in the light of the system of 'justice' which disgraced the

351 Vulliamy.
352 ibid.
353 Clarkson.
354 Webb.

period, it might well be agreed that only swords as sharp as his would avail. Indeed, it has seemed to some students of Penn that by his ruthless attacks he was deliberately seeking persecution and the martyr's crown. To have lived in peace and quietness at such a time would have seemed to him, as to the early Christians, a species of self-indulgence.[355]

The years of Penn's most numerous and most violent controversial writings were years of comparative freedom from persecution by the government, and the many religious sects utilized the opportunity of turning savagely upon one another. The rapid increase of the Quakers at the expense of the other congregations led not only to virulent spoken and written attacks upon them, but even to demands by the sectarians themselves that the persecuting hand of the state should continue to be laid heavily upon the dangerous Quakers. Such is the familiar reaction from persecution to tyranny. But throughout the fury of this contest, it is heartening to find Penn remaining steadfastly loyal to his great principle of religious toleration. He proved himself indeed as fervent a champion of toleration as he was of the other fundamental principles of Quakerism;[356] and it is due largely to his success in procuring toleration, that we of today can view with charitable indifference attacks upon our several religious faiths which would have caused Penn to fly to such methods of defending them as we may now be inclined to condemn as inconsistently violent.[357]

THE AUTHOR

OF the 157 writings of Penn which were issued from the press, there are three which were contributions to genuine literature, namely, *No Cross, No Crown, Fruits of Solitude,* and *An Essay towards . . . the Peace of Europe.* Besides these, there are eight which had to do with political and religious liberty,[358] eight which were notable for their exposition and defence of Quakerism,[359] and two relating to education.[360] Many of these twenty-one went through numerous editions

---

355 Stoughton.
356 Dobrée.
357 Fisher.
358 *Infra,* pp. 203-216.
359 *Infra,* pp. 133-150.
360 *Infra,* pp. 172 f.

A Topical Biography 155

in English, and some were translated into Dutch, German, French, Danish, and Welsh.

The volume of Penn's authorship is enormous. Forty-four years' devotion to the use of his pen — although it shared the constant use of his tongue — produced approximately one and a half million written and printed words! From 1668, at the age of twenty-four, until 1712, when he was incapacitated by illness at the age of sixty-eight, he printed an average of nearly four treatises every year. Since this large number was produced without any plan of a unified or collected edition, there is in his writing much repetition; and since most of it was called forth on specific occasions, usually for the defence of Quakerism against its opponents, its style has been severely condemned.

'Turgid masses of inchoate authority,' is one critic's condemnation.[361] 'No Quaker library complete without them, but seldom found in any other,' says another.[362] 'A tedious elegiac style,' complains a third.[363] Voluminous, but very dull; lack lucidity and conciseness. 'When he had a good thought, he usually suffocated it in an inextricable tangle of words and parentheses. His writings could be made excellent object-lessons to show how not to use the parenthesis.[364] Penn's style was the opposite of Franklin's vivid, sparkling, pointed one. Like Bunyan and Baxter, he could coin felicitous, charming titles; but like them, he could not restrain the habit of excessive amplification. 'On their short texts, they wrote long sermons. In writing they never seem to have made erasures; all which came to hand was written in full, without subsequent correction. They had vastness of conception and enormous argumentative power, and ingenious devices of arrangement; but they gave no finish to their productions. They could blast rocks, and hew marble, and strike out gigantic figures, but they had no delicate skill in the use of the chisel — all was left in the rough. Their statues half the size would have been far better.'[365]

Some of these faults of style must be candidly admitted. In Penn's case, one critic thinks that they were due to a premature departure from Oxford, and a consequent defect in training.[366] But excessive display of scholarship appears to be the usual explanation. Penn be-

361 Dobrée.
362 Buell.
363 Vulliamy.
364 Fisher.
365 Stoughton.
366 Dobrée.

came a very learned man, and he could only adopt in a half-hearted way the usual Quaker deprecation of scholarship.[367] On the other hand, it may be conceded that he was comparatively free from the excessive use of Latin and other foreign words. One of his biographers, citing this virtue of his style, remarks :[368] 'As a specimen of pure old English, without the affectation of foreign words or idioms, his diction deserves to be studied by the young.' One of his own apologies for his learning is amusingly stated in his preface to Robert Barclay's *Apology* as follows : 'The method and style of the book may be somewhat singular, and like a scholar ; for we make that sort of learning no part of our divine science. But that was not to show himself, but out of his tenderness to scholars, and as far as the simplicity and purity of the truth would permit, in condescension to their education and way of treating of those points herein handled, observing the Apostle's example of becoming all unto all.'

When the strenuous and often feverish activities of Penn's life are considered, there can be little wonder that the style of most of his writing is far below that of John Milton, who was a literary genius of the first rank, and whose *Paradise Lost* appeared two years before *No Cross, No Crown*. By none of his other great literary contemporaries, however — Pepys, Butler, Bunyan, Dryden, and Locke — is Penn at his best by any means totally eclipsed : this as to form ; while as to substance, he shines among them as does the sun among the planets. How large an influence in the deterioration of his style was due to the hurried activities of his life may be estimated from the fact that his three best books were written when he was a prisoner in the Tower,[369] or in retirement under suspicion of being a traitor.[370]

It would seem that it was not until he had written the last two books, and not until after he had become famous as the founder of Pennsylvania and notorious as a Jacobite, that his books met with much if any market. He printed and reprinted them at his own expense, and distributed them gratis as a part of his mission of service ; for, he said, he would serve the Lord both by word of mouth and by the printed page, which sometimes might go farther and last longer than the breath of his lips. That he has been justified in this belief is proved by the

---

367 Cf. Monograph Number Two (*William Penn and the Dutch Quaker Migration to Pennsylvania*, pp. 12-13); *infra*, p. 205 ; cf. Index.
368 Janney.
369 *No Cross, No Crown*, 1669.
370 *Some Fruits of Solitude* and *Essay on the Peace of Europe*, 1693.

NO
Crofs, no Crovvn:

Or several Sober

REASONS

Against
Hat-Honour, Titular-Respects, You to a
single Person, with the *Apparel* and
Recreations of the Times:

Being inconsistant with Scripture, Reason, and the
Practice, as well of the best Heathens, as the holy Men
and Women of all Generations; and consequently
fantastick, impertinent and sinfull.

With Sixty Eight Testimonies of the most famous Persons,
of both former and latter Ages for further confirmation.

In Defence of the poor despised *Quakers*, against
the Practice and Objections of their Adversaries.

By W. Penn *j.*
*An humble Disciple, and patient Bearer of the
Cross of Jesus.*

But Mordecai *bowed not,* Esth. 3. 2. Adam *where art thou?* Gen. 3. 9.
*In like manner the women adorn themselves in modest Apparel, not
with brodered hair, &c.* 1 Tim. 2. 9. *Thy Law is my Meditation all
the day,* Psal. 119. 97.

Printed in the Year, 1669.

A Topical Biography 157

fact that *No Cross, No Crown* went through twenty-four editions in England, four in America, three in French, one each in Dutch and German — within a century and a half — and through fifty editions in all, besides many reprints or 'extracts' from it.

It was during his eight months of enforced leisure in the Tower, at the age of twenty-five, that he wrote the first draft of *No Cross, No Crown*. The title of Milton's and Bunyan's great works have only two words, Baxter's three, and Penn's four; but these brief titles did indeed enshrine *multum in parvo*. Penn, not satisfied with his, added a sub-title of eighty-three words, in an endeavour to give his readers a table of contents on the title-page![371] 'Christ's Cross is Christ's way to Christ's Crown,' is the summary of its contents in the preface to the second edition, which was printed in the year of Pennsylvania's founding; this is a much enlarged edition — the real book.[372] It is divided into two parts, the first of about 200 octavo pages, and the second of about 125.

Part One contains eighteen chapters, including 246 sections. Part Two contains in four chapters the 'living and dying sayings of men [and women] eminent for their greatness, learning, or virtue, . . . collected in favor of the truth delivered in the first part.' The ancient Greek and Roman worthies quoted begin as early as Penelope, wife of Odysseus, and number eighty-eight, twelve of whom were women; the Christian witnesses number a score; the dying testimonies of two score ancient and modern celebrities, as late as that of his own father, are made to accentuate the living ones; and a final chapter summing up the thesis of 'No Cross, No Crown; No Temperance, No Happiness; No Virtue, No Reward; No Mortification, No Glorification,' ends with an exhortation and encouragement to 'the Children of Light,' and 'a brief Supplication to Almighty God.'

The weight of scholarship in citing this cloud of witnesses to the virtue of self-denial in all ages is lightened by numerous anecdotes and biographical sketches of them, a feature of the book which was largely responsible for its popularity and survival. In its first form, it was chiefly a defence of Quakerism, whose doctrines and practices had brought Penn himself into prison; but it broadened out in its second and subsequent editions into an appeal for a spiritual religion and a righteous life which met the approval of all Christendom and which

---

371 Cf. fac-simile on the opposite page.
372 The 1669 edition numbered 111 pages, the 1682 edition nearly 600.

made the book a permanent contribution to the world of literature.

The defence of Quakerism in the first Part of *No Cross, No Crown* was utilized, like the defence of the Germans by Tacitus, for chastising the follies and vices of Penn's contemporary fellow-countrymen. Pride; the conceit of knowledge; love of worldly honours and compliments, and pride in ancestry; sartorial finery: 'washes, patches, paintings, dressings, &c., the excess of which would keep the poor;' avarice; luxury in diet and apparel; intemperance; 'playhouses and stages.' These were the defects of his contemporaries of the Restoration Period which Penn weighed in the balance of pagan and Christian virtue and found sadly wanting. Quaker simplicity and plainness of speech, apparel and demeanour, he stoutly defended.

The ecclesiastical customs of his time, namely, a separate priesthood, creeds, rituals, ornamental worship, professional preaching and book prayers, were condemned as less worthy than the Quaker customs of worship on the basis of silent waiting upon the Spirit of God, and the beauty of holiness which this was capable of producing in every phase of life. These Quaker customs resulted in persecution; but this was precisely the cross of self-sacrifice which the Quakers were gladly enduring for the crown of righteousness. Penn strongly deprecated the monastic ideal of fleeing from the temptations of the world, and warmly advocated the facing of evil and overcoming it with good. Christ's cross of self-denial *in* the world is the true way to the crown of eternal glory.

There is many a touch of seventeenth century controversy in *No Cross, No Crown*, but its basic conviction of making Christianity a reality by applying it in every phase of religious worship and daily life has become (in principle) the truism of the twentieth century. Formal profession of dogmas and a dependence upon authority have been rejected (in principle) for an experimental religion based upon actual experiences and looking, not to authority for Truth, but to Truth as the sole authority.

Penn's *Fruits of Solitude* is supplementary to the ethical code of *No Cross, No Crown*. As its name implies, it was written during the years of comparative solitude when he was under suspicion after the fall of James II. But while these fruits ripened during his period of solitude, they had been growing throughout a quarter-century of ardent and strenuous social life. Perhaps the idea of placing the results of his experience in written form came to him first as he sat by the death-bed of his father and listened to the maxims which fell from his dying lips. And how varied and far-reaching had been his own training and experience since! England, Ireland, Holland, Germany, America; men of many minds, of many languages, of many customs; human cultures reaching from that of the Indian barbarian to that of the most polished courtier of St. James's and Versailles; the political and religious struggles of a quarter-century big with history : these and far more were the soil of Penn's fruits, gathered in solitude, but ripened in the sunshine and shadow of God's love and human strivings.

The first part was published in 1693, under the title of *Some Fruits of Solitude in Reflections and Maxims, Relating to the Conduct of Human Life.* In 1702, was published the second part, under the title *More Fruits of Solitude,* etc. Meanwhile, seven editions or reprints of the first part had been published, and the two parts together went through twenty-four editions, in England, within the next century and a half. In America several editions appeared; and versions in Dutch, German, French, and in English verse (1705), attested the book's wide popularity.

In our own century, it has been by no means forgotten, its abiding place in English literature being illustrated by its inclusion in Everyman's Library, and by Robert Louis Stevenson's praise. This was given in the saddest days of Stevenson's life, when he was producing his own fruits of solitude. Professor Edmund Gosse in his preface to an edition of it, says :

'Stevenson met with the little volume at a critical moment of his own career in December, 1879, while he was wandering disconsolately in the streets of San Francisco, convalescent after a very dangerous illness, yet still "somewhat of a mossy ruin," and doubtful in what spirit to face the world again. To the exile, with his hopes re-excited, his spirits grown buoyant, his moral fibers tightened by hardship and fear, the small book of Penn's maxims came with what seems a direct message from heaven. He was singularly moved by the book which he picked up on the stall of the San Francisco shop and the depth of his emotion was proved by the durability of his affection for the volume. Two years afterwards he gave that particular copy of the book to Mr. Horatio F. Brown with these words : "If ever in all my human conduct I have done a better thing to any fellow creature than handing unto you this sweet, dignified and wholesome book, I know I shall hear of it on the last day. To write a book like this were impossible; at least one can hand it on with a wrench, one to another. My wife cries out and my own heart misgives me, but still—here it is." And in a later letter to the same friend he says: "I hope if you get thus far you will know what an invaluable present I have made you. Even the copy was dear to me, printed in the colony that Penn established, and carried in my pocket all about the San Francisco streets, read in street cars and ferry-boats, when I was sick unto death, and found in all times and places a peaceful and sweet companion. But I hope, when you shall have reached this note, my gift will not have been in vain; for while, just now, we are so busy and intelligent, there is not the man living—no, nor recently dead— that could put, with so lovely a spirit, so much honest, kind wisdom into words."' 'Stevenson had intended,' Professor Gosse continues, 'to make this book and its author a subject of one of his critical essays. . . . He never found the opportunity to discourse to us about the book which he loved so much, but it has left an indelible stamp on the tenor of his moral writings. The philosophy of Stevenson as revealed to us from 1879 onwards is tinctured through and through with the honest, shrewd and genial maxims of Penn. Courage and common sense, a determination to win an honourable discharge in the bankrupt business of human life, a cheerfulness in facing responsibility, these were qualities which Stevenson possessed already, but which he was marvelously to strengthen by commerce with *Some Fruits of Solitude*. So the little Quakerish volume has a double claim upon us,—for itself so clean and sensible and manly a treatise and for its illustrious student and sedulous admirer, our admirable Robert Louis Stevenson.'

Other literary critics have compared it unfavourably with Bernard Shaw's supplement to *Man and Superman,* La Rochefoucauld's *Maximes,* Pascal's *Pensées* and La Bruyère's *Caractères*. But although it may lack the wit and brilliance of these epigrammatic collections, it would be more fair to compare it, not for style but for substance, with the Book of Proverbs and Franklin's *Sayings of Poor Richard*. The contrast between Penn's emphasis on kindness and charity and Franklin's emphasis on the shrewd and thrifty arts of making money shows the difference between seventeenth century idealism and eighteenth century 'common sense.'

Among Penn's 855 maxims (556 in Part I and 299 in Part II), there is scarcely a trace of the bitterness which might have resulted from undeserved persecution. Sweet, indeed, in his case, were the uses of

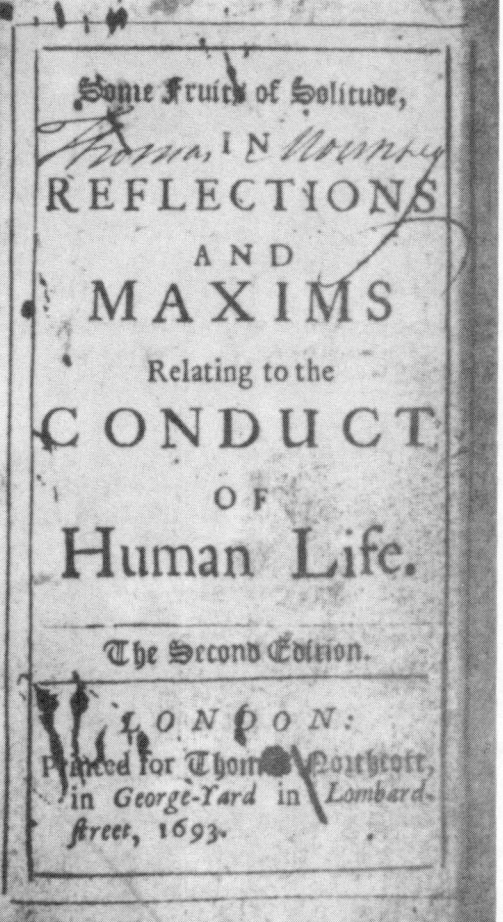

adversity. To the Reader, he says : 'The Author blesseth God for his Retirement, and kisses that Gentle Hand which led him into it : For though it should prove Barren to the World, it can never do so to him. . . . But it contains Hints, that may serve thee for Texts to Preach to thy Self upon, and which comprehend Much of the Course of Human Life ; Since whether thou art Parent or Child, Prince or Subject, Master or Servant, Single or Married, Publick or Private, Mean or Honourable, Rich or Poor, Prosperous or Improsperous, in Peace or Controversy, in Business or Solitude ; Whatever be thy Inclination or Aversion, Practice or Duty, thou wilt find something not unsuitably said for thy Direction and Advantage. Accept and Improve what deserves thy Notice ; The rest excuse, and place to account of good Will to Thee and the whole Creation of God.'

No Cross, No Crown, Fruits of Solitude, and Penn's Letters to his family on his departure for America, the first written in 1682 and the second (entitled *Fruits of a Father's Love*) in 1699, constitute a code of ethics which illustrate the best aspects of Penn's character and reveal his faith in man's destiny as being 'out of God's hand into God's hand,' and guided all the way between by that Inner Light which reveals the ripe fruits of wisdom and incites to their observance.[373]

Unlike *No Cross, No Crown* and *Fruits of Solitude,* Penn's third great book, his *Essay towards the Present and Future Peace of Europe,* has been relatively neglected. It was first published in 1693, and was reprinted three times before his death ;[374] but for nearly two centuries thereafter it was forgotten by a world which was and still is in dire need of its philosophy. Two of his fellow-Quakers recalled it in print, namely, John Bellers[375] and Jonathan Dymond ;[376] but even Janney, the careful Quaker biographer of Penn, in the mid-nineteenth century, devoted to it only one-third of a single page ; and Maria Webb (1867) gave it a single sentence, without comment. Janney's contemporary, George Bancroft, the first outstanding historian of the United States, while writing a glowing eulogy of Penn's life and character, merely says of his great *Essay:* 'Penn preserved his serenity [during his internment] and, true to his principles, in a season of passionate and

---

373 *Infra,* p. 172f.
374 In 1693, 1696, and 1702.
375 *Some Reasons for an European State* (1710).
376 *Inquiry into the Accordancy of War with the Principles of Christianity* (1823), and *Essays on the Principles of Morality* (1829).

almost universal war, published a plea for eternal peace among the nations.'

One generation later, an English non-Quaker biographer [377] referred to it as a beautiful dream, as reasonable as it was beautiful, but far from realization because of man's inborn love of fighting. Janney's chief interest in it was due to the recent holding of the Peace Conference in Paris (1848) ; his comment on this is as follows : 'It is worthy of note that a copy of this remarkable work, supposed to be the same that Penn presented to Queen Anne, was produced at the Peace Convention held within a few years at Paris, where it was received by the members with great interest as the fore-shadowing of their present plans.'

A half-century later, the Hague Conference of 1899 began in earnest the realization of Penn's dream of an international court which should settle by peaceful means disputes among the nations. The second Hague Conference (1907) and the Peace Conference in Paris (1919) carried the work still farther ; and peaceful means of settlement were applied with success many times in the first quarter of the twentieth century, despite their baleful rival, the armaments system. Recent biographers of Penn and even 'realistic' statesmen [378] have become correspondingly mindful and respectful of Penn's 'Plan.' It helps us to understand, one of these exclaims, how a disciple of George Fox could be a friend of John Locke ! Moral and idealistic, but practical and specific ; a most extraordinary book, the herald of the League of Nations two and a quarter centuries later ; it advocated what has ever since been agitating the minds first of philanthropists and finally of statesmen, namely, arbitration instead of war, and even a United States of Europe. Such are some of the commendations passed upon it by writers in our age of increasing internationalism.

Penn used as an illustration of the practicability of his plan, one which was actually and successfully being applied on the national scale, namely, the federal experiment of the United Netherlands ; but he was too modest to refer to his own Holy Experiment in Pennsylvania. The federal experiment of the United States of America came

---

377 Stoughton, 1882.
378 An edition and commentary on Penn's *Essay* was prepared and presented by the present author to the members of the second Hague Conference ; and both the Hague Court of Arbitration and the League of Nations have been desirous of receiving the gift of a statue, mural painting, or other memorial of the Plan of 1693 and of its prophetic author.

a century too late for Penn's argument; but it enabled Immanuel Kant in 1795 to advocate a 'Plan for an Everlasting Peace' based on the republican form of national government. Penn faced facts as he found them, and in the absence of large democracies argued that even monarchies could make the plan a success. Although himself under restraint for his alleged support of the Stuarts, and although writing in the midst of a half-century of warfare between the armed alliances and empires of Europe, he dared to dream of the possibility of enthroning reason, civilization, and Christianity in relations between nations.

Doubting Thomases were in the vast majority in Penn's time; and they are still strident and clamorous today. One of Penn's own twentieth century biographers, who ascribes all of his defects to Quakerism, denounces his plan as 'a sort of international Quakerism,' a dream of the millennium, as crude and as unintelligent as any one since. Riper experience of arbitration between individuals and nations, this biographer opines, has shown that arbitration will not be resorted to for any dispute that seems worth fighting for; that, when tried, it has resulted in nations with all of the cunning and none of the right cheating the eye-teeth out of nations with all of the right and none of the cunning; and that Penn's ideas must be classed among those that are ridiculous now, and were only novel then.[379]

Penn's logic in his *Essay* proceeds in quite the modern way. The great aim of statesmanship is to prevent war. Peace and security can be attained best by justice, and none of these by war. As individuals have developed society, local governments and national states, so states must develop an international government. As the Franks, Teutons, Northmen, and France, England, Germany have developed parliaments, so must Europe have its 'Sovereign or Imperial Dyet, Parliament, or Estates.' All the fifteen states of Europe, including existing enemies as well as allies, should have ninety representatives in the diet; the number of these he specified for each nation, giving to England only half as many as to the German Empire (six, as against twelve), and including the Mohammedan Turks and distant 'Muscovites,'—'as seems but fit and just.'[380]

---

379 Buell, 1904.
380 The number of representatives — each to have one vote — he based on 'the yearly value of the several sovereign countries'; and this value he believed could be estimated on current statistics as to 'the revenue of lands, the exports and entries at the custom houses, the book of rates and surveys that are in all governments to proportion taxes for the support of them.' To prevent quarrels over precedence, he made the ingenious

The diet should meet yearly; and before it should be brought 'all differences depending between one sovereignty and another that cannot be made up by private embassies before the sessions begin.' Penn evidently believed in some form of 'sanctions,' moral, diplomatic, economic, or military, perhaps all four; but his somewhat indefinite statement on this problem which is disturbing all the world at present, is as follows : 'If any of the sovereignties that constitute these imperial states shall refuse to submit their claim or pretensions to them, or to abide and perform the judgment thereof, and seek their remedy by arms, or delay their compliance beyond the time prefixed in their resolutions, all the other sovereignties, united as one strength, shall compel the submission and performance of the sentence, with damages to the suffering party, and charges to the sovereignties that obliged their submission.'

Penn was confident that such concerted pressure would succeed with any aggressor, because 'no sovereignty in Europe having the power and therefore cannot show the will to dispute the conclusion.' He apparently overlooked a possible alliance of 'aggressors'; but he realized that no sanction could succeed unless the armaments problem were solved. 'Nor is it to be thought,' he wrote, 'that any one will keep up such an army after such an empire is on foot, which may hazard the safety of the rest. However, if it be seen requisite, the question may be asked, by order of the sovereign states, why such a one either raises or keeps up a formidable body of troops, and be obliged forthwith to reform or reduce them.'

Penn could not foresee that huge armaments would continue to be maintained down to our own time, either for national 'defence,' or for the enforcement of international obligations. But he was clear that the claims of 'sovereignty' should not be permitted to block international justice, or to prevent national disarmament. Internal sovereignty, he argued, would remain intact; and if the reduction of armaments be called a lessening of the sovereign power of states, 'it must be only because the great fish can no longer eat up the little ones.'

Practical means of peaceful settlement, as a substitute for war; disarmament, so that these peaceful means shall have a fair chance to succeed; the yielding of imperial and super-national sovereignty to the

---

proposal of a 'round room with divers doors to come in and go out at.' He advocated a three-quarters vote, instead of unanimity; a large penalty for absence; no 'neutralities in debate'; and the use of Latin (for 'civilians') or French (for 'men of quality').

AN ESSAY
Towards the Present and ~~Future~~
PEACE
OF
Europe,
BY THE
Establishment of an *European*
Dyet, Parliament,
Or Estates.

Beati Pacifici.

Cedant Arma Togæ.

London, Printed in the Year, 1693.

W. Penn.

rights and welfare of the nations as a whole : What a trinity of world statesmanship for a seer of the seventeenth century to provide as a standard which the twentieth century is desperately striving to attain !

To persuade the civilized Europeans of his generation to try the experiment which he had put into practice on a small scale among the Swedes, Hollanders, Englishmen, and Indians in the wilds of his American colony, Penn analysed in masterly fashion the horrors of war as Europe had perennially experienced it, and the causes which inevitably led to it. He answered a half-dozen objections which would be made to the experiment; he enumerated a baker's dozen of the benefits which it would assuredly bring with it; and he wrote glowing words in favour of peace. 'Cedant Arma Togae is a glorious sentence,' he wrote ; 'the voice of the dove, the olive branch of peace ; a blessing so great, that when it pleases God to chastise us severely for our sins, it is with the rod of war that for the most part He whips us ; and experience tells us none leaves deeper marks behind it.'

Realizing the novelty of his proposal and the temerity with which he would be charged for venturing to advocate it, Penn wrote a modest apology by way of preface, pleading that 'they must want charity as much as the world needs quiet to be offended with me for so pacific a proposal. Let them censure my management, so they prosecute the advantage of the design; for, until the millenary doctrine be accomplished, there is nothing appears to me so beneficial an expedient to the peace and happiness of this quarter of the world.' Ignoring the sinister purpose of Henry IV of France and the fundamental differences between Henry's plan for the peace of Europe and his own, but desiring to capitalize Henry's prestige among his own monarchy-loving fellows, he concluded his essay by referring to Henry's 'Great Design' of four score years before. 'It was not only the design,' he wrote, 'but the glory of one of the greatest princes that ever reigned in it [Europe] ; and is found practicable in the constitution of one of the wisest and powerfullest states of it [the United Netherlands].—This great king's example tells us it is fit to be done ; and Sir William Temple's history [of the Netherlands] shows us by a surpassing instance that it may be done.'

But neither kingly prestige nor practical politics was the real basis of Penn's *Essay*. This he found in the necessities of men and the will of God. 'Europe, by her incomparable miseries, makes it now necessary to be done.' Thus he anticipated by a century the verdict that the experiment of 1789 for the American Union was wrung by grinding necessity from a reluctant people. And he believed heartily that man's extremity is God's opportunity : 'The voice of Heaven and judgment of God,' he declared, are against war and for peace. 'Christians, that glory in their Saviour's name, have long devoted the credit and dignity of it [Christianity] to their worldly passions,— invoking and interesting all they could the good and merciful God to prosper their arms to their brethren's destruction.'

THEOLOGY AND ETHICS

IN a century when theological argument was regarded as the chief end of man, Penn yielded to the prevalent fashion of striving to unscrew the inscrutable and indulged in the futile custom of dogmatizing about the unknowable. He did this with evident reluctance, or under obvious compulsion by the circumstances of his time ; for he shared with his fellow-Quakers their distinctive insistence upon a faith incarnated in works, and resisted the intrenched Calvinism which exalted the doctrine of 'justification by faith.' 'The devils believe, and tremble too, and yet are devils still,' he wrote ; [381] a heart dedicated to God, and a God-directed way of daily life among men in God's kingdom on earth, were his ideal of the substance and fruits of true religion. His Quaker belief in the direct communion of individual men with God necessitated both a respect for their individual convictions and a tolerance of them. 'I abhor two principles in religion, and pity those that own them. The first is obedience upon authority without conviction ; and the other, the destroying them that differ from me for God's sake.'[382] This abhorrence caused him and the Quakers to reject a creed and to strive for religious toleration, in an age when a creed was regarded as a *sine qua non* for a Christian and toleration was held to be a religious and political impossibility.

He was inclined by nature to rely more upon trust in God's goodness than upon faith in the varied attributes which theology assigned to Him. But the current charge that the Quakers were not Christians led him on to an attempt to rationalize both Quakerism and Christianity. 'I leave it with my reader,' he writes,[383] 'whether be-

---
381 *A Defence of - - - Gospel-Truths*, 1698.
382 Penn's Letter to Dr.Tillotson, 22nd 11th mo. 1685.
383 *A Defence of - - - Gospel-Truths.*

lieving in God, and Christ, and the Holy Spirit; and believing the scriptures, and the necessity of holiness, and divine worship, and finally of eternal rewards and punishments, are not points of faith chiefly to be received and professed by Christians.'

If he could have concluded this simple confession of faith by referring for its further and essential interpretation to a consistent way of life, his adventures into the chaos of theological discussion which bulk so large in his writings would have saved much labour to himself and his readers. But the fear lest he and his fellows might suffer from the terrible punishment of being called non-Christians (a fear which was realized despite all that he and Barclay and a host of other Quaker writers both ancient and modern have said) led him on to attempt definitions of the varied articles of his faith.

Primarily, he believed in the reality and imminence of God in the human soul. 'Eternal, Incomprehensible, Almighty, Allwise and Omnipresent,' were the familiar adjectives he applied to God; and yet, he says: [384] 'For professing that which is the very marrow of the Christian religion, viz. "Emanuel, God with us," we are represented as blasphemers against God.'

The doctrine of the Trinity he was accused of attacking in his *Sandy Foundation Shaken* and of defending in his *Innocency with her Open Face,*— the first of which sent him to the Tower and the second procured his release. Thirty years later, he contented himself with accepting the statement in I John v. 7: 'There are three that bear record in heaven, the Father, the Word, and the Spirit; and these three are really one.' [385] The bishop of Cork, criticizing this statement, said that it was 'far from being the sum of what the Holy Scripture teaches of them, and therefore is not a sufficient confession of faith on that head.' To this, Penn replied that it should not be necessary to defend the orthodoxy of John, since 'no other apostle has gone so far, or been so express.'

But throughout the thirty years of his exegesis, and thereafter, Penn and the Quakers were classed as Unitarians and Socinians because they would not acknowledge 'one Godhead subsisting in three distinct and separate persons.' Even one of Penn's 'orthodox' English Quaker biographers two centuries later criticized him for not stating (in his *Sandy Foundation Shaken*) 'his own full faith in the scriptural truth of

[384] *A Testimony to the Truth of God*, 1698.
[385] *A Defence of - - - Gospel-Truths.*

Christ's oneness with the Father, and his belief in the scriptural offices of the Holy Spirit ;'[386] while non-Quaker biographers of more recent years agree that while Penn accepted John's statement, he was not an Athanasian and rejected the metaphysical, scholastic doctrine that the Father, Son, and Holy Ghost were each separate and distinct persons or substances, and yet also one.[387]

The real controversy in Penn's time, as throughout all the Christian centuries, was over the definition or interpretation of Christ. The Quaker conception of the Christ Within raised the question of the relation between the Historic Christ and the Christ, or the Spirit of God, within the soul of every human being. The old controversy as to whether Jesus of Nazareth, miraculously conceived, was the Son of God or the Son of Man, or both, and how, was greatly sharpened by the distinction, if not the difference, which the Quakers drew between the Man of Galilee and the Spirit of God which is a part of all humanity's endowment.

Penn asserted repeatedly his belief in the 'Divinity of Christ' and in the 'Unity of Christ and God ;'[388] but did this mean that Jesus was wholly divine (was he God) or was he partly divine and partly human (like all other mortals, though neither divine nor human to the same 'degree') ? Did it mean, also, that Jesus was divine, like 'that of God' within every man, and that Jesus or the Historic Christ was the same as the Christ Within ?

In his controversy with Hicks, Penn would not admit that 'the manhood was a *part* of Christ,' because 'Christ is not to be divided into parts ;' but he argued that 'the holy manhood was a *member* of the Christ of God.'[389] But did this mean that the historic Jesus, or only the inward, spiritual Christ was God ? 'As for those gross terms of *human flesh* and *human blood,* I never spoke or wrote them since I knew the Lord's truth.'[390]

The lack of lucidity and scientific consistency in Penn's Christology has characterized theological discussions, both Quaker and non-Quaker, down to our own time. The most plausible explanation of the puzzle offered by the Quakers is perhaps the hypothesis of 'the subliminal self,'

---

386 Webb, 1867.
387 Fisher, 1900 ; Stoughton, 1882. The latter, an English clergyman, remarks : 'Penn was not an Athanasian ; nor are many divines who nevertheless are reputed to be orthodox.'
388 *Innocency with her Open Face* (*inter alia*).
389 Penn's letter to George Fox (Clarkson, I, 98-102).
390 ibid.

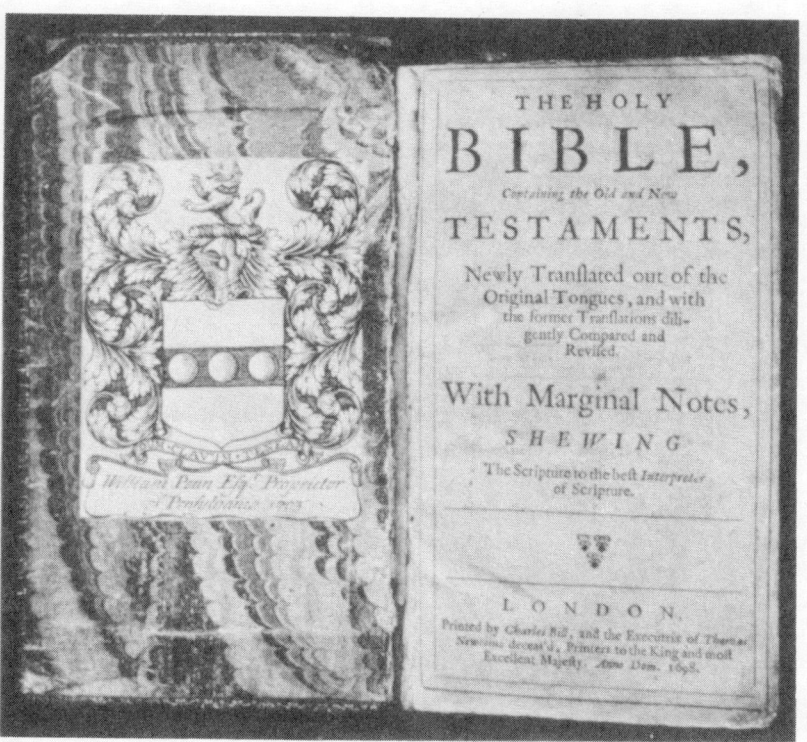

PENN'S COPY OF THE BIBLE

in accordance with which 'the subliminal mind of Jesus Christ was such that it is fitting to call him a Son of God;' and humanity's common possession of a subliminal self links men, God, and Christ into a spiritual unity which bridges the gulf between body and spirit and is independent of time and space.[391]

Some of Penn's biographers believe that the apparent inconsistency in his theology was due to a gradual development of his theories during the thirty years between 1668 and 1698. 'The consuming fire of reforming youth' became merged, they think, in 'the more pacific meditations of the older man;' there was a shift of emphasis from the iconoclast to the conciliator; and an assimilation of Penn and the other Quakers to the standard of current orthodox beliefs.[392] There are numerous passages in Penn's later writings to substantiate this theory; for example: 'Our adversaries would have us deny any Christ without us;—whereas we believe that he that is within us is also without us, even the same that laid down his precious life for us, rose again from the dead, and ever liveth to make intercession for us, being the blessed and alone mediator betwixt God and man, and him by whom God will finally judge the world, both quick and dead: all which we as sincerely and steadfastly believe as any other society of people.'[393]

The chief reason for the dispute as to Christ was the fear of eternal damnation which dominated the minds of medieval men and persisted into modern times. The 'salvation' of the soul of the individual sinner from eternal torment was regarded as the *summum bonum;* hence the other-worldliness and the non-social character of so-called Christianity; hence also the supreme importance of the metaphysical question of Christ's character and function.

Penn's first attack on the old theology included a denial of the impossibility of God's pardoning sinners without a plenary satisfaction by Jesus Christ,[394] and the justification of sinners by faith alone. While Penn included in his definition of salvation the avoidance of punishment hereafter, he laid chief stress on the avoidance of sin here and now; and he denied that Christ's 'propitiation' would suffice without

---

391 John William Graham's *William Penn*, 1924, pp. 89-91.
392 Graham, 1924; Dobrée, 1932.
393 *A Testimony to the Truth*, 1698, *passim; A Defence of - - - Gospel-Truths*, 1698, *passim.* Cf. *The Sandy Foundation Shaken*, 1668; *Innocency with her Open Face*, 1668, was so much of an 'explanation' that it came very close to being a retraction.
394 *The Sandy Foundation Shaken*, and the *Christian Quaker*, 1669.

repentance and atonement on the part of the sinner himself. He believed, apparently, that neither would suffice in itself: 'useless each without the other,' but sufficient when united. To this doctrine he adhered throughout his writings, and made a very detailed and cogent exposition of it in *Primitive Christianity Revived*.[395] In this book, he owned Christ as sacrificer and mediator for the individual from the *guilt* of sin, but insisted that the individual must free himself from the *power and pollution* of sin. 'It is impossible to be saved by Christ without us, while we reject his work and power within us.'

This belief brought him to the fundamental and the most important distinctive doctrine of Quakerism, namely, that of the Light Within. Innumerable passages in his writings both early and late are devoted to an exposition and defence of this doctrine, and he ranks with Fox and Barclay as its champion. The same divine spirit which animated Jesus shines in every man and enables him to commune directly with God, the spiritual father of all. This was the supreme lesson of Jesus to direct men's attention to the true Christ, the Christ Within, for through it they might achieve salvation from sin here and from punishment hereafter. But this would not result in an inward, personal religion alone: the Light Within every man made all humanity sacred; hence the social 'testimonies' of the Quakers were accepted by him as fully and striven for as ardently as by most of his Quaker contemporaries. '*I* am the Light of the World; *Ye* are the Light of the World:' such were the two halves of the Quaker doctrine as Penn professed and practised it.

From this fundamental belief followed others which seemed equally novel, untrue, and wicked to Penn's opponents. A mode of worship based on a 'silence' which enables the Inner Light to function;[396] the acceptance of the Bible as 'God's word,' provided it is found consistent with God's Voice Within;[397] the substitution of a spiritual baptism in the heart for a water-baptism of the body;[398] a rejection of 'the outward ceremony of breaking bread and drinking wine, which is commonly called the Lord's supper,' and a participation in 'the inward and spiritual grace thereby signified;'[399] the immortality of the

---

395 1696, Chapter VIII.
396 *A Defence of - - - Gospel-Truths.*
397 *The General Rule of Faith and Practice* (1673); *A Testimony to the Truth of God* (1698).
398 *A Defence of - - - Gospel-Truths.*
399 *A Testimony to the Truth of God.*

soul, as vital in this life as in the other:[400] these and various other parts of the Quakers' religion as expounded and exemplified by Penn all flowed necessarily out of their fundamental belief in the existence, guidance, and inspiration of the Inner Light, the Voice, or the Spirit, or the Christ Within.

Penn's theology, like that of the Quakers in general, cannot be separated from his ethics; for his religion can scarcely be expressed in any terms other than those of daily conduct. The ethical thread was prominent all through his controversial and theological writings, and he devoted his three best works to the subject of ethics alone. In his *Fruits of Solitude,* he deals with nearly one hundred virtues and their opposites, and covers nearly all of the details of private and public living. The mere catalogue of these virtues gives a clear insight into Penn's own character; and his treatment of many of them shows him to have been a seer and prophet of the highest standard of ethics in our twentieth century and beyond. For example, on the possession and use of Wealth: 'Where Charity keeps pace with Gain, Industry is blessed.— Thou art but a Steward, and another is thy Owner, Master and Judge.— Of all we call ours, we are most accountable to God and the Publick for our Estates.— If all Men were so far Tenants to the Publick that the Superfluities of Gain and Expence were applied to the Exigences thereof, it would put an End to Taxes, leave never a Beggar, and make the greatest Bank for National Trade in Europe.'

On the other hand, living a century before the Industrial Revolution and the rise of large cities, Penn naturally preferred life in the country, which is 'both the Philosopher's Garden and his Library,— his Food as well as Study, and gives him Life as well as Learning.' England then, he believed, had 'Land enough to Cultivate and more and better Manufactures [hand-made goods] to be Made.' The industrial problem, which had not then really arisen, he would have solved (in the spirit of John Woolman, two generations later) by benevolent masters and by servants who are 'diligent, careful, trusty,' thereby serving both God and master and receiving 'double Wages for Work, to wit, Here and Hereafter.'

No Cross, No Crown, as has been seen, is an eloquent and learned advocacy of human virtues; and the *Essay on the — Peace of Europe*

---

400 *A Defence of . . . Gospel-Truths*: 'The resurrection of the dead is out of all dispute with us; but with what body, will, I believe, be one [in dispute] till the dead rise. Here it is we are cautious, and tread softly.'

an epoch-making proposal for the prevention of humanity's worst vice (War, 'the sum of all evils') by the establishment of the most far-reaching of human institutions (a government of the nations by the nations, for the nations).

Posterity was central in Penn's thinking : [401] 'If we would amend the World, we should mend Our selves, and teach our Children to be, not what we are, but what they should be.— We are in this also true Turners of the World upside down : for Money is first and Virtue last and least in our care : not *How* we leave our Children, but *What* we leave them.' The most modern of educators find much of their philosophy and practice in Penn's theory of education : 'Few People know themselves; No, not their own Bodies, the Houses of their Minds, the most curious Structure of the World, a living, walking Tabernacle : Nor the World of which it is made, and out of which it is fed.— We are in Pain to make our Youth Scholars, but not Men ! To talk, rather than to know, which is true Canting. The first Thing obvious to Children is what is sensible ; and that we make no Part of their Rudiments. We press their Memory too soon, and puzzle, strain and load them with Words and Rules ; to know Grammer and Rhetorick, and a strange Tongue or two, that it is ten to one may never be useful to them ; Leaving their natural Genius to Mechanical and Physical, or natural Knowledge uncultivated and neglected ; which would be of exceeding Use and Pleasure to them through the whole Course of their Life. To be sure, Languages are not to be despised or neglected. But Things are still to be preferred.'

Underlying Penn's theory of education, was of course his everpresent sense of religion : 'The Invisible Things of God are brought to Light by the Things that are seen.— The World is certainly a great and stately volume of Natural Things, and may be not improperly stiled the Hieroglyphicks of a better.— An eternal Wisdom, Power, Majesty and Goodness, very conspicuous to us thro' those sensible and passing Forms : The World wearing the Mark of its Maker, whose Stamp is every where visible, and the Characters very legible to the Children of Wisdom.'

Penn was eager that his own children should be 'Children of Wisdom,' and he devoted two writings especially to them. These were written on the eve of his two departures for America in 1682 and 1699, and were printed under the titles, respectively, of *A Letter to my*

---

401 *Fruits of Solitude.*

A Topical Biography

Wife and Children and *Fruits of a Father's Love*.[402] Lord Jeffrey, the renowned editor of the *Edinburgh Review,* whose caustic criticism doomed many a book to oblivion, said of Penn's letter of 1682 :[403] 'There is something, we think, very touching and venerable in the affectionateness of its whole strain, and the patriarchal simplicity in which it is conceived, while the language appears to us to be one of the most beautiful specimens of that soft and mellow English, which, with all its cumbrous volume, has, to our ear, a far richer and more pathetic sweetness than the epigrams and apothegms of modern times.'

Aside from the high literary quality of these two letters, they are replete with wise and affectionate admonitions as to the practice of the many virtues he listed in his *Fruits of Solitude* and more besides : and as a solid foundation for these—the most precious treasure a father can bequeath or children inherit—he stressed the value of the religion based on the Inner Light.

On Education, he said : 'Learn, and teach your children, fair writing and the most useful parts of mathematics, and some business when young, whatever else they are taught.— Have but few books, but let them be well chosen and well read, whether of religious or civil subjects.— Measure both religion and learning by practice.— Reading many books is but taking off the mind too much from meditation. Reading yourselves and nature, in the dealings and conduct of men, is the truest human wisdom.'

Taken altogether, Penn's ethical writings raise him to the first rank of moral philosophers, and they made him a leader of Quaker thought and an inspirer of Quaker conduct during several generations. They have been rivalled in Quaker literature only by the *Journal* of George Fox and the *Apology* of Robert Barclay ; and even these great books must yield to them the palm in influencing human thought and conduct outside of Quaker circles.

402 The latter was not printed until 1726, eight years after Penn's death, and its title was probably given it by Sir John Rodes of Balber (Barlborough) Hall, Derbyshire, who edited it.
403 Jeffrey's review of Clarkson's *Life of Penn,* the *Edinburgh Review,* July, 1813 ; quoted by Janney, 1852, p. 187.

QUAKER LEADER AND ORGANIZER

It is doubtless true that William Penn was not a religious genius in the same sense and to an equal degree as were Martin Luther, John Wesley, or George Fox. But evidences of real genius are found in his early 'call,' such as the boy Samuel received; in his firm conviction that God gave him palpable assurance of direct communion with Him; in his ability to sacrifice and endure much in pursuance of the divine commission; in his idealistic vision and practical realization of a new religious society; and in his success in making a portion of the 'Kingdom of Heaven' come on earth.

Like Willem Sewel, the Quaker historian of Amsterdam, Penn became an active member of the Society of Friends nearly a score of years after that society was founded by George Fox and Penn's older contemporaries. Hence, his part in the work of organization, at least in the British Isles, was that of strengthening and development, rather than that of creation.

In the Netherlands, however, Penn was a vital factor in organizing the Society there and in Western Germany. He took a prominent part, with Fox, Barclay, Keith, and others at Amsterdam in the famous meetings of 1677, in establishing the monthly, quarterly, and yearly meetings which bound the Quakers on the Continent into corporate unity.[404] In Pennsylvania, Delaware and New Jersey, also, his influence and co-operation were far-reaching in the organization of the Society and in defending it against schism. This influence was exerted both by personal visits and by frequent open letters or Epistles to the Friends and their meetings in Europe and America.

In England, too, his pen and voice were potent in defending youthful Quakerism against not only the attacks of its opponents from the outside, but also the undermining of it from within. His voluminous controversies with outsiders have been recounted above; his participation in the difficulties with inside disturbers of the peace of the Society began as early as 1673 and continued for a score of years.

The first serious schism in the Society was due to a radical carrying out of Quaker informality in worship by one of the pioneer Friends named John Perrot. Accompanied by John Love (or Luff), Perrot went in 1660 to Italy with the purpose of converting the Pope to

---

404 Cf. Monographs Numbers One, Two, and Six.

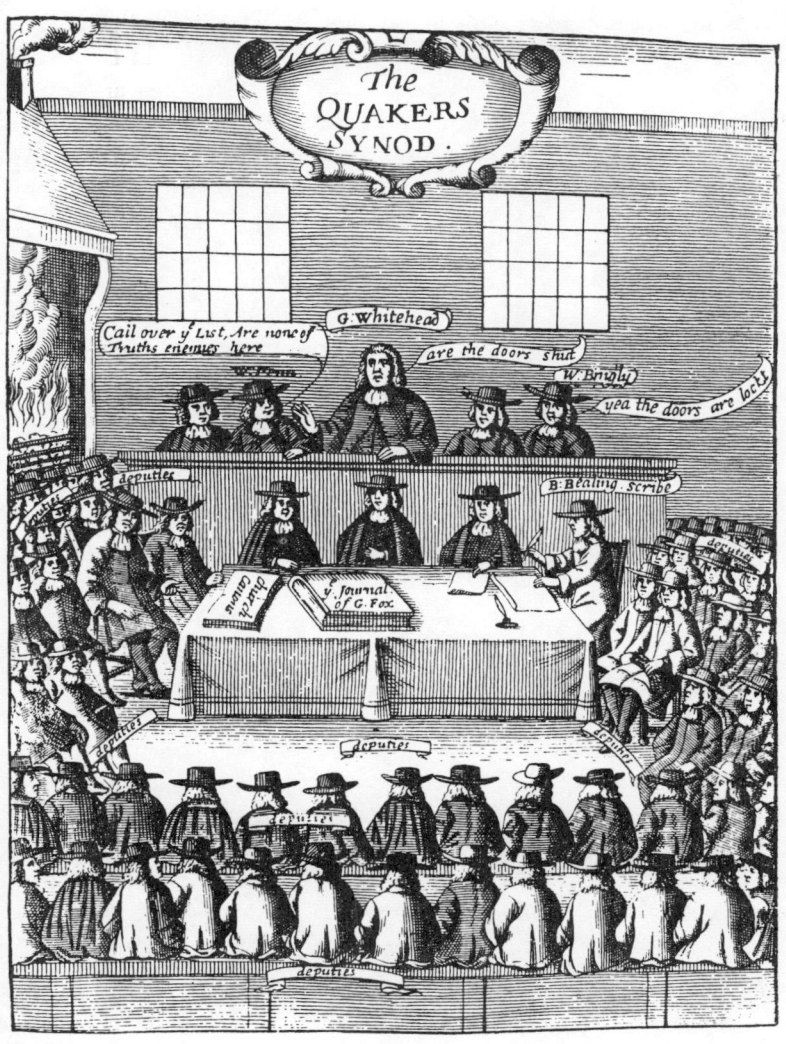

Quakerism. Having delivered their message to the Doge of Venice, they preached in the streets of Rome, where Love met with a speedy death in the prison of the Inquisition (from a hunger-fast, as the officials said, or from informal 'execution'), while Perrot was placed for a time in a lunatic asylum. Released by English official influence, Perrot returned to England, where he advanced the theory that 'hat worship'—taking off the hat in time of public prayer, unless specially 'moved' to do so [405]—was contrary to Quaker simplicity and the supremacy of the Inner Light. Many members of the Society adopted this theory and a serious split resulted from what seems like a triviality, but which was regarded as having to do with individual liberty to follow the Light.[406] The leaders of the Society had great difficulty, by means of public meetings and private conferences during a half-dozen years, in putting an end to this heresy and schism. Perrot, at length greatly outnumbered, was expelled from the Society, became a public official, administered the oaths which he had formerly denounced, abjured Quakerism, and published some violent pamphlets against the régime and morals of the Quaker leaders. Penn replied to two of these (*The Spirit of the Hat, or the Government of the Quakers* and *Tyranny and Hypocrisy Detected*) with two very caustic pamphlets entitled *The Spirit of Alexander the Coppersmith lately Revived and now Justly Rebuked* and *Judas and the Jews Combined against Christ and his Followers*. Alexander the Coppersmith, who had done Paul 'much evil' and 'greatly withstood' the apostles' words, had been delivered by Paul 'Unto Satan that he might be taught not to blaspheme;' but when Perrot did blaspheme again in his second pamphlet, Penn likened him unto Judas Iscariot, and dismissed him accordingly. Perrot was not convinced of the error of his ways, but continued to claim that he was a re-incarnation of Saint John and King Solomon, and countenanced among his followers an 'informal' marriage and the public tearing up and burning of copies of the Bible; while he himself displayed upon advertising-posts the title-pages of his defamatory pamphlets 'with torches to light them and a guard by night.'

The obvious objection to keeping on the hat in time of public prayer

---

405 Cf. the custom of the Labadist settlers in Maryland at meal-time (Monograph Number Two, p. 18).
406 Sewel (I, 374) illustrates the magnifying of the Perrot affair by his remark : 'As one error proceeds from another, so he made another extravagant step, and let his beard grow!'

was that it nullified the Quaker argument that 'hat honour' should be granted to God alone ; but the chief significance of the Perrot episode in Quaker history lies in the fact that Penn and other leaders advanced a corporate responsibility and authority as a check upon or test of the independent initiative of the individual's conscience, illumined though it claimed to be by the Inner Light.[407]

The heresy of 'Hat Worship' flared up again and again during the next half-dozen years. One of Perrot's sympathizers, Mary Pennyman, chided Penn for his severity in *Judas and the Jews Combined;* her husband, John Pennyman, forsook the Society on the same account ; William Rogers, a Quaker merchant of Bristol, attacked the Quaker system as expounded in Robert Barclay's *Anarchy of the Ranters.* To each of these, Penn wrote letters, or had public discussions with them. Another recalcitrant Quaker, named Matthew Hide, who had rebelled against the leaders' application in worship of the Inner Light and had disturbed their sermons and prayers for a score of years, died full of repentance for having done so, and Penn wrote a pamphlet, *Saul smitten to the Ground,* (1675), giving the details of his death-bed repentance, and using the opportunity to appeal to all dissidents to return to the corporate unity and harmony consistent with the 'Children of the Light.'

Another revolt against the alleged interference of church discipline with the untrammeled injunctions of the Light Within was led by John Wilkinson and John Story, in 1681. Penn aided in the moderation of this secession by writing a pamphlet against it, entitled *A Brief Examination of Spiritual Liberty* (1681), couched in dialogue form and arguing that genuine liberty is consistent with a church discipline which is itself guided by the Light Within. A dozen years later, he was still harping on the same theme in a pamphlet entitled *Just Measures, being an Epistle of Peace and Love to such Professors of Truth as are under any Dissatisfaction about the present Order practised in the Church of Christ* (1692). The chief emphasis in this was the vindication of the equality of women in the Society of Friends and the need of women having regular meetings of their own for participation

---

407 Fox utilized the opportunity by furthering the organization of local monthly and quarterly meetings, 'for the better ordering of the affairs of the church, in taking care of the poor, and for exercising true gospel discipline in dealing with any that might walk disorderly under our name, and to see that such as marry amongst us act fairly and clearly in that respect' (Thomas Ellwood's *Journal*).

in the regulation of marriages and the oversight of women members of the Society.

One of the most persistent disturbers of Quaker peace was Francis Bugg, who became a Friend in the early years of the Society, and suffered imprisonment for its sake. After twenty-five years in good standing, he began a forty years' tirade against the practices of the Quakers and the leaders who had established them. He continued his attacks as an octogenarian, fourteen years after Penn was incapacitated by paralysis; but only one of Bugg's seventy-nine pamphlets, Penn deemed it worth while to answer. This was entitled an *Address to the Parliament against the Quakers;* and as this was an attempt to bring about the repeal of toleration for the Quakers, ten years after the Toleration Act had conceded it, Penn wrote in reply *A Just Censure* (1699), which sharply denounced, not only Bugg, but also his clerical supporters for their effort to restore intolerance and persecution.

One of the misfortunes which occurred in the early history of Pennsylvania was the schism caused by George Keith, who repudiated the chief tenets of Quakerism which he had so stoutly and eloquently maintained for a quarter-century. Through Penn's influence, he went first to New Jersey as surveyor-general of the province, and then to Philadelphia as the head-master of the Friends' school founded there in 1689. Two years later, he transferred his energies to an attempt to institute a thorough-going reformation of Quaker principles, especially their belief as to the manhood and divinity of Christ, and various Quaker practices, including especially the holding of public office. Setting up a meeting of his own, he drew off not a few members, and attacked with increasingly virulent terms the motives and morals of the leaders. The Philadelphia Friends finally 'disowned' him; and when he carried his case to England, in 1693, two years after the death of George Fox, and while Penn was under restraint, the English Quaker leaders sided with the Pennsylvania Friends' verdict against him, and he was disowned by the London meeting. He then singled out Penn, and attacked his theology in a tract entitled *The Deism of William Penn . . . Plainly Open.* Quoting Penn's own words in *The Christian Quaker,* he tried to prove its author no Christian, and himself gathered a group of 'Christian Quakers' in a London meeting-house. In reply to this, Penn wrote a pamphlet entitled *More Work for George Keith* (1696), which set Keith the task of acknowledging or repudiating his own words in which he had ardently defended Quakerism in the Hicks controversy of twenty years before.

Giving up the attempt to reform Quakerism, Keith went over to the Anglican Church, became one of its agents in America for the 'Propagation of the Gospel,' tried again to break up the Society of Friends in Philadelphia, and returned to England to die as rector of Edburton in Sussex, two years before the death of Penn. This renunciation of all kinds of Quakerism was regarded as a betrayal for ambition's sake by his adherents in Philadelphia and England; most of these returned to the Quaker fold, and the ominous schism was finally healed.[408] George Keith, despite the violence of his disposition, ranked in ability of scholarly and eloquent exposition almost with Penn and Barclay; and in Pennsylvania especially, he was head and shoulders above both the rank and file and the leaders of Quakerism. Hence his attack on Quaker doctrines and Quaker control of government in America imperilled Penn's Holy Experiment in both church and state. His defeat was therefore a noteworthy triumph for Penn.

But during these same years, Penn himself became suspect with the so-called 'Foxite' wing of English Quakerism. The two outstanding leaders had themselves lived, down to the time of Fox's death, in complete accord, although they had worked in different spheres and had had relatively little personal co-operation. But immediately after Fox died, Penn was practically interned under the suspicion of treason to King William, and Fox's two step-sons-in-law, William Meade and Thomas Lower, seized the opportunity of preventing him from receiving Fox's mantle as leader of the Society. During the three years of Penn's eclipse, these two sons-in-law of Margaret Fox had considerable success in alienating English Friends from their natural leader. Margaret herself may have been fearful of the danger lest her husband's fame as Founder of the Society of Friends be eclipsed by that of the Founder of Pennsylvania, especially since Fox had cherished the dream which Penn had realized. Meade had been eclipsed by Penn in their famous trial and in Penn's account of it, when they had been

---

408 Penn had written (as early as 1692) a letter to his old friend Robert Turner, an adherent of Keith, urging him to heal the breach in Philadelphia Quakerism, and explaining in very tentative fashion his view of Christ's manhood. The original of this letter is in possession of the American Philosophical Society; it was published in Janney's *Life of Penn*, 1852, pp. 364-66. Preceding his *More Work for George Keith*, he wrote also a treatise *On Primitive Christianity*, in which he argued that the faith and practices of the Friends were a revival of those of the first Christians, and especially that the doctrine of the Inner Light was that of Jesus and the Apostles.

fellow-prisoners in 1670 and had been instrumental in establishing the rights of juries.⁴⁰⁹ Penn, too, had taken the lead and very naturally overshadowed Meade, when they went together to the Duke of York's palace in 1673 to appeal for Fox's release from Worcester Castle.⁴¹⁰

There were other, less personal, reasons why Penn was not *persona gratissima* among a section of his Quaker contemporaries. His social rank; his wealth; his conspicuous scholarship; his intimacy and influence with royalty; his sympathy with the Stuart kings' policy of toleration; his political campaign for toleration in England, and his political power in Pennsylvania; the stress which he laid on organization and 'good order' among Friends and in public life; his far-reaching fame or notoriety with the populace; his freedom from the extravagances of speech and conduct which marked some early converts, even Fox himself; his success in drawing off many Quakers from the Old World to the New; perhaps even his prosperous and imposing personal appearance and manner of living, all combined to make some of the humble and obscure members of a sect noted for its professed love of modesty and meekness uncertain as to the genuineness and stability of his Quakerism. Although he proved by his sermons, writings, and conduct in meetings that he was an enthusiastic mystic, still he was so much of a practical man of affairs and action that they could not quite reconcile the combination of the two characteristics. A Quaker statesman, and still more a Quaker courtier, appeared to them to be a contradiction in terms and in the facts of real life.

From the time of Penn's first convincement, the straitest sect of the Quakers looked askance upon this *rara avis* who had so strangely come among them.⁴¹¹ Soon afterwards, when he and a companion went to preach at a Friends' meeting in England, 'as they rod a long ye Road Wm. thought his two taild wigg which he had not yet left off, was burdensom to him took of his hatt turned his wigg of his head behind him not looking back to see what became of it he had some hair tho' but short.'⁴¹² Penn's wig continued to be regarded by his strictest fellow-members as contrary to Quaker simplicity; and as late as 1677, George Fox came to his defence in this particular by writing a letter

409 *Infra*, pp. 185-91.
410 *Supra*, p. 111; *infra*, p. 243 f.
411 *Supra*, p. 109.
412 'The Harvey MS.,' 1729 (*Journal* of the Friends' Historical Society, 1935, p. 23); cf. *infra*, p. 307.

to his critics that it was only 'a very short civil thing' and necessary because he had so little hair of his own.

After Fox's death, and at the end of his own internment in 1693, he attended the Friends' meeting at the Bull and Mouth in London, and as usual preached a sermon. 'His appearing first to preach in a public meeting' was condemned by Thomas Lower in a letter to his mother-in-law, Margaret Fox, as looking 'too triumphant and high.' Penn wrote a splendid preface for Fox's *Journal* for its publication in 1694; but Meade and Lower would not permit it to be published with the *Journal,* or even to listen to it being read in the official Morning Meeting which nevertheless read and approved it. Although his leadership against George Keith was accepted in 1695, his unpopularity with William III and Mary II militated against him; and the restoration of the royal favour under Anne came too late to mitigate his unpopularity with the Quakers in the critical decade of the 1690's; for unlike these three sovereigns, Penn's royal supporters had been not Protestant protectors, but suspected or confessed and detested Catholic persecutors.

In 1698, when Penn was in Ireland, accompanied by Thomas Story and John Everott, they received letters, telling them of an attack upon Penn's character, which was made, Story says, 'by a shameless and implacable party, being moved by envy at the honour and dignity which the Most High had pleased to confer on him.' The three travelling ministers replied to this attack, indirectly but effectively, by a joint letter to London Yearly Meeting itself.[413]

This attack came from Margaret Fox's sons-in-law, as is hinted in a letter from a London Friend to Sir John Rodes, as follows: 'Our ancient Friend M. Fox is here about town. I wish she had stayed in Lancashire or returned back soon after she came. I fear by reason of her age she will be led by her son William [Meade] into something or other which may not be of the best consequence to Truth nor the quiet of the Church, nor her own honour. This by the by to thee.' A few months later, Margaret's daughter wrote to her from London as follows: 'William Penn is in town and great crowding after him. I believe there is little alteration in him or others but much as they were when you was here.' Soon afterwards, she wrote to her mother again: 'We hope if W P be brought to condemn that which he hath been so far wrong in (to the hurt of many), though but in part, that things will grow better among Friends and Truth

413 Story's *Life,* 1747, p. 134; Penn's *Works,* 1726, Vol. I, p. 100.

come up in its ancient purity over the false wrong spirit which hath so much prevailed to its dishonour and hurt, which the truly honest will be right glad of.'[414]

But this opposition to Penn was soon forgotten or overlooked, and when he left England on a second visit to Pennsylvania, the 'Second-Day's Meeting of Ministering Friends' in London, the 'Men's Meeting of Friends in the City of Bristol,' and the Monthly Meeting at Horsham, of which he was a member, wrote to the Philadelphia Friends letters replete with eulogy and affection.[415]

But Penn's sincerity and greatness triumphed with the great majority of his fellow-Quakers, who recognized and gratefully admitted the services of varied kinds which he had conferred upon them and their Society. His memory has been venerated and cherished to this day as one of the two foremost leaders in the history of Quakerism; and it is still recognized how admirably the devotion, abilities and achievements of Fox and Penn supplemented each other in the early days of the Society and how enduring and stimulating their influence has been upon succeeding generations.

IMPRISONMENTS

PART of Penn's hold upon the affection and loyalty of his fellow-Quakers was due to the sufferings he endured in behalf of their common religion, and especially to the imprisonments inflicted upon him for it. These numbered only six, including his 'retirement' for political reasons in 1693, and his imprisonment for debt in 1708 in the Fleet. They were neither so numerous and prolonged, nor so severe, as those which Fox and others of the earlier pioneers had to suffer. But the social rank and its advantages which Penn renounced dramatized his prison experiences.

Soon after his 'convincement' by Thomas Loe's sermon in Cork, in September, 1667, he had his first taste of a British gaol. The 'Harvey Manuscript' records the story of his arrest.[416] 'When they was brought before ye Magistrate,' this manuscript reads, 'he knowing W. P. told him he did not think him a Quaker so would not send him to Goal

---

[414] *A Quaker Post Bag*, p. 134, and the Spence MSS. III (quoted by Crosfield, *Margaret Fox*, pp. 196, 230 f.
[415] Minutes of the Philadelphia Monthly Meeting, 14th of 5th month, 1699.
[416] *Supra*, p. 33 f.

but Wm told him Whether he thought him so or not; he was one and if he sent his friends to Prison he was willing to go wth them then ye Magistrate said he should Go with 'em (As he went to prison he gave his sword to his man & never wore one after) but writes a letter to ye Governer that he had commit'd W. P. prisoner among ye Quakers the Governer sent order that he should be released also another to his Father wch acquaint'd him of his son's being a Quaker wch occation'd him to send order to his son to come to him in England wch order he obeyed and landed at Bristoll where he staid some meetings to strenghen himself know[ing] his Father would not be very pleasant upon him.'

Penn's argument before the mayor naturally repudiated for the Quakers the charge that they were 'Fifth Monarchist' rebels, against whom the Act of 1660 under which they were arrested was levelled; but, in Ireland especially, the fear of Oliver Cromwell and his terrible adherents coming disguised as Quakers was still potent, and even the garb of a cavalier and the son of a loyal Stuart admiral could not wholly reassure the mayor. Penn's letter to Orrery is of peculiar interest because it marks the beginning of his struggle for religious toleration which was to be crowned with success a score of years later.[417]

Penn's imprisonment in the gaol at Cork was a very brief one, and the 'martyr's palm' which was thereby placed in his hand was not very hardly earned, nor was it at all appreciated by his incensed father who summoned him home forthwith. It played its part, however, in confirming him in that 'faith which overcomes the world,' of which he had lately heard from Thomas Loe, and which enabled him to withstand in favour of adherence to his new religion both the temptations of 'the world' and his father's endeavours to keep him in it. Within a year after his return from Ireland, he was sent to a London prison.

This was due directly, not to his publication of an attack on the Trinity in his *Sandy Foundation Shaken* (which was interpreted as a denial of the divinity of Christ), but to his publication of it without having procured the Bishop of London's license; and even this was used as an excuse by the Secretary of State, Lord Arlington, who was engaged at the time in a personal quarrel with Admiral Penn and saw a chance to strike at the father through the son. The latter admitted to Arlington his, the author's, share of the illegality, and begged the re-

417 *Infra*, p. 202.

lease of the printer; but Arlington replied by sending Penn to the Tower. This famous old prison had been reserved for political prisoners who were regarded as of grave menace to the king or state; hence, its governor, Sir John Robinson, who was also fearful of the Admiral's power, as well as of acting without the king's direct authority, refused to accept the culprit without the royal warrant which was necessary for imprisoning the king's enemies in the king's prison. To procure the warrant, Arlington first tried to frighten Penn into confessing that he had dropped a treasonable paper in Arlington's house; but when Penn repudiated this, the king was persuaded to issue a warrant on the charge of blasphemy. Charles is said to have agreed to this on Arlington's argument that a dose of imprisonment would soon cause Penn to recant, and that then he could be pardoned, and perhaps rescued from his impending Quakerism.[418]

Penn believed that the Bishop of London was responsible for his imprisonment; and when he was told that the bishop had said he must either recant or die a prisoner, he sent him word, through his father: 'My prison shall be my grave before I will budge a jot; for I owe my conscience to no mortal man.' He wrote also to Arlington an argument in defence of toleration; but as this was of no avail, the Admiral procured the good offices of the Duke of York, who induced the king, or the bishop, to send one of the royal chaplains, Edward Stillingfleet, to mediate with the prisoner. The learning and sweet reasonableness of the mediator succeeded in persuading Penn to write another pamphlet (*Innocency with her Open Face*), 'explaining' his former one largely in the spirit of Stillingfleet's own recent books on *Contra Crellius* and *Origines Sacrae, or Rational Account of the Christian Faith,* which have made their author famous. This 'explanation' was accepted by the authorities in lieu of, or as equivalent to, a recantation, and Penn was released from the Tower. The close confinement of eight or nine months had meant considerable suffering in a small room up under the roof during a hot summer, with but little fuel

---

418 Jenkins, *Family of William Penn,* 1899, pp. 255-257, quoting a paper by John Bruce, treasurer of the London Society of Antiquaries, read March 17, 1853, and published in *Archaeologia,* Vol. XXXV, pp. 72-90. Vulliamy, 1934, pp. 62-63, acquits Arlington and blames the Bishop of London, but cf. Dixon, 1902, pp. 66-88, and Brailsford, 1930, pp. 254-262, 268-275. Willem Sewel even hints that Penn's father might have desired his son to become a prisoner: 'Some thought,' he says (Vol. II, p. 173), 'it was not without his father's being acquainted with it, perhaps to prevent a worse treatment [perhaps transportation, which was actually rumoured on his release].'

during an exceptionally cold winter, constantly watched over by a keeper, forbidden to receive letters and food from outside, eating prison fare, and requiring special permission before he could receive visits from family or friends.[419]

There are several entries in the Calendar of State Papers, 1668-9 (pp. 98, 116 and 146) relating to Penn's imprisonment. Among these are warrants from Arlington to 'John Warburton Messenger to take W. Pen into his Custody & Convey him to ye Tower', and to 'S^r Jo. Robinson to receiue him & keep him close prisoner till further Order for composing ye book called The Sandy Foundation Shaken' (Dec. 12, 1668). There is a permit for 'Francis Cooke to see Wm Penn his M^r close Prison^r in ye Tower & to speake with him in ye presence of a Keeper' (Dec. 24, 1668) ; also a permit to 'Dr Stillingfleet to see Penne : Itt is his Maties Pleasure That you permitt & suffer Dr Edward Stillingfleete to haue accesse from time to time to William Penne now Prison^r und^r y^r Custody wth in y^t His Maties Tower of London, & to conferre with him in ord^r to y^e conuinceing him if it may be of his blasphemous & Hereticall Opinions' (Jan. 4 $6\frac{8}{9}$). Penn's note and long letter to Arlington, dated 'Tower of London y^e 19th off y^e month Cll^d jun 1669', are also in the Calendar of State Papers for 1668-9, p. 342.

One evidence of the impression made by Penn's arrest comes from the same papers (p. 102), namely a report to Secretary Williamson from one of his agents at 'Deale Decemb^r 15 1668', which reads : 'News also to some quakers here is that their Sain^t Penn is taken. hee is divelishly cryed vp amongest that pervers sullen ffaction'.

During his imprisonment he was permitted — apparently with a view to a recantation — to use his pen ; and from it came his great work, *No Cross, No Crown*. In the preface which he wrote for the second edition of this book, fourteen years later, he says : 'It [the Cross] is a path God in His everlasting kindness guided my feet into, in the flower of my youth, when about two-and-twenty years of age. There he took me by the hand and led me out of the pleasures, vanities and hopes of the world.' It was, thus, not 'the crown of martyrdom,' but rather of righteousness that Penn was seeking. As a result of his rigorous confinement in the Tower, and the danger of death and reality of physical suffering which it betokened, he strengthened his

---

[419] Even barbers were debarred from attending him, a circumstance to which is ascribed his permanent loss of hair !

LONDON TOWER LIBERTIES

leadership among the Quakers, and was enabled to speak with the authority of personal experience when he entered upon his great work for toleration.

Penn's next imprisonment led to one of the most famous trials and one of the most important triumphs for individual liberty in the constitutional history of England. This time, he was a sufferer and champion, not in behalf of Quakerism alone, nor even in behalf of religious toleration alone, but chiefly in behalf of 'the rights of Englishmen.' Like the patriots of the American Revolution, he subordinated particular claims to the liberty of the public in general and rested his case upon the rights which had been conferred upon English freemen by Magna Carta and the other great constitutional bulwarks of freedom. It was this significance of Penn which was in the mind of the Marquis of Lafayette when, at a public dinner in Philadelphia a century and a half later, he offered the toast : 'The memories of Penn and Franklin — the one never greater than when arraigned before an English jury, or the other than before a British Parliament.'

The story reads like a drama in three acts and seven scenes. In two of the acts, Penn and Meade played the leading parts; in the third, Penn and the jury. The first act opens with the stage-setting of Grace-church Street Friends' meeting-house, London, before which stands a company of soldiers barring entrance against all and sundry. A large crowd of Quakers and curious Londoners have gathered outside, 'as close to the meeting-house as they could get.' Penn arrives to 'attend meeting,' accompanied by another Friend, William Meade, a former Captain and Colonel in Cromwell's army, now a linen-draper, and soon to marry one of Margaret Fell Fox's daughters. Penn begins to preach to the people in the street, and is at once arrested with Meade — on a warrant signed beforehand by the Lord Mayor — and is carried off to 'the sign of the Black Dog,' a sponging-house in Newgate Market.

Scene two occurs the same evening when Penn is taken before the mayor, Sir Samuel Starling, once a supporter of Cromwell and a notorious persecutor of royalists, now an eager champion of the Stuart tyranny. Penn describes this scene in a letter the next day to his father.[420] 'He proceeded against me according to the ancient law ; he told me I should have my hat pulled off, for all I was Admiral Penn's son.— He bade his clerk write me for Bridewell, and there would see

---

420 *The Friend*, Philadelphia, Vol. VI (1833), p. 170.

me whipt himself, for all I was Penn's son, that starved seamen.—I told him I could very well hear his severe expressions to me concerning myself, but was sorry to hear him speak those abuses of my father, that was not present.' This rebuke of the mayor appeared to please the hundred auditors, for, Penn says, 'at this the assembly seemed to murmur.'

The mayor thereupon sends the prisoners back to jail, where they are kept a fortnight awaiting trial. 'The Black Dog' is described as 'the nastiest place in the most loathsome gaol in England;' and Penn declared it so 'noisome and stinking that the Lord Mayor would think it an unfit stye for his swine.'

Act II includes the trial of the prisoners, which occurred in the Old Bailey, September 1, 3, 4, and 5, 1670, Penn being at that time about twenty-six years old — just the age of John Hampden when he entered upon his championship of popular rights against the earlier Stuart tyranny.[421] So deeply was he impressed with the historic significance of the trial that just after it was finished he wrote a detailed account of it, with the questions and answers duly (and apparently stenographically) set forth. This pamphlet of eighteen pages was appropriately entitled *The People's Ancient and Just Liberties Asserted, in the Trial of William Penn and William Meade;* and there was published with it an 'Appendix' of twenty-seven pages containing a careful statement of the historic precedents from Magna Carta in 1215 down to 1667, with authoritative interpretations of the law, which Penn would have presented to the court in defence of the accused had they not been 'violently over-ruled and stopped.'

The first scene of this act begins with the appearance of the prisoners before the court, which included twelve judges and twelve jurors. The judges comprised Sir Samuel Starling, the Lord Mayor; John Howell, the Recorder; five aldermen, including Sir John Robinson, the Lord Lieutenant of the Tower; and three sheriffs. The jury of London citizens had upon it Edward Bushel, a dissenter who had already given the court trouble, and who became, next to Penn, the hero of the drama. On the first morning, the jurors were sworn to 'well and truly try . . . according to your evidence'; and the clerk read

---

[421] An interesting parallel between the characters of the youthful Penn and Hampden is revealed in Lord Clarendon's sketch of Hampden, of whom he says : 'On a sudden, from a life of great pleasure and license, he retired to extraordinary sobriety and strictness;' but even after his change, 'he preserved his natural cheerfulness and vivacity and, above all, a flowing courtesy to all men.'

the indictment. This charged that Penn and Meade and 'divers other persons to the jurors unknown, to the number of three hundred, . . . with force and arms, etc. . . . unlawfully and tumultuously did assemble and congregate themselves together, to the disturbance of the peace of the said lord and king ;' and that Penn, by previous agreement and abetment of Meade, 'then and there did preach and speak' to 'a great concourse and tumult of people' in contempt of the king and his law, 'to the great terror and disturbance of many of his liege people and subjects, to the ill example of all others in the like case offenders, . . . ' It was fortunate that the charge was not an infraction of the Conventicle Act, which could have been disposed of by the magistrates themselves, but that the charge required a trial by jury.

Summoned to plead to this indictment, Penn asked for a written copy of it, and when this was refused he pleaded not guilty. The court then adjourned until the afternoon ; but the prisoners were then 'set aside' for five hours while the court proceeded with other business, the 'trial of felons and murderers.'

That night, the next day and the following night, the prisoners spend in their filthy place of detention. The next morning the Quaker prisoners are brought back and they appear wearing their hats. The officers snatch these off, but are rebuked for doing so by the recorder, and bidden to put them on again ; a fine of forty marks is then imposed on each prisoner for contempt of court — for wearing their hats ! Witnesses then called testify that they heard Penn speaking, but because of the noise could not hear what he said. Meade appealed to the jury to note that these witnesses nevertheless testified that they heard Penn *preach ;* but Penn frankly declared that no power on earth could prevent him from preaching, praying, and worshipping God. On being told that he was there, not for worshipping God, but for breaking the law, Penn demanded to know what law he had broken, and on being told the Common Law he demanded that it should be cited. In the face of this large order, the judges resorted to bullying, and the recorder finally said : 'The question is, Whether you are guilty of the indictment ;' to which, Penn replied : 'The question is not whether I am guilty of the indictment, but whether the indictment is legal ;' and he cited Coke to show that 'common law is common right, and common right is the Great Charter privileges confirmed in successive reigns.' Denounced by the court as an impudent fellow, Penn contended that he was merely striving against their 'resolution to sacrifice the privileges of Englishmen' to their sinister and arbitrary designs. Summarily ordered to be taken to the bale-dock, he climbed to the top of it and shouted to the jury ('with a very raised voice' over the noise in the court-room) : 'I plead for the fundamental laws of England. . . . If these ancient fundamental laws . . . must not be indispensably maintained and observed . . . our liberties are openly to be invaded, our wives to be ravished, our children slaved, our families ruined, and our estates led away in triumph by every sturdy beggar and malicious informer.'

Meade also being sent to the bale-dock, after having repeated Penn's objections, the recorder charged the jury to *bring in a verdict of guilty;* whereupon Penn, 'with a very raised voice (the bale-dock being a considerable distance from the bench)' appealed to the jury and 'this great assembly' against the illegality of charging the jury in the prisoners' absence. The recorder replied that they were 'present' and had heard, and ordered the attendants to 'pull that fellow down' and take them away to 'the hole.'

After an hour and a half of deliberation, eight of the jurymen agreed, but four led by Bushel dissented ; these were sent for and severely denounced, the mayor threatening to 'put a mark' upon Bushel. Retiring to their room, the jury came to a unanimous verdict that Penn was 'guilty of speaking in Gracious-street.' They refused to add 'in an unlawful assembly,' and the judges again bullied and threatened them in vain. Sent back to their room, they reappeared with the verdict (which was now stated in writing, with all their signatures attached) that Penn was guilty, and Meade not guilty, 'of speaking or preaching to an assembly met together in Gracious-street.' This was resented by the judges 'at so high a rate that they exceeded the bounds of all reason and civility,' and they ordered the jury to be 'locked up, without meat, drink, fire and tobacco.' Penn again called out from the bale-dock demanding that the right of the jury to a free verdict be respected, that the clerk record the verdict as handed in, and that the jury remember 'You are Englishmen, mind your privilege, give not away your right :' to which Bushel, who had been the special target again of the judges' wrath, replied : 'Nor will we ever do it.' The jury declared that they had already agreed to a verdict ; and one of them asked to be dismissed on account of illness ; but they were locked up for the night, without any sanitary facilities.

At seven o'clock the next (Sunday) morning, the same scene was

A Topical Biography 189

enacted; again abuse, the threat of starvation for the jury, and of having Bushel's throat cut. A fresh charge to bring in a verdict of guilty was followed by a brief retirement, and again the same verdict and a threat to have Bushel's nose cut. Penn again clamored to have jury rights respected, and the mayor ordered the jailer to 'stop his mouth and bring fetters to stake him to the ground,' while the recorder said: 'Till now I never understood the reason of the policy and prudence of the Spaniards in suffering the Inquisition among them; and certainly it will never be well with us till something like the Spanish Inquisition be in England.' After another period of abuse and the jury's refusal to bring in the verdict demanded by the judges, the jurymen were locked up for another night without any accommodations, and the prisoners sent back to Newgate.

At seven the next morning, the scene was reënacted, this time the jury being polled and answering unanimously 'not guilty, to the great satisfaction of the assembly.'[422] But the recorder imposed a fine of forty marks upon each of them for disobeying the court, with imprisonment until paid.

Penn then demanded to be set at liberty, but was told that he too would be kept in prison until he paid his fine of forty marks for contempt of court. He replied that such a fine, not imposed by the judgment of his peers, 'expressly contradicts the fourteenth and twenty-ninth chapter of the Great Charter of England which says, "No freeman ought to be amerced, but by the oath of good and lawful men of the vicinage."' The recorder's answer to this was, 'Take him away, take him away, take him out of the court.' Penn had the last word, for he called out, as he was led away: 'I can never urge the fundamental laws of England, but you cry, Take him away, take him away. But it is no wonder, since the Spanish Inquisition hath so great a place in the recorder's heart. God Almighty, who is just, will judge you for all these things.'

Thus ended the famous trial of Penn and Meade in the Old Bailey. The prisoners and the jury were sent to Newgate; but the second day thereafter, 'some one' (probably Penn's father) sent the money to pay the prisoners' fines, and they were discharged, Penn to hasten to the death-bed of his father, who had only nine days more to live. The jurymen demanded their discharge every six hours, and were finally

---

422 In a letter to his father, Penn says: 'they were so satisfied that they made a kind of hymn' (*The Friend,* Philadelphia, Vol. VII, 1834, p. 59).

released on a writ of *habeas corpus;* they then sued the mayor and recorder for illegal imprisonment. This suit was tried soon afterwards before the Court of Common Pleas, with twelve judges on the bench, who decided unanimously that juries have a free right of handing in a verdict on their judgment of the facts, and must not be coerced in reaching and giving it. The judges, they conceded, 'may try to open the eyes of the jurors, but not to lead them by the nose.' The heroic Bushel and his eleven loyal associates were accordingly freed in open court.

This third act of the drama was not so thrilling as the first and second; but it was of vast historic importance, for, as Penn described this vindication of jury trial, it was 'the fairest flower that now grows in the garden of the Englishman's liberties.' In the London Sessions House, on the site of the Old Bailey, there has appropriately been set up a tablet to Penn, Meade, Bushel, and Vere (the jury's foreman) commemorating their contribution to the long and illustrious struggle for English liberty.

To Penn and the Quakers of his time and since, the trial illustrated at several stages both their own testimonies and the tactics of their persecutors. A copy of the indictment was denied the accused, and its terms were preposterous; for it accused a notoriously peaceful and weaponless people, intent only on worshipping God, of tumultuously assembling and riotously breaking the peace. It charged Penn and Meade with having 'conspired' to enable Penn to preach a sermon, despite the well-known requirement of Quaker ministers to respond only to 'the moving of the Spirit' within their own individual souls. It made the Quaker rejection of 'hat worship' a trick for imposing a fine upon the prisoners and thus making sure of their imprisonment for refusing to pay it, even before the trial and verdict on the main charge against them. This trick was obvious to them, Meade wittily telling the judges that since they had ordered the hats to be put on after the officers had taken them off, the judges themselves should pay the fine. The trial was unduly prolonged, both before and during the coercion of the jury, and trials of malefactors were put on both to weary and insult the highly respectable accused. A second oath was demanded of Bushel, in the hope that his reluctance to swear might remove him from the jury. Meade stated that, although once a captain in the army, he had renounced arms and violence when he became a Quaker; he proved his learning by quoting legal Latin and the writings

THE
PEOPLES
Ancient and Juſt
LIBERTIES
ASSERTED,
IN THE
TRYAL
OF

William Penn, and *William Mead*,

At the Seſſions held at the *Old-Baily* in *London*, the firſt, third, fourth and fifth of *Sept.* 70. againſt the moſt Arbitrary procedure of that Court.

Iſa. 10. 1, 2. *Wo unto them that Decree Unrighteous Decrees, and write Grievouſneſs, which they have preſcribed; to turn away the Needy from Judgment, and to take away the Right from the Poor,* &c.

Pſal. 94. 20. *Shall the Throne of Iniquity have fellowſhip with thee which frameth miſchief by a Law.*

Sic volo, ſic jubeo, ſtat pro ratione voluntas.

Old-Baily, 1ſt, 3d, 4th, 5th of *Sept.* 1670.

London, Printed and Sold by *T. Sowle,* next Door to the Meeting-houſe in *White-Hart Court* in *Gracious-ſtreet,* and at the *Bible* in *Leaden-hall-ſtreet,* near the *Market.*

of Coke; when ironically complimented for this by the recorder, who took off his hat to him, he remarked: 'Thou mayst put on thy hat, I have never a fee for thee now.' When Meade was found not guilty in the jury's first verdict, Penn argued that he be released; and since the charge was that of 'conspiracy,' he himself, an alleged fellow-conspirator, should also be freed, thus removing the stigma of conspiracy from a Quaker meeting for worship. But the outstanding significance of Penn's citations from Magna Carta and its classic expounders, and of his eloquent and repeated appeals to the fundamental rights of Englishmen, was to lift the right of Quakerism above that of a religious sect to exist and to place it upon the foundation of England's Common Law, as well as upon the duty to God owed by the human conscience.

To Penn personally, the trial and confinement were an especial grievance, coming as they did when his father lay on his death-bed. The reconciliation of father and son, after his acceptance of Quakerism, had but recently taken place; and now he was barred by prison walls from being with him in his last days. The morning after his arrest and on each day of the trial he wrote to him, briefly relating the details and giving expression to his filial affection. 'I am very well, and have no trouble upon my spirits, besides my absence from thee. . . . I am more concerned at thy distemper, and the pains that attend it, than at my own mere imprisonment. . . . I desire thee not to be troubled at my present confinement, I could scarce suffer on a better account, nor by a worse hand, and the will of God be done. It is more grievous and uneasy to me that thou shouldst be so heavily exercised, God Almighty knows, than any living worldly concernment. . . . I desire the Lord God, in fervent prayer, to strengthen and support thee, and anchor thy mind in the thoughts of the immutable blessed state which is over all perishing concerns. . . . Solace thy mind in thoughts of better things, dear father. Let not this wicked world disturb thy mind.'

Such were the efforts of the imprisoned son to console his dying father; and when, immediately after his release, he went to his bedside, we can readily imagine how those efforts were increased and made more intimate and tender. His father no doubt dictated letters or sent messages to him; and it was probably in response to one of these that he wrote from his prison: 'I intreat thee not to purchase my liberty. They will repent them of their proceedings. I am now a prisoner notoriously against law.' When they were at last together, the dying father must have rejoiced over the triumph of 'the rights of Englishmen' which his son had done so much to ensure. And even his son's despised religion had assumed new character and significance in his eyes. 'My own father,' Penn cites among many other ancient and modern worthies in his *No Cross, No Crown* [423] as saying just before his death : ' "Son William,— Let nothing in this world tempt you to wrong your conscience." Wearied to live, as well as near to die, he took his leave of us ; and of me, with this expression, and a most composed countenance : "Son William, if you and your friends keep to your plain way of preaching, and keep to your plain way of living, you will make an end of the priests to the end of the world." '

This danger from the Quakers was shared in full by the authorities of church and state, who tried to suppress them and all other dissenters by the Conventicle, Five Mile, and other acts of parliament. The fear of Puritanism and the Fifth Monarchists was still very strong and the supporters of the Stuart monarchy vied with one another in attempts to root them out. Sir John Robinson, the lieutenant of the Tower, was a nephew of Archbishop Laud, the head of High Church Anglicanism in Charles I's reign, and he regarded Penn as the head of the Quaker brand of Puritanism. His recent ignominious defeat in the Penn-Meade trial also gave more than a touch of personal revenge to his next attack upon the most prominent of the Quaker leaders. The mayor, Sir Samuel Starling, was in complete accord with Robinson, and their spies reported in February, 1671, that Penn could be caught at a meeting of the Quakers in Wheeler Street, London.

As Penn arose to speak in that meeting, a sergeant and constable accompanied by soldiers seized him, and without a warrant for his arrest, carried him to the Tower. Here he spent three or four hours and was then arraigned before Robinson, Starling, and a few other magistrates, the public this time being carefully excluded, and no jury was permitted to intervene in the trial. The 'examination' which ensued was far from being a trial, and it began with an insult to Penn.[424] Both Robinson and Starling had had frequent, recent and emphatic reasons for knowing Penn, but Robinson began by pretending not to know him and saying to him : 'I do not desire to know such as you.'

---

423 Part II, § xxxvii.
424 This examination is recorded by Besse (1726), who states that the account of it was 'given by an eye and ear witness.'

The constable would not swear that Penn had been speaking to a meeting forbidden under the Conventicle Act, and Robinson then proposed to proceed under the 'Oxford,' or 'Five-mile Act.' The latter required every clergyman to take an oath of non-resistance and support of Church and State, under penalty for refusal of five miles' exile from his former parish or an incorporated town. Penn argued effectively that, having never been ordained or inducted into a parish, he was not subject to the act. The oath of allegiance and renunciation of armed violence, demanded in that and other acts, was thereupon tendered him, but he declined to take it on the twofold Quaker ground of not swearing and of rejection of armed violence.

Robinson before imposing sentence professed sorrow that Penn, being an 'ingenious gentleman,' with 'a plentiful estate,' should render himself 'unhappy by associating with such a simple people'; to which Penn replied : 'I confess I have made it my choice to relinquish the company of those that are ingeniously wicked [the Cavaliers of the Restoration Period], to converse with those that are more honestly simple.' Robinson : 'I wish thee wiser.' Penn : 'And I wish thee better.' This brusque colloquy evidently enraged Robinson whom Penn had already proved, on the testimony of the constable, to have lied about setting spies upon him ; and he exclaimed : 'You have been as bad as other folks,— abroad and at home too.' Penn indignantly challenged him to produce evidence of this, declared that from his childhood God had preserved him 'from the power of those pollutions,' and ended by saying : 'Thy words shall be thy burden, and I trample thy slander as dirt under my feet.' One of the other magistrates backed Penn up in this, and Robinson professed that because of his friendship with Penn's father, he had a great deal of kindness for him ; but he ended by sentencing him to Newgate for six months. But Penn again had the last word by saying, when Robinson ordered an escort of a corporal and a file of musqueteers : 'No, no, send thy lacquey ; I know the way to Newgate.'

The Newgate to which he was now committed is described in the autobiography of Thomas Ellwood, who had been a prisoner in it a few years before. Part of Ellwood's description is as follows :

'The Common Side of Newgate is generally accounted, as it really is, the Worst Part of that Prison ; not so much from the Place, as the People : it being usually stocked from the veriest Rogues and meanest sort of Felons and Pick-Pockets, who, not being able to pay Chamber-

Rent on the Master's Side, are thrust in there. And if they come in Bad, to be sure they do not go out better: for here they have the opportunity to instruct one another in their Art, and impart to each other what Improvements they have made therein. . . . In the night we all lodged in one room, which was large and round, having in the middle of it a great pillar of oaken timber, which bore up the chapel that is over it. To this pillar we fastened our hammocks at one end, and to the opposite wall on the other end, quite round the room, and in three degrees or three stories high, one over the other; . . . and under the lower rank of hammocks, by the wall sides, were laid beds upon the floor, in which the sick and such weak persons as could not get into the hammocks lay; and indeed, though the room was large and pretty airy, yet the breath and steam that came from so many so close together, was enough to cause sickness amongst us, and I believe did so, for there were many sick, and some very weak. Though we were not long there, yet in that time one of our fellow prisoners, who lay in one of those pallet-beds, died. A coroner's inquest being held over the body of the deceased, one of the jury insisted upon being shown the room where he died; this was granted by the keeper with great reluctance, and when the jury came to the door, the foreman who led them, lifting up his hands said, "Lord bless me, what a sight is here? I did not think there had been so much cruelty in the hearts of Englishmen, to use Englishmen in this manner! We need not now question, (said he to the rest of the jury) how this man came by his death: we may rather wonder that they are not all dead, for this place is enough to breed an infection among them."

'These are some of the common *Evils,* which make the Common Side of Newgate in measure a Type of Hell upon Earth. But there was, at that time, something of another Nature, more Particular and Accidental, which was very Offensive to me. When we came first into Newgate, there lay (in a little Byplace like a Closet, near the room where we were Lodged) the Quartered Bodies of three men, who had been Executed some days before, for a real or pretended Plot: which was the ground or at least Pretext, for that Storm in the City, which had caused this Imprisonment. The Names of these three men were Philips, Tongue and Gibs: and the Reason why their Quarters lay so long there was, The Relations were all that while Petitioning to have leave to bury them: which at length, with much ado, was obtained for the Quarters, but not for the Heads, which were Ordered to be set up in some parts of the City. I saw the Heads when they were brought up to be Boyled. The Hangman fetch'd them in a dirty Dust Basket, out of some By-Place, and setting them down amongst the Felons, he and they made Sport with them. They took them by the Hair, Flouting, Jeering, and Laughing at them : and then giving them some ill names, box'd them on the Ears and Cheeks. Which done, the Hangman put them into his Kettle, and parboyl'd them with Bay-Salt and Cummin-Seed : that to keep them from Putrefaction, and this to keep off the Fowls from seizing on them. The whole Sight (as well that of the Bloody Quarters first, as this of the Heads afterwards) was both frightful and loathsom, and begat an Abhorrence in my Nature. Which as it had rendered my Confinement there by much the more uneasie, so it made our removal from thence to Bridewell, even in that respect, the more welcome.'

Such were some of the thousand and one scenes and conditions which Penn and his fellow-Quakers encountered in England's jails, and which gave such point to their persistent demand for prison reform, as well as for religious toleration and the prevention of such degradation and suffering by innocent persons.

Penn and the other Friends who had been sentenced with him had rented better lodgings in the 'Master's Side' of the prison ; but the extortion and brutal treatment they received there from the gaoler caused them to forsake them and to go in protest to 'the common stinking jail' among the felons. Here Penn passed six dreary months through the spring and summer of 1671 ; but with his marvellous ability to concentrate, amidst the most untoward circumstances, upon the work in hand, he wrote several treatises. These included a protest to the sheriffs of London against the condition of the prison ;[425] an address to parliament against the Conventicle Act ;[426] letters to a Roman Catholic who had severely criticized his *Caveat against Popery ; A cautionary Postscript to Truth exalted ;*[427] *Truth rescued from Imposture ;*[428] *A serious Apology for the . . . Quakers ;*[429] and a revised edition of *The Great Case of Liberty of Conscience.*[430]

425 *Works,* I, 42.
426 ibid. I, 41.
427 ibid. I, 247.
428 ibid. I, 486.
429 ibid. II, 32.
430 The preface to the second edition of this work is dated February 7, 1671, when he apparently had been in Newgate only two days ; but perhaps he went to Newgate in 1670.

At his examination, he had said to the magistrates : 'You are angry that I am considerable ; and yet you take the very way to make me so, by making this bustle and stir about one peaceable person.' This was in truth the result of his persecution ; and not only was his influence among the Quakers enhanced by it, but the literary fruits of his imprisonments — especially *No Cross, No Crown* and *The Great Case of Liberty of Conscience* — were widely read on both sides of the Atlantic and contributed largely to morals and manners within and outside Quaker circles. In Holland and Germany, also, to which he went soon after his release, his influence was increased by the prestige of suffering for his faith. 'I would have thee and all men know,' Penn had said to Robinson, 'that I scorn that religion which is not worth suffering for.'

Penn's imprisonments for his religion's sake were now, however, nearly ended. In 1681, after he had received the grant of Pennsylvania and was preparing to go there to assist in its colonization, he attended a Friends' meeting in Grace Church Street, London. A government spy or 'informer,' named Hilton, led a constable and his staff to the meeting, which was addressed by both Fox and Penn. The latter disobeyed the constable's order to stop preaching ; and so deeply impressed was the constable by the two sermons that he used the excuse of the informer's departure to refuse to execute the warrant for the preachers' arrest.

Fourteen years later, while on a preaching tour at Wells, he addressed an assembly of 'two or three thousand' standing in the market-place, and was seized in the midst of his sermon by a constable and his aids and hurried before the magistrates. But the latter released Penn because the bishop had granted a license for holding the meeting, and apologized for the disturbance of a lawful assembly ; whereupon, the Friends rented a house in the city and held a series of religious meetings, some of which were addressed by Penn.[431] Thus the church had at last come to the aid of the Quakers against local state officials in behalf of toleration.

The national state itself was responsible for one of Penn's last confinements. This was not an actual imprisonment, but an internment on the charge of giving aid and comfort to the deposed Stuart king. William of Orange landed in England, November 5, 1688, James II fled to France, and one month later Penn was taken before the king's

---

431 Cf. *supra*, p. 125 f.

council, examined and released on securities given until the following Easter, when he was 'cleared in open court.' Twice more in 1690, he was accused of holding treasonable correspondence with the exiled James, was held on bail, and again acquitted. Prevented from retiring to Pennsylvania by another accusation of treason, he 'thought it advisable to retire for a time, and accordingly appeared but little in public for two or three years.'[432] It was during this retirement—as in the case of his former imprisonments—that he wrote two of his noteworthy books, namely, *Fruits of Solitude* and *An Essay on the Peace of Europe*.

Penn's last experience of durance vile was the result, not of prosecution by church or state, but of a civil suit by creditors who procured his imprisonment in the debtors' gaol, the Fleet. Arrested once more while attending a Quaker meeting in Grace Church Street—the scene of his first arrest in London forty years before—, he spent eleven months of the year 1708 in that peculiar institution, a debtors' prison.[433] The apartments he occupied there were more spacious and more comfortable than those occupied in the Marshalsea by the immortal Mr. Dorrit; and although at the age of sixty-four he wrote no more noteworthy books in his retirement, he received his friends and visitors and held with them meetings for religious worship, in which he gave free expression to the faith that was in him. Referring to the fortitude and serenity he evinced throughout this time of trouble, one of his friends remarked: 'God darkens this world to us that our eyes may behold the greater brightness of His Kingdom.'[434]

THE PROTAGONIST OF RELIGIOUS TOLERATION

RETURNING from the falling shadows of 1708 to Penn's great decades of the 1670's and 1680's, we find him taking a leading rôle in the struggle for religious toleration and freedom of conscience. These were the decades which saw at last the triumph of toleration, and which paved the way for the triumph, in the next century, of religious liberty. In Pennsylvania, Penn inaugurated as early as 1682 almost complete religious liberty, including not only toleration of diverse

---

432 This is the indefinite statement of his first biographer, Joseph Besse, 1726. Further details are given, *infra*, pp. 266-78.
433 Besse states that it was in 'the Old Bailey, within the rules of the Fleet.'
434 Isaac Norris, of Pennsylvania.

forms of worship, but also the rejection of restrictions because of religious belief on the civil and political rights of citizenship. Fifteen years before, at the age of twenty-three, he began to advocate in England this part of the Holy Experiment which he put into practice in Pennsylvania as soon as he had the power to do so.

A century after the Catholic persecution of the Protestants in England had come to an end, the Protestant sects which claimed the right of enforcing uniformity of faith and worship entered upon a severe persecution of those which claimed the right of independence. The latter sects were on the radical fringes of Protestantism, and were so despised by the Lutheran, Anglican and Presbyterian 'established' churches that their persecution might have been as brutal and fatal to their existence had not a century of humanizing influences intervened.

The Quakers were in many ways the most radical of the Protestant sects; or, as we prefer to say now, they were the most progressive and forward-looking of them all. Their belief in the supremacy of the individual's conscience and in the corresponding duty of conceding toleration to others was well expressed by Penn as follows: 'I abhor two Principles in Religion, and pity them that own them. The first is, Obedience upon Authority without Conviction; and the other, Destroying them that differ from me for God's sake. Such a Religion is without Judgment, though not without Teeth.'[435]

Penn's own imprisonments naturally sharpened his sympathy with the sufferings of others; and those sufferings had been long and severe. The English Lollards in the fifteenth century, the German Anabaptists in the sixteenth, the Independents in the first half of the seventeenth, and the Sectarians of the Commonwealth period supplied the links in the noble line of Protestant martyrs. The Quakers were the chief sufferers in the last part of the line, for reasons which seemed wholly sufficient to their persecutors. They rejected the most cherished sacraments, baptism and the Lord's supper, and interpreted the divinity of Christ in a new and strange fashion, thus placing themselves outside the pale of Christianity; they rejected an ordained ministry for themselves, and refused to attend the services and pay tithes to the clergymen ordained by others, thus undermining the church; they broke the public peace by holding meetings in the streets, and the Sabbath by travelling outside of their own parishes to meetings held at a distance;

435 Letter to Dr. Tillotson, Archbishop of Canterbury, 1686.

whipped as vagrants for pursuing their missionary work, they were nevertheless hated for their superior workmanship and success in business; refusing to take an oath in courts, they struck at the whole judicial fabric of the state; and declining to take the oath of allegiance, they gave aid and countenance to the foreign and domestic enemies of the English Commonwealth and to the foreign allies of the despotic Stuart kings.

During the dozen years of the Commonwealth, three thousand Quakers were imprisoned, and thirty-two died in gaol; during the quarter-century of Charles II, fifteen thousand were imprisoned, and four hundred and fifty died in gaol. The official and unofficial punishments to which they were subjected resulted, Penn estimated, in the death of five thousand. Fines, imprisonment, banishment; flogging through the streets and from parish to parish; distraints on their property in shops, farms, and homes; forcible entrance to their dwellings and arrests without warrant; examinations and bullyings before magistrates; trials without indictments; sentences without juries; the employment of informers, who received one-third of the spoils. Such were some of the official means tried for dispelling the Quaker pest; while the atrocities committed by mobs and private bullies varied from place to place and in multitudinous forms.

But these methods proved in vain. The obstinacy, or devotion, of the Quakers was such that they sought rather than avoided punishment. They scorned concealment of their faith and worship; held their meetings openly; when their meeting-places were destroyed, assembled regularly on their ruins, or promptly rebuilt them; when the major part of the congregation was imprisoned, those who were left carried on their meetings, even the children stepping loyally and precociously into the breach; while those in gaol worshipped together as usual, until they were released, or until prison dirt, darkness, and disease carried them off through the portal of death to meet in the higher life.

As often before, 'the blood of the martyrs was the seed of the church.' The Quakers increased and multiplied. But the Anglican Church and the Cavalier Parliament were determined to renew the persecution of these most obnoxious and dangerous of Puritans and to make it succeed. In 1670-71, the year of Penn's imprisonment in Newgate, a vigorous attempt was made to enforce the Conventicle Acts of 1662 and 1664, which provided for fine, imprisonment and transportation of any one over the age of sixteen attending an unauthorized meeting for worship including more than five persons over and above the family in whose house it was held. Doubts as to the meaning of the act were to be construed against the conventicle, and neglectful magistrates were to be heavily fined, while a high premium was placed on the informer's trade of egging reluctant magistrates on to their duty. Under this act, more than three thousand Quakers were imprisoned, most of them in a single month. Penn denounced this act in a pamphlet which called forth the following report to Secretary Williamson from one of his agents (Calendar of State Papers, 1670, p. 219):

'Sr . . . Thursday nights pt brought to my hands A most seditious Pamphlett Covered wth a blanke pap I would haue sent you the Booke but yt I beleeve you haue seene seurall of them already peeping forth in those pts however I could not but acquaint you wth its Title wch runns thus (viz) Some Seasonable & Serious Queries vpon ye late Act against Conventicles, tending to discover how much it is against the expresse word of God ye Positiue law of the Nation, the law & light of Nature, & Principles of Prudence & Policy, And therefore Adiudged by ye law of ye Land to be voyd & Null (viz) Finch p. 3. That noe Act of Parl or Law repugnant to ye Law of God is of any force.

28. p 8 (28 H. 8). That noe man of what Estate, degree, or condition whatsoever hath power to dispense with God & Law (Gods Law).

Doct. & Stud. That agt Scripture Law, Prescription, Statute nor Custom may availe, and if any be brought in agt it, they be voyd & against Justice.

42 Ed. 3. It is assented & accorded yt ye greate Charter be holden & kept in all poynts; & yt if any Statute be made to ye Contrary, it shall be held for none.

'By A friend to truth and Peace.

[Here are quoted the verses cited on the title-page, namely, Matt: 24:48:49; Acts :9:5 [4]; and Psal. 9:16]

'Printed in the yeare 1670.

'The Pamphlett tends as much as is possible (in my Judgmt) to ye stirring vp of Sedition & Rebellion, I wish heartily that both ye Author & printer may be knowne & deservedly punished. I am sorry to troble you vpon these scores but canot avoyd it whilst I love ye Truth & Peace, & being alwayes

yor most really affectionate & humble servant
Geoffery Shakerley.'

Chestr Castle,
14 May 70.2

Two days later, Shakerley reported that he had heard that 'more of the very seditious Pamphlett are sent to oth^r Justices of ye Peace in this County in blanke papere'; and three days after this, Sir Roger L'Estrange, Surveyor of the Press, informed Lord Arlington : 'I have made a Diligent Enquiry concerning ye Queries upon ye Act ag^t Conventicles, according to y^r Lo^{ps} commande and I have traced some of them to ye Hand of a Non-Conformist minister ; But I am in hopes of a further & fuller Discovery.'

Charles II, who was a secret Catholic and desired toleration at least for his fellow-believers, was in great need of money for his courtly extravagances, and in return for a large subsidy from parliament consented to the act. But the next year, when his secret subsidies from Louis XIV were realized, he issued an order in council providing for regular trials, the right of appeal, the grant of licences for the holding of non-conformist meetings and their protection against disturbance and arrest. The next year (1672), he went farther and issued a 'Declaration of Indulgence,' which asserted his royal prerogative for dispensing with the operation of the law against both Catholics and dissenters. As a result, more than four hundred Quakers were released from gaol ; but despite the benefit that thus accrued to them, they shared the fear of their fellow-dissenters that the royal leniency might prove a Hellenic gift, and that a toleration based upon royal prerogative instead of on act of parliament would prove a "Trojan Horse."

Charles's continuing and increasing financial necessities, Louis XIV's promise of military support at the next favourable opportunity, and the growing unpopularity of his pro-French and pro-Catholic policy, induced him in 1673 to revoke his declaration ; and when the parliament neglected to provide for a measure of toleration, the persecution was revived, and during the next dozen years the informers and subservient magistrates again filled the gaols with Quaker prisoners.

It was into this religious, or rather ecclesiastical and political, imbroglio that William Penn stepped as a young man of twenty-three when he embraced Quakerism; and he began at once his struggle of twenty-one years for religious toleration. During his first imprisonment, in Cork in 1667, he wrote a letter to the Earl of Orrery, Lord President of Munster, appealing for a speedy release of all the Quaker prisoners, and remarking: 'Though to dissent from a national system imposed by authority, renders men heretics, yet I dare believe your lordship is better read in reason and theology than to subscribe a maxim so vulgar and untrue.' From this beginning of his crusade for religious liberty, he struck the note of statesmanship, as well as of the sanctity of conscience. There is no way, he wrote in this letter, 'so effectual to improve or advantage this country as to dispense with [that is, in modern English, to concede] freedom in things relating to conscience.'

The next year (1668), he went with Thomas Loe, George Whitehead and Josiah Coale to the royal court to appeal for 'tenderness of conscience' and the mitigation of 'the suffering condition of Friends in several parts of this kingdom.' The king's minister, the Duke of Buckingham, whom they interviewed, 'in his own inclination favoured liberty of conscience,' Penn wrote, but the 'application did not at that time answer our expectation.'[436] A few months later, Penn, Whitehead, and Coale repeated their visit to the court, interviewing this time the secretary of state, Sir Henry Berwick. Of this visit, Penn wrote:[437]

'I was much toucht with the sense of our Friends' many and great hardships, and the more for that they were inflicted in a Protestant country, and came from Protestant hands, and could not but think the severities they lay under for mere conscience to God, must necessarily bring the very Protestant religion under scandal abroad.[438] Being Protestants in all those points wherein the very church of England might claim that title, and whose main point was a strict and holy life. This made it seem reasonable and requisite to me, to make their sufferings and them better known to those in authority: charitably hoping that if they would give themselves the leisure to be truly informed of both, they would afford them better quarter in their new country, than Stocks, Whips, Gaols, Dungeons, Præmunires, Fines,

---

436 Penn's autobiographical fragments. Buckingham was already planning the policy of Catholic toleration or supremacy, with the support of Louis XIV.
437 ibid.
438 Penn's successful defence of toleration for the Quakers and for their release from prisons in Ireland in 1668, has been told in detail, *supra*, pp. 92-102.

Sequestrations, and Banishment, for their peaceable dissent in matters relative to faith and worship, and accordingly I had framed a scheme to myself for that purpose. But it so fell out, that towards the close of that year I was made incapable of prosecuting the resolution I had taken, and the plan I had laid of this affair, by a close and long imprisonment in the Tower of London, for a book I writ called the *Sandy Foundation Shaken*.

During this imprisonment, Penn was interviewed by the king's emissary, Dr. Stillingfleet, 'to endeavour my change of judgment,' he wrote;[439] 'but as I told him, and he told the King, the Tower was the worst argument in the world to convince me, for whoever was in the wrong, those who used force for religion never could be in the right.'

During his next imprisonment, in Newgate in 1671, Penn appealed by letter 'To the High Court of Parliament,' which was then considering more drastic means of enforcing the Conventicle Act. He first asserted that the Quakers 'own civil government, or magistracy, as God's ordinance for the punishment of evil doers, and the praise of them that do well; and though we cannot comply with those laws that prohibit us to worship God according to our consciences, as believing it to be his alone prerogative to preside in matters of faith and worship, yet we both own and are ready to yield obedience to every ordinance of man relating to human affairs, and that for conscience sake.' He then repudiated with indignation the accusation that the Quakers were rebels, plotters, or resorters to violence of any kind; and asked that 'we, or some of our Friends, may receive a free hearing from you, as several of us had upon the first act of uniformity.'[440]

During this imprisonment, also, there was published his 'Great Case of Liberty of Conscience once more briefly Debated and Defended by the Authority of Reason, Scripture, and Antiquity.'[441] This was another defence of the Quakers as a loyal and peaceable people, who held their meetings so publicly and numerously that it was impossible to make of them hot-beds of sedition. It demanded toleration of these meetings because of their innocent character, and because they were based on the rights of conscience; and it appealed for a personal con-

---
439 Autobiographical fragments.
440 This letter was signed: 'From us who are now prisoners at Newgate (for conscience-sake) on behalf of ourselves, and all our suffering friends in England, etc. W.Penn and several others.'
441 This was a revised edition of the book published in Dublin, in 1669 (cf. *supra*, p. 95).

ference with 'the Supreme Authority of England,' since 'this medium seems the fairest and most reasonable.' But it also served notice that if the existing policy should be continued, it would be met by the Quakers with a resolution, in the strength of God, 'by patience to outweary persecution, and by our constant sufferings seek to obtain a victory more glorious than any our adversaries can achieve by all their cruelties.'

The 'Great Case' for all religions Penn argued by an appeal to reason and experience. The honour of God; the meekness, suffering, promotion, and rewards of Christianity; Biblical injunctions; natural law and human rights; the aims and basis of government; peace, prosperity, and national unity;[442] the experience of the early Christian martyrs and the Protestants; a cloud of witnesses, ancient, medieval, and modern,— all these were copiously and eloquently cited, with such cogency of reasoning that it is difficult for the twentieth century mind to comprehend the necessity for stating the 'Great Case' at all.

The gleam of hope from the king's Declaration of Indulgence in 1672 was short lived; and the next year's persecution brought from Penn — after constables had broken up a meeting in which he had been preaching — letters to sundry persecuting magistrates in which he argued that 'there can be nothing more irrational than to fancy that external penalties should work right convictions;'[443] and 'there can be no reason to persecute any man in this world about anything that belongs to the next. We came not to our liberties and properties by the Protestant religion: their date rises higher; why then should a nonconformity to it, purely conscientious, deprive us of them?'[444] This appeal, of course, was in vain; as was also a letter he wrote to the king.

George Fox, refusing to take the oath of allegiance, was imprisoned for fourteen months in Worcester Castle; and Penn led the efforts of the London Quakers to procure his release.[445]

The trick of subjecting the Quakers — who would take no oath whatever — to the oath of allegiance was so prevalent, and so success-

---

[442] Penn cites here (as so often elsewhere): 'Holland, than which what place is there so improved in wealth, trade and power, chiefly owes it to her indulgence in matters of faith and worship.' To investigate this claim personally was doubtless one reason for his journey to Holland on his release from prison in 1671.
[443] To Justice Fleming in Westmorland, 1673.
[444] To Justices in Middlesex, March, 1674.
[445] Penn had his mother write to the family's friend, the lord-lieutenant of Worcestershire, to prevent the oath from being tendered to Fox, but in vain; cf. *supra*, p. 111.

ful in imprisoning them, that Penn wrote an attack upon it, in 1675, entitled *A Treatise of Oaths*.[446] Aside from its political importance, this treatise ranks in far-reaching scholarship with *No Cross, No Crown* and *The Great Case of Liberty of Conscience*. One hundred and twenty-two authorities ranging from Pythagoras to William of Orange are quoted in it to substantiate the futility and folly of exacting oaths. Penn's own argument against the practice is based on the injunctions of Jesus (Matthew, V. 34) and the Apostle James (v. 12) ; on the basis of oaths in distrust and an attempt to awe men, without any distinction between them, into speaking the truth ; the omnipresence of God in the souls of men ; the presumptuous tempting of God to summon him as a witness to 'our terrene and trivial businesses,' and to expect him to visit immediate afflictions upon perjurers ; the uselessness of oaths as a safe-guard against perjury ; and the pagan and superstitious form of kissing a book,—especially the Bible which forbids us to swear at all !

This treatise was endorsed by twelve of Penn's contemporary Quaker leaders,[447] and became and still remains the Quaker classic on the subject. It was addressed to the king and members of parliament and was possibly read by a few of the leaders. Three years after its publication, Penn represented the Quakers in a personal appeal to both houses that an affirmation be accepted in lieu of an oath, on condition of incurring the same penalties for perjury as were prescribed for those who took the oath. He made two speeches before a parliamentary committee in support of the petition, and was so far successful that the Commons complied with it in a bill which, unfortunately, was quashed in the Lords by a dissolution.[448] In 1695, Penn made another appeal to the Commons ;[449] and the next year, the Quakers' affirmation was embodied in an act of parliament. It has remained in the laws of England and the United States, being taken advantage of, not only by the Quakers, but by many others who recognize the absurdity of oaths, or who object to the superstitious and unsanitary custom of touching or kissing a court-house copy of 'the book.'

Meanwhile, persecution grew worse and worse, and Penn began his next treatise in behalf of toleration, which was entitled *England's Pres-*

---
446 *Works*, I, 612-672.
447 The name of Richard Richardson is signed with that of Penn as one of its compilers, and he may have aided in verifying the numerous quotations.
448 *Works*, 1726, I, pp. 117-120 ; cf. *supra*, p. 144.
449 ibid. I, 143-144.

ent Interest Considered (1675),⁴⁵⁰ with the following graphic picture of the Quakers' sufferings : 'Certain it is, that there are few kingdoms in the world more divided within themselves, and whose religious interests lie more seemingly cross to all accommodation, than that we live in ; which renders the magistrate's task hard, and giveth him a difficulty next to invincible. Your endeavours for an uniformity have been many ; your acts not a few to enforce it ; but the consequence, whether you intended it or no, through the barbarous practices of those that have had their execution, hath been the spoiling of several thousands of the free-born people of this kingdom, of their unforfeited rights. Persons have been flung into gaols, gates and trunks broke open, goods distrained, till a stool hath not been left to sit down on : flocks of cattle driven off, whole barns full of corn seized, threshed and carried away ; parents left without their children, children without their parents, both without subsistence. But that which aggravates the cruelty, is, the widow's mite hath not escaped their hands ; they have made her cow the forfeiture of her conscience ; not leaving her a bed to lie on, nor a blanket to cover her. And, which is yet more barbarous, and helps to make up this tragedy, the poor helpless orphan's milk, boiling over the fire, has been flung to the dogs, and the skillet made part of their prize : so that had not nature in neighbours been stronger than cruelty in such informers and officers, to open her bowels for their relief and subsistence, they must have utterly perished.'

Pointing out that persecution had failed of its object of enforcing uniformity, but on the contrary had greatly increased nonconformity, Penn advocated toleration as the best solution of the religious problem. He based his advocacy of it on three grounds, namely, the rights of Englishmen, governmental impartiality, and the promotion of general and practical religion. Trial by jury and the popular control of legislation and judicature, he naturally signalized as fundamental rights and he buttressed them by much historical learning; ⁴⁵¹ the impartiality which alone befits the enactment and administration of the law he

450 ibid. I, 672-705.

451 He even quotes the curse of 1253 given by the English clergy against any breakers of Magna Carta, and makes the comment : 'Though I am no Roman Catholic, and as little value their other curses pronounced upon religious dissenters, yet I dare declare ingenuously I would not, for the world, incur this curse, as every man deservedly doth, that offers violence to the fundamental freedoms thereby repeated and confirmed.' A century and three quarters later, an American Quaker poet, John G.Whittier, quoted this passage from Penn's book, and was inspired by it to write a poem, 'The Curse of the Charter-Breakers,' invoking it this time against clerical supporters of human slavery.

defended for eight cogent reasons; and the sincere practice of professed Christianity as a *sine qua non,* or *'unum necessarium* to felicity here and hereafter,' he advocated from the Quaker point of view that there can be no true religion unless it is practised by its individual professors in their daily lives.

Besides traversing the long road of liberty in England, Penn again cites the result of Holland's toleration and welcome to skilled artisans from abroad. 'Let the government of England,' he writes, 'but give that prudent invitation to foreigners, and she maketh herself mistress of the arts and manufactures of Europe. Nothing else hath preserved Holland from truckling under the Spanish yoke and being ruined above threescore years ago, and given her that rise to wealth and glory.'

It was apparently to this treatise that Penn referred in his autobiographical fragments (in speaking of his visit to the king's court in 1684) as follows: 'That my design might succeed the better with the King, it came into my mind to write something of the true interest of the King and kingdom, have it transcribed fair, and present it in manuscript, the times being too set, [?] and rough for print. In this I undertook to show that since it was so, that his kingdom was divided into such great bodies, opposite to each other, and near an equality in strength and value, all things considered, though not perhaps in number, and that nothing would serve either party but the ruin of the other, and that it was too great a loss to his crown to gratify either so far, he was not to suffer his authority to humor their passions, but overrule both with justice, wisdom, and goodness; that he might be King, and have the benefit of his whole people.

'Adding, that he might be easy if the uneasy are made so, and not sooner — and that the revenue was not as in old time upon tenures and in lands, but upon trade which lay much in the hands of the party he was angry with, however, that it would discourage and confound trade to be sure, if he changed the course of his government, and therefore to look upon past things as a King, and not as a man, without passion, and not suffer his own resentment or his ministers' flatteries, interests or revenges to carry him further than was good for his interest. And that upon the trial of a true liberty of conscience he would find [it] more the advantage of the crown than any private man or particular party.'

His patriotic appeal to the economic and political lessons of the past, Penn followed up by another treatise addressed to the king and parliament, entitled *The continued Cry of the oppressed for Justice.*[452] This was an appeal to the humanity of England's rulers based on a recital of the inhumanities which were being visited upon his fellow-Quakers. Specific instances of imprisonment, excessive distraints, brutal handling of men and women, for attending meetings for worship and even for burial, were catalogued one after the other without comment, and were authenticated by the statement of places and names of both victims and persecutors.

This large amount of literary labour in behalf of toleration was interrupted by a second visit to the Continent. This was undertaken in 1677, in company with Fox, Barclay, and other Quaker leaders, chiefly for the purpose of promoting and organizing Quakerism in Holland and Germany; but Penn had also prominently in mind a study of the effects of Holland's toleration which he had so often cited in his arguments in England. In western Germany, too, he found persecution of the Quakers in Emden, Dantzig, and the Rhineland and took a vigorous part in writing letters of protest to the authorities and having personal interviews with them wherever possible.[453] To the Quakers in Holland and Germany, he wrote frequent 'Epistles' of sympathy and encouragement to stand steadfast, and he did the same to those imprisoned in Scotland; while he was instrumental, as has been seen, in freeing them in Ireland. In the West Indies, Maryland, and New England, also, his letters and treatises circulated widely, even in the decade before the founding of Pennsylvania, and especially after he began to share in the government and colonization of New Jersey in 1675.

But his main struggle for toleration continued to be in England; and during the years from 1678 to 1681, his activities in its behalf led him into prominent participation in English politics. The otherworldliness of the Quakers made them look askance upon such participation; and their exclusion from public office and resentment towards a persecuting government re-enforced their subordination of politics to religion. But the condition of public affairs modified Penn's private theory, and he determined to utilize political devices for the cure of political evils. He was notably qualified in several ways for this attempt, despite his membership in a despised religious sect. His

---
452 *Works*, I, 705-710.
453 See Monographs Number Two (*William Penn and the Dutch Quaker Migration to Pennsylvania*) and Number Six (*Quaker Persecution in Holland and Germany*).

higher education, his ample means, his attractive appearance and forceful personality, his social rank, his ability as a writer and speaker, his long training in the defence and guidance of his fellow-Quakers, the royal favour, his own integrity, the fame which had come to him along with his notoriety, and perhaps an interest in public affairs inherited from, or exemplified by, his grandfather and father — the champions of Englishmen enslaved by the piratical government of Algiers : these qualifications equipped and constrained him to enter into the political arena for the promotion of religious liberty, a cause dear to the hearts of liberal-minded patriots, as well as to members of a persecuted sect that made it a prime tenet of their religion.

He turned first to the existing parliament — Cavalier and High Anglican though it was — presented petitions to both Lords and Commons, and made two speeches before a parliamentary committee.[454] This service was rendered directly on behalf of the Quakers, who were then imprisoned in large numbers and who were being fined as much as one hundred pounds a month, or two-thirds of their estates, for disobeying the old Tudor laws directed against the Catholics for not attending church. The two-fold grievance which Penn stressed in his speeches was that the Quakers were not only being persecuted, but persecuted as Catholics. 'Laws have been let loose upon us,' he said, 'as if the design were not to reform, but to destroy us, and that not for what we *are,* but for what we are *not.*' But beyond his appeal for the Quakers, Penn advocated toleration for all, including the Catholics. 'I would not be mistaken,' he continued, 'I am far from thinking it fit that Papists should be whipt for their consciences because I exclaim against the injustice of whipping Quakers for Papists ; — for we must give the liberty we ask.' Thus, nearly a century before another great Pennsylvanian, Benjamin Franklin, stood at the bar of the House of Commons pleading for freedom in government, the founder of Pennsylvania appealed to it for freedom in religion.[455]

What made the identification of Quakers with Catholics especially pernicious at this time was the popular hysteria occasioned by the alleged 'Popish Plot,' fabricated by Titus Oates. Penn strove to

---

454 *Supra,* p. 205.
455 It was in 1766 that Franklin made his plea, and it was largely as a result of it that the Stamp Act was repealed. Thomas Clarkson, who began his epoch-making opposition to human slavery, in 1784, seizes upon these speeches of Penn to expound his ideal of 'the true friend of liberty,' with Penn as his exemplar (*Life of Penn,* 1814, I, 167-177).

mitigate the ill effects of this hysteria, and its possible influence even among the Quakers, by addressing to *The Children of Light in this Generation*[456] a solemn warning of the evils which were yet to overtake Great Britain, and a fervent appeal to 'all the truly conscientious and well-inclined people in these nations.' *To thy Tents, O Israel; God is thy Tent: to thy God, O Israel!* was the keynote of this appeal; avoidance of all plots and counterplots, of all injustice and violence, would be their safeguard and their duty. But while he warned them against being influenced by the frenzy of the populace to yield to fear and a resort to 'the arm of flesh,' he admonished them that 'we cannot be insensible of their infirmities, as well as we shall not be free from some of their sufferings; we must make their case as our own, and travail alike in spirit for them as for ourselves.'

As the fear of a combined Jesuit and French attack upon England was fanned by Oates and his imitators into hotter and farther-reaching flame, and while the public were observing 'a fast and humiliation' ordered by the parliament, Penn wrote *An Address to Protestants of all Persuasions upon the present Conjuncture,* which proved its permanent value, if not its immediate popularity by requiring a second edition a dozen years later.[457] Since the official and clerical worlds had been swept off their feet by the popular and parliamentary panic, and had even become leaders and instigators of the prevalent delusion and its accompanying atrocities, Penn stated that this address was designed 'more especially [for] the Magistracy and Clergy.' The avoidance of vice, presumption, and violence, and the promotion of virtue and charity were the themes of this address, as of its predecessor. It was a voluminous one, for its author improved the occasion of public panic to denounce 'five great and crying evils of the times under the correction of the civil magistrates' and 'five capital evils that relate to the ecclesiastical state of these kingdoms.' All of these led up to persecution, which he denounced in a special 'Appendix' on seven 'causes and cure of persecution.' Perhaps the most significant of these is that 'men make too many things necessary to be believed to salvation and communion; persecution entered with creed-making.' But, setting an example of calm amidst storm, of serene wisdom amidst violent partisanship, Penn placed his address upon the placid and convincing basis of historical experiences, and the citations he made of past events and classic statements rivalled in number, learning and cogency

---

456 *Works*, I, 223-226.   457 1679 and 1692; *Works*, I, 717-818.

those of *No Cross, No Crown* and *A Treatise of Oaths*. The responsibility of the rulers in state and church Penn further enforced by some apposite words of James I and Charles I, the latter in warning to 'the then Prince of Wales, now King of England, etc.' In concrete illustration of the dire results which the neglect or misuse of this responsibility entailed, Penn next wrote three prefaces to books compiled by the Quaker meetings which recorded in tragic details the sufferings endured by their members since the Restoration in 1660.[458]

But he concluded that the printed word was not the only, or perhaps the most effective contribution he could make in the great struggle. He therefore plunged into practical, partisan politics in the campaign to elect his friend Algernon Sidney to parliament. Himself debarred by the Test Act from becoming a member of parliament, he was enthusiastic over the service which Sidney might render in that body to the cause in which they were mutually interested.

Sidney, a member of a distinguished family of English patriots, had fought in the Civil Wars against the Irish rebels and the Cavaliers, and as a member of the Long Parliament, had been appointed one of the High Court of Justice for the trial of Charles I. This he believed to be both an unconstitutional and an unwise trial, and refused to serve as one of its judges. He held no office under Cromwell, whose military dictatorship he opposed, but became a member of the council after the latter's death and was on a mission to Denmark at the time of Charles II's restoration in 1660. Because of his Roundhead activities and republican views,[459] he remained in exile until 1677, when he was permitted by the government to return to England to visit his dying father. The next year, he became a leader of the Whigs and co-operated with the Earl of Shaftesbury in demanding a successor to the seventeen year old Cavalier or Pension Parliament, and the passage of a bill by it for the toleration of non-conformists. But Shaftesbury demanded also the exclusion of the Catholic James II from the throne and the selection of the Duke of Monmouth, Charles II's illegitimate son, as Charles' successor; he also fomented the 'Popish Plot' as a means to his end. Penn and Sidney believed in the reality of an alliance between Charles and Louis XIV, and evidently believed that there was some truth in the 'Popish Plot';[460] but they were both

---

458 November and December, 1680; *Works*, I, 226-229.
459 *Infra*, p. 229.
460 Cf. *England's Great Interest in the Choice of this New Parliament, infra*, p. 212 f.

opposed to the ferocious measures adopted against the alleged plotters, and they were both opposed to Monmouth, Penn preferring the legitimate succession of his friend James, and Sidney secretly hoping for a republic.

The king having dissolved the Cavalier Parliament in January, 1679, the electoral campaign that ensued the next month was a bitter one, accompanied by the usual bribery and intimidation. Penn threw himself heartily into it, although there is no evidence that he used any but honourable methods. He was branded as a Jesuit by his opponents, and offered the oath of allegiance, which he refused on the ground that it could not legally be offered in a political meeting, even by a 'Recorder'; but the recorder is said to have caused him to be driven from the platform. Sidney was elected, but was prevented from taking his seat in the new parliament on the ground that he was not a freeman of the borough of Guildford, for which he stood. After this parliament had immortalized itself by passing the Habeas Corpus Act against illegal imprisonment, it was dissolved by Charles in July to prevent the passage of the Exclusion Bill. Shaftesbury pressed this bill in two more 'short' parliaments; but Charles was enabled, in 1682, by financial support from Louis, and a popular reaction to the fabricators of the Popish Plot and the Exclusion Bill, to dissolve these parliaments and drive Shaftesbury into exile.

Meanwhile, Sidney stood for election to the second short parliament, also in 1679, and Penn again took an active part in the campaign. The day after their first defeat, Penn had written Sidney a letter urging him to petition against his exclusion from parliament and offering to interview in his behalf the party leaders.[461] For the second election, Penn proposed that Sidney should stand for the borough of Bramber (which was in Penn's own county, a short distance from Worminghurst); he wrote letters of advice to him,[462] visited and entertained him at their respective homes, and personally visited the men who held the election in their hands.

Once more, also, he took up his pen and wrote an address dedicated to all England's 'freeholders and electors' and entitled *England's Great Interest in the Choice of this New Parliament*.[463] In this, he pointed out the seriousness of the times: 'It may be there has never happened,

461 Clarkson, I, 195-196.
462 One of these letters is quoted by Clarkson (ibid. 197-198), and the correspondence reveals the very 'practical' character of the politics involved.
463 *Works*, II, 678-682.

ALGERNON SIDNEY

not only in the memory of the living, but in the records of the dead, so odd and so strange a conjuncture as this we are under.' The long continuance of the late parliament, its sudden dissolution, the dissolution of its brief successor, 'that universal agitation that is now upon the spirit of the nation, and the reasons and motives thereof (so far as we can reach them) : — All is at stake.' Penn's insight was truly remarkable ; for he saw that it was not only a Popish, or even a French plot that was at issue, but the preservation of Englishmen's fundamental right to life, liberty and property, by means of the popular control of the legislative, executive, and judicial branches of the government.

In view of the gravity of the crisis, he said, 'I must tell you that the work of this parliament is, first, to pursue the discovery and punishment of the plot ; — second, to remove and bring to justice those evil counsellors and corrupt and arbitrary ministers of state ; — third, to detect and punish the pensioners of the former parliament ; — fourth, to secure to us the execution of our ancient laws — such as relate to frequent parliaments, the only true check upon arbitrary ministers ; — fifth, that we be secured from popery and slavery, and that protestant dissenters be eased ; sixth, that, in case this be done, the king be released from his burdensome debts to the nation, and eased in the business of his revenue.'

This certainly was a statesmanlike programme : to protect Protestantism, impeach corrupt ministers of state, eliminate bribery from parliament, provide for frequent parliaments, tolerate Protestant dissenters at least, and give financial control of the monarchy to the parliament (that is, to give to the power of the purse supremacy over the power of the sword). Toleration was made the aim and peroration of the address, although in this electoral manifesto it was not made expressly to include the feared and hated Papists ; but the sufferings through a score of years of 'your harmless neighbours'— the Quakers — were emphasized.

To carry out this programme, and 'to save poor England,' there should be a free election, without fear, flattery, or bribery, and the election of the right kind of men. The standard Penn prescribes for these is a high one, and is made specific by the statement of a dozen rules for the selection of the most fit. Sidney was not mentioned in the manifesto, but Penn's rules plainly pointed to his qualifications. Far more than Sidney's election, however, was in the mind of Penn ; for it is plain from this pamphlet that he believed the opportunity had arrived for securing by peaceful, constitutional means that limited monarchy which Pym and Hampden had worked for in parliament and which Cromwell had fought for on the field of battle. As results of a constitutional government, Penn believed, would come peace and order in public affairs, prosperity, religious liberty, and genuine Christianity in private life.

The style of this pamphlet, so different from most of his other writings, and the signature to it — not Penn's name, but *Philanglus,*— have given rise to the theory that he was not its only or its chief author, but that Sidney was mainly responsible for it. But this is too reminiscent of the other theory that Sidney was chiefly responsible for Penn's 'Frame of Government' for Pennsylvania;[464] and it rests on no basis of direct evidence. On the other hand, it is signed 'Your honest monitor and old England's true friend,' and is addressed to all of England's freeholders and electors, both of which facts suggest that Penn designed and was able to use a style of writing most suitable for such a general and political appeal, which would not have been at all well served by the style preferred in the religious literature of the time.

The result of the election was to give Sidney and his rival an equal number of votes, and its recorder cast the deciding vote for Sidney; but when the report was made to the new parliament, the Tories and landed Whig gentry were strong enough to have him again rejected. His candidate having been excluded, Penn immediately addressed to the new parliament a pamphlet entitled *One Project for the Good of England*[465] (also signed *Philanglus*), in which he argued that 'our civil union is our civil safety.' By this he meant that all Protestants were agreed as far as their civilian interests were concerned, and that they should form a united front for the preservation both of Protestantism and of England.

The existence of Protestantism in England was being threatened by Anglican persecution of Protestant non-conformists, which enabled Jesuit plots to have any seriousness and Catholicism to have an opportunity for competitive growth. England's safety against foreign conquest, its mercantile and commercial prosperity, its law and order, and above all its constitutional form of government by parliamentary and popular control, were all threatened by the religious warfare which Anglican Protestants were carrying on against their fellow-Protestants.

464 Cf. *infra*, p. 230.   465 *Works*, II, 682-691.

Catholic Englishmen had a fundamental and inalienable right to religious toleration; but since they owned allegiance to a foreign potentate, the Pope, and would probably renew their persecution of Protestants if they could regain political control, they should be excluded from holding public office.

To accomplish this exclusion, Penn proposed a new test in place of the Anglican Test of 1673. He rejected an oath, of course, and added some new and convincing reasons for doing so,— such as: 'Neither in private cases, nor yet in public transactions, have men adhered to their oaths, but their interests. He that is a knave was never made honest by an oath; nor is it an oath, but honesty, that keeps men such.' Instead of an oath, therefore, Penn proposed an affirmation, or 'New Test,' for all public officials, providing that they 'do solemnly and in good conscience, in the sight of God and men, acknowledge and declare . . .'

Aside from the form of words, this affirmation was to be made in all cities, towns, and parishes of each hundred or rape, on 'every New-Year's-day, or Ash-Wednesday rather (when the pope curses all protestants).' This last proviso was to accentuate the Protestant character of the government; and, besides acknowledging Charles II as the 'lawful king of this realm and all the dominions thereunto belonging,' the declaration specifically denounced attempts of the Pope or any papal authority to intervene in England's government; renounced such fundamental Catholic doctrines as the papal supremacy, purgatory, saint and image worship, and transsubstantiation; and acknowledged that 'the present communion of the Roman Catholic church is both superstitious and idolatrous.' Penn's purpose in these anti-Catholic provisions of the test was to prove that Quakers were not papists, and to prevent Catholics from 'disguising themselves among Protestant dissenters' by refusing to subscribe to the oath of allegiance which the Quakers had also been obliged to refuse only because it was an oath.

Penn's political and literary efforts in behalf of religious toleration were unrivalled by any writer or statesman of the time, and bore fruit eight years later in the Toleration Act.[466] To himself, however, in 1680, these efforts appeared to be fruitless. His appeals to king, judges, parliament, Anglicans, Protestants, all the electors and inhabitants of England, seemed to have been in vain. Persecution continued

---

466 John Locke's three famous 'Letters on Toleration' were not published until 1690-92, several years after the act was passed (in 1688).

rampant; fines, confiscation of property, flogging, confinement in stocks, banishment, imprisonment even unto death, were still endured by his long-suffering fellow-Quakers. Statistical records of their manifold sufferings were drawn up in 1680, and presented to one of the 'short' parliaments; and for these Penn wrote three prefaces, making one more desperate appeal.

There followed his despairing cry : 'There is no hope in England; the deaf adder cannot be charmed.' But with it came the resolution to try his Holy Experiment in the forests of the New World. Even as the Englishmen of Pym's and Hampden's days turned from their endeavour to establish political liberty at home and entered upon that marvellous 'Puritan Exodus' of 1629 to 1640 which built up a New England beyond the Atlantic, so Penn turned to his fellow-Quakers, hopeless of establishing religious liberty at home, and led them across the sea to found a great commonwealth dedicated to both political and religious liberty.

THE COLONIZER

THE England of the seventeenth century appears to us of the nineteenth to have been more cabined, cribbed, and confined than that of a century earlier. But in the days of the later Stuarts there were a few men who had visions as far-reaching as those which have immortalized the spacious days of Queen Elizabeth. William Penn was one of the foremost of these. To him as to us, no doubt, life seemed a rich and marvelous experience; but even aside from the divine discontent which sent his soul questing after things in the world of the spirit, there were things in the social world of his time which caused his mind to dwell upon a fairer and nobler social order.

Despite the deeply rooted love of country which he shared with his Puritan contemporaries, he dreamed of realizing in alien lands the ideals of a free human life, without which love of country can have no reality; and he visualized the building of another and better England beyond the seas. Accused by his enemies, and even by some of his friends the Quakers, of being influenced by a cowardly desire to escape from religious persecution in England, he might well have answered that as for himself he had not designedly sought the martyr's crown, but had willingly submitted to persecution for religion's sake and would continue to do so; but that for the sake of countless others less able to endure it, and for the sake of their posterity, he would try to create a free commonwealth abroad, where they could not only escape persecution, but where they could also build up the temples of their worship in accordance with their highest ideals. The Quaker belief also, in 'the moving of the Spirit,' the direct commission of God, was strong in him above all other reasoning.

He deeply loved the religious society for which he had toiled and suffered so much, and he longed to put an end to the wrongs and insults, the miseries, degradations, and punishments, which had checked for a quarter-century its normal growth. In England itself, he had striven his utmost to procure toleration; but the electorate, the king, the courts, the parliament had all turned against him. He estimated that fifteen thousand families had been ruined under Charles II for conscience' sake, and for it four thousand individuals had died in jail. The king had withdrawn his Declaration of Indulgence, in 1673, and had acquiesced in the policy of Anglican despotism. At the very time that Penn was recruiting his colonists during the year after he received his charter (March 4, 1681), a rigorous persecution of the Quakers was instituted in Bristol. To their meeting in that city, Penn wrote a letter of sympathy and encouragement.[467] 'Keep your ground in the Truth. — Eternal riches are before you.— O! great is God's work on earth. Be universal in your spirits.' Penn's vision was a broad one; for he believed in God's mercy beyond the wideness of the sea.

From the point of view of the civilian, too, the outlook in England looked very ominous. Sidney and Shaftesbury, with their liberal ideals had been defeated; the royal despotism had been entrenched by a split between the moderate and the extremist Whigs, and by a Tory parliament; the popular belief in the Popish Plot and the imminence of French intervention threatened another civil war, and were actually preparing the way for a revolution. The shadow of autocracy, either in state or church, or in both, lay as black across England in these days of Penn as it did in those of Pym and Hampden.

The hardships of life in an unbroken wilderness were well enough known by this time; but Penn's youthful enthusiasm and spirit of adventure, undiminished through his thirties and forties, overbalanced these. The possible profits from land-sales, agriculture, and commerce were by no means negligible in the eyes of Penn and his fellow-

467 *Works*, I, 229.

Quakers; for, aside from a comfortable livelihood for themselves, they had pressing need of profits to offset their losses due to fines and confiscations and the contributions which they were continually called upon to make to assuage the sufferings of others.

The vision of colonization in America had been shared by the seers among Penn's fellow-countrymen for a century before his time. Gilbert and Raleigh, John Smith and Winthrop, were familiar names in his boyhood. Before his birth, sixty thousand Puritans had followed the gleam. Literary accounts of America became voluminous during his early manhood, and especially after the Restoration. Boyhood tales heard from his father's sailors, and especially his father's connexion with American affairs, kindled his youthful interest. At three times before his father's death, he was actively associated with pioneering activities in Ireland. His reading of the classics at Oxford made him familiar with the dreams of Plato and More in their "Atlantis" and "Utopia"; and Harrington's widely read *Oceana* was published four years before he went up to the university. Indeed, we have Penn's own statement, in a letter of 1681 speaking of America:[468] 'I had an opening of joy, as to these parts, in the year 1661 at Oxford.'

It was at this time, as an Oxford student of seventeen, that he entered definitely upon that course of religious thinking which was soon to lead him into the Quaker fold; so that the two ideals of Quakerism and a Quaker colony beyond the Atlantic germinated together in his mind. The latter ideal had found a lodgment in the minds of other Quakers from the time when, in 1658, New England's persecution of them began. Even the location for their colony began to form itself in their minds between intolerant New England and Catholic Maryland and Anglican Virginia. In 1660, Josiah Coale, his early Quaker sponsor and intimate friend, had travelled in this region and sounded out the possibility of a settlement among the Indians on the Susquehanna. Ten years later, another Quaker worthy, John Burnyeat, and in 1671-73, George Fox, had travelled extensively through the wilds of the 'middle lands,' and brooded over their availability as a Quaker refuge. On Fox's return to England, Penn and Gulielma had welcomed him home, and doubtless talked long and earnestly about the great dream. Fox had attended a vast gathering of the Quakers at their Yearly Meeting in Rhode Island, and had incurred there the censure of Roger Williams, who soon afterwards published

---

468 A letter to Robert Turner, 12th of 2nd mo, 1681; Clarkson, I, 225.

PENN'S LANDING AT CHESTER

his *George Fox digged out of his Burrowes.* A reply to this, entitled *A New England Firebrand quenched,* was prepared by Fox, Burnyeat, and Penn, in Penn's home at Worminghurst; and the conversation during their three weeks' visit must have kindled Penn's interest still more in the New World.

Immediately after this visit, Penn went with Fox to the Netherlands, and his direct contact with the story of Dutch activities in New Netherland during the preceding half-century helped to make his own dream more tangible. The Dutch had lost their American colonies to the English in 1664; and it was doubtless a great satisfaction to Penn to welcome them at once to his colony of West New Jersey and to Pennsylvania three years later. Many of them, especially the Dutch Quakers from the Netherlands and the Rhineland, followed by many thousands of non-Quaker Germans, accepted his invitation.[469]

Two years before Penn's journey through the Netherlands and Rhineland in 1677, he had become directly and largely interested in New Jersey. Although only a young man of thirty at the time, he was invited to arbitrate a dispute over West New Jersey lands which had arisen between two Quaker purchasers of it, Edward Byllinge and John Fenwick. Penn had been especially active in inducing Fenwick to accept his award;[470] and when Byllinge fell into bankruptcy, Penn was appointed a trustee of his holdings. These included almost all the land in dispute, and Penn at once found a large task of colonization on his hands. He drew up for the New Jersey settlers a noteworthy charter of government, or *Concessions and Agreements,*[471] and issued an attractive advertisement, entitled a *Description of West Jersey.* During the four years before Penn's acquisition of Pennsylvania in 1681, Quakers and others to the number of three thousand settled in West New Jersey; and in the latter year, Penn and eleven other Quakers bought from the widow of Sir George Carteret a large tract of land known as East New Jersey. Following this union, New Jersey continued to flourish in population and material prosperity; Robert Barclay, an intimate friend and companion of Penn on his journey to the Netherlands in 1677 was appointed non-resident gov-

---

469 Cf. Monograph Number Two (*William Penn and the Dutch Quaker Migration to Pennsylvania*). An enthusiastic biographer of the Princess Elizabeth of the Palatinate and Herwerden even suggests that it was she who gave Penn the idea of founding a colony (*Biographie des Femmes Celebres*).
470 Cf. Monograph Number Two.
471 Cf. *infra,* p. 225.

ernor (holding that office until his premature death in 1690), and George Keith, another of Penn's friends and companions in 1677, carried over to it his able but disturbing activities.

New Jersey, with its one hundred and fifty shareholders, twelve partners, and twelve members of a board of control, was encumbered with too many rulers for the full scope of Penn's colonizing genius to expand as it should ; while just across the Delaware was a vast domain of almost unoccupied and ungoverned land. Here was a magnificent opportunity to plant a colony, which should open its doors freely to every kindred, tongue, and nation ; which should transplant from the Old World the best of its arts, science, and culture ; which should minimize human weaknesses by a free and full exercise of the Christian Gospel, including the benighted Indians within its beneficent light.

Circumstances favoured to an unusual degree the acquisition of this land. A Catholic proprietor, Lord Baltimore, ruled to the south ; another Catholic proprietor, Penn's warm friend, the Duke of York, ruled to the north ; and both of these welcomed the Quaker ideal of toleration. A Catholic king, although he had surrendered on toleration in England, was more than willing that Penn, who had striven for it so valiantly there, should have a chance to try it out in the New World. Penn had joined hands politically with the moderate Whigs in demanding toleration and parliamentary government ; Charles thought it wise to remove him to a distant arena, and at the same time place an ocean between the royal throne and uncounted thousands of insistent Quaker Whig petitioners for the royal clemency. Penn and the moderate Whigs did not join with Shaftesbury and the extreme Whigs in demanding the exclusion of the Duke of York from the throne ; but they united with them in opposing the French policy of the royal brothers. Moreover, England's chief concerns lay in Europe with French, Dutch, and Spanish rivals, whose strength in America would be diminished by prosperous English colonies. Even from the point of view of trade and taxes, the lands Penn asked for *might* some time become of value ; meanwhile, they were mere wild lands on the border of a savage wilderness, beyond the ken and care of a royal trifler.

Meanwhile, also, Charles got all the money he could and spent more than he got ; his debts were huge, and one of these was due to Penn's father for arrears of pay, for loans, and for the customary rewards of

PENN'S LANDING AT PHILADELPHIA

successful admirals who added to England's empire. Aside from a reward for the acquisition of Jamaica, Charles owed Admiral Penn's son about £16,000 in capital and interest. Pounds sterling went vastly farther in those days than these, and this was a sizeable sum which a grasping king would avoid paying if he could. He doubtless would have avoided paying anything, had it not been for the apparent worthlessness to him of forest lands in America. His brother James, also, to whom he had granted New Netherland, added his recommendation to the petition of the son of his friend and benefactor, the admiral: especially since Penn and the Quakers would be far more acceptable neighbours to his American lands than some powerful Anglican lord and colonists fanatically intolerant of James's fellow Catholics. Indeed, a few months after Charles granted Pennsylvania, James added to Penn's domain the territories known as Delaware, thus giving additional access to the sea.[472]

For all of these reasons, Penn desired to acquire and Charles was willing to give the territory for which he petitioned. In response to his petition, after a decent delay, the royal signatures were affixed to a charter, February 24, 1681; and the next month, Penn began to organize under it some of the most historic activities of his career.

The private motives of his prospective colonists to which Penn appealed — like the public reasons why they emigrated — were religious, political, and economic. To all of these motives he appealed by voice and pen, in conversation, public addresses, letters and numerous pamphlets.[473] The results of his appeal were of first-rate historic importance. It is true that they go far to justify the conclusion that he was, in modern mercantile parlance, a 'supersalesman,' whose

---

[472] Some of Penn's biographers lay so much stress on the part played by James in the granting of Pennsylvania as to regard him as the real founder of the province and its city of brotherly love — a strange rôle for the last embittered representative of the Stuart despots! (Cf. Buell, 107-8, and even Graham, p. 128.) Following the lead of Penn himself, of Besse (1726), Clarkson (1814), Dixon (1851), and Janney (1852), most of Penn's biographers have laid undue emphasis on the king's debt to Admiral Penn as the chief or only cause of his grant of Pennsylvania; but his latest biographer (Vulliamy, 1934) has more than redressed the balance by stressing the political circumstances of the time. The writer of a recent magazine article ('William Penn and English Politics in 1680-81', by Fuller Mood, *Journal of the Friends' Historical Society*, Vol. 32 (1935), pp. 3-21) has gone to the same extreme, in permitting the political to eclipse the financial, economic, psychological, and religious reasons for Penn's petition and the king's grant. This writer even regards Penn as being Charles's political tool, but at the same time as consciously and diplomatically concealing the king's real reasons for making the grant!

[473] Cf. Monograph Number Two (*William Penn and the Dutch Quaker Migration to Pennsylvania*, pp. 236-238, 301-392).

high-powered salesmanship might well be envied by the most successful of 'promoters' who have at their disposal all the devices of current advertising by means of newspaper and radio broad-casting.

But it is reassuring to find that Penn's appeal was directed only to the higher motives and highest welfare of his prospective colonists. He did not hesitate, on the other hand, to direct solemn warnings to them. For example, at the end of his enthusiastic pamphlet, *Some Account of Pennsylvania,* he wrote: [474] 'I desire all my dear country-folks, who may be inclined to go into those parts, to consider seriously the premises, as well the inconveniency as future ease and plenty; that so none may move rashly, or from a fickle but from a solid mind, having above all things an eye to the providence of God in the disposing of themselves; and I would further advise all such at least to have the permission if not the good liking of their near relations, for that is both natural and a duty incumbent upon all. And by this, both natural affections and a friendly and profitable correspondence will be preserved between them, in all which I beseech Almighty God to direct us; that his blessing may attend our honest endeavours, and then the consequence of all our undertakings will turn to the glory of his great name, and all true happiness to us and our posterity.'

In his 'concessions' to West Jersey, also, he wrote: [475] 'Whosoever has a desire to be concerned in this intended plantation should weigh the thing well before the Lord and not headily and rashly conclude on any such remove, and see that they do not offer violence to the tender love of their near kindred, but soberly and conscientiously endeavour to obtain their good will and the unity of Friends where they live [that is, of their local Friends meeting].'

Not to individuals alone, did Penn carry his appeal; but he made excellent use of that modern device known as the corporation, or joint-stock company, which had been devised just in time to make successful the settlement of Virginia and New England. The 'Free Society of Traders in Pennsylvania,' with Bristol as its headquarters, was one of the first of these whose organization he promoted. On the banks of the Rhine, as well as on those of the Severn and the Thames, companies to colonize Penn's province were organized under his direct or indirect supervision. Even two meetings or congregations of Dutch members of the Society of Friends in Krefeld and Krisheim folded

---

474 Clarkson, I, 221.
475 Janney, 113.

SOME
ACCOUNT
OF THE
PROVINCE
OF
PENNSILVANIA
IN
AMERICA;
Lately Granted under the Great Seal
OF
ENGLAND
TO
William Penn, &c.

Together with Priviledges and Powers necessary to the well-governing thereof.

Made publick for the Information of such as are or may be disposed to Transport themselves or Servants into those Parts.

LONDON: Printed, and Sold by *Benjamin Clark* Bookseller in *George-Yard Lombard-street*, 1681.

their tents, like the Pilgrims of Scrooby and Leiden, and sought new homes on the banks of the Delaware.[476]

Penn's eagerness to procure colonists and to promote their and his own temporal prosperity was subordinated to higher ideals by convincing measures. Among these was his refusal to sell to a company for £6,000 and 2½ percent of the profits a monopoly of the fur-trade between the Delaware and Susquehanna rivers. 'As the Lord gave it [Pennsylvania] me over all and great opposition,' was his comment, 'I would not abuse his love, nor act unworthy of his providence, and so defile what came to me clean.'

The story of the first generation of Pennsylvania's, New Jersey's, and Delaware's history under the proprietorship of William Penn has often been told, and needs not to be retold here.[477] It is a heroic one in itself; and it proves Penn a true hero, from the larger sphere of government down to the humbler one of attendance on the smallpox-stricken berths of the colonists whom he led across the Atlantic in the *Welcome*. This ship of only three hundred tons required eight weeks for its voyage from Deal to Delaware; and within its unsanitary confines, an average of four of its hundred passengers died each week from the disease which was then so prevalent and so fatal.

The *Mayflower* and the *Welcome,* more than other ships which have sailed the seas on peaceful or warlike errand, have caught the imagination of posterity. And rightly so; for they brought to the New World the founders of great commonwealths which, with their ideals of liberty, were to redress the balance of the Old.

---

476 Cf. Monograph Number Two (*William Penn and the Dutch Quaker Migration to Pennsylvania*).
477 Illustrative of the large space occupied in the biographies of Penn by the history of New Jersey, Pennsylvania, and Delaware during their first quarter-century under his guidance, are the following facts: In ten biographies of 4003 pages, 1647 pages (or 41%) are devoted to this theme; seven of these are by English authors, who devote to it from 29 to 47%, or an average of 38% of their space; two of the American authors give it 27 and 46%, while the third (a nationalistic, military propagandist) gives it 61%! On the other hand, the earliest biographers of Penn attach but scant importance to his activities in the New World. The English Quaker, Besse, 1726, devotes to them only 18 out of 115 pages, and twelve of these are filled with his letters of farewell, leaving only 6% of his space to Pennsylvania; the Dutch Quaker Sewel, 1717, tells the story in a single paragraph; the Dutch clergyman, Croese, writing in Latin, 1695, gives forty pages to Pennsylvania, but uses thirty-three of these for the Keithian secession; the French Quaker, Marsillac, 1791, gave only 6% of his 568 pages to Pennsylvania — although he himself lived three years in Philadelphia — and half of his Pennsylvania pages were filled with Penn's letters. Cf. Monograph Number Three (*Eight First Biographies of William Penn in Seven Languages and Seven Lands*).

THE STATESMAN

PROMINENT Quakers who have been also prominent statesmen are very few and far between in the pages of history — although as numerous proportionally, perhaps, as the members of any other religious denomination. William Penn was the first and the greatest of these. One of his biographers frankly and repeatedly declares his conviction that it was only when Penn laid aside the cloak of his Quakerism that he was able to assume the toga of genuine statesmanship; that it was only when he divested his mind of the vagaries of George Fox that he was able to rise to the practical common sense and statesmanlike ability which were inherent in his own character and inheritance. Born to be a political genius, he was handicapped by his Quakerism, which was responsible for none of his great achievements and for all of his weaknesses and failures.[478]

The answer to this hypothesis must be found in the author's and reader's conception of 'Quakerism' and 'statesmanship.' Penn himself believed that it was of the essence of Quakerism that its principles should be put into practice in every detail of conduct, including also and even the conduct of public affairs. He believed that a religious commonwealth, in government as well as in citizenship, was not a contradiction in terms, and that a state based on and guided entirely by Christianity was a human possibility and a divine command. Hence the 'Holy Experiment' in England which he desired and strove for, and in Pennsylvania and New Jersey which he established. *A Society of Friends,* he believed, could found a state animated by the conscious and enduring determination to yield glory to God in the highest and to act upon peace and good will toward men.

With religion at its core, it was nevertheless to be separated entirely from the medieval conception of a union of church and state. The ecclesiastical bigotry and persecution of the one and the paganism of the other were to find no place in the religious and fraternal commonwealth which he aspired to establish — a conception he expressed in the very name of its capital. The colony which he founded was to be, not the temporary theatre of military and exploiting adventure, but the permanent homes of colonists who professed and practised a religion of love and friendship. *'God* hath given it to me; He will bless it and

---

[478] Buell, p. 63, *et passim.*

make it the seed of a nation.' 'Sing unto the Lord a *new* song, ye that go down to the Sea.' The oppressed of every kindred, tongue and nation were to be invited to share in all the God-given opportunities of life ; religious toleration to be granted to all ; equality for all before the law ; law and government to be based on the consent of the governed ; democracy in government, as well as in religion.

Such were the Christian-Quaker principles and practices which Penn craved for the new experiment. While Charles stressed in the preamble of Penn's grant 'a commendable desire to enlarge the British Empire, and promote [the production of] such useful commodities as may be a benefit to the King and his dominions,' Penn cherished the hope that the success of his Holy Experiment would serve as an example to all nations and inaugurate an era of peace and righteousness and loving comradeship around the world.

To carry out this far-reaching and idealistic plan, precise and practicable specifications were requisite. Penn began them in his 'Preamble of Concessions and Agreements . . . of West New Jersey,' 1676,[479] and followed them up for Pennsylvania in the royal 'Charter' or 'Patent' of March, 1681 :[480] the 'Certain Conditions and Concessions' of July, 1681 ;[481] the 'Charter of Liberties' (or 'The Fundamental Constitutions') of April 20, 1682 ;[482] the 'Frame of Government,' of April 25, 1682 ;[483] the 'Laws' of May 5, 1682, which were ratified by the Pennsylvania Assembly as the 'Great Law' of December, 1682 ;[484] the 'Charter' (or 'Frame of Government') of April 2, 1683 ;[485] the 'New Frame of Government' of November 7, 1696 ;[486] and the 'Charter of Privileges' of October 28, 1701.[487]

Beginning with the grant of political rights by the proprietors to the colonists of West New Jersey, and by the king to the proprietor of Pennsylvania, this series of documents gradually developed from the grant of a charter by a superior power, into a genuine constitution originating with and formulated by the people themselves, with the co-operation of the proprietor. That it met the needs of the Pennsyl-

---

479 F.N.Thorpe, *Constitutions,* etc., 1909, Vol. V, pp. 2548-51.
480 ibid. pp. 3035-44.
481 ibid. pp. 3044-47.
482 ibid. pp. 3047-52. (This is only one of the versions ; cf. the 'Penn Papers' in the Library of the Pennsylvania Historical Society.)
483 ibid. pp. 3052-59.
484 ibid. pp. 3059-63.
485 ibid. pp. 3064-69.
486 ibid. pp. 3070-76.
487 ibid. pp. 3076-81.

vanians is evidenced by the fact that it endured until 1776, when the colony was converted into a state.

At the very beginning of this development, the crucial question arose, are the colonists of West New Jersey merely landowners and tenants, or are they citizens of a self-governing political community ? Penn and his fellow-proprietors answered this in the latter sense, while the agent of the Duke of York, Governor Andros, asserted that the settlers were merely landowners, under the political jurisdiction of New York, subject to the payment of taxes and customs-dues levied by the governor of New York, and with no right to set up a representative legislature of their own. During the years 1679-1680, when Penn was striving for the election of Sidney to parliament as a champion of toleration and parliamentary government, and when the Duke of York had retired to Scotland in the midst of the excitement over the Popish Plot and the Exclusion Bill, Penn prevailed with the Duke, in August, 1680, to release all his powers of sovereignty over West New Jersey to its proprietors. The chief argument which he used was that such a concession on the Duke's part would prove to Englishmen that their future king was swayed by justice and generosity.

Four years before this, the West New Jersey proprietors, under Penn's leadership, had issued their famous 'Concessions' which provided that the settlers should elect annually by ballot (not by acclamation) their representatives to an assembly which should be a genuine legislature ; that the legislature should make, alter and repeal laws ; that every male adult free from crime should be eligible both to vote and to be elected to office (*suffragium et honores*) ; that the executive power should be in the hands of ten commissioners chosen by the legislature and responsible to it ; that the judicial power should be exercised by judges and constables elected by popular vote ; that trial by jury should be unrestricted and untrammeled : the triumph of the Penn-Meade trial !

Religious, as well as civil, liberty was provided for in this great document, which established freedom of conscience and the right of every man to worship without interruption or molestation, because, it declared, 'no men nor number of men upon earth hath power or authority to rule over men's consciences in religious matters.' [488]

These Concessions of West New Jersey, antedating by a hundred years the Declaration of Independence, laid the foundation of democracy

[488] *Concessions*, Ch. XVI.

and were recognized by Penn himself as epoch-making. 'In the fear of the Lord and in true sense of his Divine Will,' he wrote, 'we try here to lay foundations for after ages to understand their liberty as Christians and as men, that they may not be brought into bondage, but by their own consent ; for we put the power in the people.[489]

When Charles II's charter for Pennsylvania was granted to Penn, it was made by the king's ministers (mainly by the Chief Justice, Lord North, who had in mind the twenty years' struggle with an independent legislature in Massachusetts) more royal and less liberal than than that which another proprietor, Lord Baltimore, had received from Charles I before the Civil War and the Commonwealth. It provided, for example, that the laws passed by the Pennsylvania legislature and proprietor should be subject to the royal veto ; and the right of parliamentary taxation was expressly reserved.[490] But when Penn had received his charter, he proceded to grant to the prospective citizens of Pennsylvania a government established on a democratic basis entirely alien to the despotism of the Stuarts.

Over against the Stuart conception of 'the divine right of kings,' he placed his conception of 'the divine right of government.' In a preface to his 'Frame,' he wrote : 'When the great and wise God had made the world, of all his creatures it pleased him to choose man his deputy to rule it ; and to fit him for so great a charge and trust, he did not only qualify him with skill and power, but with integrity to use them justly. This native goodness was equally his honour and his happiness ; and, whilst he stood here, all went well ; there was no need of coercive or compulsive means ; the precept of divine love and truth in his bosom was the guide and keeper of his innocency. But lust, prevailing against duty, made a lamentable breach upon it ; and the law, that had before no power over him, took place upon him and his disobedient posterity, that such *as would not live conformable to the holy law within,* should fall under the *reproof and correction of the just law without in a judicial administration.* . . . [He quotes here the Epistles of Paul to Timothy.]

'This settles the divine right of Government beyond exception, and that for two ends : first, to *terrify* evil-doers ; secondly, to cherish those that do well ; which *gives Government a life beyond corruption,* and

---

[489] In the public letter distributed in West New Jersey and throughout England with the *Concessions*.

[490] This was one of the reasons why opposition to the Revolution of 1776 was so strong in Pennsylvania.

makes it as durable in the world as good men shall be, so that Government seems to me a part of religion itself, a thing sacred in its institution and end; for, if it does not directly remove the cause, it crushes the effects of evil, and is, as such, though a lower, yet an emanation of the same divine Power that is both author and object of pure religion; the difference lying here, that the one is more free and mental, the other more corporal and compulsive in its operation; but that is only to evil-doers, Government itself being otherwise as capable of kindness, goodness, and charity, as a more private society. They *weakly err, who think there is no other use of government than correction, which is the coarsest part of it.* Daily experience tells us, that the care and regulation of many other affairs, more soft and daily necessary, make up much the greatest part of government.'

Proceeding from what he thought was the origin of government, he discussed the hands in which it had been placed. 'I know,' he wrote, 'what is said by the several admirers of monarchy, aristocracy, and democracy, which are the rule of one, of a few, and of many, and are the three common ideas of government when men discourse on that subject. But I choose to solve the controversy with this small distinction, and it belongs to all three : Any government *is free to the people under it,* whatever be the frame, *where the laws rule and the people are a party to those laws; and more than this is tyranny, oligarchy, or confusion.*

'But, lastly, when all is said, there is hardly one frame of government in the world so ill designed by its first founders, that in good hands would not do well enough; and history tells us, that the best in ill ones can do nothing that is great and good. . . . *Wherefore governments rather depend upon men, than men upon governments. Let men be good, and the government cannot be bad. If it be ill, they will cure it. But if men be bad, let the government be never so good, they will endeavour to warp and spoil it to their turn.'*

Since the king had decreed a proprietary government for Pennsylvania, its proprietor proceeded to popularize it. Writing of the 'Frame,' he said : 'For the matters of liberty and privilege, I propose that which is extraordinary, and to leave myself and successors no power of doing mischief; so that the will of one man may not hinder the good of the whole country.'

Religious liberty he made the 'first or great Fundamental' of Pennsyl-

PENN'S CHARTER OF LIBERTIES, 1682

vania's Frame. 'In reverence to God, the father of light and spirits, the author as well as object of all divine knowledge, faith, and worship, I do, for me and mine, declare and establish for the first fundamental of the government of my province, that every person that doth and shall reside therein shall have and enjoy the free profession of his or her faith and exercise of worship toward God, in such way and manner as every such person shall in conscience believe is most acceptable to God. And so long as every such person useth not this Christian liberty to licentiousness or the destruction of others, that is to say, to speak loosely and profanely or contemptuously of God, Christ, the holy Scriptures, or religion, or commit any moral evil or injury against others in their conversation, he or she shall be protected in the enjoyment of the aforesaid Christian liberty by the civil magistrate.'

This last reservation was followed by a 'Law' which excluded atheists and malefactors from freedom of worship, and all non-Christians from voting and office-holding; thus, Pennsylvania's Frame was more restrictive of religious liberty and democracy than was New Jersey's Concessions. Moreover, Pennsylvania's council, which was to be chosen by popular vote, had the right of preparing and proposing bills, while its assembly could merely 'pass them into laws or reject them as it shall see meet.'

These conservative changes made in the government between the 'Charter of Liberties, or Fundamental Constitutions,' and the 'Frame of Government' were severely criticized by Penn's staunch republican friends, Benjamin Furly of Rotterdam and Algernon Sidney. Furly wrote to Penn very frankly about them; and among other things, he said:[491] 'To have a great nation bound up to have no laws but w^t two thirds of 72 men [that is, the Provincial Council, and not the Assembly] shall think fit to propound . . . is not consistent with the public safety.'

Sidney's precise objections are not known; for our knowledge of them comes from an indefinite statement in a letter of Penn which refers to rumours that Sidney had said that 'I [Penn] had a good country, but the basest laws in the world, not to be endured or lived under, and that the Turk was not more absolute than I.' The language of the rumours was doubtless exaggerated; but it is probable that

---

491 Cf. Monographs Number Two (*William Penn and the Dutch Quaker Migration to Pennsylvania*) and Number Five (*Benjamin Furly and Quakerism in Rotterdam*).

Sidney, like Furly, objected to the legislative initiative being withheld from the Assembly and given to the Governor and Council. The restriction of the suffrage to freemen (land owners or tenants), and the powers of the 'Governour' (as Penn was careful to call himself, and not 'Proprietor'), with his 'treble vote' in the council, and his right to veto any amendments to the constitution, these two were inconsistent with Sidney's strict republican principles.

In his letter to Sidney, Penn asked for a reply in confirmation of his version of the story, which was as follows : [492] 'This made me remember the discourse we had together, at my house, about me drawing constitutions, not as proposals, but as if fixed to the hand. And that as my act, to which the rest were to comply if they would be concerned with me. But withal, I could not but call to mind, that the objections were presently complied with, both by my verbal denial of all such constructions as the words might bear, as if they were imposed and not yet free for debate. And, also, that I took my pen, and immediately altered the terms, so as they corresponded (and truly, I thought more properly) with thy objection and sense. Upon this thou didst draw a draft, as to the frame of government, gave it me to read, and we discoursed it with a considerable argument ; it was afterwards called for back by thee to finish and polish ; and I suspended proceedings in the business ever since (that being to be done after other matters), instead of any further conference about it.'

Upon the basis of this letter, some of Penn's biographers have assumed that Sidney was a co-author, or probably the chief author of Pennsylvania's frame of government ; but they are obliged to admit that 'so intricate, so continuous, was this mutual aid [the assertion of which is based on no evidence], that it is now impossible to separate the work of one legislator from that of the other — Penn's share from Sidney's — Sidney's share from Penn's.' [493] But here we are in the realm of conjecture, with little or no historical evidence to support us ; for Sidney's reply to Penn, if he ever wrote one, is not extant.

Another, even greater Englishman than Sidney, is supposed to have had a hand in the framing of Pennsylvania's government, namely, John Locke. But although Locke was certainly an outstanding liberal in many ways, the 'Fundamental Constitutions' which he drew up in 1669

---

492 Janney, 192.
493 Cf. especially Dixon, 178, 180, 181-2, 267, 280.

The FRAME of the
GOVERNMENT
OF THE
Province of Pennsilvania
IN
AMERICA:
Together with certain
LAWS
Agreed upon in England
BY THE
GOVERNOUR
AND
Divers FREE-MEN of the aforesaid
PROVINCE.

To be further Explained and Confirmed there by the first *Provincial Council* and *General Assembly* that shall be held, if they see meet.

Printed in the Year MDCLXXXII.

A Topical Biography   231

for the government of Carolina were far more feudal than Penn's proprietorship.[494] While the popular assembly of 'the Palatinate' of Carolina was given by Locke control over money bills, the government officials were made financially independent of it; and the large degree of feudalism in it is illustrated by the provision for sub-infeudation, for a permanent division of the people into social classes, and for the granting of titles of nobility, provided these were given names differing from those in England.

Locke, like Penn, was a great advocate of religious toleration, and this was provided for in large measure in Carolina's constitution; but neither Locke nor Penn prohibited the existence of slavery. Indeed, Locke's constitution specifically provided that 'every freeman of Carolina shall have absolute power and authority over his negro slaves' (Article 110). On the other hand, Locke's and Penn's friend, the Dutch Quaker Benjamin Furly, wrote Penn condemning the omission from Pennsylvania's 'Frame' of the clause in West New Jersey's 'Concessions' which provided that 'all and every person and persons inhabiting the said Province shall, as far as in us lies, be free from oppression and slavery.' Furly proposed to apply this principle for Pennsylvania by the following Law (XXIII) : 'Let no blacks be brought in directly. And if any come out of Virginia, Maryld. [sic] in families that have formerly bought them elsewhere Let them be declared (as in ye west jersey constitutions) free at 8 years end.[495]

The Dutch Quaker settlers of Germantown, also, protested against slavery and advocated its entire abolition in 1688.[496] While Penn did not accept this proposal, he did provide in the articles granted to the Free Society of Traders that Negro slaves, after fourteen years' service, should at least be bound to the soil, and not be subject any longer to indiscriminate buying and selling, transportation, separation of families, etc. He continued to own slaves and employ them from their owners, on his estates at Pennsbury; but before leaving Pennsylvania the last time, he made a will providing for their manumission.

The movement for manumission or abolition among the other Quakers in Pennsylvania was so feeble at the time of Penn's first visit

---

494 Thorpe, op.cit., V, pp. 2772-2786. Locke provided also for oaths of allegiance and for compulsory military training and service between the ages of seventeen and sixty.
495 Monograph Number Two, p. 344, and Monograph Number Five.
496 Cf. Monograph Number Two, pp. 212 f, 217, 219, 222, 294-300, 344.

as to defeat in the assembly Penn's proposal to legalize slave-marriages; but four years later, the assembly laid a duty on the importation of slaves, and a half-dozen years before Penn's death, it passed an act prohibiting their importation altogether. By this time, however, the iniquitous *asiento* in the Treaty of Utrecht had given to England a monopoly of the slave-trade, and the Pennsylvania act was disallowed by the Crown.

Penn's dealings with another 'coloured' race, the North American Indians, have been sufficiently and justly signalized; but those with white aliens are usually overlooked. On his arrival in his province, he found about three thousand Dutch, Swedish, and German settlers along the Delaware. They flocked in to Newcastle to see their new governor; and the day after his arrival, he 'took possession' by old feudal formalities, and made them a speech promising them full civil, religious, and political rights. He renewed their former officers' commissions and naturalized, by act of the first assembly in 1682, all the non-English European settlers. Soon after his own arrival, Dutch Quakers founded Germantown, and in July 1684, sixty-four of its settlers became naturalized citizens by means of papers issued by Penn's deputy-governor.

After England's next war with France and its allies had begun, naturalization papers were again granted to Pennsylvania citizens of non-English origins (in 1691); and again, in 1709, when Louis XIV's fourth war of aggression (or the War of the Spanish Succession, or Queen Anne's War), was running its course and arousing deep hatred among Europe's peoples, the Pennsylvania Assembly passed another general naturalization act.[497] This met with opposition from the British government, as is evidenced by the following passages from two of Penn's letters. Writing to Logan from London, 29th 7th mo., 1708, Penn says:[498] 'For the naturalization of strangers I being now at liberty, and the Parliament to sit fear it not; yet send me per first a list of all in the country, for the Speaker's profit contests it, no man endeavouring it more under a personal confinement than I did. But bid them be easy. Do as formerly, and heed not the empoisoned breath of our enemies. They are safe from me and mine by my charter, and I shall get them either naturalized or endenizened by the Queen.'

A half-year later (from Reading, 3d 1st mo., 1708-9), he writes to

---

497 Cf. Monograph Number Two, pp. 221, 418-421.
498 *Memoirs* of the Pennsylvania Historical Society, Vol. X (1872), p. 292.

PENN'S 'TREATY WITH THE INDIANS'

Logan :[499] 'Tho' we have here a bill for naturalization in the House, and I think I never writ so correctly, as I did to some members of Parliament, as well as discoursed them on that subject, yet that point being a fair flower in the Speaker's garland, it moves but slowly ; and lest it should miscarry, fail not, pray, to send me over the names of all our foreigners not born in the country, and I will put them into one Act, or at least patent, for denization, to put them out of their trouble that villain Lloyd put the Saxons and others into, as the chiefest of them told me, and gave it under his hand, which I have to shew. . . . Peace is yet dubious ; yet I think it will be the last campaign, which is ready to open, and the mighty preparations on all hands and sides, rather confirm me in my opinion, as well as our vehemences, and calling out too much at home.'

By this time, negotiations for peace were opened in The Hague, Louis XIV had been beaten, and the war-hatred of foreigners subsided to a degree which enabled the British government not only to tolerate them as desirable settlers in the colonies, but to permit the colonial government of Pennsylvania to admit them to full citizenship. In this respect, also, Penn's wise statesmanship was manifest.

Penn's plans of government included those for counties, townships, cities, the province of Pennsylvania, the 'territories' of Delaware, and a federal union of all the British colonies in America. Unlike the county system of local government in the Southern colonies and the township system in New England, Pennsylvania's was neither exclusively one nor the other, but a mixture of both. Thus a centralization of rural administration was made possible side by side with a large degree of local self-government. Three counties were set up in the province (Philadelphia, Bucks, and Chester), and three in the territories (Newcastle, Kent, and Sussex), courts, sheriffs, and other officials being established in each. By the time of his departure for England in 1684, the rural population had increased to about seven thousand and Penn had set up twenty townships for their government. The towns, too, were to be linked together by a system of 'high-ways' at least forty feet in width.

By this time, Philadelphia's population numbered about 2,500, and it too was provided with local self-government. The site selected by Penn for this, his capital city (and paid for to both Indians and Swedes), was a fortunate one in every respect except, perhaps, its distance from

[499] ibid. p. 323.

the seaboard. The plan which he conceived for it was on a generous scale, comprising ten thousand acres at the junction of the two rivers, the Delaware and the Schuylkill,[500] with a checker-board arrangement of streets, four of these one hundred feet wide and twenty-eight, crossing them at right angles, fifty feet in breadth.

Penn's pride in his 'City of Brotherly Love,' which he hoped would always remain 'a greene country town, which will never be burnt and always wholesome,' was manifested in the first year of his residence in it, when he wrote to the Free Society of Traders : 'I say little of the town itself ; . . . but this I will say, for the good providence of God, of all the places I have seen in the world I remember not one better seated ; so that it seems to me to have been appointed for a town, whether we regard the rivers, or the conveniency of the coves, docks, and springs, the loftiness and soundness of the land, and the air, held by the people of these parts to be very good.'

A central public square of ten acres, and four more of eight acres each in the four quarters of the city were provided 'for the comfort and recreation of all forever.' A school was opened in 1683, and a printing press set up in 1685.

Penn's quite modern ideas of city-planning included also the granting of a charter to Philadelphia (at least as early as 1691, and probably earlier), which gave it a government of its own separate from that of Philadelphia County.[501] But his conception of a democratic city government ended with giving it its own, instead of an outside government. He did not place the selection of its mayor and councilmen in the hands of its citizens, but provided that they should be selected by the successors of the officials whom he himself appointed in 1701. And since these appointments were for life, Philadelphia's government remained until the Revolution a close corporation, like those which ruled the boroughs in contemporary England.

Realizing that 'except the Lord build the house, they labour in vain that build it : except the Lord keep the city, the watchman waketh but in vain,' Penn strove to place his beloved city upon a high moral and religious basis. He gave instructions against intemperance and im-

---

500 The river banks he considered 'as a common from end to end,' and he 'would not sell the shore nor the land in the water to any man' (Penn's reply in 1683 to some Philadelphia land-owners).

501 Penn's charter of October 25, 1701, is the one under which Philadelphia exercised its self-government for many years. The original has been deposited in the library of the Pennsylvania Historical Society.

'THE PENN ELM TREE'

morality of various kinds — probably going to the Puritan Quaker extreme in this; and on his departure for England, he included in his letter of farewell the following prayer:

'And thou, Philadelphia, the virgin settlement of this province, named before thou wert born, what love, what care, what service, and what travail, has there been to bring thee forth and preserve thee from such as would abuse and defile thee!

'"O that thou mayest be kept from the evil that would overwhelm thee; that, faithful to the God of thy mercies, in the life of righteousness thou mayest be preserved to the end! My soul prays to God for thee, that thou mayest stand in the day of trial, that thy children may be blessed of the Lord, and thy people saved by his power. My love to thee has been great, and the remembrance of thee affects my heart and mine eye.... The God of eternal strength keep and preserve thee to his glory and peace!"'

The political union between Pennsylvania and Delaware occasioned difficulties both political and financial, and called for a tactful, statesmanlike solution. At first, the Delaware 'territories' were incorporated in the Pennsylvania 'province,' since they had been granted to Penn by the Duke of York under deeds of feoffment, and numbered only four thousand inhabitants. A boundary dispute with Lord Baltimore was decided in Penn's favour by the British Privy Council in 1685 and again in 1732, 1750 and 1760.

The first Pennsylvania assembly in 1682 passed an act uniting 'the three lower counties on the Delaware,' as the 'territories' were also called, to Pennsylvania. But the demands of the 'territorials' for equal representation in the 'provincial' assembly, for their choice of their own judges and other officials, and for a privileged status in regard to taxes, soon threatened disunion. Penn met the difficulty by appointing their leader, Colonel Markham, the deputy-governor of the territories, and by making a concession on taxes. This arrangement lasted for another decade (except during the two years when both Pennsylvania and Delaware became royal colonies), and then Penn met renewed demands by the agreement that an entirely separate government should be set up in Delaware, after three more years of union, should its people so desire. The people did so desire, and in 1703 the 'lower counties' were separated from the province and thereafter (until the Revolution in 1776) had their own provincial or proprietary government, except that they had the same men as governors who were governors of Pennsylvania, thus constituting a 'personal' as opposed to a 'political' union, such as existed between England and Scotland before 1707.

Penn tried his hand, also, in planning a far more important union or federation of all the British colonies in North America. He did this under the stress of the third of Louis XIV's wars of aggression, or King William's War as it was called in America. William III, to promote this war, appointed in 1696 a committee, The Lords of Trade and Plantations, which promptly advised him to pool all the military resources of the colonies under the command of a captain-general, who should also assume the powers of the governors in those colonies into which his military activities might lead him in person.

To meet this threat of a military dictatorship, Penn appeared before the Lords of Trade, on December 11, 1696, as a proprietor of East New Jersey. After protesting against the collection of customs by New York on goods sent to Jersey, 'he spoke also of the Quota required from the neighbouring Colonies for the defence of New York And said that he conceived the best way of regulating it would be, by stated Deputies from each Province, to meet in one common Assembly : The effecting of which was observed to require one Captain General or Vice Roy to preside. But upon these heads he was desired and he promised to draw up a scheme more fully in writing.'[502]

In conformity with this promise, on February 8, 1696 [1697], he submitted the following :

'William Penn's Plans for a Union of the Colonies,
8th February, 1696/7

'A Briefe and Plaine Scheam how the English Colonies in the North parts of America Viz : Boston Connecticut Road Island New York New Jersey, Pensilvania, Maryland, Virginia and Carolina may be made more usefull to the Crowne, and one anothers peace and safety with an universall concurrance.

'1st. That the severall Colonies before mentioned do meet once a year, and oftener if need be, during the war, and at least once in two years in times of peace, by their stated and appointed Deputies, to debate and resolve of such measures as are most adviseable for their better understanding and the publick tranquility and safety.

'2. That in order to it two persons well qualified for sence sobriety and substance be appointed by each Province as their Representatives

[502] 'New York Colonial Documents,' Vol. IV, p. 246.

A Topical Biography 237

or Deputies, which in the whole make the Congress to consist of twenty persons.

'3. That the King's Commissioners for that purpose specially appointed shall have the Chaire and preside in the said Congresse.

'4. That they shall meet as near as conveniently may be to the most centrall Colony for ease of the Deputies.

'5. Since that may in all probability, be New York both because it is near the Center of the Colonies and for that it is a Frontier and in the Kings nomination, the Govr of that Colony may therefore also be the Kings High Commissioner during the Session after the manner of Scotland.

'6. That their business shall be to hear and adjust all matters of Complaint or differences between Province and Province, As 1st where persons quit their own Province and goe to another, that they may avoid their just debts tho they be able to pay them, 2^d where offenders fly Justice, or Justice cannot well be had upon such offenders in the Provinces that entertaine them, 3dly to prevent or cure injuries in point of commerce, 4th, to consider of ways and means to support the union and safety of these Provinces against the publick enemies. In which Congress the Quotas of men and Charges will be much Easier, and more equally sett, then [than] it is possible for any establishment made here to do; for the Provinces, knowing their own condition and one anothers, can debate that matter with more freedome and satisfaction and better adjust and ballance their affairs in all respects for their common safty.

'7^{ly} That in times of war the Kings High Commissioner shall be generall (or Chief Commander) of the severall Quotas upon service against the Common Enemy as he shall be advised, for the good and benefit of the whole.'[503]

Penn's thoughts on this subject may have been directed or crystallized by a letter which he had received from a New York correspondent, P. D. La Noy, under date of June 13, 1695. After complaining of the actions of the royal governor Fletcher, La Noy said:[504] 'I wish his Maj^{ty} would place a Generall Govern^r over New England, New York and the Jerseys, so as the Assemblys, Courts of Judicature and Laws of the respective colonys may remaine and be kept separate

---

[503] ibid. p. 296. There is no date given in this collection to the paper, but it is supplied in *Memoirs of the Historical Society of Pennsylvania*, vol. iv., part ii, p. 265.
[504] ibid. p. 224.

and entire as they now are; for our laws & manner of trade are different from one another and the distance betwixt us would make very uneasie for the rest of the Provinces to resort to any one for comon justice. But a Union under one Govern^r would be very convenient and particularly in time of war, and be a terrour to the French of Canada who assume a boldness purely from our divisions into separate bodyes and the piques that are to comon amongst the several govern^{rs} of which the French don't want a constant intelligence.'

La Noy's letter was evidence of the strong and growing demand for colonial union against the French and their Indian allies; but whether Penn yielded to this demand for a common military defence because he desired that the colonies should be kept 'separate and entire as they now are'; or whether he considered it impossible to persuade the white Christians of England and France to deal with one another without the defence of armed force, as the white Quakers were successfully dealing with the heathen Indians of Pennsylvania, New Jersey, and Delaware: which of these was the controlling reason for his action is left to conjecture. To have departed from his Quaker principles and practice for the sake of suggesting 'a compromise within the realm of practical politics' would have been bad enough; but to have done so for the sake of preserving his province from a second confiscation would have been still worse. Perhaps Louis XIV's foreshadowing of a Hitler and Mussolini terrorized Penn lest a similar military dictatorship should arise out of the long and sanguine warfare and put an end to all hope of democracy in the New World.

The union of the colonies did come, a half-century after Penn's death and after another famous Pennsylvanian, Benjamin Franklin, had championed it at Albany and Philadelphia;[505] but when it came, it was directed, not against the 'old enemy,' France, but against the Mother Country herself, and it resulted in the loss of the fairest jewels in her colonial crown. Could William III have foreseen this result, he probably would not have regarded colonial union on the military basis as within the realm of 'practical politics.'

The most statesmanlike and successful feature of Penn's 'Plan of Union' was the suggestion of a permanent congress in which 'all matters of Complaint or differences between Province and Province' might be heard and adjusted. In this, we find repeated the proposal of 'a dyet or congress' of the nations, which made his 'Essay' of 1693

---

505 See Monograph Number Three, pp. 115-117.

so memorable and which was to be realized in the Supreme Court of the United States and the two international courts at The Hague. Pennsylvania's mixed juries of whites and Indians, and Penn's plan for 'three Peace-makers chosen by every County Court, in the nature of common Arbitrators, to hear and end differences between man and man,' are interesting stepping-stones towards the peaceful international settlement of international disputes. His institution of 'Arbitrators' was doubtless suggested by the *Vredemakers* of Holland; and thus was completed the circuit from The Hague back to The Hague, by way of the City of Brotherly Love.

The severely critical, and cynical, assessors of Penn's Holy Experiment write it off as a failure during his life-time because of his chimerical Quaker ideas, and a success after his death only in spite of them. Complete religious liberty; a government without war and without oaths; a religion without an established church or a professional, salaried ministry, without dogma or ritual; a refuge for the downtrodden and despised of every nation and race; reformatories, instead of prisons; a chance for reform, instead of capital punishment; no aristocracy by birth or wealth; an earthly paradise, with all these ideals realized side by side with a prosperous agriculture and commerce, pursued by enterprising and efficient pioneers and adorned by the beauty of art and exalted by righteousness. These were the ideals which Penn had in mind when he wrote:[506] 'As my understanding and inclinations have been much directed to observe and reprove mischiefs in government, so it is now put into my power to settle one.'

Severely critical biographers have also insisted that Penn was not a *Quaker* statesman; that this characterization is a contradiction in terms; that it was only when he ceased to be a Quaker that he became a statesman, and vice versa; that all the failures and futilities of his career as a statesman were due to the dry rot of Quakerism; and that if he could have got farther away from Quakerism and stayed there, his 'experiment' might not have been so 'holy,' but would have been a statesmanlike success. But this is merely to say that he would have been an entirely different man, and not William Penn at all. For the ideals of government which he sought to realize were precisely the ideals of Quakerism. Although he was certainly a leader of Quakerism, he was, like all true leaders, a follower or an exponent of the ideals cherished by his fellow-members, or fellow-citizens, or fellowmen.

506 Letter to Robert Turner, 1681.

The Quaker attitude towards 'all prizes, stage-plays, cards, dice, may-games, masques, revels, bull-baitings, cock-fightings, bear-baitings, and the like, which excite the people to rudeness, cruelty, looseness, and irreligion,' as well as towards 'all offences against God, such as swearing, cursing, lying, profane talking and drunkenness,' and towards 'all scandalous and malicious reporters, backbiters, defamers, and spreaders of false news,' was reflected in the penal code of Pennsylvania. In the higher realm of government, Penn practised the Quaker ideals of religious liberty, a congregational church-government, civil freedom and democratic equality for men of every nation, race, and colour, and the rejection of military force and oaths. He adopted the ideal of prison reform and the treatment of criminals which the Quakers had developed through their own long and hard experience. A rejection of capital punishment, for example, was a part of this idea; for he excluded from his list of capital crimes about two hundred which stood (and were continuing to stand for a century) on the statute-books of England, and retained only the crime of wilful murder to be punished by death. Even this was retained, apparently, as a concession to the British government — a kind of sop to Cerberus — which without it might have vetoed the rest of his criminal code.

Indeed, it would seem to have been not so much the defects of Quakerism which prevented Penn's statesmanship from being a complete success, as it was the spurious statesmanship of the British rulers who exercised a partial control upon Penn's efforts, and whose continual warfare abroad and suppression of democracy at home constantly interfered with Penn's great experiment in the New World of America for a new world of human life and society. The very framework of the Society of Friends — with its democratic control in monthly, quarterly, and yearly meetings, its methods of settling disputes and establishing justice among its members, its devotion to moral and social reform, its insistence on at least a 'practical' elementary education for every boy and girl, and a subordination of political citizenship to religious conviction and duty — was incorporated at many points in Penn's polity for Pennsylvania.[507] Puritanism was not more potent in shaping New England practice than was Quakerism in shaping the conduct of life in Pennsylvania, New Jersey, and Delaware.

It was largely because of the invincible traits of the Quakers that Penn had so much trouble during his later years with the conflict

---

507 Cf. Isaac Sharpless, *A Quaker Experiment in Government*, 1898, *passim*.

between his governors and their assembly, with the collection of government taxes and proprietary quit-rents, with his brief essays in retaining the initiative in legislation, in setting up a 'hydra-headed' executive, in threatening the use of the suspensory power, and especially with his struggle with the British government over the question of military 'defence.'

While Penn's feelings were hurt and he was mentally vexed and financially embarrassed by these unexpected difficulties with his Quaker colonists, he realized that, beneath the superficial and unnecessary irritants which they launched against him, there was a profound movement of democracy. He yielded to it and conceded what they desired, because he knew that he shared fully in his inmost soul Quakerism's conviction that democracy is God's will and man's possibility, and that all the things in this world, including government itself, are insignificant or irrelevant in comparison with the spirit of God as revealed in the souls of men.

'JESUIT' AND COURTIER

THE three years and nine months of James II's reign are regarded as the darkest period of Penn's career, although they were spent within the halo that surrounds a royal court. In the public mind, Penn was regarded as a Jesuit in disguise; but in the palaces of the king, he was a welcome and powerful courtier, and almost revived the unpopular institution of royal favourite.

It seems preposterous that any Quaker, especially William Penn, should ever have been regarded as a 'Jesuit'; but in the national hysteria which made the Popish Plot accepted as a reality, even such an illusion was possible. There were circumstances too which made such a belief plausible. Rumours concerning Penn were accepted as facts. One of these was his alleged reply to a fellow-traveller in a coach who asked him how, though a Quaker, he could converse so learnedly; perhaps with a smile of amusement, Penn replied: 'It may come from my having studied at Saumur in France.' Since this name sounded to his unlearned questioner like Saint Omer, the report spread that he had received his education at the famous Jesuit seminary at that place. It was also reported that he had received holy orders at Rome; that he regularly performed mass in the royal chapel at Whitehall; that he had been able to have a wife and family only by special papal dispensation; that he had written (over his familiar initials, 'W.P.') some verses lamenting the death of Charles and congratulating James on his succession, which were replete with devotion to the pope.

Penn wrote a denial of this last rumour in a letter entitled *Fiction found out*.[508] The mingled contempt and humour of his letter may be seen in the following quotation from it: 'For the verses — if it be considered, the two letters W.P. begin five hundred names besides mine; and I that pretend not to *poetry* at any time, should hardly have done it then, when I must needs look to have such sad company as the dull flattery of all the suburbs of the town. But that I did not write them, the stuff itself shows; and they must be bereaved of sense, as well as charity, that can think it. For to own myself a Quaker and jeer the profession; to use their phrases and profane them; to promise as Quakers to live peaceably, and yet engage to be no more such; to make ourselves loyal in one stanza, and ask pardon for not being so in another; be now a mistaken and wilful rout, and presently the loving and loyal friends of Charles and James; make up a jarr and a nonsense that I have not been used to be guilty of in prose; and whenever I turn such a penny-poet, let such confusion be my judgment.'

Denials, of course, never overtake such rumours; and what seemed to verify them were the unconcealed religious practices of Penn's great friend and patron, James II. Unlike his brother Charles, James openly avowed himself a Catholic; he and his queen regularly attended mass at Whitehall and gathered round them their fellow-Catholics;[509] he sent an ambassador to the papal court at Rome; a papal nuncio came to England as in 'Bloody Mary's' reign, and like Mary, James knelt before him — the first step, alarmed Protestants said, to following her example of surrendering England to the pope and receiving it back as a papal fief. While several Catholic orders established themselves in London, the Jesuits opened a school in the palace of Savoy; and a Jesuit, Father Petre, became the king's confessor.

The friendship of James and Penn was deep-seated and of long

508 Dated Worminghurst, 2nd month (April) 30, 1685; *Works*, I, 125.
509 Penn in a letter of 16th of 1st month (March) 1685, to Thomas Lloyd says: 'The Popish lords and gentry go to Whitehall to mass daily, and the Tower, or Royal Chapel is crammed by vying with the Protestant lords and gentry.'

KING JAMES II

standing. For twenty-five years as Duke of York, James had frequently showed his fidelity to the promise which he had made to the dying Admiral in his son's behalf. He had helped Penn out of prison in 1670, and did what he could to shorten or prevent other incarcerations. Three years later, Penn called on James in behalf of another Quaker prisoner, George Fox, and the story of his very kindly reception is told in his autobiographical fragments as follows:[510] 'The third time I came to court was in '73, having not frequented it for five years. The business that drew me thither, was the imprisonment of that servant of God, my worthy friend George Fox, in Worcester Castle; .... it was resolved amongst us at London to remove him by habeas corpus to the King's bench, and try what we could do at the court to procure his discharge.

'It fell to my lot to go on this errand, in which solicitations William Mead accompanied me. The person we first addressed ourselves to was the Earl of Middlesex, now also Dorsat, who advised us to make our application to the Duke of York as most powerful with the king, and that if he would receive us, that nobody would be more zealous to perform what he undertook, adding that he would speak to him, and that Fleetwood Shepherd should introduce us.

'The time being fixt, we found that gentleman as was agreed, and went with him to the Duke's palace, where he endeavoured our admission by the means of the Duchess' Secretary; but the house being very full of people and the Duke of business, the said Secretary could neither procure our nor his own admission; but Colonel Aston, of the bedchamber, then in waiting, and my old acquaintance and friend (yet I had not seen him in some years before) looking hard at me, thinking he should know me, asked me in the drawing-room, first my name and then my business, and upon understanding both, he presently gave us the favour we waited for, of speaking with the Duke, who came immediately out of his closet to us.

'After something I said as an introduction to the business, I delivered him our request. He perused it, and then told us That he was against all persecution for the sake of religion. That it was true he had in his younger time been warm, especially when he thought people made it a pretence to disturb government, but that he had seen and considered things better, and he was for doing to others as he would have others do unto him; and he thought it would be happy for the world

510 Cf. *supra*, p. 111.

if all were of that mind; for he was sure, he said, that no man was willing to be persecuted himself for his own conscience. He added that he looked upon us as a quiet, industrious people, and though he was not of our judgment, yet he liked our good lives, with much more to the same purpose, promising he would speak to his brother, and doubted not but that the king's counsel would have orders in our friend's favour.

'I and my companion spoke as occasion offered, to recommend both our business and our character, but the less because he prevented us in the manner I have expressed.

'When he had done upon this affair, he was pleased to take a very particular notice of me, both for the relation my father had had to his service in the navy, and the care he had promised him to show in my regard upon all occasions.

'That he wondered I had not been with him, and that whenever I had any business thither, he would order that I should have access; after which he withdrew and we returned.

'This was my first visit to the court after five years' retirement; and this the success of it, and the first time I had spoken with him since '65. That it should be grateful to me was no wonder; and, perhaps, that with some was the beginning of my faults at court, but what impression it made upon my companion, and the expressions he used to declare it, cannot well escape the memory of F. Shepherd, to whom, in the garden, he presently related what had past, and his own extraordinary satisfaction, both in that and the Duke.'

For New Jersey and Delaware, Penn owed much to James; and the latter's aid in procuring the charter for Pennsylvania was so great that a Quaker biographer of Penn flatly declares: 'William Penn would never have got his charter but for the friendliness and support of the Duke of York . . . ; so that Philadelphia after all owes its existence to that misguided man, King James II!'[511] To these reasons for gratitude, Penn added the greatest of all, namely, James's expressed belief in religious toleration and the clemency which he extended to Quakers imprisoned for religion's sake.

On James's part, there was an acknowledged liking for Penn, and probably a real though suppressed respect for his integrity and idealism. 'The King loved him,' says the non-Quaker Croese,[512] 'as a singular

---

[511] Graham, 1924, p. 128.
[512] *Historia Quakeriana*, 1695, p. 369 (1696, Book II, p. 106).

A Topical Biography 245

and entire friend, and imparted to him many of his secrets and counsels. He often honoured him with his company . . . discoursing with him of various affairs, and that, not for one, but for many hours together, delaying to hear the best of his peers who at the same time were waiting for an audience.' When one of these ventured to remonstrate with the king for his partiality, Croese says that he received the reply : 'Mr. Penn always talks ingenuously, and I listen to him with pleasure.' Amidst so many false and doubtful courtiers, and without apparently any other real friend, even a king might welcome the friendly companionship of a great and kindly man like Penn, who had no axe of his own for the royal grindstone and sought no favours for himself.[513]

Indeed, the name of 'courtier' seems as inappropriate for Penn as does that of Jesuit ; for, although he took a mansion in Hyde Park and was almost continuously calling on the king in one or other of the royal palaces, the business which he transacted with him, aside from their friendly conversations and Penn's appeal for general toleration, was in behalf of others. The name of mediator, rather than courtier, would best fit him ; and the number of his clients was very large. 'His house and gates were daily thronged by a numerous train of clients and suppliants,' Croese wrote, 'desiring him to present their appeals to his majesty ; there were sometimes two hundred and more.'

This personal contact with the king was the usual method of conducting public business in the days before the Revolution of 1688 had subordinated the royal power to government by parliamentary committees, the cabinet, and permanent departments. It was the common practice for his courtiers to obtain the king's necessary initiative or referendum, and they were a special kind of attorney, agent, or middleman, who amused the king as well as received the fees of their clients. Penn, while he may have interested, if not amused, the king, accepted no fees from his numerous and varied clients. Most of his intercession appears to have been for the victims of religious persecution ; but there are evidences of other kinds of work, as in the dispute between a Whig leader, Sir Robert Stuart, and the Earl of Arran. Penn procured

---

[513] There were, of course, differences and contrasts between the two men, although the following caricature scarcely does justice to them : 'No two men could have been more flatly unlike each other. There was James with his green supercilious face, the mask of cruelty and weakness ; and there was Penn, softly important, a rounded parsonic figure (though only forty-one), an elderly cherub in a round hat, beaming with idealised humanity' (Vulliamy, 1934, p. 210).

Stuart's pardon and return from exile; and then, finding that Arran was unjustly retaining Stuart's estates, he successfully threatened the king's displeasure unless the earl settled a yearly payment upon him.[514]

We hear also of other Whig exiles, namely, John Trenchard and Aaron Smith, whose pardons Penn obtained — even though they had to be passed upon by the infamous chancellor, Lord Jeffries. The influence of the Quaker courtier, who had been also a prominent Whig, is strikingly emphasized by the fact that he actually induced the king to pardon Smith, after at least one angry refusal, although Smith was accused of complicity in the Rye House Plot and refused to give evidence against his leader, Algernon Sidney. He even induced the king to receive other suspected Whigs and to listen to recitals from them of the Whig policy of toleration, Anglican supremacy, and civil liberties.[515]

The greatest of the Whig exiles was John Locke, whom James as Duke of York had been largely instrumental in having expelled from his Oxford professorship and driven into exile in Holland; but at Penn's earnest request, James as king cancelled his antipathy as duke and granted Locke a full pardon. Locke expressed his deep sense of obligation to Penn, but like George Fox before him was true to his own sense of justice and refused to accept the pardon, since he had not been guilty of any crime. In later years, when Penn was under a cloud during the reign of William III, Locke was glad to intervene in his behalf; and against the charge of Penn's Jesuitism, Sir William Popple was able to be of service, in return for the pardon which Penn had procured for him also.

The Whig revolt which led to Monmouth's Rebellion at the beginning of James's reign, led also to Penn's greatest activity in procuring pardons and to the worst accusations that have ever been made against him. Lord Macaulay, the son of a Quaker mother, utilized one episode in the prosecutions following this rebellion, that of the 'Maids of Taunton,' to decorate and give a piquant flavour to his historical drama by making unsubstantiated and unrepented-of charges against William Penn; but that eminent statesman, Right Honourable William E. Forster, the son of a Quaker father, has so conclusively disproved these charges that the empty straw needs no further threshing.

514 *Memoirs* of the Pennsylvania Historical Society, IV, 183.
515 Charlewood Lawton's narrative (ibid. III, 2).

Macaulay made eight other baseless accusations against Penn,[516] and they were greeted with vast indignation by the admirers of Penn and the lovers of historic truth; but even his fellow-Quakers — after the charges were disproved — were enabled to say with their poet, John G. Whittier:

> How vainly he labored to sully with blame
> The white bust of Penn in the niche of his fame!
> Self-will is self wounding, perversity blind,
> On himself fell the stain for the Quaker designed.
> For the sake of his true-hearted father before him,
> For the sake of the dear Quaker mother that bore him,
> For the sake of his gifts and the works that outlive him,
> And his brave words for freedom, we freely forgive him!

Of the thousand victims of the rebellion who escaped the massacre committed by 'Kirke's Lambs' and the gibbets of Jeffreys, Penn begged of the king the pardon of twenty who had been sentenced to death or transportation, and he may have succeeded in having them sent to Pennsylvania, instead of into slavery in Barbados.[517] He was brave and honest enough, even Bishop Burnet admitted,[518] to protest to the king against the butchery of 'the Bloody Assize,' and that in the face of the fact that Monmouth's Whig followers regarded him as a friend and listed him as one of those who could rally the colonies to their support.

For some of the victims executed in London, also, Penn showed his sympathy. This was noticeably the case with Henry Cornish and Elizabeth Gaunt, for whose pardons Penn appealed in vain. Cornish had been one of the London sheriffs elected in 1680 by the Whigs, and was accused of complicity in the Rye House Plot; evidence of the latter was found, and Cornish was hanged in front of his own house in Cheapside. Penn, the friend of both Cornish and Sidney, stood

---

516 Cf. John Paget's *Paradoxes and Puzzles*, 1874, *The New Examen*, 1858 and 1861.
517 Buell (p. 195) asserts that he did, and that 'their descendants have been governors of American States and Senators in the American Congress. One of their descendants, on his mother's side, was a general officer in the American Revolution; his name was Nathaniel Greene — a name not unknown to the history of England!' Penn merely says (speaking of the prosecutions): 'About 300 hanged in divers towns in the West, about 1000 to be transported. I begged twenty of the King. Colonel Holmes, young Hayes, the two Hewlings, Lark, and Hicks' (Letter to Thomas Lloyd, 2nd of 8th month (October, 1685).
518 *History of his own Times*, III, 66.

manfully by him at his death, when one of Cornish's closer friends feared to do so.[519] Burnet says that it was given out that Cornish 'died in a fit of fury; but Pen who saw the execution said to me, there appeared nothing but a just indignation that innocence might very naturally give.'[520] Elizabeth Gaunt, who appears from her piety, charity, and interest in the reformation of prisons to have been an earlier Elizabeth Fry, had sheltered in her house one of the fugitive rebels. The fugitive himself testified against her, and she was sent to Tyburn and burnt at the stake! 'Pen the Quaker told me,' says Burnet, 'he saw her die. She laid the straw about her for burning her speedily, and behaved herself in such a manner that all the spectators melted in tears. . . . Pen might well be relied on in such matters, he being so entirely in the king's interests.'

The reason why the cruel death by fire was meted out to Elizabeth Gaunt was probably the fact that she was regarded as not only a political rebel, but also as an ardent Protestant. 'She rejoiced,' Bishop Burnet continues, 'that God had honoured her to be the first that suffered by fire in this reign; and that her suffering was a martyrdom for that religion which was all love.' Although Macaulay sneers at Penn—'for whom exhibitions which humane men generally avoid, seem to have had a strong attraction'—because he went to witness these executions, he fails to point out that it was usual *then* and for a long time afterwards for the most humane of men to attend public executions; and he fails to note Penn's fearless honesty in standing by those who were suffering for the principles which he himself cherished, although he was strongly opposed to their methods. It is apparent, also, that while Penn was attached to Cornish because of political principle, he admired Elizabeth Gaunt because of her religious steadfastness.

James's own attitude towards the ruthless prosecution and savage punishment of the rebels was one of approval, and perhaps of incitement as well, and against this, Penn vigorously protested; but Burnet says that he told him: 'The king was much to be pitied, who was hurried into all this effusion of blood by Jeffrey's impetuous and cruel temper.'[521] Penn would now doubtless admit the justice of Burnet's

---

519 *Life of Galmany*, I, 61 (Quoted by Grant, p. 168).
520 loc.cit.
521 Burnet, op.cit., I, 651.

comment that the tragedy would not have occurred if James and his priests had opposed, or at least not approved it ; and he would probably emphasize the historical explanation that it was due, not so much to James's ruthless nature as to his alarm at the very critical character of his position, with plots and rebellions behind him, an Anglican Church and Protestant people around him, and with an impending revolution casting its shadow before.

For both political and religious factors dominated the course of James's reign, and William Penn was deeply concerned in both ; in fact the two strands of its history were so intricately entangled as to constitute a single unit, and this accounts chiefly for Penn's apparent two-fold activity. His chief religious concern was, of course, toleration for both his fellow-Quakers and all his fellow-Englishmen. His first need, therefore, was to disabuse the popular mind, if possible, of the strange belief that his advocacy of toleration was due to his being a Jesuit and therefore eager to restore England to the papal fold. He had begun to meet the charge of Jesuitism hurled against him as early as 1668, in which year he denounced Roman Catholicism with youthful vigour in his pamphlet entitled *Truth Exalted*.[522] But as he exalted in this Quakerism only and denounced all other religions, his first controversialist opponent, Thomas Vincent, insisted that he — though not his Quaker companion, George Whitehead — was a 'Jesuit in the pay of the pope.'[523]

Two years later, he again belaboured the papists and Jesuits[524] in such vigorous fashion that his opponents said that he did protest too much, and were confirmed in their belief that his denunciation was designed to cover up his own complicity. In the same year, too, Charles made his secret treaty of Dover with Louis XIV ; and although Englishmen did not know of this at the time, they were deeply suspicious of Louis's and the Jesuits' designs upon their crown and their religion.

Moreover, Penn, while denouncing Roman Catholicism, strangely and suspiciously insisted that it, equally with all religions, must be conceded complete toleration. A Catholic Englishman took him at his word and felt aggrieved at his rough handling of the Mother

---

522 *Supra,*, p. 140.
523 *Supra*, p. 133.
524 In his *Seasonable Caveat against Popery* ; *supra*, p. 139.

Church; but the *Letter to a Roman Catholic* which he wrote and had published in 1675 did not convince his fellow-Protestants, although it may have soothed his Catholic correspondent.

Even the acquisition of Pennsylvania was attributed to a design on the part of the Jesuit Penn and the Catholic James to make of it a Catholic bulwark and possible base of operations against Protestantism at home and in the colonies. Penn's English agent, Philip Ford of Bristol, found it necessary after the *Welcome's* departure in 1682 to publish *A Vindication of William Penn,* in which he had to deny not only the reports of his Jesuitism while alive, but also the rumour which appeared in the London *Gazette* of January 15, 1683, that he had died a confessed Jesuit! [525]

The belief or assertion that Penn was a Jesuit spread to the Continent, also, and his friend and translator, Willem Sewel of Amsterdam, published refutations of it.[526] But it does not appear to have been widely accredited there; for there is no evidence that it affected adversely the stream of Dutch and German Protestant emigration to Pennsylvania.[527]

When James became king and Penn a courtier at his court, it was all the more impossible to lay the charge of Jesuitism. Some of the best and wisest in the land were for a time misled by it. Even the benign Dr. John Tillotson, Dean of St. Paul's and appointed by William III in 1791 Archbishop of Canterbury, accepted and helped to spread the report that Penn was a Jesuit and kept up a secret correspondence with the Jesuits in Rome. A very frank and kindly correspondence between Penn and Tillotson set all of the Dean's doubts at rest, and he candidly admitted his error and promised to do what he could to put an end to the falsehood.[528] At Penn's request, he gladly gave permission for his letters to be shown to others, which Penn took care to do.

But two years later, it was still necessary for Penn and his friends to deny the fantastic rumour. This time, Sir William Popple, an old-time friend and then the secretary to the Privy Council's Committee on

---

525 *Pennsylvania Magazine,* VI (1882), 176.
526 See Monograph Number One, p. 80.
527 See Monograph Number Two (*William Penn and the Dutch Quaker Migration to Pennsylvania*), p. 90.
528 Penn wrote three of the letters and Tillotson two (all under date of January and April, 1686). Besides a straight denial of the report, Penn referred in his letters to his *Address to Protestants,* 1679, and the first four chapters of *No Cross, No Crown.*

A Topical Biography 251

Trade and Plantations, wrote to him a long letter relating the details of the Jesuit story, and Penn replied in another letter denying and disproving these details one by one. The two letters were published under the title, *A Letter to Mr. Penn, with his Answer*;[529] and they must have been convincing to every fair-minded person who read them. But by this time James had fallen and the Dutch William had taken his place on England's throne; so that it was no longer a question of 'Penn the Jesuit and Courtier,' but of 'Penn the Jacobite and Traitor.'

Meanwhile, during all these twenty years of denunciation as a Jesuit, Penn had been striving for religious toleration, first, for the so-bitterly-persecuted Quakers, and then with increasing urgency, for Englishmen in general.

The persecution of the Quakers under Charles II has been cited above;[530] but bad as their condition was then, their worst estate was during the first year of James II. One month after his accession, the Quakers presented to him a petition for clemency, in which they stated that about 1640 of their members, of both sexes and various ages, were still in prison in England and Wales—where "some hundreds" of them had died during the past five years—under punishment for holding religious meetings of their own, or for declining to take oaths. Penn himself estimated that since 1660 'above 15,000 families' had been ruined, and 'more than 5,000 persons dead under bonds for matters of mere conscience to God.'[531] It was for their sake, primarily, that Penn returned to England in 1684; and immediately after his arrival on October 6—'after some days of refreshment' at home, Penn says—he repeated his visits of 1668 and 1673 to King Charles and the Duke of York. 'They received me very graciously,' Penn records,[532] 'as did the ministers very civilly; yet I found things in general with another face than I left them : sour and stern, and resolved to hold the reins of power with a stiffer hand than heretofore, especially over those that were observed to be State or Church Dissenters, conceiving that the

---

529 See Monographs Number One (pp. 88-90) and Two (pp. 303-306). Sewel translated them into Dutch and published them from an Amsterdam press, adding to them a preface of his own which cited the recent appearance of the Jesuit stories about Penn in the *Utrechtsche Courant* and in a book entitled *Engeland Beroerd*.
530 *Supra*, p. 199.
531 *Good Advice to the Church of England* . . . , 1687. His estimate probably included non-Quaker as well as Quaker sufferers, especially the Catholic victims of the 'Popish Plot.'
532 Autobiographical fragments.

opposition which made the government uneasy, came from that sort of people, and, therefore, they should either bow or break.

'This made it hard for me, a profest Dissenter, to turn myself — for that party having been my acquaintance, my inclination, and my interest too; to shift them I would not, to serve them I saw I could not, and to keep fair with a displeased and resolved government, that had weathered its point upon them, humbled and mortified them, and was daily improving all advantages against them, was a difficult task to perform.

'Finding myself narrowed in this manner, that one day I was received well at court as proprietor and governor of a province of the crown, and the next taken up at a meeting by Hilton and Collingwood, and the third smoakt [?] and informed of for meeting with the men of the whig stamp. After informing myself of the state of things, I cast about in mind what way I might be helpful to the public, and as little hurtful to my concerns as I could, for I had then a cause depending about bounds of land in America with the Lord Baltimore, before the council, that was of importance to me.

'Upon the whole matter, I found no point so plain, so honest, so sensible, that carried such weight, conviction, and compassion with it, and that would consequently find an easier reception and more friends, than liberty of conscience, my old post and province. I therefore sought out some bleeding cases, which was not hard to do, Bristol, Norwich, &c., being ready at hand in bloody letters — barbarities never used certainly in a Protestant country — especially at Bristol.'

The result of Penn's appeal to Charles was evidently very meagre, as he mentions only his success in procuring the release of one Richard Vickris. This success Penn attributes to James's influence; and within two months after James came to the throne, he ventured to issue a proclamation freeing those who had been imprisoned for refusing oaths. The Anglican parliament, however, opposed this clemency at once; and on the day when the Quakers presented their petition to James, it voted 'that the laws be put in execution against all Dissenters whatever.' In face of parliamentary opposition, and that of the Anglican Church; also because of James's desire to prevent the election to the new parliament of some of the imprisoned Whig leaders; and because of the rise of Monmouth's rebellion, James abstained from issuing a general pardon on his coronation and postponed it until March, 1686. Then he issued a general jail delivery, and some thirteen hundred

A Topical Biography 253

Quakers were released from prison—just in time to revisit their families before going up to London Yearly Meeting, where they were joyously welcomed by their fellow-Quakers after having sat in darkness for terms lasting in some instances as long as fifteen years.

Penn's share in this great success could not fail to be recognized and praised; but he was blamed by some critics for neglecting Pennsylvania in order to bask in the sunshine of the royal court. The lure of his province and of his beloved Philadelphia was strong indeed; but his sense of duty to his suffering Friends in England and to the cause of general toleration was stronger still. The king pressed him to remain in England, and held out to him strong hopes of the toleration he craved and stressed the useful part he could surely play in its establishment.

Charles II's attempts at toleration had not been wholly a failure,[533] and James might carry them to complete success. Penn had made his plea to parliament in 1678,[534] and in two speeches before a committee of the House of Commons had strenuously denied that he and the Quakers had anything in common with the Jesuits and other Catholics. But the excitement over the Popish Plot put an end for a time to all hope of parliamentary relief. During three years of the excitement, Penn was a leader in the Whig campaign to elect Sidney to parliament, and this alone should have proved both his non-Jesuitism and his sincerity in advocating complete toleration.[535] But it too was regarded as a clever camouflage; and to defend himself against the old charge of Jesuitism and the domination of England by anybody except its own parliament, as well as to help Sidney in his second campaign, he published, *An Address to Protestants* and *England's Great Interest in the Choice of this New Parliament*.[536] After Sidney's second defeat, he published *One Project for the Good of England,* which was addressed to the new parliament and suggested a new Test Act which should exclude Catholics only from public office.[537] Still, he insisted on religious toleration for them; and the severe denunciation of them in the pamphlet was again regarded as hypocritical pretence, or as being inconsistent with his general policy, or even as a bait to allure the persecuted Protestants of France to Pennsylvania. There is no doubt of his desire to have the Huguenots go to his province, and it was frankly stated in his letter to James Harrison, his Pennsylvania steward, in a

---

533 *Supra,* p. 201.   534 *Supra,* p. 209.   535 *Supra,* p. 213.
536 *Supra,* pp. 210-3.   537 *Supra,* p. 214 f.

letter dated in October, 1685.[538] In this he says : 'In France, not a meeting of Protestants left, they force all, by not suffering them to sleep, to conform ; they use drums or fling water on the drowsy till they submit or run mad. They pray to be killed, but the King has ordered his dragoons to do anything but kill. . . . Such as fly are caught, are executed or sent to the galleys to row. Thus they use all qualities, from dukes and duchesses to the meanest of that way. Many [persons] and much wealth will visit your parts. Be wise, weighty, and strict against looseness. Believe me it is an *extraordinary day,* such as has not been since generations ago. *Read this to weighty Friends* and magistrates, in private, and gird up your loins and serve the Lord in this juncture. No matter in what part they settle in our country, let not *temporal interest* sway, on my land or on theirs that have bought of me ; no matter, the public will [gain] in a while by their establishment.'

Penn was now to add to his other rôles that of diplomacy. As a severe denunciator of the cruelties perpetrated by Louis XIV's revocation of the Edict of Nantes, and as an English Protestant and Whig foremost in the struggle for religious toleration, James naturally believed that he would be *persona grata* to William of Orange, James's nephew, but the chief opponent of Louis on the Continent and a well-known champion of religious liberty in the Netherlands. James's object was to ascertain if William, whose wife was at that time (1686) the heir presumptive to the English throne, and who was in correspondence with leading English Whigs, would support the repeal of the Test Act and thus give full citizenship as well as toleration to the Catholics.

Penn's purpose in going to the Continent was to visit the Quaker meetings there and to procure colonists for Pennsylvania. He was glad also to accept James's commission as a promising step towards toleration. He had several interviews with William and Mary at The Hague, which were entirely friendly but fruitless, since William had insight enough to realize that the mass of Englishmen were wedded to Anglican supremacy and opposed to full Catholic and dissenter citizenship. His views were influenced by Bishop Burnet, also, who took a dislike to Penn and his far-reaching policy of religious liberty.[539] William was then midway in his thirty years' struggle against Louis

538 *Pemberton MSS.* (quoted by Janney, pp. 258-9).
539 See Monograph Number Two, pp. 118-122.

XIV, and had no patience with Quaker pacifism — a fact which Penn discovered a half-dozen years later when William deprived him for a time of Pennsylvania's government. His sentiments as to pacifism are thus reported by Dr. Montanus in his *Leven van Willem III* :[540] 'Prince William spoke with particular warmth of the so-called scruple of the Quakers against force of arms. He said it was a doctrine without sanction of any law in statute or in morals, human or divine. Those who professed it pretended to teach more than God had taught in His own Word, in Testament Old or New. They pretended to exceed Christ in holiness, and to revise the Ten Commandments by certain inventions of one Fox ; a low, unlettered fellow, claiming new apostleship and impiously asserting particular revelation from God Himself. This, Prince William declared, was a doctrine he would never defend ; those who pretended to believe it placed themselves without the pale of protection by laws which they refused to enforce.'

Little did the protagonists of the method of national security and of international justice, respectively, dream that two centuries later a conference of the nations would be held in The Hague to inaugurate the method of William the Quaker and to begin the repudiation of the method of William the Prince. Nor did they foresee that within two years, William the King would establish religious toleration in England, and thus begin the long process of destroying the Anglican supremacy in political affairs.

Returning to England, Penn continued his work for toleration. He had presented to the king and council, in the spring of 1686, a treatise entitled *A Persuasive to Moderation to dissenting Christians*.[541] In this, he answered the political argument against toleration, namely, that it would endanger the state, and the religious argument, namely, that it would continue to prevent church unity, which was essential to national union. According to his usual method, he backed up reason by experience, and gave a detailed review of ancient and recent history, and quoted an astonishing list of political and literary authorities. Citing his favourite Holland, he wrote : 'Holland, that bog of the world, neither sea nor dry land, now the rival of tallest monarchs ; not by conquests, marriages, or accession of royal blood, the usual ways to empire, but by her own superlative clemency and industry ; for the one was the effect of the other : she cherished her people, whatsoever were their opinions, as the reasonable stock of the country, the heads

540 Quoted by Buell, p. 187.   541 *Works,* II, 727-49.

and hands of her trade and wealth ; and making them easy in the main point, their conscience, she became great by them ; this made her fill with people, and they filled her with riches and strength.'[542]

On the religious side, he argued that toleration and church disunity were entirely consistent, and alone consistent, with genuine national unity. In his historical proofs of this assertion, he referred to Monmouth's Rebellion and the Rye House Plot, and he cited his father's policy of disregarding religious differences in the appointment of naval officers, which was successful when adopted, and disastrous when neglected. He also warmly defended Charles II's ill-fated Declaration of Indulgence of 1671, and may have hoped that it would persuade James to repeat the experiment. At all events, most of his biographers believe that it was largely or chiefly responsible for James's jail delivery in the spring of 1686. Penn himself, writing at that time to James Harrison, said : 'My *Persuasive* works much among all sorts, and is divers spoken of. I have been thrice taken at meetings, but got off, blessed be the Lord.'[543]

One year later (April, 1687), James issued his first Declaration of *Indulgence,* as its opponents called it, or for *Liberty of Conscience,* as he preferred it. In this, he utilized the royal prerogative of dispensing with acts of parliament, and abrogated the Test Acts and all the penal laws for their enforcement. Although the judges of the king's courts had unanimously, with one exception, decided in the king's favour the much disputed question of his constitutional right to take such action, Penn realized that toleration could not be permanent on such a basis.[544] When a Quaker address of thanks was presented to the king therefor, Penn inserted a clause expressing the hope that the Declaration would be sustained by an act of parliament ;[545] and James, responding to the address, said : 'Some of you know (I am sure you do, Mr. Penn), that it was always my principle, that consciences ought not to be forced, and that all men ought to have the liberty of their consciences. And what I have promised in my declaration I will

---

542 He also praises the example of William the Silent,— probably for the behoof of his successor and namesake.
543 *Pemberton MSS.* (quoted by Janney, p. 271).
544 This was the chief constitutional question at issue in the Great Revolution of 1688-89, which was answered by it, of course, in favour of parliamentary supremacy.
545 The phrase was : 'We hope the good effects thereof for the peace, trade, and prosperity of the kingdom will produce such a concurrence from the Parliament as may secure it to our posterity, in after times.'

continue to perform so long as I live. And I hope before I die, to settle it, so that after ages shall have no reason to alter it.'

So far as religious toleration was concerned, it was settled by the Act of 1688; but the repeal of all the test acts, and full religious liberty, had to wait for many a weary year. James had already begun the appointment of Catholics to public office, and Penn evidently approved of this; but he continued to warn the king in their private interviews of the necessity of getting parliamentary sanction for both religious toleration and political appointments. To support publicly this position, Penn wrote the last of his great treatises on toleration, namely, *Good Advice to the Church of England, Roman Catholics and Protestant Dissenters.*[546]

As himself a recent victim of persecution, and as a well-known intimate of the king, Penn published this treatise at first anonymously. Its purpose was to persuade all Englishmen of every sect to accept the policy of toleration and political equality, and to establish it permanently by the election of a parliament which would give it parliamentary as well as royal and judicial sanction. Since this was far in advance of the public opinion of his time, it became later one of the reasons for his condemnation as 'a tool of King James.' The fear of a French and papal despotism still dominated the minds of the English, Anglicans and Dissenters alike; and all the logic and history which Penn crammed into his *Good Advice* failed to shake their determination to reject it *in toto*. Even though he stated that there were only thirty thousand Catholics in England's population of eight million, and suggested an 'equivalent' to the Test Acts in the form of a law making it a capital crime to attempt any repeal of religious liberty, his advice was rejected, Lord Halifax expressing the popular sentiment by saying:[547] 'Look at my nose; it is a very ugly one, but I would not take one five hundred times better as an equivalent, because my own is fast to my face.'

As a former Oxford student, Penn must have been especially interested in the case of the Magdalen College fellows. As leaders of public opinion, Oxford and Cambridge Universities were of great importance even at that time, and James determined to capture them

---

546 *Works*, II, 749-73. His pamphlet, entitled *The great and popular Objection against the Repeal of the Penal Laws*, appeared soon afterward; but it was a brief supplement or summary of *Good Advice*.
547 Mackintosh, *History of the Revolution*, 219 (Quoted by Stoughton, 242).

from Anglican control. Christ Church and University Colleges passed under Catholic control; and when Magdalen's presidency became vacant, he ordered its fellows to elect a Catholic to fill the vacancy. When the fellows refused to do so and chose an Anglican, Dr. Hough, the royal officers took charge of the buildings and excluded president, fellows and students. Penn, in the course of a preaching tour, was in Oxford at the beginning of the dispute and, just as he was leaving the city, wrote a letter of remonstrance to the king, which the fellows delivered to him. His subsequent part in the affair was sufficiently threshed out by Macaulay, his accuser, and William E. Forster, his vindicator, four score years ago.[548] The chief item in it was an anonymous letter to one of the fellows, advising submission to the king's will for fear of serious consequences to themselves and the college. This letter was attributed to Penn by its recipient, and Macaulay accepted it as his, although the contemporary copy of it preserved in Magdalen's archives bears on its margin the words, 'Mr. Penn disowns this'; and although Macaulay could offer no proof whatever that it was Penn's. Macaulay also grossly perverts an account (written by the ousted president, Dr. Hough himself) of a subsequent interview the fellows had with Penn at Windsor, the object and result of which was to obtain Penn's promise to make further efforts with the king in their behalf.

Six out of nine of Penn's biographers accept fully the refutation of Macaulay's version of the Magdalen story — Clarkson writing a generation before it was published, but citing material which was later to discredit it; three of them appear to acquit Penn of intentional dishonesty, but are sceptical of his intelligence. One aspect of the story is indicative of Penn's insight, perhaps of his prescience, namely, his statement to Magdalen's president and fellows : 'I hope you would not have the two Universities such invincible bulwarks for the Church of England that none but they must be capable of giving their children a learned education.' In this conversation, and in the presence of the king at several of his religious meetings and sermons which had preceded it, Penn must have reflected on the dramatic turn of events which had brought him from the condition of a student expelled from Oxford University for his heretical leanings, and from that of a mem-

---

548 Janney, following Forster and another contemporary criticism in *The Tablet* of March 10, 1849, devoted fourteen of his pages to it. Dixon gives seven pages to it, and 'supplementary chapter' of thirty-two pages refuting Macaulay's charges against Penn.

ber of the despised and proscribed sect of the Quakers (who had been treated with such barbarity by Oxford's students), to the position of a mediator with the king in behalf of the proudest and richest of the university's colleges !

James's next attack on parliament by means of 'regulating' the counties, boroughs and corporations so that he might procure the election of the men whom he could trust, met with Penn's disapproval. What action he took, if any, to induce the king to give up the plan is not known. The only evidence we have, is a passage in the narrative of Charlewood Lawton, an ardent Whig and advocate of toleration under James, and Penn's London agent for Pennsylvania during his second visit to his province under William. In this narrative, Lawton said:[549] 'Soon after this, Mr. Penn went into Yorkshire, and during his absence, that justly suspicious and offensive measure of regulating corporations was resolved on. At this I was excessively alarmed, and therefore, went, with a design to take my leave of him, to meet Mr. Penn at his lodgings at Kensington, the day I was told he would return. He did return at the time he had set, and after common civilties, and being by nature very passionate, and then very young, I fell into a vehement declamation against regulations. Mr. Penn let me spend my fury, and after it was over, told me he did not know what I meant, but desired me to tell him coolly what had so disturbed me. I then talked over the matter with more temper, and when I had done, he assured me that was the first time he had ever heard any thing of it. . . . "What thou hast said, hath made impression upon me, and I entreat thee to send me thy thoughts by the penny post, without setting thy name to thy letter, but prithee write with as much vehemence as thou spokest at first; for that warmth will make them enter more into my mind." This request, I must confess, convinced me that he had no hand in setting on foot that measure; and I complied with it, but little imagined what use he intended to make of that letter. That, and several other anonymous letters which he, by honest artifice, from time to time got from me, he showed to the King. . . . Mr. Penn told me the King liked me for my sincerity, and I would have thee (said he) think of some place. The King hath a mind thou shouldst be in commission of the peace, and a member of the next Parliament, and a corporation will be found where some honest gentleman will bring thee in. . . . As to being a member of Parliament, I told him I should

[549] *Memoirs* of the Pennsylvania Historical Society, Vol. III, part 2 (1839).

be glad, if a regulated Parliament did any good, but by the help of God, I would never make one amongst them.'

In defence of James, it has been argued that since it was the usual custom to 'pack' parliament, and a custom in which his political foes were adepts, he was entirely justified by the rule of the political game as played in his time to do his best to 'unpack' it by procuring members who would vote against the dominant party of the Anglican church. Penn's disapproval was based, not so much on the political method employed by either party as on the grave constitutional objection to striking at the roots of popular government through an attack on the units of local self-government.

James having failed, by coercion of the corporations and annulment of borough charters, to procure a compliant parliament, issued another royal Declaration for Liberty of Conscience in April, 1688. This was strengthened, and made more unpopular, by a threat to appoint to public office only those who supported it, and by a demand that it be read on two successive Sundays by the clergy in all the churches of the kingdom. Penn told the king flatly that this was a violation of the very liberty of conscience he had declared, and pleaded with him to withdraw the order, and to rely upon parliament for its passage.

James did promise to summon parliament in the following November, but insisted that his declaration and orders in council should be observed meanwhile; and when the clergy almost unanimously refused to obey, he acted on the advice of Jeffreys and sent as prisoners to the Tower the archbishop of Canterbury and six of the bishops who had presented to him a petition against reading the declaration in the churches. The bishops immediately became popular heroes and were hailed, not so much for defending the prerogatives of the Anglican Church, as for defending English liberty. At the end of June, they were tried before the Court of King's Bench, and the popular excitement was so menacing that the king's judges and jury acquitted them amidst the vast acclaim of the people.

Meanwhile, in June, the Catholic queen (Mary Beatrice of Modena) gave birth to a son — after fifteen years of married life during which several children had died in infancy — and the English people lost their hope of a Protestant successor to the throne in the person of Mary, the wife of William of Orange, and daughter of James by his first, Protestant wife. Immediately the rumour spread that the new Prince of Wales was not the queen's son, and this was strengthened by the fact that only Catholics or the king's most trusted servants were invited to the levée which witnessed the boy's birth. Penn was not present on the occasion; but it was widely believed that he was a party to the deception, as is evidenced by a Dutch cartoon which appeared soon afterwards. This was entitled *Europe alarmed for the Son of a Miller*,[550] and it portrayed the birth of the prince in the presence of his real mother, of Father Peters, James II, the queen, Panurge, Louis XIV and his son, and some Quakers who were *on their way to Pennsylvania*. This last touch was a sly allusion to the deceitfulness of the Quakers and to the mission of Penn to Holland in 1686.[551]

That Penn was at the palace on the prince's birthday is stated by Lawton, who says in his narrative quoted above: 'But before I go further, I must set down Mr. Penn's own behavior that summer, in relation to the bishops who were sent to the Tower. He was not only against their commitment, but the day the Prince of Wales was born, he went to the King, and pressed him exceedingly to set them at liberty, and to order, in council, a general pardon to be issued out, as soon as it could pass the seals. He pressed, most heartily, to have both done, and told his majesty, that on that happy day, every body ought to rejoice, which they would do, if the bishops were let out; and it was generally known such a pardon would soon be proclaimed. Mr. Penn hoped the occasion would have made him succeed in both proposals; and I suppose all men must own, it was unhappy for the King that he did not follow Mr. Penn's advice.'

Since this advice was given in private, and it was only known in public that Penn frequented the court during these critical days, the suspicion against him was strengthened and appeared to be confirmed. The birth of the prince was the signal for the invitation to William of Orange to invade the kingdom; and after a bloodless revolution, James abdicated, and Penn ceased to be a favoured courtier and became suspected of Jacobitism at the royal court, as well as in the country at large.

No one any longer believes, of course, that Penn was a Jesuit, but his conduct as a courtier has continued to this day to be a subject of controversy. Hypocrisy and selfish ambition are urged upon him by some critics; others see in him a kindly mediator in behalf of others;

---
550 *l'Europe Allarmée pour le fils d'un Meunier.*
551 *Zinspeelende op hun bedrog en de missie v.d. Kwaker W.Penn naar Holland.* (F.Muller, "De Nederlandsche Geschiedenis in Platen," Vol. 1 (1863), p. 422, No. 2760).

while his own supreme interest was to procure religious toleration for all. Judged by James's public actions and by his oft-repeated professions to Penn, he was an earnest believer in religious toleration for Catholics and Protestants alike; at any rate, Penn believed so, and in this their policy was alike. The two men agreed also in condemning the Anglican autocracy in church, university, and parliament; but while James strove to substitute for it his own royal autocracy, Penn advocated reliance upon a parliament which he hoped would be instructed by an enlightened electorate to place toleration upon a constitutional, that is, a parliamentary, basis. James had no faith in popular government, and accepted the totalitarian philosophy of his friend and ally, Louis XIV, who summed it all up in the words, *L' état c'est moi!*

Was James the tool of Louis for the establishment of the autocracy of king and pope in England's state and church? And was Penn the dupe and tool of James? Or was he the dupe of his own too enthusiastic hopes? His fellow-courtiers, like Sunderland and Buckingham (whose published views on toleration he wrote a long treatise to commend[552]), were on the lowest level of private and public corruption; Penn, of course, was far above them. 'Would I have made my market of the fears and jealousies of the People,' he wrote,[553] 'when this King came to the crown, I had put twenty thousand pounds into my pocket, and an hundred thousand into my province; for mighty numbers of people were then upon the wing; but I waived it all; hoped for better times; expected the effect of the King's word for liberty of conscience, and happiness by it.'

Posterity has fully accepted his plea and acquitted him entirely of dishonesty and hypocrisy. But was he justified in striving with such men and James's other courtiers for even a great good? Statesmen answer yes; compromises with men and measures they regard as necessary to success; politics makes strange bed-fellows, they reluctantly admit, but they console themselves with the thought of the approaching dawn. Penn's contemporary Quakers thought otherwise — at least for a time, while the clouds of suspicion were lowering against them in the days of James and William because of their con-

---

552 In *A Defence of the Duke of Buckingham's Book,* 1686. Buckingham was himself accused of having become Penn's tool — of having let 'the Pennsylvanian enter him with his Quakeristical doctrine.'
553 Letter to Sir William Popple (*supra,* p. 251).

spicuous leader.[554] This, of course, was more pronounced after the revolution; but even in James's time, 'several Friends manifested their uneasiness at his being so much at Court, expressing their fears that in such a place, and in such company, he would be in great danger of departing from that simplicity of demeanour which Friends believed it their duty to maintain.'[555] The cloud of 'quietism' which blanketed the Quakers during the eighteenth and early nineteenth centuries was already casting its shadow over their motives and actions, and even as late as 1852, one of their ministers and one of the best of Penn's biographers, Samuel M. Janney, wrote as follows:[556]

'Among the few who have maintained their integrity while mingling with the incumbents of high political station, William Penn affords a most remarkable instance, and yet the professors of religion should hesitate to expose themselves to the temptations incident to such an intercourse, without an imperative necessity. His circumstances were peculiar: born to the possession of wealth and rank, introduced in early life to the society of the most distinguished men, possessed of great learning and talents, he had the power to render effectual relief to thousands who were suffering under the iron rod of persecution; and he could not exert the influence he possessed, without appearing at court and exchanging civilities with men whose principles were as opposite to his own, as darkness to light. Nor can it be supposed that the king considered him as a partisan of the court, for his political writings, as well as the course he pursued at the hustings in Guilford, had identified him with the Whigs.

'There is another point in which the professors of religion, and especially ministers of the Gospel, should closely examine themselves, before they venture to follow the example of Penn. The share he took in obtaining votes, and speaking at the hustings to promote the election of Algernon Sidney. It cannot be denied that the political arena, both in England and America, is a most unfavorable field for the growth of religious principles. Men of all parties who mingle in the

554 One of Penn's biographers goes so far in his condemnation of Penn's activities as to claim that they were not only immoral, or unmoral, but that they were unnecessary, since Barclay and Whitehead admirably and worthily represented the Quakers in the crisis. 'Penn was a figure at Court; he was not an influence,' this writer opines (Vulliamy, 1934, pp. 223-4; but cf. Clarkson II, 34-35).
555 *Journal* of the Friends Historical Society, XIX (1922), p. 31. This anecdote, by a near-contemporary of Penn, relates that Penn thereupon offered to take one of his critics to court as an unofficial observer. The result of the ensuing visit was to reassure the critics of Penn's propriety as a Quaker in the royal presence.
556 Janney, p. 150.

strife generally attendant on elections, are too much in the habit of using means to promote the success of their candidates, which are not consistent with Christian principles. And, moreover, the very excitement which prevails at such times, is unfavorable to that quiet contemplative spirit, which peculiarly becomes the station of those "who minister about holy things."'

At the same time, this author, Janney (following Forster and Dixon) refutes Macaulay's charge that the Society of Friends as a whole [557] 'looked coldly on him and requited his services with obloquy.' But he accepts as true Clarkson's statement that many of the Friends thought 'he had meddled more with politics, or with the concerns of government, than became a member of their Christian body, though they allowed that he took such a part often out of pure benevolence to others.' Janney was himself, within the next score of years after writing his biography of Penn, to become a very active and useful agent in President Grant's administration of Indian affairs; and with the passing of the Quakers' age of quietude and the rise of their vigorous participation in public affairs, the part that Penn took in attempting to realize his noble dream of toleration, during the exceedingly difficult and inauspicious years of James II's reign, has become a cause of admiration and gratitude.

A non-Quaker biographer of a half-century ago believes that Penn's court experience was harmful to himself. 'I cannot but think,' he says, 'that it was a good thing for William Penn when King James abdicated the throne and retired from England. Though in one respect the favour of the sovereign helped him to serve the Quakers, the influence of the sovereign could not be favourable either to his political or his religious character. It tended to warp his judgment in some points, and to impair the beauty of his life in others. He must have been more than man if his exposure to the temptations of a Court like that of James II. left him perfectly unharmed and entirely untouched. It could hardly fail to rub off the fresh bloom of his early piety. It certainly has had a detrimental effect on his historical fame. All the most serious charges against him spring from *this one source*. Those charges are, when fully examined, found to be unsustained; yet occasion and colour were given to them by the unfortunate circumstances in which patronage such as that of the popish prince placed this excellent person over and over again. Some of the reports circulated respecting him

---

557 Macaulay's rather ambiguous words are: 'his own sect.'

might have been silenced at once but for his uncommon intimacy with the monarch, and the means he adopted to maintain and increase it.'[558] On the other hand, a non-Quaker biographer of 1850 [559] believes that 'it was after all James's greatest glory that his name should have been associated with that of the benignant founder of the Utopia of the new world, Pennsylvania. That the royal admiral with his passion for naval glory, the despotic monarch with his stately ideas of the "divinity that hedges in a King," and all the hot zeal of a convert to Romanism about him, could enter with sympathy and delight into the enlightened views of that pure-minded Christian philosopher, William Penn, is an interesting fact, and not less strange than true.' And, finally, Penn's latest Quaker biographer declares that 'he was the good, often ineffectual, angel of the King, and he was able to bring relief to many sufferers. That was his task. Had James finally been guided by him, instead of by Father Petre, his Jesuit Confessor, he might have died a king in London, and Britain would have been spared the wars of William against Louis XIV and the National Debt'! [560]

'JACOBITE' AND TRAITOR

However difficult it may be to understand and justify Penn as a courtier in the court of James II, the charges of Jacobitism and treason made against him in the reign of William III can be readily disposed of. As for his Jacobitism, there is no question that he felt kindly and grateful to James after his downfall, and was honest and brave enough to admit it. No doubt he was bitterly disappointed by the apparent failure of his hopes for religious liberty. When William landed in November, and James fled in December, 1688, he could not have dreamed that within the next five months toleration would be established, and established by act of parliament. With religion as the mainspring of his own life, he had not sufficient political acumen to realize that William's chief interest in England was as an ally in his wars against Louis, and that his desire to unite all Protestants in the Grand Alliance would cause him to insist, even against Anglican opposition, upon a substantial measure of toleration.

558 Stoughton, 1882, p. 244. Later non-Quaker biographers are severe in their condemnation (Cf. Dobrée, 1932, and Vulliamy, 1934).
559 Agnes Strickland, *Lives of the Queens of England* (*Mary Beatrice of Modena*).
560 Graham, 1924, p. 167.

[The Act of 1689 was by no means all that Penn had striven for. It excluded the Unitarians and the Catholics from toleration, and it preserved the tests which excluded all Non-Anglicans from public office. Quaker persecution concerning tithes and military service was to be long continued. But persecution for holding public meetings to worship God came to an end. The Act made a special concession to the Quakers, permitting them to substitute for the oath of allegiance an affirmation, or solemn promise to be loyal; and it was accompanied by a Bill of Rights which confirmed the liberties of Englishmen for which Penn had so often and so eloquently contended.] Was this the triumph of William the Quaker, or of William the King? Perhaps the verdict of history is that they both played essential parts. As William Lloyd Garrison and the Abolitionists were to Abraham Lincoln and the Republican Congress, in the abolition of slavery, so were William Penn and his long-suffering Quaker associates to William III and the English Parliament, in the abolition of religious persecution. The popular sentiment which William Penn had kindled and fanned into a blaze, and which William III utilized for political action, grew steadily for the next two centuries, until another William — Gladstone, in 1873 — completed the task by removing the last handicap because of religious belief on the civil, political and educational equality of Englishmen.

Meanwhile, Penn entered into a dark and distressing period of his life. He scorned to follow the example of some of James's adherents, like Jeffreys and Sunderland who tried to escape, in sailor's or woman's disguise, to France and there rejoin James in the Court of Louis XIV; he would not play the part of others of James's courtiers, who speedily made their peace by supine submission to and fulsome adulation of the new ruler; least of all would he withdraw to Pennsylvania while he himself was under suspicion and thus draw the wrath of the victors in the Revolution upon his innocent province. He might have become a political Jacobite and remained in England to engage in plots for the restoration of James to the throne; and this was what his enemies accused him of doing, but what the true story of his actions proves him not to have done.

During the fortnight after James's and his courtiers' ignominious flight, Penn continued his daily visits to Whitehall; and there, on the 10th of December, 1688, he was arrested by order of the king's temporary Council and brought before them. In reply to their questions, he stated that 'he had done nothing but what he could answer before God, and all the Princes in the world; that he loved his country and the Protestant religion above his life, and had never acted against either; that all he had ever aimed at in his public endeavours was no other than what the Prince himself had declared for; that King James had always been his friend, and his father's friend; and that in gratitude he himself was the King's, and did ever, as much as in him lay, influence him to his true interest.'[561]

Although no evidence was forthcoming to refute this frank statement, the council, hoping to avoid William's censure and to secure his approval, bound Penn over by a bond of £6,000 to appear if called for at the next term of the king's court. Before this date, he was again summoned, but refused to appear, on the ground that it was not so noted in the bond. He took the precaution, however, to write to one of his friends, the Earl (later Duke) of Shrewsbury, who was a pillar of the new régime. In this letter he protested his innocence of sharing in any conspiracy against William, and his ignorance of any one who did; and he explained why he declined to yield himself up 'an unbailable prisoner.'[562] This plea, or Shrewsbury's influence, was sufficient to leave him unmolested until the court met; and then, no accusers appearing against him, he was acquitted.

This release occurred in March, 1689; but three months later, the Irish rebellion under James's leadership was in full swing, and amidst the public excitement in London Penn was again arrested and brought before the council. A letter from James to Penn had been intercepted (in a cave on the Flintshire coast!) and on the basis of it he was accused of treasonable correspondence. He denied all guilt, and appealed to the king himself. William gave him a two hours' interview, and satisfied himself of Penn's innocence; for it was obvious that he could not prevent James from writing to him, and there was no evidence that Penn had written to James or any of his agents. But on the insistence of the council, he was again bound over for the next term of court, and kept under surveillance during the next five months.[563] When

---
561 Clarkson, II, 29.
562 *The Friend*, Philadelphia, Vol. VI (1833), p. 194; *Memoirs* of the Historical Society of Pennsylvania, Vol. IV (1840), part I, p. 190.
563 Fox, in his *Itinerary Journal*, under date of the 27th of 7th mo: 1689, says that he 'went to meet W: P: who was y^n under ye Messingers hand in picadilly.' Narcissus Luttrell, in his contemporary *Brief Relation* of the Revolution of 1688, states that **Penn's release occurred on the 28th of November** (quoted by Vulliamy, pp. 226-7).

the court met at its Michelmas term (September 27 to November 30) he was again acquitted for lack of evidence. The intercepted letter from James had requested Penn to come to his aid 'and to express to him the resentments of his favor and benevolence.' This last cryptic phrase appears to mean : 'express to Penn assurances (*renseignements*) of James's favor and best wishes (*sa faveur et sa bienveillance*).'[564]

The interest of the Dutch and French in this episode is indicated by its inclusion in Bernard Picart's *Cérémonies et Coutumes Religieuses de tous les Peuples,* which was published in French in Amsterdam and Paris, and in Dutch in The Hague, between 1724 and 1743. In it, appears the statement : 'Penn was strictly examined concerning this correspondence ; his answer was noble, generous and wise ; but party animosity made it looked upon in the hurry of spirits at that time as a bare-faced espousing of King James's cause.'[565]

By July, 1690, the war of Louis and James against William had become very bitter and very ominous. Not only had James made great head in Ireland, but the combined Dutch and English fleet was defeated on June 30 by the French and Spanish off Beachy Head. The next day, William's victory at the Boyne caused James to flee to France, and the Irish revolt to subside. But, one week before, Queen Mary, alarmed by the course of events and hoping to prevent an uprising in England, ordered the arrest of eighteen suspects, chiefly noblemen and military men, and the last name on her list was that of William Penn. The other accused men were sent to Newgate or the Tower, several were convicted of treason, and one was executed ; but Penn, because of illness, was released on bail. July 31, he wrote a letter to his old friend, Henry Sidney (Algernon's younger brother), who was now Earl of Romney and secretary of state. In this he said :[566] 'As soon as I heard my name was in the proclamation, I offered to surrender myself. . . . It is now six weeks that I have laboured under the effects of a surfeit and a relapse, . . . and it is not three days ago that I was fitter for a bed than a surrender or a prison.' He wrote another letter to Romney (—22d A. 91.), through whom he appealed to the king for justice : 'Pray him to reflect on what past the last time I saw him, and whatever anybody tells him, I am neither more culpable, nor less sincere and candid than he was pleased to think me at that time.'[567]

564 Clarkson, 1814 (II, 46), Buell, 1904 (p. 207, note).
565 Clarkson, II, pp. 46-7.
566 Historical MSS. Commission, Finch, II, 391 (quoted by Dobrée, 309).
567 *Memoirs* of the Pennsylvania Historical Society, IV, I, 192-5.

KING WILLIAM III

A Topical Biography 269

Romney apparently prevented his imprisonment; and when he came before the court of king's bench in November, he was acquitted for the third time because of lack of evidence.

He now decided that he had been sufficiently examined, tried, and acquitted, and that he would be justified in placing the Atlantic between himself and the 'informers' who were constantly on his trail. He therefore prepared to go to Pennsylvania and procured a ship for the voyage, and the government provided a convoy for defence against French privateersmen. But at this juncture (January 30, 1691), George Fox died; Penn attended the funeral and delivered the chief sermon, and when he returned to his home was informed that officers had been sent to the grave-yard with a warrant to arrest him, and had failed to do so only because they had mistaken the hour of the funeral and had arrived too late! This time, it seems, an informer by the name of William Fuller, had charged him with more treasonable correspondence. A few months later, parliament itself denounced Fuller as 'a cheat and a notorious impostor'; and a few years later, the government pilloried him at Charing Cross, Temple Bar, and the Royal Exchange, the mob beat him unmercifully, and he was fined and sent to a house of correction.

But at this time, the armies of Louis were ravaging the Rhine Palatinate, and James was preparing for an attack on England. How widespread and lasting was the belief in Penn's complicity in James's planned attack is indicated by a cartoon of May 6, 1692, published in the *European Mercury*.[568] This represents James leaning against a broken pillar, mourning over his *breuk* ('landing' in English, *descente* in French), to whom 'William Penn the Quaker' is offering a *breukband*, or truss, for support. Bishop Burnet and other one hundred percent 'Orangemen' believed the accusation against Penn; and after one of the real conspirators had been tried and executed, the government once more bowed to popular excitement and in February, 1691, ordered the arrest of the Bishop of Ely, James Grahame (the brother of Lord Preston, who had been sent to the Tower), and William Penn.

Burnet assumes that Penn was guilty of complicity in the plot, and states that he 'absconded.'[569] One of Penn's recent non-Quaker, American biographers shares this belief; but argues that Penn had a perfect

---

[568] Volume for 1692, p. 311. It is cited in F. Muller's *De Nederlandsche Geschiedenis in Platen*, Amsterdam, 1863, Vol. I, p. 436 (No. 2852).
[569] Cf. Clarkson's refutation of Burnet, II, 283-289; also of Nairne, James's secretary in France, II, 289-292.

right to endeavour to restore James to the throne; he also implies that Penn did abscond to France, and probably remained there at least a year.[570] Two more recent, non-Quaker, English biographers lead their readers to believe that Penn was surely guilty of *something,* and that he was afraid or ashamed to make a clean breast of the whole matter.[571] A non-Quaker, English biographer of 1882,[572] the non-Quaker Clarkson,[573] and the American and English Quakers, Janney[574] and Graham,[575] all dismiss the charges, suspicions, and innuendoes as altogether unsustained by any authentic evidence.

If even twentieth-century biographers of Penn accept the charges of treason, or near-treason, against him, there is no wonder that he realized how impossible it was to clear himself entirely amidst the perfervid war propaganda of the 1690's, how assuredly he would be subjected to the continual attacks of venal 'informers,' and how useless even judicial trials and acquittals — as he had thrice experienced — would be as security against fresh accusations. He could no longer honourably carry out his plan to retire to Pennsylvania; and of course he would not 'abscond' to France. He therefore decided to retire completely from public view, and permit better times and calmer minds to establish and acknowledge his innocence.

It is not certain that the place of his retirement, or 'the sanctuary of my solitude,' as he himself called it, was one or more lodgings in London, or that he left London occasionally to meet his family at Worminghurst or some other place nearer the city. 'A private lodging in London;' 'some obscure alley among the crowded lanes of old London;' 'close seclusion — most of the time in London;' 'a hidden dwelling-place in the heart of London, and often at Worminghurst;' 'hunted up and down, and never allowed to live quietly in city or country;'[576] 'he bolted into a hiding, like a rabbit into a burrow:' Such are the varied guesses of biographers as to the place of his retreat.

Of more interest and importance is the question, What of his activities and attitude of mind during his three years of retirement (Feb-

570 Fisher, 1900, pp. 317-328.
571 Dobrée, 1932, pp. 311-314, and Vulliamy, 1934, pp. 228-231.
572 Stoughton, pp. 259-262, 271-272.
573 1814, Vol. II, pp. 55-6, 285-292.
574 1852, pp. 355-6.
575 1924, p. 195.
576 Penn himself wrote, in a letter without address or date, but sometime in 1693: 'I have been above these three years hunted up and down, and could never be allowed to live quietly in City or County' (*Memoirs* of the Pennsylvania Historical Society, IV, I, 198).

ruary, 1691, to November, 30, 1693) ? King William had become personally convinced of Penn's candor and integrity during his visit to The Hague in 1686 and in the long interview he had with him in London in 1689;[577] and the government, having no real evidence against him, including also several of his friends and admirers, was evidently glad to have the problem solved by his retirement from public notice until the storm should blow over. He was therefore left at peace, but was probably kept under surveillance. Sidney (Lord Romney), who visited him in February, 1691, and reported on his visit to the king, said:[578] 'I went to the place at the time [agreed upon] where I found him just as he used to be, not at all disguised, but in the same clothes and the same humour I formerly have seen him in.'

This was in the early part of his retirement; but it is probable that he retained the same 'humour' or serenity of mind and constancy of spirit throughout; for, without it, he could not possibly have utilized those three years in writing such admirable books as *Fruits of Solitude* and *Essay on the Peace of Europe*.[579] In his preface to the first of these, he writes: 'The Author blesseth God for his Retirement, and kisses that Gentle Hand which led him into it: For though it prove Barren to the World, it can never do so to him. He has now had some Time he could call his own; a Property he was never so much Master of before.... There is nothing of which we are apt to be so lavish as of Time, and about which we ought to be more solicitous; since without it we can do nothing in this World. Time is what we want most, but what, alas! we use worst; and for which God will certainly most strictly reckon with us, when Time shall be no more.'

The best philosophy and truest religion he surely needed, not so much because of his retirement from the world, as because of the blows

577 One of Penn's biographers (Buell, pp. 94-5), without citing any evidence, states that 'Mary shared her father's regard for Admiral Penn and, like him, was disposed to transfer the good-will to his son. William of Orange also took a fancy to Penn, whose maternal grandfather, John Jasper of Rotterdam, had befriended him in his boyhood.'

578 Dalrymple's *Memoirs*, III, 183 (quoted by Dixon, 333-5). A few months later (August, 1691), he wrote a letter 'To the Lord Romney, to show to King William,' which contained a brief, but manly and moving appeal to the king's justice and goodness, requesting permission 'to live quietly any where, either in this kingdom, or in America,' and offering as security for 'inoffensive behaviour' both his own solemn promise and 'the security of a society of honest, sober people, that I dare believe will be the pledges of my peaceable living' (*The Friend*, Philadelphia, Vol. VI (1833), p. 211).

579 Besides these, he wrote also: Prefaces to Barclay's and Burnyeat's *Works; The New Athenians; Just Measures; A Key opening the Way; and A Brief Account of the People called Quakers*, the last of these being as excellent as it is brief.

which continued to be inflicted upon him by the world. One of these came from Ireland. Writing in 1693, he says:[580] 'And before the date of this business which is layd to my charge, I was indicted for high Treason in Ireland before the Grand Jury of Dublin, and a bill found upon the Oaths of three scandalous Men—Fuller—one Fisher and an Irishman whom I know not, and the last has not been in England since the Revolution, nor I in Ireland these 20 years, nor do I so much as know him by name, and all their evidence upon hearsay, too. It may be it is the most extraordinary case that has been known ; ... But that an Englishman in England walking about the streets should have a Bill of High Treason found against him in Ireland for a fact pretended to be committed in England, when a man cannot legally be tryed in one County in England for a Crime committed in another—And the others are at ease that were accused for the same fault, and that Fuller is nationally staged and censured for an Imposter, that was the Chief of my Accusers—my Estate in Ireland is, notwithstanding lately put up among the Estates of Outlaws to be leased for the Crown, and the Collector of the Hundred where it lyes ordered to seize my Rents and lease it in the name of the Government, and yet I am not convicted or outlawed.'

The confiscation of the rents of his Irish estates followed soon after his payment of £30,000 in consequence of the cancellation of his intended voyage to Pennsylvania in 1690 and his preparations for the settlement of five hundred families on the Susquehanna.[581] By 1688, he told Sir William Popple in his letter denying the charge of Jesuitism, Pennsylvania had cost him £120,000 ; so that his financial resources were greatly depleted, and poverty was added to the other misfortunes of his retirement.

The worst blow of all was the loss of his province, which was confiscated by order of the king, in October, 1692, and annexed to New York. A royal governor took the proprietor's place and united New England, New York, New Jersey, Pennsylvania, Delaware, and Maryland for the purpose of using them against the French and Indians in the third war of Louis XIV's aggression, or King William's War, as it was called in America. William did not inflict this punishment upon Penn because of any suspicion of treason to himself, but because the Quaker rule in Pennsylvania meant that he could look for no mili-

580 *Memoirs* of the Pennsylvania Historical Society, IV, I, 198-200.
581 Penn's letter to Thomas Lloyd, 14th of 4th mo. (June), 1691.

tary and but very little financial assistance from it in the prosecution of his duel with Louis.

The militarist biographer of Penn, whose real hero is William III, and whose bête noire is Quakerism, comments upon this transaction as follows :[582] 'Every Quaker historian has denounced this measure as "tyranny," "despotism," "usurpation"—in short, has exhausted the thesaurus in search for synonyms of that meaning. As a matter of fact, it was wise, salutary, and patriotic. It was made indispensable by the pusillanimity and parsimony of the Quakers themselves. The Indians of Count Frontenac and the buccaneers of Jean Bart could not be persuaded to a policy of peace by Saltmarsh's Inward Light or by George Fox's special decalogue. They needed cannon-balls or muskets, and such King William proposed to give them.'

The Quakers, on their part, believed it their religious duty to abstain from every kind of war, whether it was one of defence, as William claimed it to be, or one of struggle for empire, as his critics discerned it to be.[583] Their religion and their ten years of experience in Pennsylvania declared it to be both practicable and right to attain security and justice by means of peace and friendship ; and they pointed to the glaring failure of warfare during the previous century to attain either security or justice in America, to say nothing of its centuries-old failure in Europe. To Penn, both as Quaker and as colonizer and statesman, the loss of his province was a grievous blow, for not only would it become the scene of bloody strife between his colonists and his friends the Indians, but it would cease to be the scene of his Holy Experiment, and his dream of a New World land of peace and freedom would be shattered.

Especially grievous under these circumstances must have seemed to him the loss of confidence which he suffered among certain circles of the English Quakers. Both political and personal reasons were responsible for this. Quietism forbade participation in politics of any kind ; and antipathy to the Catholic James, and aversion to, or jealousy of, Penn's prominence at a royal court, as well as his prominence as a Quaker and a colonizer, added fuel to the flame of censure.

An 'epistle general to the people of God called Quakers,' which Penn wrote—without date, but evidently just before the passage of the

---

582 Buell, 1904, p. 214.
583 Even Buell stresses—and glories in—the stakes of empire which William strove for and won (pp. 210-216) ; Vulliamy, 1934 (pp. 234-5) coincides.

Toleration Act on May 24, 1689—contains the following interesting defence of his conduct:[584] 'It is now about twenty-two years since I embraced the testimony of the blessed truth, and the fellowship of it among you, which is *Christ, the light of the world, in us, the hope of the glory that is to come*. I cannot repine, notwithstanding the many sort of troubles and afflictions I have met withal on that account, whether they came from my near relations, or the governments of the world, or my neighbours, or my enemies, or my false friends. . . .

'And now, my friends, as concerning the present tossings and revolutions of things that are in the world, *let your eye be to God, believe not every spirit, nor lay hands suddenly on persons or things,* but be humble and sober, and do to others as you would that they should do to you, and stand still that you may see the salvation of God come in his own way, for so you are to receive it, and share in it. And for those *clamours* that have almost *darkened the air* against me, your suffering friend and brother, be neither troubled nor captivated by them, but keep your minds *chaste* in the dwellings of truth, and possess your souls in patience, and in this true frame of spirit, remember me, as I have never forgotten you ; but of one thing be assured, I AM INNOCENT both of the imputation of *Jesuitism, popery*, and *plots*, and my God will in his good time confound their devices that trouble you and me with these false things, though I beseech him to forgive the authors of them, as I desire mercy for my own soul. I have *little deserved* this measure and usage from any of the people of this nation. The Lord God Almighty knows, I have universally sought the liberty and peace of it, and that nothing may take place to spoil or hinder that good work, nor can any one upon earth justly tax me with advancing any one thing that unbecomes a Christian and an Englishman, neither popery, blood, money, nor slavery can be laid at my door. I wrought, as well as I could, with the strength and instruments I had, for a general good ; if some things were done that were not well and pleased not, it was no fault of mine, and that is well known to many persons of unquestionable truth. I never accepted of any commission, but that of a free and common solicitor for sufferers of all sorts, and in all parties, which made my conversation very general. I thought that *charity* which gave me that office, should know no man after the flesh, nor suffer bounds to any that needed it. Nor do I find

---

584 Penn MSS. in the library of the American Philosophical Society, Philadelphia ; published in *The Friend*, Philadelphia, Vol. VI, 1833, pp. 257-8.

in my conscience that doing what good one can, under any government, is a sin or a fault, for which a man ought to be *stigmatised* or evilly entreated. I acknowledge I was an instrument to break the jaws of persecution, and to that end, I did take the freedom to remember King James of his frequent assurances in favour of liberty of conscience, and with much zeal used my small interest with him, to gain that point upon his ministers, that he told me were against it; that so the doors of our prisons and meeting-houses, until that time cruelly shut against us, might be opened, and the poor, and the widow, and the orphan might come forth, and praise God in the use of a just freedom. This and personal good offices were my daily business at Whithall, of which I can take the righteous God of heaven and earth to witness. Nor can I yet see that providence of liberty and peace, which we enjoyed under him, was such a *trick or snare,* as some have represented it — harm is to them that harm think. We sought but our just and Christian privilege, and I heartily wish that they that thought so, may do better, and answer that great expectation that has been raised in the people's minds about it. One thing, I know, could I have apprehended that the good days, we had in his reign, were a trick to introduce evil ones, all obligations would have ceased with me, and no man have more earnestly and cheerfully engaged, after my manner, against his government than myself. For, alas! what did I seek, or what have I got? What I have *spent* and *lost* is much harder to tell: but I leave that with a just and good God, to reprise to me and mine in his own way and time, as I do to *vindicate my oppressed innocence* against my implacable adversaries, of whom, with David, I can say *they have hated me without a cause.* . . . The Lord God Almighty rebuke the *wrath* and *wickedness* of man, and look down from heaven upon this *broken* and *sinful* nation in his great mercy, and *heal* it of all its *distempers,* that we, notwithstanding the judgments of God that seem to gather over our head as a *dark cloud,* may yet see *righteousness* and *peace,* break forth in this land as the sun in the fulness of his strength and glory. And, for you, my dear brethren, in whose cause, and for whose sakes, I have been as one killed all the day long, have your conversation, let me entreat you, according to the gospel, in *sobriety* and *humility,* in *patience* and *brotherly kindness.'*

To the Friends Yearly Meeting of 1691, also, he wrote a short letter of appeal, which contains the following paragraph: 'Receive no evil surmisings: neither suffer hard thoughts, through the insinuations of any, to enter your mind against me, your afflicted, but not forsaken friend and brother. My enemies are yours, and, in the ground mine for your sakes ; and that God seeth in secret, and will one day reward openly. My privacy is not because men have sworn truly, but falsely, against me ; *"for wicked men have laid in wait for me, and false witnesses have laid to my charge things that I knew not."'*

Two years later, a leader of the dissatisfied Quakers, namely, Thomas Lower, one of Margaret Fell Fox's sons-in-law, proposed to Penn that he should write a 'tender, reconciling epistle to all Friends,' and close it with the following words : 'And if in any things during these late revolutions I have concerned myself either by words or writings (in love, pity or goodwill to any in distress,) further than consisted with Truth's honour or the Church's peace, I am sorry for it ; and the Government having passed it by, I desire it may be by you also, that so we may all be kept and preserved in the holy tie and bond of love and peace.'

Penn rejected this suggestion ; for he was not conscious of any guilt, and would therefore not ask pardon of either his fellow-Quakers or of the king. His friends (with the little *f*) were eager to see him released from what they considered disgraceful and unmerited bondage ; among these was the illustrious philosopher, John Locke. Returning to England from his exile when William landed in 1688, Locke was *persona grata* with the king ; and when he heard of Penn's difficulties, he sought him out and offered to procure a pardon for him. This offer had been made by Penn to Locke at The Hague, in 1686, but in both instances the answer had been the same : since no guilt had been incurred, no pardon would be acceptable.

What Penn desired, of course, was a full and public acquittal ; and this came to him in November, 1693. In a letter to Thomas Lloyd, dated at 'Hodson' (Hoddesdon), the 11th of 10th mo (December), Penn wrote :[585] 'It hath pleased God to work my enlargement, by three lords representing my case as not only hard, but oppressive ; that there was nothing against me but what impostors or those that are fled, or that have, since their pardon, refused to verify, (and asked me pardon for saying what they did,) alleged against me ; that they had long known me, some of them thirty years, and had never known me to do an ill thing, but many good offices ; and that for not being thought to go abroad in defiance to the government, I might and would

---

585 Janney, 375.

have done it two years ago; and that I was, therefore, willing to wait to go about my affairs, as before, with leave; that I might be the better respected in the liberty I took to follow it.

'King William answered, "That I was his old acquaintance, as well as theirs; and that I might follow my business as freely as ever; and that he had nothing to say to me,"— upon which they pressed him to command one of them to declare the same to the secretary of state, Sir John Trenchard, that if I came to him or otherwise, he might signify the same to me, which he also did. The lords were Rochester, Ranelagh, and Sidney; and the last, as my greatest acquaintance, was to tell the secretary; accordingly he did; and the secretary, after speaking himself, and having it from King William's own mouth, appointed me a time to meet him at home; and did with the Marquis of Winchester, and told me I was as free as ever; . . . The lords spoke the 25th of November, and he discharged me on the 30th. From the secretary I went to our meeting, at the Bull and Mouth; thence to visit the sanctuary of my solitude; and after that to see my poor wife and children.'

Even this seemed to Penn a private liberation, and he asked for a full acquittal, which was formally granted him by the King in Council, after he had made another detailed answer to the charge of treason. Since he was desirous now of going to Pennsylvania, he would not do so without a formal acquittal.

Writing to Lord Rochester, he said: [586] 'In reference to my going to America, I humbly say, that thither I intend and must go, if God and the King please. My concerns there suffer beyond imagination, by a constrained absence. . . . To America I was going in April '91, if this misfortune had not hindered the January before, which is known to a hundred honest and substantial people in the city, and I had printed an intelligence to all concerned, and made a proposition to others therein, to that effect, ready to have engaged with me in a new settlement. And the like I purpose now, with God's help. But as I am not to trifle with the government that can so easily see whether I do or not, I desire it understood that *I will not receive my liberty to go as a condition to go there, and be there as here looked upon as an article exile.'*

Some of his caustic critics suggest that the government gave him his acquittal for the purpose of getting rid of him by sending him to Penn-

586 *Memoirs* of the Pennsylvania Historical Society, IV, I, 196-7.

sylvania, or that it was due to the fact that he was considered harmless.[587] Macaulay, characteristically, without the slightest authentic evidence to support his accusation, utilized the opportunity for administering his last sting to Penn's memory. 'The return,' he writes, 'which he made for the lenity with which he had been treated does not much raise his character. Scarcely had he again begun to harangue in public about the unlawfulness of war, when he sent a message earnestly exhorting James to make an immediate descent on England with thirty thousand men'!

By 1694, the French and Jacobites had been ousted from Ireland, defeated at sea, checked in the Netherlands and Italy, and in America. There was now no pressing military reason why Pennsylvania should not be restored to him and the Quakers;[588] the political excuse for its confiscation, namely, that disorder and misrule had been rampant, was now whitewashed by the government's assertion that this had been due entirely to Penn's own absence from it. Hence the rule of right and justice was permitted to have sway; a petition of the privy council was presented to the king asking for the restoration to Penn of the rights granted him in his charter; and a royal order under date of August 20, 1694, restored Pennsylvania to its founder.

The last alleged connexion of Penn with Jacobitism concerns his wife, Gulielma. The story is told by Agnes Strickland, who quotes it from a supposititious though undiscovered biography of Penn by 'Kennersley'; but the improbability of Kennersley's story is matched by the impenetrability of Kennersley himself. If he really published a *Life of Penn* in 1740, it appears to have fallen into oblivion.[589]

Gulielma lived long enough to rejoice with her husband over his acquittal and liberation, but died six months before the restoration of his province. The loss of his wife cast a permanent shadow over his spirit, and from this time, despite his two public triumphs of 1693 and 1694, he entered into the clouds which enclosed the later years of his life.

---

587 Fisher, 328; Dobrée, 325-26.
588 In 1701, when William was about to embark on the fourth war against Louis (the War of the Spanish Succession), he was again keen for the acquisition of Pennsylvania (*infra*, p. 286).
589 *Supra*, p. 37.

LAST YEARS

WHEN Penn's loyalty was vindicated and his province was restored to him, he was still only fifty years of age, and he had another quarter-century of life. But it was a different Penn whom we have to follow to the grave. Indeed, it was a new age upon which England itself had entered since the Great Revolution of 1688-89. Political supremacy had been regained by parliament; toleration to Dissenters had destroyed the monopoly of the Anglican Church in ecclesiastical affairs; the moral tone and manners of the court and nation had swung back from the decadence of the Restoration towards the Puritan conviction of individual responsibility to God and conscience; violence and brutality had subsided in private and public life; a literature of common sense, utility, and the public welfare had replaced the sensual nonsense of the dramatists of the later Stuarts; science and journalism had begun to take on their modern guise.

The Quaker ideals of peace and brotherly love for all men were still a long way from realization, however; and there is no evidence that Penn recognized and rejoiced in the dawn of a new and better era. John Milton, who had died twenty years before at the age of sixty-six, had written his *Paradise Regained* and *Samson Agonistes* three years before his death; but it was not an earthly paradise that he had found, and the autobiographical Samson whom he portrayed was the dying and defeated champion of the lost cause of Puritanism insofar as the middle years of the Restoration period reflected its failure.

No more great literature (except for *More Fruits of Solitude,* 1702) was to come from the hand of Penn — not even tragedies of despair; for, although he did not sense the coming of a better era for mankind, he was not depressed by a sense of human failure, and he retained his trust in the goodness of God. The survival and growth of Quakerism was one factor in his optimism, and he gave expression to it in an excellent and widely read history of *The Rise and Progress of the people called Quakers.*[590] The characteristic sub-title of this work is 'A Summary Account of the Divers Dispensations of God to Men, from the Beginning of the World, to that of our present age, by the

---

[590] Entitled at first *A Preface to George Fox's Journal,* 1694 : reprinted the same year under the second title, and sixteen more times within the next century and a half in England, Ireland, and America, with three editions in French, two in German, and one each in Welsh and Danish. *Works,* I, 858-892.

Ministry and Testimony of his Faithful Servant George Fox.' Its value is enhanced by its wealth of personal retrospection and reminiscence of Penn himself; and it included a noble and unequalled tribute to his co-founder of Quakerism.

This book included also a brief explanation of the Quakers' 'fundamental principle (the Light of Christ Within), doctrines, worship, ministry and discipline'; and it was followed by further clarifications of these in *Primitive Christianity Revived*,[591] *The Quaker a Christian, Gospel-Truths, A Defence of a paper entitled Gospel-Truths, A Testimony to the Truth of God*, and *Just Censure of Francis Bugg's Address to the Parliament against the Quakers*.[592] The last five of these were called out in reply to criticism of the Quakers by the Bishop of Cork and other opponents, including the notorious Francis Bugg.[593] Another controversy, this time within the Society of Friends, led to still another pamphlet, entitled *More Work for George Keith* (1696), which set Keith to the task of replying to his own former defence of the Quakers whom he now abused. The year before, Penn had met Keith in person in the Friends' Meeting at Ratcliffe, East London, and had severely censured a sermon delivered by him there.

Penn's writings grew fewer and fainter with advancing years; but as late as 1709 and February, 1712, he published an account of the *Life and Writings of Sir Bulstrode Whitlocke*, and a preface to a *Journal of ... John Banks*. Whitlocke was an eminent Puritan lawyer during the Commonwealth, whose persecution and close sympathies with Quakerism after the Restoration led to an intimate friendship with Penn. The learning and abilities of the two men made them congenial friends as long as Whitlocke lived; and soon after his death, Penn wrote a glowing paragraph concerning him in *No Cross, No Crown*.[594] John Banks was one of the 'first Publishers of Truth'; and forty years before Penn wrote this preface to his Journal, he had been, Penn says, 'a strength to my soul in the early days of my convincement.' This last of Penn's publications was finished shortly before his final illness, and he 'dictated it to a Person that wrote it from his Mouth (as he walked to and fro with his Cane in his Hand,

591 1696; *Works*, II, 853-875. This was reprinted six times within the next century, and was translated into Welsh and German.
592 *Supra*, p. 177.
593 *Supra*, p. 177.
594 Edition of 1682, paragraph XXXV. In 1711, Penn wrote an 'Epistle to the Reader' for Whitlocke's *Discourses to his Family*, in which he again paid tribute to the author as 'a Great Man.'

and gave occasional Answers to other Matters intervening).'[595] It is to be hoped that his cane helped him, not only to sustain his faltering footsteps and to mark the emphasis on his words, but also to retain the thread of his thought amidst the 'other Matters intervening!'

The spoken as well as the printed word, Penn still resorted to in his preaching tours (from 1694 to 1709) in southern and western England and in Ireland, where his fame as a statesman and colonizer and his notoriety as an alleged Jacobite drew huge audiences of farmers and woolen-workers to the meeting-places of various kinds which he visited.[596] The catholicity of his missionary appeal, even in these later years, is shown by the 'Visitation' which he addressed to the Jews, and in which he sought to vindicate the divine authority of the New Testament as well as the Old.[597] After his incapacitation, he made no more preaching tours; but in 1714 and 1715, he 'often went in his Chariot to the Meeting at Reading, and there sometimes uttered short, but very Sound and Savoury Expressions.'[598]

Meanwhile, public services were mingled as always among his private affairs. In 1695, he presented in person to the House of Commons a petition which once more stressed the wrong and ineffectiveness of oaths and requested that the Quakers should be permitted to make affirmations instead. The next year, with the sturdy aid of George Whitehead, who quoted to William III Holland's precedent of a hundred years before in the case of the Mennonites, an Affirmation Act was passed which permitted a declaration acceptable to the Quakers in many classes of cases before the courts.[599]

Another bill, relating to 'oaths' of another kind, was the Blasphemy Bill of 1697, which Penn opposed in a 'Caution humbly offered about Passing the Bill against Blasphemy.'[600] The purpose of the bill was to punish all who denied the doctrine of the Trinity as guilty of 'blasphemy'; and Penn's protest was against such interpretation of the word as would permit parliament to enact a creed in violation of the Toleration Act and cause many sincere Christians to be 'brought by

---

[595] Besse, 1726, I, 148.
[596] Some of the sermons which he preached in these years (1694, 1696 and 1699) were preserved in print (cf. *supra,* p. 131).
[597] 1695; *Works,* ii, 848-53.
[598] Besse, I, 150.
[599] Braithwaite, *The Second Period of Quakerism,* 1919, p. 183.
[600] This was published anonymously, but reprinted with Penn's name as author under the title of *Some Considerations upon the Bill for the more Effectual [Ly] Suppressing Blasphemy and Prophaneness : Humbly offered ; Works,* II, 883-4.

invidious Informers under Severe Suffering for a Circumstance of Words and Terms.' He circulated his protest among members of the House of Lords, where the bill originated, and it was one of the influences which caused it to be dropped.

Having dealt with England's king, lords and commons, Penn next interviewed the Czar of all the Russias. This was Peter, so-called the Great, who was then (in 1698) a young man of twenty-six years. He had come in the course of his study of west European civilization to the ship-yards of Deptford, and Penn accompanied by Whitehead and three other Friends, visited him there, or in his London lodgings at York House. In their two interviews, Penn conversed fluently with him in German and gave him some Quaker literature translated into that language. In their two conversations, Penn the admiral's son, may have talked navigation, and Penn the Quaker undoubtedly talked religion ; but not satisfied with these opportunities, he wrote the Czar a letter, in which among other things, he said :[601] 'May thy example show thee to be as good as great, that thou mayest bear his image by whom kings reign and princes decree justice, which without goodness, power itself can never do.' Penn's letter was in fact an eminently Quaker variant of Shakespeare's immortal dictum : 'The quality of mercy . . . is mightiest in the mightiest ; it becomes the throned monarch better than his crowne. . . . But mercy is above this sceptered sway ; it is enthroned in the hearts of Kings, it is an attribute to God himselfe ; and earthly power doth then shew lik'st Gods, when mercy seasons justice.' It was signed : 'So prays a little man, but thy great friend and well wisher, William Penn.' Which of these two men — Peter the Great and William the Little — does the historical philosopher rank the greater : the master of the sword, or the servant of the pen ?

The Czar was sufficiently impressed by the Quaker envoys to attend their meetings for worship at Deptford ; and although he renewed his attendance on them at Frederikstad fourteen years later and behaved in a modest and sympathetic manner,[602] there could be no real chance of converting such a man to Quakerism. One of the fundamental

---

601 The original English is published in *The Friend,* Philadelphia, Vol. VII (1834), p. 45. A German translation was probably sent to the Czar ; or it is possible that by this time Peter was able to converse with Penn in Dutch and to read Dutch Quaker literature.
602 Cf. Monograph Number Eight (*The Friesland Monthly Meeting and the Society of Friends in the Netherlands*).

differences between them was illustrated by the question he put to one of his Quaker visitors, namely : 'What use can you be in any kingdom or government, seeing you will not bear arms, and fight ?' [603] The significance of this question was enhanced in Peter's case by the fact that one of his chief aims at that time was to procure an armed alliance with the western European powers against the Turks.

Recalling Penn's relations with King Charles II, King James II, the Princess Elisabeth of the Palatinate,[604] Queen Mary II, King William III, Czar Peter the Great, and Queen Anne, it is noteworthy how well he illustrated the truth of the proverb : 'Seest thou a man diligent in his business ? he shall stand before kings.' Mary may have conceived a dislike for Penn at what was probably their first interview, in Holland, in 1677, when she was the fiancée of William of Orange ; [605] but more probably she was jealous of Penn's intimacy with her father, James II, and feared from him some adverse influence against her own and her husband's succession to the English throne. After she had him arrested, in June, 1690, she probably did not see him again before her death by smallpox in December, 1694. William, in spite of his imperial ambitions, had been obliged in all honesty to acquit Penn of treason and to restore to him his province when his own military necessities became less pressing ; but he too appears not to have admitted Penn to an audience after June, 1689 ; and he was preparing at the time of his death in March, 1702, another grand alliance for the war which, if he had lived to conduct it, might well have cost Penn the permanent loss of his province.

Queen Anne was more loyal to her father than was Mary, and shared his respect for Admiral Penn and his friendship for the admiral's son. Ulterior motives have been suggested for this friendship, such as the claim of Penn that there were '40,000 quaking freeholders [and *voters*] in England ;' [606] and the influence of the Duchess of Marlborough on Anne in behalf of her friend, Hannah Penn, whose husband paid the duchess handsomely for her good offices with the Queen ! But even after the break between the queen and the duchess, Anne continued throughout her reign to protect Penn and his colony against the demands of the militarists in their conduct of Queen Anne's War. In response to this fact, the argument is urged that Anne treated Penn

603 Thomas Story's *Journal*, 1747 (pp. 123-27).
604 Cf. Monograph Number Two, pp. 21-56, *et passim*.
605 ibid. pp. 56 f.
606 *Reliquiae Hearnianae*, March 29, 1706 (quoted by Dobrée, p. 378).

kindly so that she might acquire Pennsylvania by purchase, rather than by William's plan of confiscation. There certainly were negotiations for the purchase and sale of Penn's proprietary rights, after 1703 until Anne's death ; but these negotiations were initiated and carried on by Penn quite as much as by the queen and her ministers.

Anne proclaimed on her accession to the throne her determination to maintain the Act of Toleration, and the address of thanks which the Quakers returned for this was presented by a delegation of which Penn was the head. In reply to the address and Penn's presentation speech, Anne said : 'Mr. Penn, I am so well pleased that what I have said is to your satisfaction, that you and your friends may be assured of my protection.'

Penn, says his first biographer,[607] 'being in the Queen's favour, was often at Court, and for his Conveniency took Lodgings at Kensington' — in the realm of high fashion, and near the queen's favourite palace ; he lived also 'for some years' at 'Knightsbridge, over against Hide-Park Corner,' which was also near the palace. Once again, he was a welcome guest at court — a courtier of a strange type ; and he had varied business affairs in connection with his province to transact with the queen and her ministers. Although toleration had been won and ratified, office-holding by Dissenters had still to be struggled for, and indeed toleration itself was threatened by the High Church party ; Penn contributed to the struggle a treatise entitled *Considerations upon the Bill against Occasional Conformity* (1702), and doubtless opposed the bill in his conversations with the many influential friends he had at court. Among these, were Robert Harley, speaker of the House of Commons and later Earl of Oxford, a staunch opponent of the Occasional Conformity Bill ; the Duke of Ormond, Lord Lieutenant of Ireland, his life-long friend ; the Earl of Sunderland, Lord Godolphin, and the Earl of Dartmouth.

It can only be conjectured how much he knew and conversed with that scintillating circle of wits and literature of 'the Age of Queen Anne,' such as Bolingbroke (colleague of Oxford), Defoe (whom he tried to save from pillory in 1703),[608] and Dean Swift. The last-named refers to Penn in several of his books in such manner as to indicate a rather close acquaintance. For example, in his remarks on Bishop Burnet's history, Dean Swift quotes the latter's characterization of Penn

607 Besse, 1726, I, 147.
608 Paul Dottin, *Life of Daniel DeFoe*, English translation, 1929, pp. 103-105.

as 'a talking vain man, . . . who had a tedious luscious way that was not apt to overcome a man's reason, though it might tire his patience;' and Swift adds the comment: 'He spoke very agreeably, and with much spirit.' Again, in his *Journal to Stella,* Swift says: 'I was very deep with the Duke of Ormond to-day at the Cockpit, where we met to be private; but I doubt I cannot do the mischief I intended. My friend Penn came there, Will Penn the Quaker, at the head of his brethren, to thank the Duke for his kindness to their people in Ireland. To see a dozen scoundrels with their hats on, and the Duke complimenting with his off, was a good sight enough.'

But Swift's liberality or cynicism permitted him (in his *Discourse of Mr. Collins on Freethinking*) to take the following much more favourable view of Penn's religious activities: 'It is a great hardship and injustice, that our priests must not be disturbed while they are prating in the pulpit. For example: Why should not William Penn the Quaker, or any Anabaptist, Papist, Muggletonian, Jew, or Sweet-Singer, have liberty to come into St. Paul's Church, in the midst of divine service, and endeavour to convert first the aldermen, then the preacher, and singing-men? Or pray, why might not poor Mr. Whiston, who denies the divinity of Christ, be allowed to come into the Lower House of Convocation, and convert the clergy? But, alas! we are overrun with such false notions, that, if Penn or Whiston should do their duty, they would be reckoned fanatics, and disturbers of the holy synod, although they have as good a title to it as St. Paul had to go into the synagogues of the Jews; and their authority is full as divine as his.'

If Swift's knowledge of Penn, however, was no greater than his knowledge of Pennsylvania, there could not have been much intimacy between them. In his *Answer to Several Letters from unknown Persons,* Swift's geographical deficiencies are thus revealed: 'Neither was I at a loss to know the reasons why so many people of this kingdom were transporting themselves to America. And if this encouragement were owing to a pamphlet written, giving an account of the country of Pennsylvania, to tempt people to go thither, I do declare that those who were tempted, by such a narrative, to such a journey, were fools, and the author a most impudent knave; at least, if it be the same pamphlet I saw when it first came out, which is above 25 years ago, dedicated to Will Penn (whom by a mistake you call "Sir William Penn,") and styling him, by authority of the Scripture, "Most Noble

Governor." For I was very well acquainted with Penn, and did, some years after, talk with him upon that pamphlet, and the impudence of the author, who spoke so many things in praise of the soil and climate, which Penn himself did absolutely contradict. For he did assure me that his country wanted the shelter of mountains, which left it open to the northern winds from Hudson's Bay and the Frozen Sea, which destroyed all plantations of trees, and was even pernicious to all common vegetables.' One of Swift's editors (Temple Scott, 1905) makes a comment on the above as follows : 'Swift betrays a lamentable knowledge of the geography of this part of America. Penn, however, may have known no better' !

Penn certainly knew more accurately the geography even of northern Pennsylvania ; but he was painfully aware also, during these last years, of the troubles and difficulties that came to him with almost every wind that blew or ship that sailed from across the Atlantic. Financially, instead of taxes and revenues being provided for the government, and quit-rents paid to the proprietor, 'bills payable at sight' were drawn upon him. Animosities and quarrels arose among the members of the council, which caused a lax administration, and Penn was besieged to assuage them. The assembly struck at the administration by impeaching a judge, a councillor, and the proprietor's trusted agent and secretary. Delaware demanded and obtained practical independence of Pennsylvania. A riot broke out in East New Jersey, during Penn's visit in 1699-1701, and had to be severely suppressed.[609] A 'popular' party arose under the leadership of an able politician, David Lloyd, which dominated at times the popular elections and the assembly. The Quakers were divided by the Keithian Schism, and one faction denounced the proprietor on public and even religious and moral grounds. An Anglican party grew strong enough to threaten to establish the supremacy and intolerance of the Anglican Church. Of the six lieutenant governors whom he appointed, five proved inefficient or hostile to Quaker principles. His son, William Junior, caused him more trouble in Pennsylvania than at home. War taxes, militia, and quotas of troops were demanded by the British government for 'defence' in two virulent wars. Pirates and privateers preyed upon the coasts and upon commerce. King William confiscated his province for two years, during one of the wars, and was planning to do so again in preparation

609 Cf. Penn's original letter of instruction for suppressing this in the *Journal* of the Friends' Historical Society, Vol. III (1906), pp. 93-95.

for another one when he was killed by being thrown from his horse.

All these difficulties caused many of Penn's last years, even before his strokes of apoplexy, to be spent in a 'twilight' zone; and some of his critics go so far as to declare that his holy experiment was a flat failure. They think that it was an impossibility that he had attempted : either that it was impossible for a political democracy to be established on the basis of a lord proprietorship of the soil; or, that any union of church and state, even on the basis of Penn's principle of wide toleration and even in an age of reason, is premature this side of the millennium. When Penn had compromised some of his Quaker principles, these critics think he was saved from complete defeat : 'Penn the Quaker failed; Penn the statesman finally succeeded.' But this judgment is qualified, or negatived, by the conclusion that Penn was too far ahead of his time; and that when his success was finally accomplished, it was found to be the realization of his Quaker ideals.

His accumulated political, financial, and personal difficulties caused Penn at last to consider the voluntary surrender of his province to the crown. From the time when William III threatened to take it from him, in 1701, down to his own illness in 1712, he negotiated from time to time with the government, not only in regard to the sale of his proprietary rights for a sum which would pay off his debts, but especially in regard to the political rights which he had conceded to his colonists.

His financial difficulties, which had been enormously increased by the fraud of others, caused him great mental anguish and at last brought him once more within prison walls. Philip Ford, a Friend and lawyer of Bristol, who had been one of the first purchasers of Pennsylvania land, became at some time in the 1680's Penn's English land and financial agent, and acted in that capacity for a dozen years before his death in 1702. Penn, with characteristic confidence in the integrity of others, trusted him entirely and was very lax in examining Ford's reports and in signing the various papers he presented to him. By devious and dishonest methods, such as excessive commissions, fees, interest on advances but none on receipts, compound interest on advances charged at eight per cent and calculated every six months, Ford gradually built up an account against Penn which amounted to £14,000, although Penn was kept in ignorance of this until after Ford's death. When Penn was preparing for his second journey to Pennsylvania, in 1699, he received an advance from Ford of £2,800; for this he signed what he thought (and Ford verbally agreed) was a *mortgage* on his Pennsylvania lands, but which was in reality a *deed of sale* for them to Ford, and soon afterwards he signed a document by which he leased them back again at a yearly rental !

When Ford died, his widow, Bridget (a bed-ridden invalid, resembling in character Mrs. Clennam in *Little Dorrit*) and her son Philip Junior (a chip off the old block) presented Penn with the bill for £14,000. Fortunately, when Penn received this bill, he found accounts — which he had never opened [610]— which showed that Ford had received on Penn's account £17,859 and had paid out for him £16,200 ; but this balance of £1,659 in Penn's favour had been converted — by the jugglery cited above — into a debt of £14,000.

Penn thereupon offered to submit the claim to the arbitration of Friends chosen by each party ; but the Fords, secure in the legality of their deed of sale, refused arbitration and carried the case to the Court of Chancery. They employed able lawyers, Sir Simon Harcourt in England and Penn's political adversary in Pennsylvania, David Lloyd, while Penn was represented by Henry Gouldney, a prominent London Friend, and Herbert Springett, a relative of Gulielma. The suit in Chancery was characteristically prolonged, but in November, 1707, the court declared the deed of sale to be valid, and gave judgment against Penn for £3,000 (including 'rents' and costs). But since this was only the law and not the equity of the case, Penn refused to give the double security required. The Fords thereupon caused his arrest, in January, 1708, as he was leaving a meeting for worship in Gracechurch Street Meeting-house ; and when he was bound over by the security of two friends, he was placed in lodgings in the Old Bailey, within the liberties of Fleet Prison.[611] Various rumours or legends were reported of Penn during the progress of the trial and after he was in prison. One of these was that, fearing arrest, he had a peephole made in the door of his lodgings so that he might scrutinize all comers ; and that on one occasion, a visitor kept waiting for a long time asked Penn's servant or companion : 'Will not your master see me ?' To this came the reply : 'Friend, he has seen thee, and does not like thy looks.' One of

---

610 Writing of this to Logan, December 28, 1705, Penn says : 'Their accounts, though so voluminous, have been, through Providence, rather than by my carefulness, preserved entire ; having never opened them since the father delivered them sealed to me, 'till on this occasion' (Penn-Logan Correspondence, II, 99).
611 *Supra,* p. 197.

these legends persisted down to the time of Edmund Burke, who stated that William Penn died in the Fleet Prison! [612]

Penn stayed in the Fleet until the following December, when he was released on a compromise with the Fords to pay them £6,800 in full quittance. Meanwhile, the Fords had petitioned Queen Anne for a new charter, confirming 'Governor Philip and Governor Bridget' as proprietors of Pennsylvania! But this was too much for the queen's Lord Chancellor Cowper, who decided that the government of Pennsylvania had not passed to the Fords by the bill of sale, and that even the lands must be restored to Penn when he found funds with which to redeem them. Some of the swindling sources of the claim had also come to light, which the chancellor denounced in no uncertain terms. With these rebuffs, the Fords were glad to settle for less than half of their original claim ; and Penn's father-in-law and other friends were glad to lend him the required sum.

One of the unpleasant aspects of this case was that it was used by Penn's political enemies in Pennsylvania ; and so pressing did his difficulties become that, as has been stated above, he negotiated at several times with Queen Anne's government for its relinquishment. But, however pressing his financial and other difficulties, he was determined not to surrender his dream of 'a free colony for all mankind' unless the queen would guarantee its safeguards — especially its safeguard against an Anglican suppression of toleration. William Junior was eager for his father to sell, and the father realized how unfitted his son was to succeed him. James Logan varied his counsel, but on the whole advised the sale. The war-policy of the home government harassed the Quaker rule ; and Penn prophesied that all the charter and proprietary governments would be annexed to the crown by act of parliament during the winter of 1712-13.[613]

Hence, finally, in the summer of 1712, Penn made terms with the queen's lord treasurer. 'I have not actually sold my government to our truly good queen,' he wrote to Logan, the 24th of 5th mo (July), 1712, 'yet I have agreed it. . . . But I have taken effectual care that all the laws and privileges I have granted to you shall be observed by the queen's governors. . . . I hope I have made an end with my lord treasurer about my business (twelve thousand pounds, payable in four

---

612 *Account of the European Settlements in America* (quoted by Clarkson, II, 222).
613 Penn's Letter to Logan, 24th 5th mo (July), 1712.

years, the price), with *certain stipulations* which I recommend to thy great care and diligence.' Hannah Penn, writing to Logan (in January, 1715), after Penn's illness, said : 'I am persuaded, that had my husband minded his own and his family's interest, but as much as he did the country's, it had been finished years ago ; for the answer I receive from all the great men is, that my husband might have long since finished it, had he not insisted so much on gaining privileges for the people.'

An 'earnest' payment of £1200 was made by the government, arrangements were made for an act of parliament to ratify the transaction, and it would probably have been completed had not Penn been stricken by paralysis. Writing his last letter to Logan from Bristol on the 4th of 8th mo (October), 1712, his mind suddenly ceased working at the beginning of a sentence, and he was troubled no more by the cares of this world. The crown lawyers decided that he was not able to complete the agreement, and his wife was able within a few years to repay the earnest money and to pass on the proprietorship of Pennsylvania to the Penn children and grandchildren.

Penn had himself written at various times since 1705 of his desire and intention to settle permanently with his family in Pennsylvania.[614] Only six weeks before his last letter to Logan, he wrote to some Pennsylvania Friends : 'I purpose to see you, if God give me life, this fall, but I grow old and infirm, yet would gladly see you once more before I die, and my young sons and daughters also settled upon good tracts of land, for them and theirs after them, to clear and settle upon, as Jacob's sons did.' He had had a striking proof in 1710, of the esteem and affection which the settlers in Pennsylvania cherished for him ; for, after he had written to them a long letter of loving expostulation in June of that year,[615] the election of the ensuing autumn returned to the assembly not a single member of the opposition, and the 'proprietary party' was unanimous in the legislature. Two years later, the assembly passed an act which was very close to his heart — a prohibition of the importation of Negro slaves into the province.

But the angel of death interposed to prevent his eyes from looking again upon his beloved wood-lands and his body from resting in a

---

614 Cf. Penn-Logan Correspondence, II, 69, 72, 106, 291-2, 303, 308, 310, 322, 354-5, 420.
615 Cf. Proud, Clarkson, and Janney.

Pennsylvania grave. In May, 1712, he had received in London, while interviewing officials in regard to Pennsylvania affairs, an admonitory stroke of 'lethargic illness,' as his wife called it, or an attack of 'fever,' as he called it in a codicil to his will; the stroke of paralysis on October 4, when he was writing his last letter to Logan, was much more severe; and on October 13, he was able to add as a postscript to a letter from Hannah Penn to Logan only the few broken words: 'Farewell and pursue former exact orders, and thou wilt oblige thy real friend, W. Penn. My dear love to all my dear friends.'

Hannah Penn writing to Logan two months later, referred to the letter from her husband from Bristol, and said: 'He was then very ill there, but recovered so as, by easy journeys, to reach London, and endeavoured to settle some affairs, and get some laws passed for that country's ease, and his own and family's comfort; but finding himself unable to bear the fatigues of the town, he just reached Ruscombe, when he was seized with the same severe illness that he has twice before laboured under. And though, through the Lord's mercy, he is much better than he was, and in a pretty hopeful way of recovery, yet I am forbid, by his doctors, to trouble him with any business till better.'

He did not grow better, but on the contrary the third stroke permanently impaired his memory and dulled his intellect, although his strong constitution carried him through nearly six more years. An old and faithful friend paid him annual visits during these years,[616] and reported that in May, 1713, he was 'pretty well in health, and cheerful of disposition, but defective in memory; so that though he could relate many past transactions, yet could he not readily recollect the names of absent persons; nor could he deliver his words so readily as heretofore; yet many sensible and savoury expressions came from him, rendering his company even yet acceptable, and manifesting the religious settlement and stability of his mind.

'At a second visit made him in the spring, 1714, he was very little altered from what he had been the last year. The friend accompanied him in his chariot to Reading meeting, where he spoke several sensible sentences, but was not able to say much. At parting he took leave

---

616 This account is from Besse, 1726, Vol. I, p. 150. The two friends referred to in it may have been Henry Gouldney and Joseph Besse himself. Cf. also Thomas Story's account of his visits to Penn in 1714, 1716, 1717 and 1718, and of the funeral at Jordans, ten days after his last visit (*Life*, 1747, pp. 463-4, 529-30, 578, 606-7).

of his friends with much tenderness and affection. In the year 1715, his memory became yet more deficient; but his love to, and his sense of, religious enjoyments, apparently continued.'

His wife, writing to Logan in February, 1714, said: 'Let Thomas [Wilson] know that my husband is better than when he was here. He was at Reading meeting last first-day, as also two or three times before, and bore it very comfortably, and expressed his refreshment and satisfaction in being there, as he frequently does in the enjoyment of the Lord's goodness to him in his private retirements. He frequently expresses his loving concerns for that country's good, and sends his love in a general manner to all its well-wishers.'

In 1715, he frequently attended the Friends' meeting at Reading, and even 'went to the Bath, but the waters there proved of no benefit to his long-continued distemper.' The next year, 'the said friend and another went to visit him, at whose coming he seemed glad; and though he could not then remember their names, yet, by his answers, it appeared he knew their persons. He was now much weaker than last year, but still expressed himself sensibly at times, and particularly took his leave of them at their going away in these words, "My love is with you: the Lord preserve you, and remember me in the everlasting covenant!" In the fifth month, 1717, being the last visit the said friend made him, he found his understanding so much weakened, as that he scarce knew his old acquaintance, and his bodily strength so much decayed, that he could not well walk without leading; nor scarce express himself intelligibly.'

But amidst these distressing signs of decline, there are gleams of light and happiness. The few years between his release from the Fleet and his first stroke of paralysis had been filled with the tranquil joy of recalling the stirring times of the valiant and successful struggle for religious toleration and the founding of Quakerism; while the evidences of the growth and prosperity of his province and the love and gratitude of its colonists made his heart rejoice in the present and fill with hope for the future. Even after illness struck down his physical and mental vigour, he became like a little child among his young children and grandchildren, watching and sometimes participating in their games, and wandering with them through the spacious rooms and gardens of his beautiful home at Ruscombe.[617] His

617 Indicative of the malignant gossip of his enemies, even after his death, was the story that he had died, a lunatic, at Bath! This story was embellished with the

JORDANS MEETING-HOUSE

wife writing to Logan in January, 1715, speaks of these years as follows : 'When I keep the thoughts of business from him, he is very sweet, comfortable, and easy, and is cheerfully resigned to the Lord's will, and yet takes delight in his children, his friends, and domestic comforts, as formerly. It is the public and his family who feel the loss, and myself the trouble of his (I may say) translation. However, I bless the Lord, who has hitherto upheld me.'

Again, in a letter to Logan in March, 1717, she wrote : 'I have, for these last three or four years, continued on in this large house and expense, only to keep him as comfortable as I can ; for he had all along delighted in walking and taking the air here, and does still, when the weather allows ; and, at other times, diverts himself from room to room ; and the satisfaction he takes therein is the greatest pleasure I have in enjoying so large a house, which I have (with the necessary expenses and loads I bear) long found too much for me and our shrunk income.'

Hepworth Dixon [618] gives of these last years an idealized picture which recalls the character of Mr. Dick in *David Copperfield,* except that instead of the head of King Charles I which constantly interrupts Mr. Dick's mental processes, we may hope that Penn's were cheered and softened by happy recollections of the province which Charles II had granted to him and which he had done so much in a generation of loving toil to start upon its prosperous career.

Finally, says his first biographer, 'on the 30th of 5th mo [July], 1718, in the seventy-fourth year of his age, his soul prepared for a more glorious habitation, forsook the decayed tabernacle ; which was committed to the earth on the fifth of the sixth month [August] following, at Jordans in Buckinghamshire.' [619] Thus passed William Penn, the

detail that his 'lunacy was of the nature of Nebuchadnezzar's of old, which terminated in rage and madness before the end of his days.' As late as 1730, Joseph Besse was obliged to deny this story on his own evidence and on that of a neighbouring gentleman (Simon Clement, Hannah Penn's uncle by marriage) and of a nurse who had attended Penn 'from the beginning of his last indisposition, which was a palsie, occasioned by a third apoplectic fit.' (Clarkson, II, pp. 261-3).

618 Edition of 1902, p. 303 ; cf. also Dobrée, 411-92, and Vulliamy, 288-89.

619 In the year that Penn was imprisoned in Newgate for his religon's sake (1671), a Quaker farmer named William Russell conveyed to the Friends the land at Jordans to be used as a burial ground. The meeting-house beside the grave-yard was built in 1688, and Penn frequently attended meeting there. The first member of Penn's immediate family to be buried at Jordans was an infant daughter, Gulielma Maria, in 1673 ; his wife, Gulielma, was buried there in 1694, and her son Springett in 1696. The graves were unmarked — in deference to Quaker custom — until about seventy years ago.

builder of a City of Brotherly Love on earth, to the City of the New Jerusalem. At his grave might well be repeated his own words in *Fruits of Solitude*: 'The truest end of Life, is, to know the Life that never ends. He that makes this his Care, will find it his Crown at last. . . . And he that lives to live ever, never fears dying. Nor can the Means be terrible to him that heartily believes the End. For though Death be a Dark Passage, it leads to Immortality, and that is Recompense enough for Suffering of it. And yet Faith Lights us, even through the Grave, being the Evidence of Things not seen. And this is the Comfort of the Good, that the Grave cannot hold them, and that they live as soon as they die. For Death is no more than a Turning of us over from Time to Eternity.'

On several occasions during the last half-century, attempts have been made by Pennsylvanians, both officially and unofficially, to procure the consent of the Friends of Jordans Meeting to remove the bones of the Founder to Philadelphia; [620] but these attempts have proved unsuccessful, and Philadelphia's giant statue of its founder which stands on the top of its city hall must continue to satisfy its citizens, while his remains repose in the peaceful English countryside in the lowly grave marked by a simple Quaker tombstone.

PENN'S PERSONAL APPEARANCE

THE physical changes of all men between the cradle and the grave are numerous and striking; even within their adult years, most men develop numerous and varied traits — as is evidenced by the portraits, for example, of George Washington, who achieved that union of the colonies which Penn dreamed of. Washington's portraits are so numerous and varied as to make even a composite photograph of them untrustworthy. We have no such embarrassment of riches in the case of Penn, not one of whose portraitures is of entire authenticity.

The earliest of Penn's extant portraits comes nearest to being genuine. It is the so-called 'portrait in armour,' which portrays him at the age of twenty-two. This is said to have been painted in Dublin by

---

[620] One of these attempts was made in 1382, when Governor Hoyt of Pennsylvania commissioned George L. Harrison to perform the service. Harrison reported among other things that when Penn's grave was opened to receive the body of his second wife (in 1726), a bystander recorded the fact that he had seen the leaden coffin which contained Penn's remains; Jenkins, 96.

A Topical Biography 295

an unknown artist, when Penn was planning to enter a military career. There are at least three exemplars of it, all of which claim to be the original. One of these hangs in the library of the Pennsylvania Historical Society, which received it as a gift from Penn's grandson, Granville, in 1833.[621] Another is in 'Pennsylvania Castle' on the Isle of Portland (in the English Channel), a residence of Granville's brother John. A third version of the 'armour' portrait was retained in Bedfordshire (Tempsford Hall) by the Stuart family, descendants of Granville Penn's sister, Sophia Margaretta; and one school of critics claim that it is a replica of this which hangs in the library of the Pennsylvania Historical Society.

To add to the uncertainty as to the 'armour' portrait, there is extant a portrait of Penn the admiral which resembles that of Penn the son.[622] Pepys the Diarist gives us authentic information of this portrait. Under date of April 18, 1666—when Penn the son was 'at the age of twenty-two' and the admiral was forty-five—Pepys writes: 'To Mr. Lilly's, the painter's [Sir Peter Lely's]; and there saw the heads, some finished, and all begun, of the Flaggmen in the late great fight with the Duke of York against the Dutch. The Duke of York hath them done to hang in his chamber, and very finely they are done indeed. Here are the Prince's . . . and will be Sir. W. Pen's.' One of the admiral's old seamen, Gibson, told Penn: 'Your late honoured father was fair-haired; of a comely, round visage.' This vague description and the two portraits appear to fit either or both of the Penns; but it is possible that when the father was having his portrait done by Lely in London, he had the son's painted in Dublin.

On the basis of this portrait, various descriptions of Penn's youthful person have been written by zealous biographers. For example: he was tall in stature, and of athletic make; a fresh-faced, rosy-lipped, but very serious minded English youth; pleasing in person, and graceful in manners; an exceedingly handsome officer, in the style and uniform of a royalist soldier, of port and mien as martial as any cavalier, with hair parted in the middle, profuse dark locks falling in gallant fashion over his shoulders, and a neckcloth of fine lace wound several times around his neck, with the ends gathered in a bunch at the throat and hanging down the front of his polished breastplate; his eyes large,

---

621 The reproduction in this book (*supra*, p. 000), is from a photograph of the Pennsylvania Historical Society's portrait. Several engravings of it have been made, which idealize the original. Cf. Monograph Number Three, pp. 82 f.
622 *Supra*, p. 24.

clear, and lustrous, with a depth of intensity in them; a face strong and serious, showing character and purpose; the face and eyes look straight at you with intense and almost startling earnestness. 'A portrait whose youthful nobility and brooding strength has much in common with Rembrandt's ideal picture of "The Man in Armour."' [623] 'The features are rather full and beautifully moulded, the countenance combines energy and sweetness happily blended, and we read in that calm and earnest expression the index of a mind formed for high designs and noble achievements.' [624] Much more is read in this 'index' by another critic: 'There is no sense of humor in the features, or even youthful gayety. At first sight you might say that the face was melancholy; but close inspection leads you to describe it as over-serious, too earnest for the time of life. There is great determination expressed in it,—that sort of wild determination which, when combined with a lack of education, makes what is called the fanatic. But, at the same time, every line in the portrait shows that the young man is of cultured and good associations, and belongs to the best class of his time. The eyes are very large, and it is in them that this wild determination principally resides; and, at the same time, they have an appealing, soft, lustrous look. Gentle, sympathetic, and ideal qualities are evidently combined in a tumultuous way with some sort of an heroic soul. It is precisely the sort of picture one would paint after a careful study of Penn's life. There is no trace of shrewdness, subtle tact, or deep sagacity, so characteristic of Franklin's face.

'We can easily imagine that Penn might have looked like this. We know that he was very religious; and the face of this portrait is not the hard, cunning face of the ecclesiastic, nor the sour face of the Puritan. It belongs to another type of that strangely religious age, the type of the smaller sects, who were more radical than either Puritan or Churchman, who were not plotting for political control, who took their mystical religion to heart with simple, unworldly, reckless earnestness, and went with it to the prison or to the stake. Whatever decision may be reached as to the authenticity of these armor portraits, they will always be valued by Penn's admirers as idealizations of his qualities. It is, indeed, hard to resist the fascination of pictures which take all the heroic and intellectual qualities of the mature man and depict them in his boyish face, as foreshadowing what he was to be.' [625]

Still another critic of this portrait takes a somewhat different

---

[623] Brailsford, 165-6. [624] Janney, 22. [625] Fisher, 13-14.

view : [626] 'The only portrait of William Penn which was certainly painted during his lifetime, at a period when he admitted being susceptible to the vanities of this world, does not give us the impression of a very simple man. It is a beautiful, generous head, that of a youth inclined to learning, to the graces of life, to the arts ; the well-combed locks hanging to the shoulders indicate bodily refinement. The eyes are striking, looking wide but unmovingly beyond you — steadfast eyes, not fanatical, but obviously idealistic. The well-shaped nose tells us nothing ; but then the noses of young men are not usually very revealing. The mouth is secure ; it is not that of a man with doubts, yet is it not, yes, just a trifle prim ? The chin is firm, well modelled, but it is not a strong one, not that of a dominating man of action, as is, for instance, that of John Wesley. A handsome young man, attractive, with, one would say, great possibilities ; but what kind of possibilities it would be hard to guess. From his armour, and the way he wears it, one might think he would be a soldier ; a certain meticulousness makes one suppose he would adorn a Court ; his eyes suggest that he would be a seer. But whatever we may make of it, it is certain that it is not a simple face.'

Two or three years earlier than this armour portrait, it is said that another one, a miniature, of Penn had been made when he was only nineteen, 'whilst he was sojourning at the French court ;'[627] and Pepys gives us a description of his appearance on his return from the Grand Tour.[628]

The next supposed attempt (after the ages of nineteen and twenty-two) to portray the person of Penn is found in a picture of 'A Quaker Meeting' by Egbert van Heemskerk. This meeting was held in Rotterdam in 1677, when Penn was thirty-three ; and there is, in the portrait of Penn, a decided indication of energy and worldly shrewdness, but little of the spiritual quality and religious devotion which his recent experiences would lead one to expect.[629]

Five years after this visit to Holland as a missionary and colonizer,

---

626 Dobrée, 1.
627 It is said to have been preserved at Huntingdon Castle, Clonegal, County Carlow, the seat of Alexander Durdin, Esq., LL.D., whose grandfather, Alexander Durdin, married the widow of Penn's grandson, William Penn III. (*The Daily Express*, Dublin, September 18, 1868 ; quoted in *Notes and Queries*, 4th series, Vol. II, p. 382, October 17, 1868.)
628 *Supra*, p. 83.
629 See Monograph Number Five (*Benjamin Furly and Quakerism in Rotterdam*). The English dress and pointed nose help to identify Penn in the picture.

Penn set foot on Pennsylvania soil. To celebrate the 150th anniversary of that event, a portrait of Penn was painted by a very popular portrait-painter of Philadelphia, Henry Inman.[630] This painting is a pleasing one and is preserved in the National Museum in Independence Hall, Philadelphia; but its artist was born a century after Penn's last visit to Pennsylvania, and it was painted more than a century after his death.

Inman evidently owed much of his portrait to the conception of Penn in the famous painting of 'The Great Treaty' by Benjamin West.[631] West himself had no portrait of Penn for his guidance, and since his painting was made a half-century after Penn's death, he was obliged to draw upon his imagination for details of person and costume; or, perhaps, he made of him a composite of the Quakers whom he had known in his own life-time. The chief objection to West's portrait is that it represents Penn at the time of the 'treaty' as a man well on in middle age, although he was only thirty-eight; and instead of being the extremely sedate and portly figure of the painting, he was in real life full of energy and able to compete with the Indians themselves in jumping and running. The costume, also, with which Penn is clothed in the picture, is not the Quaker costume of 1682, but that of Pennsylvania Quakers of some seventy years later. The painter who gave a great impulse to realism in art by refusing to depict General Wolfe in a Greek helmet or Roman toga, might have come a little closer to reality in depicting William Penn; but we are grateful for his conception and painting of a great aspect of Penn's career, and we may regard the care with which he painted the Indians in his picture as his tribute to those who are said to have taught him the use of colours in his boyhood.

The sculptor who designed the huge bronze statue of Penn that stands on Philadelphia's city hall,[632] represented him at the age when

630 *Supra*, the frontispiece.
631 *Supra*, p. xiiif.
632 The colossal size of this statue is indicated by the following figures: weight, 52,400 lbs.; height, 37 ft.; hat, 3 ft. in diameter, rim 23 ft. in circumference (the crown has a large glass window on its top supplying light for the stairway within); eyes, 12 in. long, 4 in. wide; mouth, from corner to corner, 1 ft. wide; face, from hat to chin, 3 ft. 3 in.; hair, 4 ft. long; shoulders, 28 ft. in circumference, 15 ft. diameter; waist, 24 ft. circumference, 18 ft. 9 in. diameter; hands, 6 ft. 9 in. circumference, 3 ft. diameter, 4 ft. long; fingers, 2 ft. 6 in. long; finger nails, 3 in. long; legs, from ankle to knee, 16 ft.; ankle, 5 ft. circumference; calf of leg, 8 ft. 8 in. circumference; feet 22 in. wide, 5 ft. 4 in. long. It was said when erected (1892) to be the largest cast statue in the world; it stands now at an altitude a few feet lower than Washington's statue on his monument in Washington, D.C. At

PENN'S STATUE ON PHILADELPHIA'S CITY HALL

he came to his province; and the right hand extended in greeting to the Indians and in welcome to prospective colonists is another touch of verisimilitude. The costume, too, is that of the cavaliers of Penn's time and social rank, with its sword and extreme decorations on hat and coat omitted in deference to Quaker sensibilities and also to historic truth.[633]

A representation of 'Penn at the age of fifty-two' comes from the pencil or crayon of Francis Place, an eccentric but gifted amateur artist, about fifty years old when he is alleged to have made Penn's portrait.[634] About 1874, this portrait was found in the collection of a Mr. Allan, of Blackwell Hall (or Grange), County Durham, England.[635] It is held by some critics to resemble the 'armour' portrait; while others think that it was really a portrait of Admiral Penn.[636] On the basis of this portrait, Penn is described as 'eminently handsome, the expression of his countenance remarkably pleasing and sweet, his eye dark and lively, and his hair gracefully flowing over his shoulders.'[637]

Two distinguished London painters, contemporary with Penn, are also supposed to have made extant portraits of him. One of these was Sir Godfrey Kneller (or Kniller), born in Lübeck in 1646, resident in London from 1674 until his death in 1723. He was the foremost portrait painter of his time, and painted 'almost every person of note in London.' His alleged portrait of Penn is said to have been 'taken from a rectory in Westmorland, where it has hung for over eighty years [before 1907];' it was exhibited in the Graves Galleries, London,

night, it is lighted by a circle of electric lights, and, alas, many hundreds of birds of many varieties hurl themselves against it in the course of the year. Penn's right hand rests on the trunk of a tree [an elm?], holding a scroll inscribed with part of his Charter from Charles II; his right is extended towards Kensington (or Shackamaxon), as if blessing his Indian friends.
633 Another statue of Penn, made of bronzed lead, which was made for Lord Le Despenser and stood in his park at High Wycombe, England, was presented in 1804 to the city of Philadelphia by John Penn, the Founder's grandson, who purchased it from a plumber, to whom it had come as old lead. (Cf. Monograph Number Three, pp. X, 42, 120). The head of this statue may have been an imitation (plus a *hat*) of Bevan's bust.
634 Cf. Monograph Number Three, p. 93. A copy of it hangs in the National Museum in Independence Hall, Philadelphia.
635 A portrait of Penn and one of Hannah Penn, 'by Francis Place,' were listed at a sale in July, 1822 (*Journal* of the Friends' Historical Society, IV (1907), p. 130.
636 If the companion portrait is really that of the *Admiral's* wife, it is of exceptional interest as being the only representation of Penn's 'Dutch' mother. Mr.J.M.Rigg, in his article on William Penn in the *Dictionary of National Biography*, judges Place's portrait to be one of Admiral Penn; but it is doubtful that Place was making portraits before the admiral's death.
637 *Notes and Queries*, 7th. series, VI (September 29, 1888), p. 245; cf. Frank Etting's article in *Scribner's Magazine*, XII (1876), 1.

in the summer of 1907, and a large reproduction of it was published in *The Sphere,* London, July 20 of that year. An engraving by a German named Kuhner is supposed to be from Kneller's original; but its resemblance to Bevan's bust of Penn makes this doubtful.

A contemporary rival of Kneller was Jonathan Richardson (1665-1745), who became the head of his profession after Kneller's death. His portraits have been described as 'solid, steady-going and heavy-handed, but not deserving the oblivion into which they have fallen.' This description applies to the portrait of Penn which is attributed to him. The pointed nose and double chin of the Bevan bust appear to be the chief reliance for accepting it as authentic. The portrait was exhibited in 1892, and purchased by an American, Mr. E. G. Kennedy; it is now owned by Mr. Morris L. Clothier of Philadelphia.[638]

Illustrative of the attempted supply of the perennial demand for Penn's portrait, is the so-called 'Whisker,' or Lord Kames's portrait of him, which excited Benjamin Franklin's interest in 1760, but which was so obviously unauthentic that it fell entirely into oblivion.[639] Another alleged 'find' was made in 1888 at the sale of 'a Quaker lady's effects,' in which there was 'a portrait of William Penn in 1715, when he was at Bath for his health.' This was said to have come down 'through two or three generations in the Sturge family at Bath,' and is described as that of 'an elderly, good-looking man, firm-jawed, with well-cut nose and sharp, thoughtful eyes, bewigged, large-hatted, and wearing an eight-buttoned coat of mauve velvet, with a white stock atop.[640]

A portrait of Penn which rivals the 'armour' portrait in authenticity — at least in the eyes of many students — is the small ivory bust of him made by Sylvanus Bevan, a London Quaker apothecary.[641] Bevan, in fact, made three busts of Penn, one of which was sent to James Logan, and was burned in a fire in the Philadelphia Library in 1831; but fortunately, it had been engraved in 1773 by John Hall, and a marble copy of it had been made for the Pennsylvania Historical Society.[642] Clarkson, writing in 1813, says:[643] 'We have no portrait

---

638 Cf. Wilfred Whitten's account of this picture in *The Friend,* Vol. 32 (1892), 414.
639 Cf. Monograph Number Three, pp. 118 f.
640 *Notes and Queries,* 7th series, VI (September 29, 1888), pp. 245-6.
641 Cf. Monograph Number Three, pp. 118, 120.
642 The photograph in this book is from Bevan's ivory bust, which descended to Alfred Waterhouse, R.A. (of Yattendon Court, Berkshire, England), from his grandfather, Paul Bevan.
643 Vol. II, pp. 266-7.

PENN AT THE AGE OF FIFTY-TWO

taken of Penn while alive. Silvanus Bevan, a chemist of eminence
in London, who when young had known him well, took great pains
to form a bust of him some time after his decease, in which he was
assisted by the recollection of others familiarly acquainted with
him. . . . Bevan was in high repute as a man of science and literature,
and possessed a talent of taking striking likenesses from recollection
and carving them in ivory, though he indulged it but sparingly.'

This is all very unsatisfactory evidence of authenticity, but it is
helped a little by the testimony of some of Penn's friends. Lord
Cobham of Stow, for example, on seeing Bevan's carving without
knowing for whom it was intended exclaimed, as soon as he saw it:
'Whence comes this? It is William Penn himself.'[644] Robert Proud,
the first good historian of Pennsylvania, while visiting Bevan in 1750,
was told that 'the likeness is a real and true one,' not only by Bevan
himself, but also by 'other old men in England of the first character in
the Society of Friends, who knew him in their youth.' Richard Penn
also (probably the son of the Founder, 1706-1771) is quoted as having
said of an engraving (by Smithers) of Du Simitière's drawing of
Bevan's carving that it was 'a good likeness.'[645]

From such uncertain representations of Penn's person, his biographers have tried to give verbal descriptions of him. From the age
of twenty, when Pepys described him as 'a most modish person, grown
quite a fine gentleman,' and from the age of twenty-two, when the
armour portrait was taken, down to three years before his death, they
have done their best; but it is natural that discrepancies should exist.
Some think him tall; one calls him short — on the report of 'an old
woman who said she saw him in Pennsylvania, and declared that he
was of rather short stature, but the handsomest, best-looking, lively
gentleman she had ever seen.' Beauty of form and face, the mirror
both of gentleness and strength — an exceedingly handsome young
man: tall and lithe and strongly built, with wide and lustrous eyes
under wide arching brows, a refined and sensitive mouth, but a powerful chin indicative of the strength of will and purpose characteristic of
his whole life; eyes of an intense earnestness, with a determined look
in them, settled and steady, but with a soft and lustrous gentleness.
'Penn was somewhat above the middle height, well built and agile,

[644] Benjamin Franklin's letter to Lord Kames, 1760; (Monograph Number Three, 118 f).
[645] The engraving was published in the *American Universal Magazine* for January 2, 1797; and under it is printed Richard Penn's comment (Fisher, 17).

with a fine forehead, a short protuberant nose, a heavy chin, large lustrous eyes, and luxuriant hair.'[646]

But on the other hand—based on Bevan's picture : 'the features of an enormously corpulent person with a dangerously thick neck, a little mouth, a tilted nose, and a general expression of blank benevolence, with a touch of the autocrat ;'[647] 'the honeyed, drawling voice, the candid and sometimes rather puzzled being that dwelt behind the corpulent figure, of which something was revealed by the nose that had grown questingly tip-tilted amid the ample folds of the cheeks, and the dreamy blue eyes floating out from under the well-smoothed wig, enlarged to fifty-shilling size ;[648] 'Bevan's delineation was drawn when old age, sedentary habits and a decayed intellect left little in his countenance but its good nature.'[649]

But in the same bust, others read a different story : 'There appear in the eye deep reflection and strength of intellect, and in the mouth a sort of calm benignity ; the face is not an usual one, and there is in the countenance throughout a great sweetness and a general look of benevolent feeling.'[650] Even a modern critic says :[651] 'The serene, cheerful face of the Bevan portrait conforms to the tradition and the assertions of his biographers that he took all his difficulties, his imprisonments and his loss of fortune very lightly, and was fully sustained in his worst trials by his sanguine and courageous temperament.' Perhaps the truth lies between these extremes in the words of a mid-nineteenth century writer :[652] 'William Penn was "tall in stature, and of an athletic make." When a young man, he was handsome in his person and graceful in his manners : later in life, he was inclined to corpulency, but using much exercise, retained his activity : "a fine, portly man."'

As for Penn's costume, we have some general descriptions of it, and some of its special features are much and frequently emphasized. It was, during most of his life, the garb worn by his fellow-Quakers ; and of this, one of his biographers, himself a minister in the Society of

---

646 J.M.Rigg, article on William Penn in the *Dictionary of National Biography*.
647 Vulliamy, 273.
648 Dobrée, 329.
649 Philadelphians writing in 1836 ; cf. Monograph Number Three, p. 120. The editor of the Penn-Logan Correspondence, Edward Armstrong, found that even the 'Place' portrait of Penn gave him 'a weak expression, inclining to imbecility.' (*Notes and Queries*, 4th series, II, 37 (July 11, 1868).
650 Clarkson, II, 267.
651 Fisher, 18.
652 Janney, 549.

PENN IN OLD AGE

Friends during its most 'quietistic' period, remarked : [653] 'It is worthy of remark, that no peculiar form of dress has ever been prescribed by the discipline of Friends. The first members of the Society wore the dress then common among serious and religious people in England; it was much more simple than that worn in fashionable society, and when, in the reign of Charles II., the nation became infected with that passion for gaudy and extravagant apparel which distinguished his court, the Friends still adhered to their plain and simple costume, and thus became peculiar by refusing to follow the changeable fashion of the world. They maintained that the only proper objects of dress are decency and comfort, and that useless ornaments and gaudy apparel are inconsistent with the Christian profession.'

Another Quaker biographer, writing of Penn in the early days of his Quakerism, says : [654] 'At first, they [his family] were a little cheered on noticing no particular change in his manners or dress, except in not uncovering his head when he addressed them. He continued to wear the fashionable cavalier costume; the long curls, the plume and the rapier were still in their wonted places, as were the rings and other gold ornaments. No thought had as yet been directed by him to these customary decorations; but in after times they were all laid aside for what was more simple, though not for any style of dress peculiarly distinguishing the Quakers from other strictly religious people of those times.'

A Pennsylvania biographer of recent years comments : [655] 'Penn was rather fond of good clothes. He altered the dress which marked his class and station in life only by making it somewhat plainer than that of the gay cavalier. This seems to have been the practice of all the early Quakers. They did not adopt a distinctive dress, but made the one they were accustomed to plainer. The broad-brim hat and straight-cut coat were not the original Quaker costume. It was the shifting and changing of fashions, and excessive ornamentation, that they particularly disliked. Many of them, especially in Pennsylvania in colonial times, while adhering to one fashion wore clothes of the most handsome and expensive materials.'

In contrast with the Quaker costume, the same writer gives the following picture of the costume usual in Penn's time : 'We should

---

653 Janney, 1852, p. 43.
654 Webb, 1867, p. 162.
655 Fisher, 1900, pp. 21, 113-14.

naturally expect that the dress of the people would conform to their surroundings, or be of color that would least show the accidents through which they might have passed. But, on the contrary, they travelled their rough roads, during half the year almost impassable with mud, ran the gauntlet of highwaymen or the showers of filth in London's streets in most fantastic clothes of scarlet, blue, and yellow, with feathers in their hats. "I saw," says Pepys, "the King, the Dukes and all their attendants go forth in the rain to the City and it bedraggled many a fine suit of clothes." Pepys' description of his clothes, with the long list of their now meaningless names, and the way in which he developed his costume with his increasing prosperity, seems ludicrous enough now, but was an important matter with him.

'All sorts of fashions broke out among them. French clothes became an extravagant tyranny which Charles II. determined to break ; and as clothes were then as important as politics, he announced his resolution to his council. He would start a new and modest fashion which should never be altered : "a long cassock, close to the body, of black cloth, and pinked with white silk under it, and a coat over it, and the legs ruffled with black riband like a pigeon's leg." But Louis XIV. and the French nobility, to check this revolt against the supremacy of their nation, put their footmen in the new costume. It became a livery, and no English gentleman dare wear it. These gay people, with their embroidered and velvet coats, fringed gloves, camlet cloaks, gold and silver buttons, and huge wigs, which were bedraggled in the rain and mud of London, were not so particular when they went to bed.'

A critic of 'the fairer sect' states the sartorial contrast as follows :[656] 'Much has been written about the dress of the Quakers, and it is a common error to suppose that William Penn was attired in the costume worn by the sect in the eighteenth century, when they rendered themselves conspicuous by the dress in which they are generally represented. Penn did not follow the changes of fashion, or wear the brilliant colours in vogue at the time, but dressed as befitted one who wished ever to preserve a grave and serious demeanour. His own maxim was, "Choose thy clothes by thy own eyes, not another's. Plain and simple, not fantastical nor unshapely." The dress he usually wore was far from inelegant, and although the Puritans were preaching against the use of wigs and buckles, William Penn wore both.

656 Grant, 1907, pp. 93-95.

THE BEVAN BUST OF PENN

'In the latter part of Charles II.'s reign collarless coats were the fashion, straight fronted, with many buttons, showing no waist, nor cut into skirts, having only a short buttoned slit behind. The sleeves a little below the elbow, with large cuffs, showing full shirt sleeves. The vest was as long as the coat, full breeches open at the sides and tied with ribbons. Hats were worn high crowned, flat, or broad brimmed, according to fancy.

'The only mark of the Quaker among those who wished to appear particularly austere, was an absence of linen and cambric, and very sad-coloured garments. The Quaker lady, on the other hand, dressed with considerable richness. The restrictions imposed obliged her to wear much white, and delicate shades of gray and dove colour, she was invariably a pattern of cleanliness, so that her clothes never appeared to have been worn before, and rich plain silks, and fine muslins, were her favourite article of apparel. The ugly close bonnet did not exist at the time I am speaking of, and when going abroad a hood was generally drawn over the head.'

Penn's own opinion of apparel is stated in his *Fruits of Solitude,* the key-note of it being struck as follows : 'Excess in apparel is another costly folly. The very trimming of the vain world would, clothe all the naked one.'

In view of the notoriety visited upon the Quakers by their rejection of 'hat honour,' it is natural that much stress has been laid in the descriptions of Penn's costume on the hats he wore. He shared fully in the rejection of 'hat honour,' as is evidenced by his ninth chapter of *No Cross, No Crown,* and by the anecdotes told of him in connextion with Charles II and his own father. The latter begged him, when a young man of twenty-three, at least to uncover his head in the presence of himself, the King, and the Duke of York. But Penn felt in conscience bound to keep his hat on even before them. When he appeared thus before Charles II, the latter is said to have uncovered *his* head, with the jesting remark that it was the custom for only one person to wear a hat in the royal presence. Another anecdote relates that once when he was conversing with James II, the king asked him to explain the difference between Roman Catholicism and Quakerism, and he not wishing to offend unduly the royal susceptibilities and yet desiring to make some significant reply, pointed to their respective hats, 'which were exactly alike except that the king's was covered with feathers and ribbons,' and said: 'The only difference lies in the ornaments that have been added to thine.' This reply may illustrate the tact as well as the sincerity of Penn's statement: 'I know no religion which destroys courtesy, civility and kindness.'

Typical Quaker justifications of wearing the hat are given by two of Penn's biographers as follows : 'Penn had, after mature deliberation, adopted the views of the Friends, among whom nothing which had the least relation to religious duty, was deemed trivial or unimportant. They considered the uncovering of the head an act of reverence or of worship, that was due to none but Deity. In their public ministry, and in vocal prayer, they uncovered their heads, agreeably to the Apostolic injunction, but they could not pay the same mark of homage to a mortal like themselves. Although this refusal, especially in courts of justice, subjected them to great abuse, and even to fine and imprisonment, they persevered in adhering to their convictions of duty until their constancy gained them an exemption from the general usage, and perhaps has been one means of diminishing a practice which was then considered indispensable. In addition to their objections to this custom, as an act of homage improper to be offered to a human being, they believed that it was very generally adopted without sincerity.

'Like the expression, "Your humble servant," which generally accompanied the hat honor,— it was, in fashionable life, offered to all equals or superiors, when, in most cases, there was no corresponding feeling of reverence or humility entertained by those who made the profession. The primitive Friends felt it their duty to bear an uncompromising testimony against this custom, as well as all others, which had been adopted for the purpose of flattering human pride.'[657]

A more recent Quaker biographer comments :[658] 'Hat honour can only be judged fairly when we realise that it stood then for much more. People wore their hats at meals. Pepys took cold by dining without one. They were worn indoors all the time. In church they were only taken off at the solemn utterance of the name of God. But French fashions had come in, and the habit of doffing the hat was one. It stood as the central symbol of a wicked way of life. To reserve the act for reverence to God alone was simply to stand for the conservative upright English Puritan way of life. It was really an unquakerly error to stiffen a symbol into the substance; but there were extenuating circumstances. We know from other evidence that the men to whom

[657] Janney, 1852, p. 27.
[658] Graham, 1924, pp. 32-33.

this apparent crotchet appealed were neither bigots nor fools.'

That he was not careless as to the appearance of his own or his friends' hats is shown by the following extract from one of his letters to James Logan : [659] 'I have sent some hats [to Philadelphia], one for Griffith Owen, and the other intended for Edward Shippen, which thou mayest take with this just excuse, that the brim being too narrow for his age and height, I intend him one with a larger brim ; for as soon as I saw it I told the Friend who made it [the MS. deleted] [660] I thought it handsome, though I pinch here, to be sure.'

In regard to what lies under the hat (or did in that age), the wig, the Penn-Logan Correspondence gives some indications of his opinion of it. Writing to Logan, Penn inquires : [661] *'Periwig.*— Did not a fine new wig come to thy hands for me ? It cost fifty shillings sterling ; made by Watson. S. V. puts it to my account.' And Logan, replying, says : [662] 'Thou received a new wig thyself some little time before thy departure [from Pennsylvania, for England], as I remember, which cost either forty or fifty shillings, and N. Puckle would put an ill-favored one on me, which thou gave him he said to dispose of his last voyage ; but I sent it forthwith to my wig-maker's to sell to the best advantage.'

By this time, Penn was nearly three-score years of age, and the Quakers had become used and reconciled to seeing him wearing a wig ; but in the early days of his Quakerism, there was some caustic criticism of it.[663]

Penn evidently continued to wear a wig, for in his Irish Journal of 1669-70, under date of September 25, 1669, he writes : 'I caus'd my hair to be Cutt off & putt Into a wigg because of Baldness since my Imprisonment [in London Tower].' February 12, 1670, he writes : 'I shau'd my head ;' and March 25, 1670 : 'I gaue order for my little wig to be made into two Cap borders.' A half-dozen years later, the criticism of his wig grew stronger, and George Fox took it upon himself to defend Penn for wearing the obnoxious article ! [664]

Although Penn continued for very practical reasons to wear a wig — and increasingly expensive ones — to the end of his life, he discarded

---

659 6th mo., 1703 (Penn-Logan Correspondence, Vol. I, p. 214).
660 Perhaps he referred to its expense, but his determination to buy a good one.
661 21st 4 mo. [June], 1702 (Vol. 1, p. 114).
662 1st 10th mo. [December], 1702 (ibid, p. 149).
663 Cf. *supra*, p. 167.
664 Cf. *supra*, p. 66.

his sword as a part of his costume very soon after becoming a Friend. Two versions of this story are given. One of these refers to the first Quaker meeting he attended in Ireland, in 1667. Here, according to this story, after threatening to throw a soldier down stairs, he submitted to arrest, and 'as he went to prisson he gave his sword to his man & never wore one after.'[665]

The more familiar story of Penn discarding his sword is given by Janney, as follows:[666] 'When William Penn was convinced of the principles of Friends, and became a frequent attendant at their meetings, he did not immediately relinquish his gay apparel; it is even said that he wore a sword, as was then customary among men of rank and fashion. Being one day in company with George Fox, he asked his advice concerning it, saying that he might, perhaps, appear singular among Friends, but his sword had once been the means of saving his life without injuring his antagonist, and moreover, that Christ has said, "he that hath no sword, let him sell his garment and buy one." George Fox answered, "I advise thee to wear it as long as thou canst." Not long after this they met again, when William had no sword, and George said to him, "William, where is thy sword?" "Oh!" said he, "I have taken thy advice; I wore it as long as I could." This anecdote, derived from reliable tradition, seems to be characteristic of the men and the times. It shows that the primitive Friends preferred that their proselytes should be led by the principle of divine truth in their own minds, rather than follow the opinions of others without sufficient evidence.'

Penn the Quaker adopted no substitute for the sword of the cavalier, but in his old age he carried a cane and, according to Clarkson, used it for a two-fold purpose. 'William Penn was very neat, though plain, in his dress. He walked generally with a cane. This cane he was accustomed to take with him in the latter part of his life into his study, where, when he dictated to an amanuensis, as was frequently his practice, he would take it in his hand, and walking up and down the room would mark, by striking it against the floor, the emphasis on points which he wished particularly to be noticed.'[667]

Penn's use of lace was very sparing, and he gave up his cuffs and ruffles in deference both to his own ideal of simplicity and to the

665 *Supra*, p. 109.
666 1852, pp. 42-43. He states in a footnote that this story was related to him by 'J.P. of Montgomery County, Pa., who had it from James Simpson [born in 1743].'
667 Vol. II, p. 267.

A Topical Biography 309

action taken by a Friends' meeting in his neighbourhood. Isaac Penington's *Papers* record this action as follows: [668] 'We do, in ye name and authority of God unanimously and with one consent, judge, condemn, deny, and declare against that practice and employment of making or in any way dealing in Band Lace, as a thing wholly useless in the Creation, as a hindrance and obstruction to the spreading and prosperity of Truth, and as a support of Pride and Vanity, which the Fire of the Lord is Kindled against.' They accordingly gave up their trade of lace-making and sought other means of livelihood.

There is a tradition, however, that Penn conceded to his position as governor in Pennsylvania the wearing of 'a sky-blue sash,' which was afterwards owned by 'Thomas Kett of Seetingh-hall near Norwich,' and which is portrayed in West's 'Treaty with the Indians.'

PENN'S CHARACTER

IN considering the character of William Penn, it should be remembered first of all that he was a man — 'no angel, but a dearer creature still.' If he had had no faults, he would not have been human; and being human, he had defects. The question of real importance is: did he correct his faults as he passed through life, and did his virtues at all times outweigh them?

He has left us in his writings his own ideal standard of character and conduct, and it is fair to estimate how nearly he applied them in himself and in his career. Of the nearly one hundred human virtues he signalized in his *Fruits of Solitude* [669] there can be no question that he exemplified fully half; and of the score or more of vices which he excoriated in his *No Cross, No Crown* [670] and *Address to Protestants*,[671] he avoided or overcame nearly all.

The foundation stone of his character was surely an unaffected piety. 'Serving God concerns the Frame of our Spirits, in the whole Course of our Lives . . . God is better served in resisting a Temptation to Evil, than in many formal Prayers. . . . The truest end of Life is to know the Life that never ends. . . . Nothing in us unlike God can

---

668 P. 116: the minute adopted on the 31st of 3rd month, 1669, by the meeting at Weston Turvey (quoted by Brailsford, 284-5).
669 *Supra*, p. 160.
670 *Supra*, p. 158.
671. *Supra*, p. 210.

please him. . . . He that lives in Love lives in God, says the Beloved Disciple : And to be sure a Man can live no where better.' God with us, here and hereafter : out of God's hand into God's hand, and all the way between never out of touch with him ; Love of God shown by love and service of man. Such were the two halves of Penn's religion. Our modern world accepts as axiomatic its second half ; but how difficult it is for it to accept even in theory the practice of the *presence* of God. And how difficult, even, for twentieth century minds to avoid a feeling that a frank and constant profession of it by such men as Penn or Cromwell smacks of pretence and hypocrisy. 'The knowledge of God from the living witness within' was Penn's invincibly assured and perpetually declared belief.

'A Quaker, or some very melancholy thing,' Pepys called him in his youth. The thing which appealed to this Diarist of the Restoration Period as melancholy was Puritanism. Penn shared fully the Puritan belief in the responsibility of every human being to his Creator for the special commission with which God himself had charged him. He believed that God had spared him amidst the Great Plague and the varied vicissitudes of his life to do his part of the work in the kingdom of God on earth. Not only as a protagonist of Quakerism in the field of religion, but also as proprietor and governor of Pennsylvania and in all the secular affairs of his life, he sensed the compelling hand of God and devoutly believed that he was God's instrument in the service of humanity. 'My God hath given it [Pennsylvania] me, in the face of the world.'

To this Puritan trait, he added the Quaker faith that God's very presence can be experienced within every individual soul. In public and in private worship, and in the pursuit of every day's affairs, both small and great, he consciously sought, and rejoiced in the belief that he found in all verity, God's living presence. Three times daily, he assembled his household for private worship ! Innumerable public meetings and multitudinous sermons, thousands of letters and of printed pages, attest this conviction ; and out of it blossomed the fragrant flowers of his character and conduct. It was to this, also, that critics have attributed some of his defects.

'A dreamer of dreams' has been both his praise and his censure. Not so much a seer of unrealizable ideals ; but, 'sustained by faith and matchless fortitude,' he made his dreams come true. His faith was kindled by Thomas Loe's sermon in the days of his youth on the assurance that 'there is a faith which overcomes the world'; and this faith was sustained through both the joys and the sorrows of his life. Alike when he set sail in *The Welcome* to try his holy experiment in the New World beyond the Atlantic, and when his province was taken from him because of 'military necessity;' alike when he saw thousands of his fellow-Quakers released from prison by the religious toleration of which he was the foremost champion, and when he was himself imprisoned by debt incurred on behalf of the land of refuge he had established, his enthusiasm for his ideals remained undimmed. The dirt, darkness, and disease of dungeons; the hardships of slow and tedious travel in Ireland and on the Continent; the nervous strain and fervid emotion of missionary journeys; the intellectual expenditure required for a vast mass of writing and controversy; financial pressure; political vicissitudes of royal favour and charges of treason, of party success and failure; family bereavements and the loss of friends by death and estrangement; incessant toil over public laws and constitutions for three American colonies; the advertising and sale of enormous tracts of land: all the varied and exacting demands of a most strenuous life attest both his extraordinary physical and mental vigour and the endurance which did not fail until near the term of three score years and ten. 'The more he is pressed, the more he rises,' wrote an intimate friend;[672] 'he seems of a spirit to bear and rub through difficulties and . . . his foundation remains.' 'I bless the Lord,' wrote Penn himself, 'I am yet upon my Rock, a lasting foundation.'

Joined with this strength of religious faith, there was in Penn a natural, buoyant optimism which sustained his hope of happiness and prosperity, whether in the American forest, or in an England ruled by wastrels or bigots. This irrepressible optimism has been attributed both to a sanguine temperament and to a childlike immaturity which enabled him to ignore or suppress gloomy doubts and discouraging realities. Hence semi-conscious self-delusion, it is alleged, showed itself in a passion for self-justification, and prevented him from realizing that his dreams were made of the unsubstantial stuff of failure; that he was but an impracticable visionary. He dreamed of a pure democracy, without counting on the defects of human nature; and when his theories were shattered on the stones of practical government, he still continued to declare them valid and successful.

However visionary he may have been in great things, say other

[672] Isaac Norris to James Logan.

critics, in details he was minutely practical. When he planned a vast city, utility replaced ideal beauty, and Philadelphia emerged as prosaic and mathematical as a checker-board. He urged rural colonists to start commerce and manufactures on the Delaware, to trade with the Indians, to develop iron mines on the Schuylkill, and to establish vineyards of wild 'fox-grapes' for the making of claret; but he himself had no true sense of business. This was natural, say his defenders, because he was an aristocrat and had the training of a landlord. Was it not extraordinary that such a man, with a score of years' experience as a religious proselyte behind him, should have laid down such minute and detailed regulations for the founding of a colony overseas in an unknown land?

In fact, some critics regard him as a first-rate man of business. His genius for giving books titles worthy of best sellers showed itself, they think, in his advertising ability as a colonial promoter, and a sense of land values which would put to shame up-to-date real estate experts. While admonishing his land agents to deal fairly and generously with the Indians, he warned them to 'hearken by honest spies if you can hear that anybody inveigles them not to sell, or to stand off and raise the value upon you.' He was keen, also, to receive the full amount of quit-rents and adequate revenue for government expenses which were due him from colonists and citizens. In fact, he had a worldly ambition that his province should be profitable to his own and his family's fortune and should contribute to their power and prestige.

Against this, it may be noted that he did not sell his books, but printed them at his own large expense and gave them away; that he suffered in fame and fortune because of his union with Quakerism, incurring such contemptuous pity as that of Sir John Robinson: 'I vow, Mr. Penn, I am sorry for you; you are an ingenious gentleman — all the world must allow that — and you have a plentiful estate: Why should you render yourself unhappy by associating with such a vulgar people?' As for Pennsylvania, he put into it far more than he got out of it during his life-time; he rejected large offers for monopolies of trade with the Indians and in other industries; and, like another illustrious 'speculator' in American lands, George Washington, he saw not only legitimate profits for himself, but also and chiefly, the development of wild lands, the advance of culture and Christianity. 'Had I indeed sought greatness,' Penn said to one of his contemporary critics, 'I had stayed at home, where the difference between what I am here, and what was offered and I could have been there in power and wealth, is as wide as the places are.'

Beyond such disinterestedness, generosity and benevolence show forth both in the magnanimity of his public aims and in his own daily conduct. Even his most severe critics admit that 'cupidity is the last vice of which anyone can accuse Penn.'[673] Instead of exploiting the Indians, he protected them against monopolies, alcoholic liquors, and mistreatment, and was bountiful of hospitality towards them; he made many liberal donations of land to individuals and for public purposes; he declined the offer of revenue from the first colonial assembly; he was generous in his charity towards his poor neighbours and dependents in England — as his cash-book abundantly testifies; and the parish registers of baptism in his neighbourhood reveal the gratitude and esteem in which he was held by the number of children who were given his name and various combinations with 'Pennsylvania.'[674] The same care and consideration he extended to the emigrants settling in his colony; and in every generation since his time, the name of William Penn has been gratefully bestowed and proudly worn by uncounted Americans.

His first three commissioners in October, 1681, he instructed to 'take an especial care of the people that shall embark with you, that they may be accommodated with conveniences as to food, lodging, and safe places for their goods, . . . that so none may be injured in their healths or estate, in which, if you find the Dutch, Swedes, or English of my side hard or griping, taking an advantage of your circumstances, give them to know that they will hurt themselves thereby, for you can for a time be supplied on the other side, which may awe them to moderate prices.'

When he himself went over with *The Welcome,* he devoted himself to the care of the victims of smallpox, and his fellow-voyagers told with gratitude many incidents of his benevolence in other ways. He assisted many colonists to emigrate, and supplied them with the necessaries of life while they were getting established in their new homes. Kind usage by others — as in the case of distressed immigrants in the West Indies[675]— brought tears to his eyes.[676]

673 Dobrée, 158 ; cf. Fisher, *et al.*
674 Clarkson, II, 274.
675 Clarkson, II, 273.
676 The charge of callousness, over against such evidence of his tender sensibilities, has been considered *supra,* p. 248.

William Penn

His modesty was illustrated by his lowly seat in Quaker meetings, his praise and preferment of the young, the uneducated, the poor, and the gifted ministers; and his persistent but unsuccessful effort to have his colony named New Wales, instead of Pennsylvania. But over against this personal modesty, must be placed his conviction—shared by George Washington and many another professed democrat—that some ceremony was due to the appreciation and strengthening of his public office. As proprietor and governor and the personal representative of his sovereign, he brightened up the wilds of Pennsylvania by going in procession to the opening meetings of the assembly, with a mace-bearer before him. At his gate on audience days, an officer with a long silver-tipped staff stood on duty. His fellow-governors of Maryland, Virginia, and New York were received or visited with similar ceremony, in which numerous horse-back riders played a part. With a love of horses typical of the English gentry, he rode through Pennsylvania's forest on a large white horse, and on state occasions was driven in a coach by a negro coachman. Often he was rowed down the Delaware in a stately six-oared barge. 'Above all dead things, I love my barge,' he frankly confessed; 'I hope no one uses it on any account, and that she is kept dry in dock, or at least covered from the weather.' [677]

This official ceremoniousness, his critics believe, was an outcropping of personal exhibitionism.[678] 'He liked to play his part well, especially to himself; and since the part was a good one, and that he played it in all directness and simplicity, there is no reason for any one to object.' His Quaker censors in London Yearly Meeting did object, however, to his 'undue fondness for honour and dignity and for the things of this world.' Even in his religious labours, he is accused by his modern critics of having a strong desire to be conspicuous, and of not being content to buckle down to the obscure work of the varied committees of the Quaker society; he delighted to be proved the beneficent father of his people, the heroic patron of the Indians, the centre of a dramatic and historic panorama; self-importance, a desire to be regarded as the patron and protector of the Quakers, was his chief motive in attaching himself so conspicuously to the court of James II.

This defect of Penn's character, these critics think, grew into or out of a desire to dominate. 'On the upper levels of consciousness, in his

---

677 Penn-Logan Correspondence.
678 Cf. especially Dobrée and Vulliamy, *passim*.

brain, he was democratic, but fundamentally he believed in autocracy.' 'If he had not been a Quaker, he might have been a Cardinal or a Bishop.' A contemporary critic, Bishop Burnet, says bluntly : 'He is a man of good parts, but extremely vain ; he loves mightily to hear himself talk ; he has a flourish of learning, and with it a copious fluency ; and his head is much turned by the notion of government.'

But the bishop was jealous and prejudiced ; and the modern critics are inconsistent. For example, one accounts for the defects of Penn by attributing them to his physical break-down in old age ; while another thinks that he grew gentler, warmer, more lovable, and more possessed of genuine simplicity. That he had the simplicity of greatness in his earlier years as well, is attested by his delight in rural life ; [679] later also by his affable condescension to the Indians (although, as one critic admits, 'we can be sure he did not feel he was being condescending'), and by his whole-hearted participation in their homely meals of maize and in their athletic sports ; by his courteous acceptance of a poor woman's invitation to dine with her on bread, butter, and cheese, when wealthier members of the meeting he was attending feared that their repast would not be adequate to a great man's and governor's needs. At this time, too, he appears to have been a good trencherman. The wild turkeys and venison of Pennsylvania's woods, the smoked haunches of pork and beef, obtained from his Swedish settlers, the 'rare shad' caught by 'the old priest at Philadelphia,' pleased him better than delicate French dishes which, he said, subordinated the meat to the sauce. Beverages which in our time have fallen out of the Quaker menu, such as wines (especially his father's favourite Madeira), ale, and cider were never lacking at his table.

On the other hand, he had no liking for tobacco, and he tolerated no extravagance. 'Waste destroys hospitality and wrongs the poor,' was one of his maxims similar to many others. Both disillusionment with the pleasures of luxury, which he had known in his youth, and regard for the necessities and sensitive feelings of the poor made frugality a religious principle and moral duty in his eyes. His dislike of the tobacco habit was well known and respected by his friends, as is illustrated by the story of a visit which he made to the governor

---

679 'Divine pleasures,' he often declared, 'are found in a Free Solitude'. In a letter which he wrote from Chester to a Friend in England, soon after arriving in Pennsylvania, he said : 'Here is what an Abraham, Isaac and Jacob would be well contented with. . . . O, how sweet is the quiet of these parts, freed from the anxious and troublesome solicitations, hurries, and perplexities of woeful Europe !'

of New Jersey, who retired with his friends for a smoke behind the barn, while Penn was taking a nap in the house; but when Penn came upon them and reproached them for not smoking openly in his presence, the governor replied: 'We only refrained from doing so out of regard for a weaker brother'!

That Penn was capable of biting irony, many passages in his controversial writings and some in his maxims reveal; for example: 'It too often happens in some Conversations, as in Apothecary-Shops, that those Pots that are Empty, or have Things of small Value in them, are as gaudily Dress'd and Flourish'd, as those that are full of precious Drugs.' But of humour, there are very few evidences. His writings are almost entirely devoid of it, and his conversation, though probably genial, had in it little or no wit. 'Wit is fitter for Diversion than Business, being more grateful to Fancy than Judgment. Less Judgment than Wit is more Sail than Ballast. Yet it must be confessed that Wit gives an edge to Sense and recommends it extreamly. Where Judgment has Wit to express it, there's the best Orator.' Such is the balanced judgment of his 'Maxims.' Some anecdotes do betray a homely humour; for example, he called a Welsh friend's attention to a goat chewing a broom and remarked: 'What hardy fellows the Welsh are,' and then made amends by relating a tale of a Welsh ancestor of his own — John Tudor, by name — who lived on the top of a hill and was therefore called John Penmurrith, or 'John on top of a hill: hence the name of Penn!' Another anecdote tells of Penn advising a drunkard to give up his drinking habits, and when asked *how,* replied: 'It is as easy as opening thy hand; when thou findest in thy hand any cup of intoxicants, open thy hand before it reaches thy mouth and thou wilt never be drunk again.'

Probably a Puritan mind and a Quaker mission were partly responsible for Penn's lack of humour, but his own personality was far removed from trivialities in thought and speech. Orderliness, system, sobriety ranked high among his virtues and rather overshadowed the undergrowth of lighter vein. The rules he laid down for his household [680] divided the day into hours of work; the rising hour was seven, six, five, and six, according to the four seasons of the year; breakfast, dinner, and supper at nine, noon, and seven; to bed at ten; family worship before breakfast, and again at eleven A.M. and six P.M.;

---

680 'Christian Discipline; or, Good and Wholesome Orders for the Well-governing of a Family.'

a specific regimen for the children and servants, the latter to report after supper on how they had carried out their instructions of the evening before, and if they had observed the strict rules for their daily conduct; and specific rules for the behaviour, conversation, and self-control of the children. Philadelphia's checker-board arrangement betrayed his 'geometrical mind, abhorring the sensuality of curves.'[681]

But undue rigidity was not compatible with his geniality and sociability in friendly intercourse. He was very pleasant and strikingly animated in conversation; Dr. Tillotson, Dean Swift, James II, as well as a chance fellow-traveller in a stage-coach took much pleasure in his company; the Philadelphia Friends testified that 'his behaviour was sweet and engaging, and his condescension great even to the weakest and meanest; affable and of easy access; tender to every person and thing that had simplicity of truth or honesty for a foundation.'[682] Such are the almost universal encomiums that have come down to us from his contemporaries. Bishop Burnet alone sneers at him as 'a talking vain man, . . . with a tedious luscious way of talking, not apt to overcome a man's reason, though it might tire his patience;' but this judgment was based on suspicion and prejudice.[683] Perhaps, also, the bishop did not relish in the despised Quaker a knowledge of 'sacred and profane history' which by far overmatched his own.

That Penn's profound scholarship shone forth in his conversation as well as in his writings is attested by the anecdote of an unknown fellow-traveller who, after listening to his discourse for many miles of weary jolting in a stage-coach, asked him how, since the Quaker society despised human learning, he had acquired so much knowledge. In addition to his grasp of history, his scientific knowledge was sufficient to procure him election as a Fellow of the Royal Society; while his keen and comprehensive observations of Pennsylvania's soil and climate, fauna and flora, and aborigines enabled him to write, and doubtless to talk, most interestingly and instructively about them.

Beyond an extraordinary fund of knowledge, Penn had the modesty and teachableness of the truly wise. His appreciation of this trait of wisdom is well expressed in his Maxims as follows: 'Perhaps the worst Part of this Vanity is its Unteachableness. Tell it any Thing,

681 Vulliamy, 189.
682 Infra, p. 324.
683 Supra, p. 254. A friendly Quaker biographer, however, admits: 'I should say that he was an expansive man, hearty, sociable, conversational, and both in speech and writing more apt to begin than to stop.' (Graham, 186).

and it has known it long ago; and out-runs Information and Instruction, or else proudly puffs at it. Whereas the greatest Understandings doubt most, are readiest to learn, and least pleased with themselves; this, with no Body else. For tho' they stand on higher Ground, and so see further than their Neighbours, they are yet humbled by their Prospect, since it shews them something so much higher and above their Reach.' As John Milton escaped from straight-laced Puritanism into the realm of beauty and culture, so William Penn's spirit shook off the trammels of a narrow Quakerism and found its way into the realm of sweetness and light.

Marked courtesy was evidently a part of his sociability, both in theory and practice. The plainness of his costume and simplicity of his address did not dull the polish of his manners, whether among his courtly friends of the English aristocracy or in the company of simple colonists or the untutored red men. 'The Indians do not love to be smiled upon,' was his discerning caution to his commissioners; and when 'the pipe of peace' was passed, he waived his dislike of tobacco, and took one draw upon it.

Whatever may be thought of Penn's democracy in government, he was — for an English 'gentleman' of the seventeenth century — remarkably democratic in his mental outlook; and this was due to the religion which bade him seek and find God in himself and in his fellow-men. 'Man would have others obey him, even his own kind; but he will not obey God, that is so much above him, and who made him. He will lose none of his Authority; no, not bate an Ace of it : He is humorous to his Wife, he beats his Children, is angry with his Servants, strict with his Neighbours, revenges all Affronts to Extremity; but, alas, forgets all the while that he is the Man; and is more in Arrear to God, that is so very patient with him, than 'they are to him with whom he is so strict and impatient. . . . If he be to receive or see a great Man, how nice and anxious is he that all things be in order? And with what Respect and Address does he approach and make his Court? But to God, how dry and formal and constrained in his Devotion?' This humility and friendliness he carried with him from royal palaces on the Thames to peasant homes on the Rhine and forest huts on the Delaware. Despite his words and his conduct, some modern critics will have it that 'Penn never lost his middle-class reverence for mere rank — it is abundantly shown in his letters to princes or noblemen — and he was undoubtedly flattered by the attention of the

King.' These incisive comments are from critics who live in a land wherein divinity doth still hedge a king; how many of their twentieth-century fellow-citizens who pride themselves on their democracy, or how many of the fellow-countrymen of Jefferson and Lincoln—even within the democratic Quaker fold—would *not* be flattered by the attention of a king?

Not undemocratic, but merely diplomatic, has been another verdict. This alleged evasive trait of his character has been pushed especially by Penn's militaristic biographer who had a frankly expressed contempt for Quaker pacifism.[684] 'Not quite daring to disobey the commandment of George Fox [not to use or countenance the use of force],' Penn permitted the military defence of Pennsylvania to 'be settled affirmatively, provided some one else would shoulder the sin of it. . . . In this transaction Penn appears more discreditably than in any other of his career. It serves to exhibit the grip that Fox had fastened upon him, an influence capable of making him tread so closely upon the verge of dissimulation as almost to obliterate the line between that and dishonesty.' The harshness of this criticism, his biographer seeks to palliate by explaining that 'even William Penn had learned some lessons during ten years in the grim school of William of Orange;'[685] and that at the height of his evasiveness, 'it is probable that the weakening of his mind and will, which Hannah Penn not long afterward described as "a lethargic illness," was at this time beginning to affect him.'

Another critic[686] illustrates Penn's artful, or artless, diplomacy by quoting one of his letters to the Earl of Rochester—'my noble Friend' —, in which he appeals for a boundary settlement in his favour, and mentions a gift of 'beavers and otters for hats and muffs' to the king, the Duke of York, and Rochester, concluding with the sentiment: ' 'Tis the heart, not the gift, that gives acceptance.' Upon which, his critic comments: 'Quite so; and the heart that accepts the gift will be all the clearer to judge boundary questions.' Quoting from an alleged letter of Penn in 1684 to Charles II—it is alleged to be 'now [1934] printed in full for the first time'—another critic comments:[687] 'There is nothing adroit or subtle here; it is the fulsome address of a courtier, rounded off with luscious piety.' And finally, an undoubtedly able

---

684 Buell, 242-252.
685 Cf. *supra*, p. 255. Penn's compromise with militarism is discussed *infra*, p. 332.
686 Dobrée, p. 201.
687 Vulliamy, 197.

American diplomatist, Benjamin Franklin, remarked: 'William Penn united the subtlety of the serpent with the innocence of the dove.'

Evidently, students and practitioners of diplomacy differ as to whether subtlety or innocence predominated in Penn's. All seem agreed that he was of a remarkably, indeed lamentably, unsuspicious character. This unsuspiciousness is attributed to the broad charity which naturally arises from a belief in 'that of God in every man.' The choice of suitable agents, for example, 'was not one of Penn's strong points,' an admiring Quaker biographer admits;[688] 'he was too trustful and optimistic. That went with his general character, and was the source of much of his strength. To be a Quaker at all you have to have faith in human-kind, and to be an apostle of Quakerism does not go well with even moderate and prudent suspicion of others. We cannot all do everything, and in the point of employing subordinates, whether for his own affairs or for those of Pennsylvania, William Penn had the defects of his qualities.' Too great liberality militated against good judgment, and despite his far-reaching knowledge of men in the past, he could not read the character of living men and was often disappointed or deceived by them. Like the sundial that responds only to sunshine, he marked only the good in his fellow-men and was oblivious to their evil. He believed James II, for example, to be a far better man than he was; and the men whom he appointed to govern in his absence in Pennsylvania fell beneath his expectations, while his relations with Philip Ford showed that he was not only unsuspicious, but downright gullible.[689] However much other-worldly wisdom was conceded to him, men believed that he had little or no worldly wisdom. Had it been otherwise, he would not have toiled so long and ardently for religious liberty under the ægis of kings who were despots at heart.

Of his loyalty to family and friends, there could be no question. In an age when, as he said, lack of loyalty and affection was the great fault in families, he was pre-eminently a loving and devoted husband and father, and his loyalty to his scape-grace son and namesake survived many a sad disillusionment. At a time when friendship was worn most lightly and betrayed for the sake of place and power, he stood manfully by suspected traitors such as Sidney and worked unselfishly

---

688 Graham, 216.
689 Cf. Fisher, 373: 'The great Quaker, as he was called, the proprietor and governor of her Majesty's colony of Pennsylvania, had been juggled out of his province by a bookkeeper!'

for their political restoration and advancement at the risk of his own private and public welfare. His gratitude, affection, and loyalty to James, as duke and king, never wavered in the days either of James's power, or after his downfall when the dread charge of Jacobitism might have cost Penn his province and his life.

His physical and moral courage remain practically unquestioned. At unnumbered meetings for worship, beset by constables, soldiers, or mobs, he steadfastly 'held on, declaring Truth in the Power of God.'[690] In London Tower, he declared : 'My prison shall be my grave before I will budge a jot ; for I owe my conscience to no mortal man ;' Luther's 'Ich kann nicht anders, hier stehe ich ; so hilf mir Gott', thus found in a young English Protestant a noble echo a century and a half later. He withstood his father's stern displeasure and his associates' contempt — more formidable than any physical menace. He lived unarmed and trusted his colonists without military defence in the midst of Indian 'savages,' believing that their truest defence would be found in God's own spirit within the Indians' hearts. Before this evidence of sublime courage, even his severest critics bow in homage. 'It was not,' writes one of these,[691] 'that he was the first to buy their land ; others had done that with excellent results in other colonies, and indeed failure to do so had been visited with the ghastly retribution of massacres. But Penn was the first to go towards them with hands empty of weapons. He treated them as equals before God, not as blood-thirsty savages, and on no account would he fight them. He would put the Quaker doctrine to the test, he would have the courage to go among them unarmed. The faith, and the valiance of faith, needed to do this were stupendous.' In the smallpox stricken cabins of *The Welcome,* as in England's courts of justice intent on persecuting the heretical Quakers and urged on by all the power of church and state, Penn's courage blazed as a beacon-light of hope for the victims of disease and hatred.

It may be justly claimed for Penn that, like Sir Galahad, his courage and his moral strength were as the strength of ten because his heart was pure. Perhaps the chiefest glory of his character was that, in the midst of Restoration England, his heart and life were clean. Only once was this even challenged, and he replied to his persecutor's (Sir John Robinson's) accusation, 'You have been as bad as other folks,' with

---

690 George Fox's *Journal.*
691 Dobrée, 155.

the indignant demand : 'When and where ? I charge thee tell the company [at the trial] to my face.' And when Robinson answered, 'Abroad and at home too,' Penn launched the challenge to 'all Men, Women and Children upon Earth justly to accuse me with ever having seen me Drunk, heard me Swear, utter a Curse, or speak one Obscene Word (much less that I ever made it my Practice). I speak this to God's Glory that has ever preserv'd me from the Power of those Pollutions, and that from a Child begot an Hatred in me toward them. . . . Thy Words shall be thy Burden, and I trample thy Slander as Dirt under my Feet.' Even one of his other judges endorsed this indignant denial with the exclamation, 'No, No, Sir John, that's too much ;' and Sir John apologized.[692]

Even Pepys marvelled at his own jealousy of the youthful Penn ;[693] and his latest critic admits that 'a moderate foppery in youth marks the full extent of the Restoration influences upon his character ;[694] while his Quaker-hating biographer[695] grudgingly admits that Penn's life may have been 'irreproachable in the sense of freedom from wrong and scandal,' and concludes his volume with the words : 'If, with the facts we have deployed before him, the reader is unable to form an estimate of his own, nothing within our power to say further could help him. But we are confident all will agree that William Penn, in every aspect of character and in every relation of life, was a good man. It is, we think, equally apparent that he was a great man. Sometimes he was a great statesman ; at other times he was a great Quaker ; but he was never both at the same time.' In public as in private life, Penn practised the conviction that it is righteousness alone that exalteth a nation ; if this be Quakerism, his critics have made the most of it.

Summing up the traits of Penn's character in general, it may be granted that he fulfilled the requirements laid down by Micah in doing justly, loving mercy, and walking humbly with his God. 'A kind Husband, a tender Father, a noble Patriot, and a good Man :' such is his characterization by another, non-Quaker Englishman of the finest type.[696] He realized most of the ideals which he so anxiously and prayerfully prescribed for his children. Since his life was both noble and pathetic, full of varied and even thrilling adventure, his character

692 Besse, I, 38-39 ; *supra*, p. 192.
693 *Diary*, under dates of September 5 and 14, 1664.
694 Vulliamy, 43.
695 Buell, 301, 363-64.
696 Clarkson, II, 276.

was correspondingly many-sided. It is also correspondingly difficult to grasp and comprehend in its entirety; and suspicious or superficial students have called it two-sided, contradictory, even two-faced. It is difficult to reconcile at once the mental picture of a stout, somnolent figure, clad in the plain drab clothes and broad-brimmed hat of Bevan's bust and West's painting, with the gallant founder of a commonwealth and the champion of religious liberty. Hence the contradiction, or even hypocrisy, that has been found or imputed in the Puritanical youth and the gay cavalier of the French and Irish courts; in the Quaker preacher and the Stuart courtier; in the author of books which advocated the noblest ideals of individual, national and international conduct which were far in advance of his time, during the very years when he was hunted and in hiding for having co-operated with the worst of the Stuart despots and received from his hands extraordinary royal favours; in the placid lover of sylvan solitudes and homely, rustic pleasures, and the stirring, ambitious favourite moving with conscious power among the bedizened throngs of royal palaces; a trimmer in politics and a rock in religion; the perfervid seeker after earthly glory, and after eternal verities.

Indicative of the difficulty of grasping firmly the varied threads of Penn's character, of seeing it sanely and seeing it whole, is the following estimate by his latest critic: [697] 'It would be possible to compose unimpeachable obituaries of Penn from several points of view and in several manners. Did he fail? Did he conquer? Did he fail at one time and conquer at another? Was he uniformly good, unquestionably great, a grand historical figure, a rather unfortunate visionary? You can make out a good case, either for a positive or a negative answer to each of these questions, and that without taking a too prejudiced view of the evidence. And one difficulty about Penn is that he is obviously made up of bits and pieces, he is not definable in a single term, he is not uniform, clear, and consistent like George Fox or Calvin or John Wesley. . . . You cannot say that he is good or bad, clever or stupid, the advocate of this or that policy; you do not know what he is doing; he wanders away, vaguely though hugely benevolent, into a cloud of intrigue; he appears dimly, from time to time, making uncertain gestures on a darkened stage. . . . Was there a trace of the humbug in Penn? He was a man of honest principles, of noble principles. But he was also a man of woolly doggedness, imperfectly

[697] Vulliamy, pp. 207, 210, 290.

aware of the meaning of other men, blindly tenacious of opinion, entirely uncritical in his attitude to himself, and never unduly restrained by humility.'

Very different obituaries were written a few months after his death by Penn's own Quaker monthly meeting at Reading, by the Indians of Pennsylvania, and by the Philadelphia Yearly Meeting of Friends.[698] The last of these is as eulogistic as the restrained habits of the Friends permitted them to write; but it is noteworthy that it was signed by fifty of their leaders, among them that David Lloyd who, as speaker of the Pennsylvania Assembly, and in other offices, had given Penn and his friends such prolonged difficulty and anxiety. Perhaps a Quaker poet, midway between Penn's first eulogists and his last critic, may have expressed the most significant and fundamental trait of his character in a poem entitled 'The Quaker of the Olden Time:'[699]

> With that deep insight which detects
> All great things in the small,
> And knows how each man's life affects
> The spiritual life of all,
> He walked by faith and not by sight,
> By love and not by law;
> The presence of the wrong or right
> He rather felt than saw.

And yet, this does not mean that Penn thought with his heart, and not with his brain, but that both heart and intellect were illuminated by the Light that shines, not on land or sea, but in the soul, and were warmed by an abiding sense of the immediate presence of God.

---

698 *The Friends' Library,* Philadelphia, Vol. V (1841), pp. 327-8, and *The Friend,* Philadelphia, Vol. XXIX (1856), p. 227.
699 John Greenleaf Whittier.

PENN'S ACHIEVEMENTS

THAT William Penn was one of humanity's truly great men in achievement is proved by the things which he accomplished and by those which he attempted or promoted and left as unfinished business for posterity. Generation by generation since his time, the ideals which he cherished and partially realized more than two and a half centuries ago are being carried through in public and private life and, like all profound truths, are becoming the commonplaces of human thought and belief.

As a young man he saw visions, and as an old man he continued to dream dreams. Had it not been so, he and his people might indeed have perished. The liberal ideas which he cherished far in advance of his time were linked in his mind with that far-off divine event towards which the whole creation moves. Hence, he was not deterred from their advocacy even though all of worldly wisdom denounced them as impractical.

The voices of his contemporary critics and assailants have long since been silent. Those of a later and milder age have mingled high praise with their blame. His various biographers declare: 'His place in history is as sure as it is unique;'[700] 'an agent and promoter of secular civilization in its broadest sense;'[701] 'he played no ordinary part in the history of religion, politics and empire.'[702] Historians have joined in the chorus of praise. Even Macaulay, his most virulent and unconvinceable defamer, acknowledged: 'To speak the whole truth concerning Penn is a task which requires some courage: for he is rather a mythical than a historical person. Rival nations and hostile sects have agreed in canonizing him. England is proud of his name. A great commonwealth beyond the Atlantic regards him with a reverence similar to that which the Athenians felt for Theseus, and the Romans for Quirinus. The respectable society of which he was a member honours him as an apostle. By pious men of other persuasions he is generally regarded as a bright pattern of Christian virtue. Meanwhile admirers of a very different sort have sounded his praise. The French philosophers of the eighteenth century pardoned what they regarded as his

---

700 Dobrée, 417.
701 Buell, 5.
702 Vulliamy, VII.

superstitious fancies in consideration of his contempt for priests, and of his cosmopolitan benevolence, impartially extended to all races and to all creeds. His name has thus become, throughout all civilized countries, a synonym for probity and philanthropy. Nor is this high reputation altogether unmerited.'

Macaulay's great predecessor among historians and statesmen, Edmund Burke, declared: 'But what crowned all [in Penn's work as a statesman], was that noble charter of privileges, by which he made them as free as any people in the world, and which has since drawn such vast numbers of so many different persuasions and such various countries to put themselves under the protection of his laws. He made the most perfect freedom, both religious and civil, the basis of his establishment; and this has done more towards the settling of the province, and towards the settling of it in a strong and permanent manner, than the wisest regulations could have done on any other plan.'

America's distinguished historian and statesman, George Bancroft, wrote (while Macaulay was writing his mingled praise and denunciations): 'This is the praise of William Penn, that, in an age which had seen a popular revolution shipwreck popular liberty among selfish factions; which had seen Hugh Peters and Henry Vane perish by the hangman's cord and the axe; in an age when Sidney nourished the pride of patriotism rather than the sentiment of philanthropy, when Russell stood for the liberties of his order, and not for new enfranchisements, and Shaftesbury and Locke thought government should rest on property—Penn did not despair of humanity, and though all history and experience denied the sovereignty of the people, dared to cherish the noble idea of man's capacity for self-government. . . . There is nothing in the history of the human race like the confidence which the simple virtues and institutions of William Penn inspired. . . .

'Every charge of hypocrisy, of selfishness, of vanity, of dissimulation, of credulous confidence; every form of reproach, from virulent abuse to cold apology; every ill name, from Tory and Jesuit, to blasphemer and infidel, has been used against Penn; but the candor of his character always triumphed over calumny. His name was safely cherished as a household word in the cottages of Wales and Ireland, and among the peasantry of Germany; and not a tenant of a wigwam from the sea to the Susquehanna doubted his integrity. His fame is now wide as the world; he is one of the few who have gained abiding glory.'

Another eminent American historian, John Fiske, has written: 'We have to view the career of a man of extraordinary and varied powers, uniting after a fashion all his own the wisdom of the serpent with the purity of the dove, who was able at once to be a leader of one of the most iconoclastic and unpopular of Christian sects, and to retain the admiring friendship of one of the most bigoted kings that ever sat upon a throne. We must make the acquaintance of William Penn, who, take him for all in all, was by far the greatest among the founders of American commonwealths.'

The specific achievements — aside from his character — on which Penn's fame is based are by no means so few as is commonly supposed. Macaulay admits that 'on one or two points of high importance, he had notions more correct than were in his day common, even among men of enlarged minds'; and these one or two points have generally included Penn's laws and government for Pennsylvania and his dealings with the Indians. But a round dozen of achievements must be included in the list.

As a founder and leader of Quakerism and an outstanding exponent of its faith and practice, Penn stands side by side with Fox. They do indeed supplement each other; and it is possible that Quakerism would have disappeared at the end of the seventeenth century, or during the Age of Reason, had not the enthusiasm of Fox, the religious genius, been shared and organized and made politically and socially serviceable by Penn, the Quaker statesman. 'Be universal in your spirits, and keep out of all straitness and narrowness,' was his appeal to the Quaker prisoners at Bristol in 1682 and to all subsequent generations of the Society of Friends.

Together with the religious and organizational aspects of Quakerism, Penn coupled indissolubly its 'testimonies,' or struggles for social reforms. Some of his biographers, it is true, declare that it was only when Penn ceased to be a Quaker in spirit that he became a social reformer. One of them, for example, declares:[703] 'Though the sect [of the Quakers] is at this writing (1903) two hundred and sixty years old, it has never produced a man who made any permanent impress upon human affairs or accomplished anything worth enduring record except William Penn. Fortunately he was great enough to monopolize the earthly grandeur of a sect never very large itself, and his life glorifies the sect far more than sectarian biographers can exalt him.'

703 Buell, pp. 76-77.

Another insists : [704] 'Penn was indeed a trifle too much addicted to the things of this world; besides being overmuch the statesman, he was also too readily the courtier, and too zestfully the theologian — speculative endowments have their snare — and perhaps he was not altogether free from vanity. He was not, therefore, great though he might be, the perfect Quaker, the ineluctable model; he is not to be put on the same plane as Fox. To those, however, who are not of his Society, these deficiencies are not even flaws; they are, on the contrary, necessary parts of his complicated structure, the essential springs of his action. Without the combativeness, without the delight in worldly things, without the sense of glory — weaned from the impulse to argue, free of the touch of vanity — Penn would, no doubt, have been the worthiest of Quakers; but he would not have been the desire-impelled visionary, the creative man, simple, complex, self-contradictory, even self-deluding, whose place in history is as sure as it is unique.'

But as a matter of historic fact, and not of prejudiced fancy, Penn's work for social reforms was rooted in Quakerism, and sought to give expression to its fundamental tenet that the Divine spirit lives within the souls of men and makes them capable of moral regeneration. The insistence of Quakerism that religion has no reality unless it is embodied in conduct caused Penn to reject Locke's system of government for Carolina, which was based on privileged classes, and to establish one recognizing the value of the individual and the viciousness of class legislation. Just laws applicable to all, a code of individual and social morality, freedom of conscience and religious liberty, the rejection of oaths, the repudiation of war, and international jurisdiction as its substitute — all these and other features of his government were the flower and fruit of his Quaker convictions.

The Quaker 'concern' for the welfare of the Negro had not yet gone so far as to demand the complete abolition of slavery; but Penn manumitted by will his own slaves, and provided (for his Free Society of Traders) that slaves were to be emancipated after a service of fourteen years and on payment of two-thirds of their produce to receive land, live stock, and tools from the society. To prevent the unrestricted sale of slaves in his colony, he tried to stabilize marriage relations among the Negroes by passing through the Council a bill

---

[704] Dobrée, p. 417.

substituting, for the prevailing concubinage and bastardy, legal marriage and the legitimacy of offspring; but the Assembly rejected the bill. He induced the Philadelphia Quaker meeting to provide for the religious and physical welfare of the Negroes; and in 1705, the Assembly yielded to his wishes insofar as to tax the owners of imported slaves forty shillings per head. Seven years later, the Assembly laid a prohibitive tax on imported slaves of £20 per head; but paralysis had by that time overtaken Penn, and he was incapacitated from persuading the British government to ratify the act.

The care for the welfare of the Indians, which the American Quakers were to contribute in the nineteenth century towards counterbalancing 'a century of dishonour' on the part of the American government, was given a great stimulus by Penn. The genius of Quakerism supplied the principle for this, and Penn had a great and dramatic opportunity for carrying it into practice. Not only did he buy their land, instead of seizing it by conquest, and treat them justly in government and generously in barter and in hospitality (forbidding the sale of alcoholic liquors to them, and giving them equal representation on juries); but he also regarded it as an essential part of his Holy Experiment to live with them as a good neighbour, renouncing all show of armed force, and endeavouring by friendship and example to civilize and Christianize their barbarous manners and nature. He desired, he said, 'to reduce the savage nations, by gentle and just means, to the love of civil society and the Christian religion.'

The year before his first visit to Pennsylvania, he wrote them through his commissioners as follows : [705] 'My Friends, There is a Great God and Power that hath made the World and all Things therein, to whom you and I must one Day give an Account for all that we do in the World: This Great God hath written his Law in our Hearts, by which we are taught and Commanded to love and help, and do good to one another. . . . If in any Thing any shall offend you or your People, you shall have a full and speedy Satisfaction for the same by an equal Number of Just Men on both sides that by no means you may have just Occasion of being offended against them?

The first biographers of Penn, in seven languages and seven lands, unanimously extol his relations with the Indians as one of his greatest achievements and as one of the outstanding facts on the credit side of

---

705 October 18, 1681; *Works*, I, 121-2.

human history.[706] His later critics, also, bow before this verdict. Macaulay, for example, said: 'He will always be mentioned with honour as the founder of a colony, who did not, in his dealings with a savage people, abuse the strength derived from civilization.'

And his latest critic adds this (characteristically qualified) tribute:[707] 'It is the Shackamaxon treaty, which marks the highest level of Penn's fame. And rightly so, for it is the most perfect and the most productive of all his gestures. That speech by the elm tree was the speech of no bouncing imperialist bloated with false pride of race; it was the plain speech of an honest man with a true vision of human brotherhood, even if he had at the same time an equally true vision of the peaceful way to prosperity.'

The Quakers' 'testimony' against cruel and unjust treatment of prisoners — which was born out of their religious theory and their tragic sufferings — was shared fully by Penn, and for both reasons. The barbarous condition of prisons in seventeenth century England, and the punishment of death in several cruel ways even for scores of petty crimes, impelled Penn to make a civilized treatment of crime and punishment a part of his code for Pennsylvania. He denounced 'the wickedness of exterminating, where it was possible to reform'; accordingly, he consented to the death penalty for only two crimes, those of murder and treason. Before it could be inflicted, two witnesses of the fact and proof of premeditation were required, and the governor's sanction was necessary. Under these restrictions, only one criminal (a murderer) was executed in Pennsylvania before 1700.[708]

Imprisonment for theft was to be avoided if possible by making the thief restore double the amount of his theft, or work for the victim until full compensation was made. Where imprisonment was imposed, it was carried out under the dictates of humanity and common sense. Prisons were to be workhouses — in fact, as well as in name; while the reformation of the prisoner's morals and his restoration to normal society were to be the controlling principle of their manage-

---

706 Cf. Monograph Number Three (*The First Eight Biographies of William Penn in Seven Languages and Seven Lands*), passim.
707 Vulliamy, 187.
708 One of Penn's apologists for retaining capital punishment for *any* crime suggests that it was due to the influence of the Biblical text: 'Whoever shall shed man's blood, by man shall his blood be shed;' while another suggests that it was due to the knowledge that if it were entirely abolished, and especially if it were not imposed for the crime of treason, the English government would intervene to have it imposed for many and perhaps all of its own two hundred capital crimes.

PENN'S 'TREATY WITH THE INDIANS'

ment. Colonial Pennsylvania departed for a time from Penn's salutary penal code, but restored it when independence was attained; and Penn's biographer of 1813, Thomas Clarkson (who was also an authority on prison reform), declared that Pennsylvania was the only state in the world with a really enlightened penal code. Since that time, England, says Bancroft, 'confesses Penn's sagacity, and is doing honor to his genius. . . . After more than a century, the laws which he reproved, began gradually to be repealed; and the principle which he developed, sure of immortality, is slowly, but firmly, asserting its power over the legislation of Great Britain.' That such was the case in England a century ago, when Bancroft wrote, was due partly to the exemplification of Penn's and the Quakers' principle by Elizabeth Fry; and the spread of Pennsylvania's prison system throughout many parts of the United States has been due to the persistence of the Quaker 'concern' for the criminal, inspired as it has been by the example of William Penn.

The Quaker 'testimony' against war and preparations for war and in favour of exclusively peaceful means of settling disputes between communities of people, of whatever character and origin these disputes and communities may be, was exemplified most fully and dramatically by Penn in his dealings with the Indians. 'That of God' within the soul of every human being was Penn's assurance of success in appealing to the Indians by word and example for the preservation of peace and friendship; and this appeal was entirely successful. During three-quarters of a century, Pennsylvania was entirely free from Indian wars; but when the Quakers lost control of the government, and a military policy was adopted by their successors, Pennsylvania suffered many of the worst massacres and miseries experienced in border warfare. Thus, the practicability of Penn's policy of peace was proved by the experience both of that policy and of its opposite.

In the warfare between Great Britain and France — its rival in imperialism and colonization — which continued from 1628 until 1763, Penn's peace-policy became more dubious and even devious. Two of the worst wars in the long series (those of the Grand Alliance and the Spanish Succession) were waged during his connexion with Pennsylvania affairs; and, together with their prelude (Louis XIV's Chambers of Reunion and Revocation of the Edict of Nantes), they covered all the years between Penn's charter in 1681 and his paralysis in 1712. The threat of the French and their Indian allies to invade the British colonies from Canada, as well as the British government's determination to oust the French from America, put a sword of Damocles over the head of the proprietor of Pennsylvania. Constant pressure to supply money and troops for the wars, and persistent threats to revoke Penn's charter unless this were done—the threat being carried out during two years—compelled Penn to choose between a strict observance of the Quaker peace-policy and a compromise with militarism for the sake of saving his 'Holy Experiment.' His position was far more difficult than that of Woodrow Wilson in Paris, in 1919; for Wilson was not under a religious compulsion to reject the sanction of armed force for the sake of saving the League of Nations. The moral conflict in Wilson's mind and the religious one in Penn's was the chief cause, it may well be conceived, for the paralysis with which they were both afflicted. Wilson yielded to 'practical necessity,' and tried to justify his action to the world and to himself; Penn strove long and painfully against the compromise constantly pressing upon him, and tried in the end to escape from the issue by offering to surrender his government to the crown.

Meanwhile, he yielded insofar as to appoint non-Quaker governors of Pennsylvania, who persuaded the Quaker Assembly to grant to the government supplies called by non-military names, but used for military purposes. The moral and religious conflict in the minds of these Quaker legislators became too intense for them also, and at the beginning of the next great war in the series, which began in 1755, they resigned their seats in the Assembly, conceded the government of Pennsylvania to the military party, and for a time they and their fellow-Quakers virtually retired from politics. Hence, it was *war* that threatened to destroy Penn's 'Holy Experiment' at its beginning, and did seriously cripple it at the end.

Penn's experience with the inveterate militarism of European Christians, as compared with the sweet reasonableness of the uncivilized heathen of Pennsylvania, caused him also to leave a loop-hole, or excuse, for the use of force in his proposal of 1693 for a European Dyet,[709] and also in his proposal of 1696 for a union of the American colonies.[710]

Non-Quaker biographers of Penn stress, as is natural, those of his achievements which were not specifically identified with the Quaker faith and 'testimonies.' His achievements in scholarship and author-

709 *Supra*, p. 164.
710 *Infra*, p. 237.

ship are notable; and while some Quakers have contributed somewhat in this field, Penn's contributions transcend the bounds of Quakerism and give him an assured place in the wide world of learning and literature.

Religious toleration had been an ideal of sectarian martyrs long before the time of William Penn; but it was he who seized a great opportunity of embedding it in the political structure of a commonwealth. In his three American colonies, he established complete toleration, and forbade all persecution and discrimination for conscience' sake. He did not, it is true, establish complete religious liberty; for a professed belief in Christ was made a requisite of suffrage and office-holding. But the advanced position which he took may be estimated by the fact that even during the Puritan Commonwealth in England, the death penalty was prescribed for the denial of the trinity, the divinity of Christ, bodily resurrection, the Day of Judgment, and the Bible as the word of God.[711] Pennsylvania's advanced stand was in striking contrast, also, with that of the other American colonies, most of which were founded by fugitives and exiles for conscience' sake, but all of which imposed restrictions of varied kinds upon religious worship and the inviolability of conscience.[712] Even as late as 1776, Pennsylvania and Delaware alone conceded social and political equality to all Christian sects.[713]

While the Quakers advocated religious toleration both because of their faith and of their own and others' sufferings under persecution, Penn lifted his demand for religious liberty to the plane of the historic rights of Englishmen. The leading part which he played, in the spoken and written word and in the political arena, in basing toleration upon these rights, has immortalized his name as one of the great heroes in the long struggle for liberty. A non-Quaker, English author, in estimating the lasting importance of this aspect of his career, regards him not so much 'as the outstanding figure of Quaker history, but as the greatest Englishman and the greatest European of his time.'[714] In

[711] Graham, 264.
[712] Cf. Isaac Sharpless in the *Friends Intelligencer*, Philadelphia, November 4, 1916.
[713] Fiske, II, 99.
[714] Brailsford, IX. Indication of Penn's broad vision of the rights of Englishmen is the fact that the first publication of Magna Carta in America was translated into English by Penn and published in Philadelphia in 1687, 16 mo., 63 pp. it is entitled *The Excellent Privilege of Liberty & Property Being the Birth-Right of the Free-born Subjects of England,* and contains, besides Magna Charta and comments upon it, two other English state papers and Penn's Patent and Charter of Liberties.

partial justification of this claim, it might be noted that the demand for 'the rights of Englishmen' overthrew the reactionary Stuart dynasty and paved the way for a period of England's progress along many lines comparable with that of Queen Elizabeth's spacious days.

A dozen years, and again a half-dozen years, before the Grand and Glorious Revolution occurred in England, Penn had secured the opportunity of transplanting liberty to the soil of New Jersey and Pennsylvania. Nobly did he utilize that opportunity, and noteworthy indeed was the crop which sprang from the seed he sowed. As a colonizer of trans-Atlantic lands, he met with phenomenal success. Penn himself lived to see and give thanks for it. As early as 1684, at the end of his first visit to Pennsylvania, he wrote with pride:[715] 'I have led the greatest colony into America that ever any man did upon a private credit, and the most prosperous beginnings that ever were in it are to be found among us.'

Writing in 1710 a letter of expostulation to his 'Old Friends' in Pennsylvania, for some things that had gone wrong, he said:[716] 'When it pleased God to open a way for me to settle that colony, I had reason to expect a solid comfort from the services done to many hundreds of people; and it was no small satisfaction to me, that I have not been disappointed in seeing them prosper, and growing up to a flourishing country, blessed with liberty, ease, and plenty, beyond what many of themselves could expect, and wanting nothing to make themselves happy, but what with a right temper of mind and prudent conduct they might give themselves. . . . Friends, the eyes of many are upon you; the people of many nations of Europe look on that Country as a land of ease and quiet, wishing to themselves in vain the same blessings they conceive you may enjoy.'

At the time of Penn's death fifty thousand colonists had settled in 'Penn's Woods' and ten thousand in the City of Brotherly Love — chiefly as the result of his direct and indirect leadership;[717] a half-century later, the tide of immigration had brought two hundred thousand settlers to his province and twenty thousand to Philadelphia. Penn's ideal of his capital city as 'a green country town,' his far-reaching 'town-planning' views which would convert it into 'a garden city,' the care which he took, as America's first 'conservationist,' of

715 Pa. Hist. Soc. Memoirs, I, 448-9.
716 Sharpless, I, 98-101.
717 Cf. Monograph Number Two (William Penn and the Dutch Quaker Migration to Pennsylvania), Ch. V, and passim.

PHILADELPHIA ABOUT THE TIME OF PENN'S DEATH

Pennsylvania's forests, are very congenial to our most progressive twentieth-century practices and illustrate Penn's insight and vision; and although the great city has spread over a large space in order to accommodate its two million inhabitants, and the province has departed lamentably in some respects from its founder's plans, it still cherishes as its most conspicuous memorial Penn's statue on the top of Philadelphia's city hall in the heart of its business district.

As a maker of constitutions and laws, Penn has taken high place in the line of illustrious statesmen. Even one of his most caustic non-Quaker critics has said of his Preamble of Concessions to West Jersey: 'It was a simple code. Yet it was, crudely, the greatest code in popular government that has fallen from the pen of mortal man. It was the pioneer of all codes that now express, under various conditions and in diverse forms, the essential doctrine of self-government, "of the people, by the people, and for the people."'[718]

Of the frame of government and laws Penn provided for Pennsylvania, an eminent non-Quaker lawyer of Philadelphia, on retiring from the speakership in Pennsylvania's Assembly in 1739, said: 'It is not to the fertility of our soil or the commodiousness of our rivers that we ought chiefly to attribute the great progress this province has made within so small a compass of years in improvements, wealth, trade, and navigation, and the extraordinary increase of people who have been drawn from every country in Europe; it is all due to the excellency of our Constitution. Our foreign trade and shipping are free from all imposts except those small duties payable to His Majesty by the statute laws of Great Britain. The taxes are inconsiderable, for the sole power of raising and disposing of public money is lodged in the assembly. . . . By many years' experience we find that an equality among religious societies, without distinguishing one sect with greater privileges than another, is the most effective method to discourage hypocrisy, promote the practice of moral virtues, and prevent the plagues and mischiefs which always attend religious squabbling. This is our Constitution, and this Constitution was framed by the wisdom of Mr. Penn.'

Even Macaulay joins in the chorus of the critics' praise; he writes: 'As the proprietor and legislator of a province, which, being almost uninhabited when it came into his possession, afforded a clear field for moral experiments, he had the rare good fortune of being able to carry

[718] Buell, 97.

his theories into practice without any compromise, and yet without any shock to existing institutions. He will always be mentioned with honour as the founder of a colony, who did not, in his dealings with a savage people, abuse the strength derived from civilization, and as a lawgiver, who, in an age of persecution, made religious liberty the corner-stone of a polity.'

Thomas Jefferson, the father of democracy in America, writing of William Penn,[719] expressed his sincere pleasure 'that a day will at length be annually set apart for rendering the honours so justly due to the greatest lawgiver the world has produced; the first, either in ancient or modern times, who has laid the foundation of government in the pure and unadulterated principles of peace, of reason and right; and in parallelism with whose institutions, to name the dreams of a Minos, or Solon, or the military and monkish establishments of a Lycurgus, is truly an abandonment of all regard to the only legitimate object of government, the happiness of man.'

James Madison, the father of the Constitution of the United States, declared:[720] 'Pennsylvania may well be proud of such a founder and lawgiver as William Penn, and an obligation be felt by her enlightened citizens, to cherish by commemorations of his exalted philanthropy, and his beneficent institutions, their expanding influence in the cause of civil and religious liberty.'

Rising above Philadelphia and his three American colonies, Penn's vision embraced some of the fundamental ideas upon which the United States of America was to be built a century after his Plan of Union was proposed, and upon which, after still another century, international courts of arbitration and justice were to be founded and a League of Nations was to be attempted. A total rejection of war and armaments, was Fox's word; union, co-operation, pacific means of settlement and disarmament, was Penn's addition. And this united and implemented message of the eternal negative and the eternal positive may yet be regarded — when the nations shall recognize it as the eternal truth and shall learn war no more — as the supreme achievement of Penn and Quakerism alike.

Penn's Quaker biographers are naturally inclined to revert from the political, economic, and other social achievements of Penn to that one

---

[719] A letter dated 'Monticello, Nov. 16th, 1825,' on the commemoration of the landing of Penn in Pennsylvania; quoted from *Poulson's Daily Advertiser*, October 28, 1826, in *The Friend*, Philadelphia, Vol. I (1828), p. 104.
[720] A letter dated 'Montpellier, Nov. 12, 1825,' ibid.

which was the ruling passion throughout his life, namely, the religious. The *holy* experiment of founding a modern commonwealth on the principles of applied Christianity is in their eyes his supreme achievement. Janney, for example, writes that 'Pennsylvania affords the only example of a state, where the executive power was upheld without military force, justice administered without the use of oaths, and religion sustained without a priesthood or salaried ministry. . . . The enterprise of Penn and his associates in the colony of Pennsylvania, by demonstrating the feasibility of peaceable principles, has served to confirm the faith of the wavering, and to encourage the true-hearted disciples of Christ. As an example of Christian principles, applied to the government of a state, it stands without a parallel in the history of the world; and will, doubtless, continue to be more admired and imitated as time advances, until that happy period shall arrive when "nation shall not lift up sword against nation, neither shall they learn war any more."'

But non-Quaker biographers also stress the realization of this religious ideal as Penn's supreme achievement. He said in his preface to the Frame of Government that 'governments rather depend upon men, than men upon governments'; and commenting upon this, one of these biographers wrote:[721] 'The fact that for seventy years Pennsylvania endured as a Christian state, ruled and defended by love and not by force, was due in the first place to the constitution settled upon it by its founder. But it was due in equal measure to the loyal working out of those laws in the daily life of the men and women who were its first settlers. For the only time in the history of the world, a whole country had accepted the Sermon on the Mount for its working policy, and found it neither impossible of performance, nor unpractical in operation.'

Another biographer, speaking of the holy experiment as an ideal not fully realized, comments:[722] 'He would show how people would flourish under it in agriculture, commerce, and all the arts and refinements of life. He would show that government could be carried on without war and without oaths, that the pure, original, primitive Christianity of the times of the apostles could be maintained without an established church, without a hireling ministry, without cruelty or persecution, without ridiculous dogmas or unmanly ritual, simply by

---

721 Brailsford, 351.
722 Fisher, 210-211.

its own innate power, the spirit of Christ, the inward light. He would do this through the aid of his followers, the Quakers, who would never desert him, through his own sincerity of purpose and energy of mind, through his feudal ownership of a vast domain, and through the power which wealth would give. It was a stupendous plan, an heroic grasp for a whole world of light and truth by one who had been living for centuries in darkness; for Penn was typical of his time; he was the voice of his time crying passionately, recklessly, for light after the long night of the Middle Ages.'

Still another, more critical biographer, who believes that Penn the idealist was defeated in his plans, nevertheless declared:[723] 'But the ideal was not defeated; and if ever it is defeated, then the Holy Experiment of Christianity will have come to an end.'

While Senator Charles Sumner paid this tribute: 'To William Penn belongs the distinction of first, in human history, establishing the law of love as a rule of conduct for the intercourse of nations.'[724]

Penn himself showed plainly in several of his writings that he was primarily intent on founding a religious commonwealth: by no means a theocracy, but a state based on the universality — in belief and practice — of genuine religion. In a letter to an American friend soon after receiving his patent for Pennsylvania, he wrote:[725] 'For my country I eyed the Lord in the obtaining of it, and more was I drawn inward to look to him and to owe it to his hand and power, than to any other way. I have so obtained it, and desire that I may not be unworthy of his love, but do that which may answer his kind providence, and serve his truth and people; that an example may be set up to the nations; there may be room there, though not here, *for such an holy experiment.*'

Biographers who have toiled long and carefully through a study of the writings, the career, and the character of William Penn may well feel when their task is ended as John Morley felt when he had finished his biography of Gladstone: not relieved and rejoicing, but saddened and lonely. Readers of these biographies, also, must miss the companionship of great-hearted Penn, even though it come inadequately revealed, as through a glass darkly. But both alike may be grateful for the large psychological, political, literary, and religious interest and

---

[723] Vulliamy, 294.
[724] *The True Grandeur of Nations,* Boston, 1845.
[725] To James Harrison, 6th month (August) 25, 1681 (*The Pemberton MSS.*).

ISAIAH'S PROPHECY

instruction which a study of him affords, and for the inspiration and encouragement which he bequeathed to posterity. In many a subsequent social crisis, it may still be said of William Penn, in behalf of all humanity, as was said of his great contemporary, John Milton, in behalf of England : Thou shouldst be living at this hour ! The world hath need of thee.

WILLIAM PENN—A CHRONOLOGY

1644 (October 14) Birth	Civil Wars in England Battle of Marston Moor, 1644
1644–48 Infancy Smallpox at age of three	Roger Williams and John Eliot in New England Pieter Stuyvesant in New Netherland Thirty Years' War in Europe (1618–48) Louis XIV in France (1643–1715)
1648–56 Chigwell School	Charles I executed (1649) The Commonwealth of England (1649–60) John Lilburne's two trials (1649–53) : the rights of juries England's first war with Holland (1651–54) Cromwellian Settlement of Ireland (1652-56) Jamaica seized by the English (1655)
1656–60 Private tutors	Four Quakers hanged on Boston Common (1659–61)
1660–62 Oxford University (October 26, 1660 to about March 1, 1662)	Restoration of the Stuart Kings, the Parliament and the Anglican Church (1660) Religious persecution under the 'Clarendon Code' (1661–85) England's empire in India (1661–)
1663–64 The Grand Tour (July, 1662, to about August 26, 1664)	New Netherland to the Duke of York (1664) German wars against the Turks (1661–64)
1664–65 Lincoln's Inn (About August 1664, to early spring, 1666)	England's second war with Holland (1664–67) The Plague (1665)
1666–67 Ireland (Early spring, 1666, to about Christmas, 1667)	The Great Fire (1666)
Quakerism The first imprisonment (Cork) Expelled from home	The Dutch in the Medway (1667) England's first war with Louis XIV

1668–69 A Quaker preacher Imprisoned in the Tower *No Cross, No Crown*	Louis XIV's first war of aggression (1667–68)
1669–70 Ireland Penn-Mead Trial	John Locke's Constitution for Carolina
1670–71 Imprisoned in Newgate Death of his father (1670) Holland and Germany (1671)	
1672 Marriage with Gulielma Maria Springett	Declaration of Indulgence
1673–74 Religious Controversies	England's third war with Holland (1672–74) Louis XIV's second war of aggression (1672–78)
1675 New Jersey	King Philip's War (1675–76)
1677 Holland and Germany	
1678–81 The Struggle for Toleration	The Popish Plot (1678–81) Rise of Political Parties (1679) Habeas Corpus Act (1679)
1681–82 Charter for Pennsylvania (March 14, 1681) Fundamental Constitution of Pennsylvania (1681) Death of his mother (1682)	Louis XIV annexes Alsace and Lorraine
1682–84 First visit to Pennsylvania Frame of Government for Pennsylvania Founding of Philadelphia (1682) Founding of Germantown (1683)	Forfeiture of London and other town charters Forfeiture of Massachusetts Charter Execution of Algernon Sidney German wars against the Turks (1682–99) Turks repulsed from Vienna (1683)
1685–88 'Jesuit' and Courtier Holland (1686)	Monmouth's Rebellion (1685) Stuart absolutism in England Andros ruler of New England, New York and New Jersey Revocation of the Edict of Nantes (1685) Devastation of the Palatinate (1688) 'The Grand and Glorious Revolution' (1688)

A Chronology

1689–90 'Jacobite' and 'Traitor'

    Declaration and Bill of Rights (1689)
Toleration Act (1689)
Louis XIV's third war of aggression, 1689–97 ('King William's War' in America)

1690–93 Internment
Essay . . . Peace of Europe
Some Fruits of Solitude
Pennsylvania annexed by the Crown (1693)

    Death of Robert Barclay (1690) and George Fox (1691)
'Pacification' of Limerick (1691)
Salem Witchcraft Frenzy (1692)
The National Debt (1693)

1694 Death of Gulielma Penn
Pennsylvania restored to Penn
The Keithian Separation

    The Bank of England
Censorship of the Press abolished

1696 Marriage to Hannah Callowhill
Death of Springett Penn

    Recoinage Act (Isaac Newton)

1697 Interview with Peter the Great
Plan for American Union

    The Peace of Ryswick

1698 Ireland

1699–1701 Second visit to Pennsylvania
Pennsylvania's new charter (1701)

    The Great Northern War (1700–21)

1702–4 William Penn Junior's disgrace

    Louis XIV's fourth war of aggression, 1702–13 ('Queen Anne's War' in America)
English take Gibraltar (1704)

1705–8 Lawsuit and Debtors' prison (1708)

    Union of England and Scotland (1707)

1712–18 Paralysis
Death: 30th of 5th Mo (August), 1718
Jordans

    Treaty of Utrecht (1713)
The Hanoverian Kings succeed the Stuarts (1714)
The Old Pretender (1715–16)
Italian and Austrian Wars with the Turks (1714–18)

AN ALLEGED PORTRAIT OF GULIELMA PENN

The story of this portrait is given by Webb (1867) as follows : [726]

'The original of this portrait is a painting on glass in the possession of the descendants of Henry Swan of Holmwood, Dorking, who died in 1796. It was given to him by John Townsend of London, at an unknown date, and along with it one of William Penn. Jemima Swan, the present owner of these portraits, kindly gave permission to have copies of them engraved for this work. The artist had the portrait of the lady nearly completed, when my friend John Thompson, of Hitchin, informed me that he had engravings of the great-grandparents of the late Joseph Gurney in his possession, closely resembling the photographic copies of the reputed portraits of William and Gulielma Penn, and he very kindly took them out of their frames and sent them for my inspection. I found points of dissimilarity as well as of resemblance. The busts were different, and there was some difference in the attitude of the lady; but the dresses were so exactly alike,— each button, fold, and slope being the same,— that there was evidently some original connection between the paintings and engravings. A correspondence ensued between John Thompson and Daniel Gurney, the senior representative of the Gurney family, from which it was ascertained that the portraits of the Gurneys were first engraved in 1746, and that subsequently two copies of different sizes were executed. These engravings have always been regarded by the family as authentic likenesses, but they have never known of the existence of any paintings from which they were taken. Two sets of engravings were executed in the lifetime of Joseph and Hannah Middleton Gurney; but without their names, and probably without their knowledge; the first set being styled *A Sincere Quaker* and *A Fair Quaker*. Family tradition speaks of Hannah Middleton Gurney as having been surpassingly handsome.

'Joseph Gurney and his wife were contemporaries of the Penns, and though much their juniors in age, it is probable that up to the time of their marriage in 1713, the style of their dress was not materially different from that of the Penns. From all these circum-

[726] Webb, "Penns and Peningtons of the Seventeenth Century," pp. VI-VII. The "Swan" portrait of Penn is not reproduced in Maria Webb's book.

stances it appears to me most likely that both sets of *portraits* are genuine as regards the heads and faces, but that the *dresses* of the Gurneys, except hat and hood, are copied from those of the Penns, possibly because he who employed the artist had only *busts* of the Gurneys.

'I am aware of the statement made by Granville Penn, and repeated by other writers, that the portrait of William Penn in armour, painted in Dublin in 1666, was the only likeness of him ever executed. But a second portrait might be in existence without his knowledge; as it is not probable any likeness of William Penn, accompanying (as this does) that of his first wife, should come into the possession of the children of his second wife, from whom Granville Penn was descended. Any such portraits would naturally be left to Letitia Aubrey, Gulielma's only daughter; and as she died childless and always remained amongst Friends, is it not most likely that after her death they became the property of the Friend who gave them to Henry Swan?'

ANOTHER ALLEGED PORTRAIT OF GULIELMA

'The Friends' Institute, London, possesses an oil painting said to be Gulielma Penn in middle life; but there is very little evidence as to its genuineness' (Graham, *William Penn*, p. 331).

THE PENN FAMILY

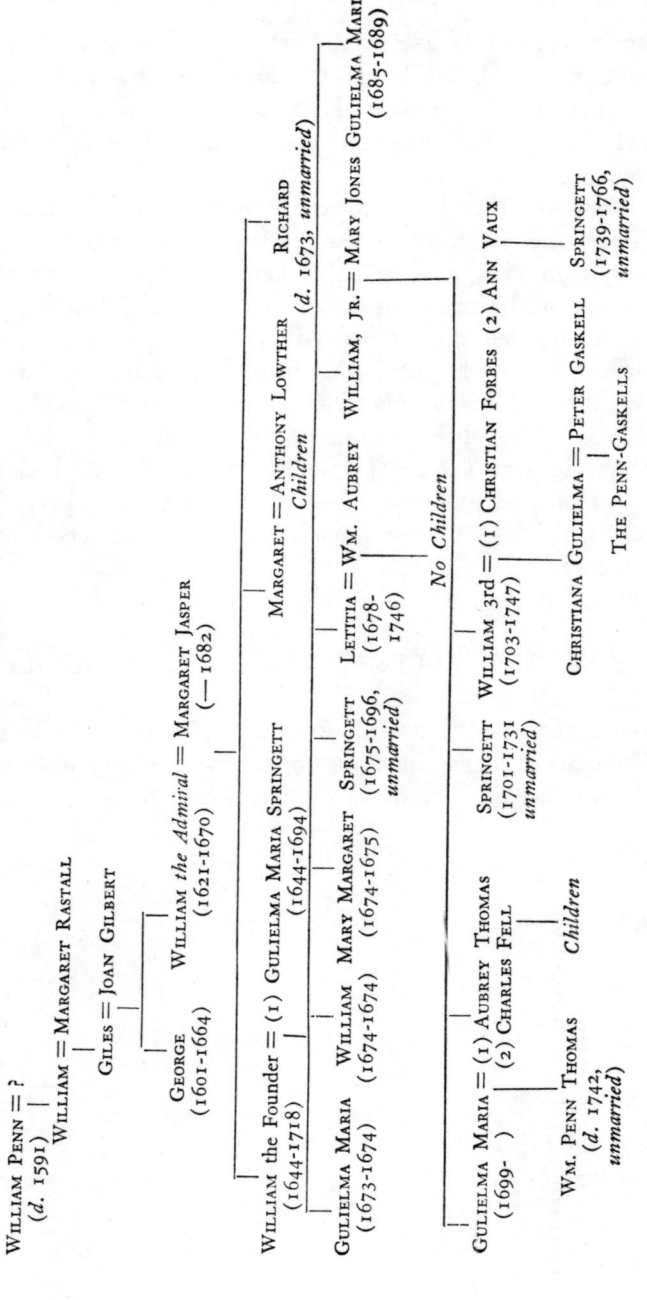

THE PENN FAMILY

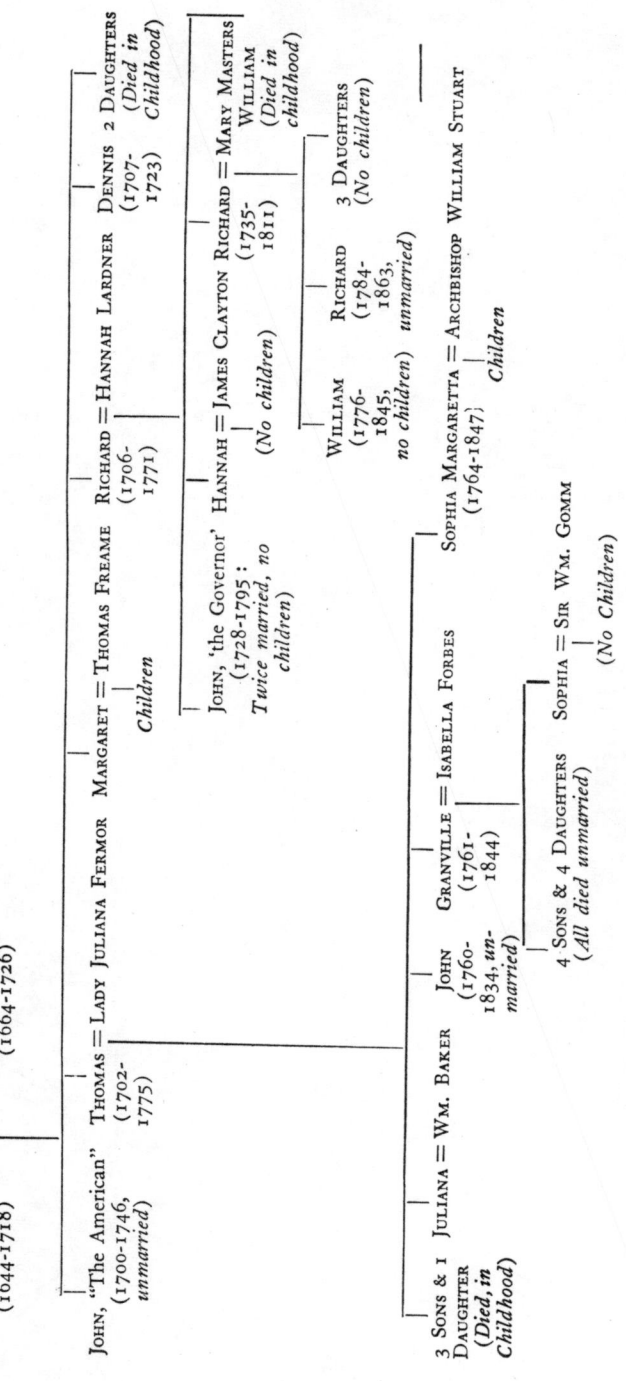

BOOKS AND MANUSCRIPTS CITED IN THIS VOLUME

Beck and Ball, *London Friends' Meetings*, London, 1869.
Bellers, John. *Some Reasons for an European State*, London, 4to, 1710.
Besse, Joseph, Ed., *The Works of William Penn, to which is prefixed a Journal of His Life*, London, 2 vols., folio, 1726.
Besse, Joseph, *Sufferings of the . . . Quakers*, London, folio, 1753.
Brailsford, Mabel Richmond, *The Making of William Penn*, London and New York, 1930, 8vo, 24+368 pp.
Braithwaite, William C., *The Beginnings of Quakerism*, London, 1912.
Braithwaite, William C., *The Second Period of Quakerism*, London, 1919.
Buell, Augustus C., *William Penn as the Founder of two Commonwealths*, New York, 1904, 8vo, 368 pp.
Burnet, Gilbert, *History of his own Times*, London, folio, 1724-34.
Clarendon, Earl of, *The History of the Rebellion*, Oxford, 1702.
Clarkson, Thomas, *Memoirs of the Private and Public Life of William Penn*, Philadelphia, 1814 (London, 1813), 2 vols., 12mo, 441 and 390 pp.
Croese, Gerard, *Historia Quakeriana*, Latin ed., Amsterdam, 16mo, 1695, English ed., London, 12mo, 1696.
Crosfield, Helen G., *Margaret Fox of Swarthmoor Hall*, London, 1913.
Davies, Godfrey, *Bibliography of British History, Stuart Period, 1603-1714*, Oxford, 1928.
Dixon, W. Hepworth, *A History of William Penn, Founder of Pennsylvania*, New York, 1902 (London, 1851), royal 8vo, 337 pp.
Dobrée, Bonamy, *William Penn, Quaker and Pioneer*, London, 1932, 8vo, 428 pp.
Dottin, Paul, *Life of Daniel DeFoe*, English Trans., London, 1929.
Dymond, Jonathan, *Essays on . . . Morality*, London, 1829.
Dymond, Jonathan, *Inquiry into . . . War . . . Christianity*, London, 1823.
Ellwood, Thomas, Autobiography, London, 1714.
Fisher, Sydney George, *The True William Penn*, Philadelphia, 1900, 8vo, 385 pp.
Fiske, John, *The Dutch and Quaker Colonies in America*, Boston, 1899, 8vo, vol. II, pp. 92-167.
Forster, William E., Preface (pp. XVII-LX) to a new ed. of Clarkson's *Life of William Penn*, London, 1849 (A Refutation of Macaulay's charges).
Fox, George, *Journal* (Cambridge, 1911, 2 vols., 8vo), *Short Journal* and *Itinerary Journals* (Cambridge, 1925, 8vo).

Friend, The, London, *passim*.
Friend, The, Philadelphia, *passim*.
Friends Intelligencer, Philadelphia, *passim*.
Friends Library, The, Philadelphia, vol. IV, 1841.
Fuller and Holme, *Sufferings of the . . . Quakers in Ireland*, n.pl., 1672.
Graham, John W., *William Penn, Founder of Pennsylvania*, London, 1924 (1917), 8vo, 332 pp.
Grant, Mrs. Colquhoun, *Quaker and Courtier: The Life and Work of William Penn*, London, 1907, royal 8vo, 11 + 259 pp.
Grubb, Isabel, *Quakers in Ireland*, London, 16mo, 1927.
Harvey MS., The Thomas.
Huckel, Oliver, *A Dreamer of Dreams . . . The Love-Story and Life-Work of Will Penn, The Quaker*, New York, 1916, 8vo, 27 + 249 pp.
Janney, Samuel M., *The Life of William Penn*, Philadelphia, 1852, 8vo, 11 + 560 pp.
Jenkins, Howard M., *The Family of William Penn, Founder of Pennsylvania, Ancestry and Descendants*, Philadelphia and London, 1898, royal 8vo, 288 pp.
Journal of the Friends' Historical Society, London, *passim*.
Locker-Lampson, Mrs. G., *A Quaker Post Bag*, London, 1910.
Macaulay, T. B., *History of England*, London, 1849-1861.
Mackintosh, Sir J., *History of the Revolution*, London, 1834.
Marsillac, Jean de, *La Vie de Guillamne Penn, etc.*, Paris, 1791, 2 vols., 12mo, 264 and 304 pp.
Muller, F., *De Nederlansche Geschiedenis in Platen*, Amsterdam, vol. I, 1863.
Myers, Albert Cook, *Immigration of the Irish Quakers into Pennsylvania*, Philadelphia, 1902.
New York Colonial Documents, Albany, vol. IV.
Notes and Queries, London, 1868, 1888.
Paget, John, *Paradoxes and Puzzles*, Edinburgh, 1874.
Pemberton MSS., The.
Penn-Forbes MSS., The.
Penn MSS., The Granville.
Penn, Granville, *Memorials of the Professional Life and Times of Sir William Penn, Knt.*, London, 1833, 2 vols., 8vo.
"Penn-Logan Correspondence" (*Memoirs* of the Pennsylvania Historical Society, vols. IX and X), Philadelphia, 1870 and 1872.
Penn, William, Writings; cf. Index, *infra*, pp. 359f.

Books and Manuscripts Cited in This Volume

Penney, Norman, Ed., *Extracts from State Papers relating to Friends*, London, 1910-1913.
Penney, Norman, Ed., *First Publishers of Truth*, London, 1907, 8vo, 410 pp.
Penney, Norman, Ed., George Fox's *Journals* (cf. Fox, George).
Pennsylvania Historical Society MSS., The.
Pennsylvania Historical Society *Memoirs*, Philadelphia, vol. 1, 1826.
Pennsylvania Magazine of History and Biography, The.
Pepys, Samuel, *Diary*, H.B.Wheatley's ed., London, 1904, 8 vols.
Picart, Bernard, *Cérémonies et Coutumes Religieuses*, Amsterdam, 1724.
Plimpton, George A., *The Education of Shakespeare*, New York and London, 1933.
Proud, Robert, *The History of Pennsylvania, in North America*, Philadelphia, 2 vols., 8vo, 1797.
Purdie, Samuel A., Trans., *Memorias de Guillermo Penn*, H. Matamoros, 1879, 12mo, 131 pp.
Quaker Meeting Records: Bucks, Surrey, Sussex, Horsham, Bristol, London, Weston Turvey and Reading, England, and Upper Merion and Philadelphia, Pennsylvania.
Rigg, J.M., 'William Penn' (Article in the *Dictionary of National Biography*).
Rutty, John. *The Quakers in Ireland*, Dublin, 4to, 1751.
Sewel, Willem, *Histori van de Opkomste, Aanwas, en Voortgang der . . . Quakers*, Dutch ed., Amsterdam, folio, 1717; English ed., London, folio, 1722.
Sharpless, Isaac, *A Quaker Experiment in Government*, Philadelphia, 1898, vol. II.
Smith, Joseph, *A Descriptive Catalogue of Friends' Books*, London, 2 vols., 8vo, 1867, 1027 and 984 pp.
Spence MSS., The.
State Papers (See Penney, Norman, ed.).
Story, Thomas, *Journal*, Newcastle upon Tyne, folio, 1747.
Stoughton, John, *William Penn, the Founder of Pennsylvania*, London, 1882, 8vo, 364 pp.
Strickland, Agnes, *Lives of the Queens of England (Mary Beatrice)*, Philadelphia, vol. 9, 1846.
Sumner, Charles, *The True Grandeur of Nations*, Boston, 1845.
Swift, Dean, *Journal to Stella; Notes on Burnett; Discourses . . . on Freethinking ; Letters from Unknown Persons.*
Thirnbeck MSS., The.

Thompson MSS., *The Sylvanus.*
Thorpe, F. N., *Federal and State Constitutions,* vol. v, Washington, 1909.
Trevelyan, George M., *England under the Stuarts,* New York and London, 1925.
Vulliamy, C.E., *William Penn,* New York, 1934, 8vo, 12 + 303 pp.
Watson, John F., *Annals of Philadelphia and Pennsylvania,* Philadelphia, 1844.
Webb, Maria, *The Penns and Peningtons of the Seventeenth Century,* London, 1867, 8vo, 15 + 430 pp. (Philadelphia, 1868, 8vo, 446 pp.).
Weems, Mason L., *The Life of William Penn, the Settler of Pennsylvania, etc.,* Philadelphia, 1822, 8vo, 219 pp.
Whiting, John, *Memoirs (Persecution Expos'd),* London, 4to, 1715.
Whittier, John G., *Poems,* Boston, 1892.
Wood, Anthony, *Life and Times,* 1632-1695, London, 1891.

INDEX

Abrahamsz, Galenus, 132
Affirmation, 205, 215, 266, 281
Aggs, William Hanbury, Mr. and Mrs., XIV, 12
All Hallows Church Barking, XIII, 6, 65f
American Philosophical Society, 178 n 408, 274 n 584
American Universal Magazine, 301 n 645
Amsterdam, 121, 123, 132, 174
Amyraut, Moïse, 81f
Anabaptists, 198
Andros, Governor, 226
Anglicans, 4f, 73, 141, 144ff, 214f, 255, 257f, 262, 286
Anne, Queen, 162, 180, 283ff
A Quaker Post Bag, 181 n 414
Arc, Joan of, 71
Archaeologia, 183 n 418
Arlington, Earl of, 85, 182ff, 201
Armstrong, Edward, 302 n 649
Arran, Earl of, 88f, 93, 97
Arran, Earl of, 245f
Aston, Colonel, 243
Athenian Mercury, The, 144
Aubrey, William, 45, 47f, 56

Baker, Humfrey, 68 n 154
Baltimore, Lord, 220, 227, 235, 252, 319
Bancroft, George, 161f, 326, 331
Bandon, 96
Banks, John, 280
Baptism, 170
Baptists, 5, 134ff, 147f
Barclay, Robert, 41, 56, 82f, 123, 130, 167, 170, 173f, 176, 219f, 263 n 554
Barrymore, Lord, 97
Broderick, Sir St. John, 97
'Basing House,' 11
Bath, 292, 300
Batten, Admiral, 70
Baxter, Richard, 135f, 149ff
Beck and Ball, 56 n 123
Beckham, Edward, 144
Bellers, John, 161
Berwick, Sir Henry, 202
Besse, Joseph, 25, 29 n 45, 39 n 70, 43 n 77, 77 n 168, 110, 116f, 126-29, 138, 145 n 321, 146f, 192 n 424, 197 n 432-3, 221 n 472, 233 n 477, 281 n 595 & 598, 284, 291 n 616, 293, 322 n 692
Bevan, Sylvanus, XV, 129, 300ff
Bible, The, 170, 175, 205
Bigland, Percy, XIII
Billingsley, H., 68 n 154
Bishops, The Seven, 260f

Blake, Admiral Robert, 17
Blue Idol Meeting-house, XIV
Boate, Gershon, 98
Bolingbroke, Viscount, 284
Brailsford, Mabel R., 19, 20 n 21, 23 n 25, 25 n 29, 28 n 36 & 38, 29 n 42, 30 n 47, 69 n 155, 108 n 224, 112 n 235, 152 n 345, 183 n 418, 296 n 623, 309 n 668, 333, 337
Braithwaite, Wm. C., 77 n 168, 281 n 599
Brentford, 13
Bridewell, 185f, 195
Bridgwater, 126
Bristol, 1, 13, 22, 58f, 114, 124f, 217, 222, 252
Broghill, Lord, 97
Brown, Horatio F., 159
Bruce, John, 183 n 418
Bryan (O'Brien?), Lord, 97
Buckingham, Duke of, 202
Buell, Augustus C., 19 n 18, 21 n 22, 25 n 30, 28 n 40, 71 n 158, 107 n 223, 108 n 224, 111 n 230, 113 n 237, 117 n 241, 129, 138 n 300, 155 n 362, 163 n 379, 221 n 472, 224 n 478, 247 n 517, 255 n 540, 271 n 577, 273 n 582-3, 319, 322, 325 n 701, 327
Bugg, Francis, 177, 280
Bunyan, John, 6, 156
Burke, Edmund, 289, 326
Burnet, Bishop Gilbert, 247ff, 254, 269, 284f, 315, 317
Burnyeat, John, 149, 218f
Burrough, Edward, 112
'Bury House', 11
Bushel, Edward, 186-91
Butler, Samuel, 156
Byllinge, Edward, 219

Calendar of State Papers, 19 n 17, 20 n 21, 25 n 29, 121 n 247, 123, 133f, 184, 200
Callowhill, Thomas, 57, 60, 62, 289
Calvin, John, 323
Cambridge, 77 n 168, 78
Camm, John, 77
Carlyle, Thomas, 19
Carpenter, Samuel, 46, 51
Carrickfergus, 89
Carstares, William, 37 n 67
Carteret, Sir George, 219
Cashel, 104
Catholicism, Roman, 76, 139, 142, 150, 209f, 213ff, 220, 242, 249, 253, 257, 305f
(*see* PENN, WILLIAM: Jesuit)
Charing Cross, 12
Charles I, 211

353

Index

Charles II, 8, 18f, 21f, 73ff, 85, 183, 199, 201, 207, 211, 220f, 225ff, 251, 305
Chasles, Philarète, XVI
Chesne, J. de Beau, 68 *n* 153
Cheyney, John, 146f
Chigwell School, XIII, 7, 67-72
Chorley Wood, 11, 33
Christ, 129, 135, 142, 148f, 168ff, 177 (*see* Light Within)
Christchurch College, *see* Oxford
Clapham, Jonathan, 141
Clarendon, Earl of, 18ff, 186 *n* 421
Clark, Lt. Edward, 102
Clark, John, 136
Clarkson, Thomas, 19 *n* 18, 29 *n* 45, 30 *n* 51, 70 *n* 157, 74 *n* 164, 109 *n* 226, 125 *n* 258, 130f, 135 *n* 293, 138, 149, 153 *n* 353, 168 *n* 389, 173 *n* 403, 209, 212 *n* 461-2, 221f *n* 472 & 474, 258, 263 *n* 554, 267f *n* 561 & 564-5, 269 *n* 569, 270, 289 *n* 612, 293 *n* 617, 300f, 302 *n* 650, 308, 313 *n* 674-5, 322, 331
Clarridge, Samuel, 99
Clement, Simon, 293 *n* 617
Cleynaerts (Clénard), Nicholas, 68
Clothier, Morris L., XV, 300
Coale, Josiah, 112ff, 120, 202, 218
Cobham, Lord, 301
Colbert, Jean, 80
Conventicle Acts, 187, 192f, 199f
Cooke, Francis, 184
Cooper, Peter, XVI
Cork, 93-105, 107f, 181f
Cork, Bishop of, *see* Wetenhall, Edward
Cornish, Henry, 247f
Corporations, Attack upon, 259f
Cowper, Lord Chancellor, 289
Crawford, Earl of, 80
Cremorne, Viscount, 61
Crisp, Steven, 135
Croese, Gerard, 25, 132, 233 *n* 477, 244f
Cromwell, Oliver, 7f, 18-21, 70, 72, 182
Crosfield, Helen G., 181 *n* 414
Curtis, Thomas and Ann, 120

Dalrymple, Sir John, 271 *n* 578
Darrell, Major A., 123f
Dartmouth, Earl of, 284
David, ———, 69 *n* 156
Declarations of Indulgence, 201, 256, 260
Defoe, Daniel, 284
Delaware, 174, 221, 235f
Demsey (Dempsey?), Jonathan, 97
Deptford, 282
Derry, Dean of, 103
Devizes, 125
Dixon, Hepworth, 16 *n* 13 & 16, 19 *n* 18, 28 *n* 39, 55 *n* 112, 109 *n* 226, 117 *n* 241, 138, 151f (*n* 343, 348, 350), 183 *n* 418, 221 *n* 472, 230, 258 *n* 548, 264, 271 *n* 578, 293
Dobrée, Bonamy, 19 *n* 18, 28 *n* 35 & 40, 129, 138 *n* 300, 152 *n* 346, 154f (*n* 356, 361, 366), 169 *n* 392, 265 *n* 558, 268 *n* 566, 270 *n* 571, 293 *n* 618, 297 *n* 626, 302 *n* 648, 313f *n* 673 & 678, 319 *n* 686, 321, 325 *n* 700, 328
Dottin, Paul, 284 *n* 608
Drogheda, Earl of, 93
Dryden, John, 156
Dublin, 88, 90, 93f, 97ff, 103, 294f
Durie, John, 123
Dyck, Peter van, XIII
Dymond, Jonathan, 161

Ealing, 13
Eccles, Solomon, 95f, 100ff
Eclipse of the sun, 71
Education, 172f
Elisabeth, Princess, 110, 219 *n* 469
Ellwood, Thomas, 32 *n* 54, 33ff, 112 *n* 234, 134f, 176 *n* 407, 193
Ely, Bishop of, 260
England, 17th. Century, 1f, 216
Epping Forest, 7
Etting, Frank, 299 *n* 637
European Mercury, The, 269
Evans, John, 53
Evelyn, John, 142
Everet (Everott), John, 103, 148, 180

Faith, 166f
Faldo, John, 20, 143 *n* 314, 146f, 149, 151 *n* 342
Familism, 148, 150
Fell, Charles, 56
Fenwick, John, 219
Fifth Monarchy Plot, 76, 182, 192
Fire, The Great, *see* London Fire
First Publishers of Truth, 77 *n* 168
Fisher, Sidney G., 19 *n* 18, 138 *n* 300, 152 *n* 347, 154 *n* 357, 155 *n* 364, 168 *n* 387, 270 *n* 570, 278 *n* 587, 296 *n* 625, 302 *n* 651, 303f, 320 *n* 689, 337f
Fiske, John, 327, 333 *n* 713
Five Mile Act, 192f
Fleet, The, 13, 197, 288f
Fletcher, Elizabeth, 77, 108
Fletcher, Governor, 237
Ford, Bridget, 288f
Ford, Philip, 250, 287f, 320
Ford, Philip, Jr., 288f
Forster, William E., 246, 258, 264
Fox, George, XII, 5f, 39 *n* 72, 66f, 71, 82, 110f, 113, 117 *n* 241, 121, 124, 129f, 135, 149, 151, 162, 170, 173f, 176 *n* 407, 178-81, 196, 204, 218f, 243, 246, 255, 267 *n*

Index

563, 269, 273, 279f, 308, 319, 321 *n* 690, 323, 327f, 336
Fox (Foxe), John, 141 *n* 303
Fox, Margaret Fell, 36, 112 *n* 234, 178, 180
France, 79-82, 104 *n* 219
Franklin, Benjamin, 14, 81 *n* 175, 160, 185, 209, 238, 296, 300, 301 *n* 644, 319f
Freame, Thomas, 61f
Frederikstad, 282
Friend, The, London, 127 *n* 264
Friend, The, Philadelphia, 45 *n* 82, 185 *n* 420, 267 *n* 562, 274 *n* 584, 282 *n* 601, 324 *n* 698, 336 *n* 719-20
Friends' House, London, XIII, 36 *n* 63 & 65
Friends' Institute, London, 345
Friends Intelligencer, The, 333 *n* 712
Friends' Library, The, 324 *n* 698
Friends' Reference Library, London, XIV, 34 *n* 56, 107 *n* 223
Fry, Elizabeth, 248, 331
Fuller, Abraham, 98f
Fuller, William, 269, 272
Furly, Benjamin, 83, 121, 229ff

Galloway, Earl of, 104f
Galway, 101
Garrison, William Lloyd, 266
Gaskell, Peter, 57
Gaunt, Elizabeth, 247f
Gazette, London, 258
Germany, 121ff, 174
Gibson, P., 7 *n* 1, 9 *n* 2, 83, 295
Gilbert, Sir Humphrey, 218
Gilbert, Joan, 17
Gladstone, William E., 266, 338
Gloucester, Duke of, 74
God, 167
Godolphin, Lord, 284
Gosse, Edmund, 159f
Gouldney, Henry, 288, 291 *n* 616
Graham, John W., 19 *n* 18, 169 *n* 391 & 392, 221 *n* 472, 244, 265, 270, 306f, 317 *n* 683, 320, 333 *n* 711, 345 (note)
Grahame, James, 269
Grand Tour, The, 78-84
'Grange, The', 11, 32
Grant, Mrs. Colquhon, 19 *n* 18, 58 *n* 127, 60 *n* 130, 71 *n* 158, 143 *n* 312, 248 *n* 519, 304f
Grevill, Samuel, 144
Grubb, Isabel, 99 *n* 210
Gwynedd, Pa., 45

Hague, The, 162, 239, 254f
Hainault Forest, 7, 67, 71
Hale, Sir Matthew, 111f
Halifax, Lord, 257
Hall, John, 300
Hallywell, Henry, 148f
Hammersmith, 39
Hampden, John, 186, 214
Harcourt, Sir Simon, 288
Harrington's *Oceana,* 218
Harrison, James, 253, 256, 338 *n* 725
Harsnett, Samuel, 67
Harvey, Thomas, 107 *n* 223
Harvey MS., 33f, 77 *n* 170, 107, 109, 114ff, 179, 181f
Harwich, 85, 121
Harwood, S., 48
'Hat Honour', 117f, 187, 190
'Hat Worship', 174ff
Haverford College, XIV
Hedworth, Henry, 148
Heemskerk, Egbert van, 297
Henry IV, 165
Hicks, Edward, XVI
Hicks, Thomas, 134f, 147f, 151 *n* 342, 168
Hide, Matthew, 176
Hilton, ———, 196
Hispaniola, *see* Santo Domingo
Historical MSS. Commission, 268 *n* 566
Hoddesdon, 13, 38
Holland, 26, 29, 32, 83, 165, 174, 204 *n* 442, 207, 255f
Holland House, 12f
Hollister, Dennis, 60 *n* 132, 64
Holme, Thomas, 99
Horny, Lady, 93
Hough, Dr., 258
Howell, John, 186-91
Hubberthorne, Richard, 77
Huckel, Oliver, 28 *n* 37, 30 *n* 50
Huguenots, 81, 253f
Hull, J., 95 *n* 206
Hyde Park, 13 *n* 10, 245

Immortality, 170f
Independents, 5, 198
Indians, 61, 298
Industrial Problem, The, 171
Inman, Henry, XIII, 298
Ireland, 8, 9f, 55, 60, 72, 88-105, 107, 114
Italy, 82f
Ives, ———, 134
Ives, Jeremy, 134f, 146

Jamaica, 7f, 18f, 88, 221
James I, 211
James II, 9, 21f, 37f, 75, 85, 125, 183, 196f, 211f, 220f, 226, 241-70, 295, 305f, 320f
'James III', 260f
Janney, Samuel M., 16 *n* 16, 19 *n* 18, 37 *n* 67, 109 *n* 226, 131, 138, 156 *n* 368, 161f, 173 *n* 403, 178 *n* 408, 221f *n* 472 & 475,

230 *n* 492, 254 *n* 538, 258 *n* 548, 263f, 270, 296 *n* 624, 302 *n* 652, 303, 306, 308, 337
Jasper Family, 69f, 99
Jasper, John, 25-26, 271 *n* 577
Jasper, John Baptist, 25 *n* 29
Jasper, Marie, 26f
Jefferson, Thomas, 336
Jeffrey, Lord Francis, 173
Jeffreys, Lord George, 246ff, 260, 266
Jenkins, Howard M., 19 *n* 18, 26 *n* 31, 34 *n* 58, 39 *n* 71, 55 *n* 113 & 115, 56 *n* 117, 59 *n* 129, 63 *n* 146, 69 *n* 155, 183 *n* 418, 294 *n* 620
Jenner, Thomas, 145f
Jesuits, *see* PENN, WILLIAM
Jews, 119, 122f
Jordans, XV, 14, 34, 39, 43, 48, 61, 63f, 291 *n* 616, 293 *n* 619, 294
Journal of the Friends' Historical Society, London, 26 *n* 31, 34 *n* 56, 59 *n* 128, 66 *n* 152, 107 *n* 223, 109 *n* 227, 124 *n* 257, 221 *n* 472, 263 *n* 555, 286 *n* 609, 299 *n* 635
Jury Trial, 185-91

Kant, Immanuel, 163
Keith, Charles P., 26 *n* 31
Keith, George, 130, 135, 174, 177f, 180, 220, 280
Kennersley, ———, 37 *n* 67, 278
Kensington, 12f, 284
Kent, 123f
Kett, Thomas, 309
Kingston, Earl of, 93
Kinsale, 10, 21, 89f, 94
Kneller, Sir Godfrey, XV, 299f
Knightsbridge, 13, 284

Lafayette, Marquis of, 185
La Noy, P. D., 237f
Latin, 42, 68, 74, 164 *n* 380
Lawson, Sir John and Lady, 86
Lawton, Charlewood, 246 *n* 515, 259, 261
Leavens, Elizabeth, 108
Lely, Sir Peter, XIIIff, 295
L'Estrange, Sir Roger, 201
Letitia Court and Cottage, 14, 44f
Light Within (The Inner), 106, 113, 120, 123, 127, 129, 134f, 140, 144, 153, 161, 168f, 170f, 173, 175f, 178 *n* 408, 274
Lily, William, 68
Lincoln, Abraham, 30, 266
Lincoln's Inn, 9, 32, 86
Lloyd, David, 233, 286, 288, 324
Lloyd, Thomas, 38 *n* 68, 242 *n* 509, 272 *n* 581, 276
Locke, John, 75, 156, 162, 215 *n* 466, 230f, 246, 276, 326, 328

Loe, Thomas, 76f, 107-113, 120, 150, 182, 202
Logan, James, XIII, 14, 46-56, 60, 232f, 288 *n* 610, 289-93, 300, 307
Lollard, 198
LONDON, I
  Bishop of, 182f
  Great Fire, 65, 92
  Navy Office, 9
  Quaker Meetings, 126f, 131 *n* 281, 185, 192, 196f
  Yearly Meeting, 125
Lord's Supper, The, 170
Louis XIV, 80, 121, 201, 211f, 232f, 236, 238, 249, 254, 262, 265, 272f, 304
Love (Luff), John, 174f
Lower, Thomas, 178ff, 276
Lowestoft, Battle of, 9, 21, 86
Ludgate Parish, 13
Ludlow, Edmund, 83 *n* 179
Luther, Martin, 174
Luttrell, Narcissus, 267 *n* 563
Lysons, Daniel, 69 *n* 155

Macaulay, Lord, 246ff, 258, 264, 278, 325f, 327, 329, 335f
Mackintosh, Sir J., 257 *n* 547
Macroom, 8, 20, 72
Madison, James, 336
Magdalen College Fellows, 125, 257f
Magna Carta, 185-91, 200, 206 *n* 451, 333 *n* 714
Markham, Colonel, 235
Marlborough, 125
Marlborough, Duchess of, 283
Marsillac, Jean, 30, 223 *n* 477
Mary II, 180, 254, 260, 268, 271 *n* 577, 283
Masters, Thomas, 51
Masters, William, 45f, 48
'Mayflower, The', 223
Meade, William, 66, 111, 178ff, 185-91
Melksham, 136
Mennonites, 281
Middlesex and Dorset, Earl of, 243
Milton, John, 12, 68, 149, 152, 156, 279, 318, 339
Minety, 15
Monmouth, Duke of, 211f
Monmouth's Rebellion, 246-9, 256
Montanus, Dr., 255
Mood, Fuller, 221 *n* 472
Moore, Thomas, 112 *n* 234
More (Moore, or O'More?), Rev., 96
More (O'More?), 96
More's *Utopia*, 218
Morley, John, 338
Morse, John, 148
Mt. Alexander and Clancarty, Countess of, 93

Index

Muggleton, Ludovic, 150f, 153
Muller, F., 261 *n* 551, 269 *n* 568
Myers, Albert Cook, XIII, 26, 47 *n* 88, 99 *n* 211, 105 *n* 220

Nairne, Lord, 269 *n* 569
Newgate Prison, 121, 185-91, 193ff, 203
New Jersey, 87, 122, 174, 219, 226f, 229, 231, 236, 286
Netherlands, see Holland
New York, 226, 236f, 272
New York Colonial Documents, 236 *n* 502
Norris, Isaac, 47 *n* 88, 51, 54, 197, 311
North, Lord Chief Justice, 227
Northleigh, Dr. John, 128
Notes and Queries, 297 *n* 627, 299f, *n* 637 & 640, 302 *n* 649

Oaths, 193, 199, 204f, 212, 215, 266, 281
Old Bailey, The, 186ff, 197 *n* 433, 288
'Orchard, The', 13 *n* 10
Ormond, Duke of, 88f, 93f, 97f, 284f
Orrery, Earl of, 202
Owen, Griffith, 307
Owen, Dr. John, 73, 79, 108f
Oxford, Earl of, 284
Oxford and Mortimer, Earl of, 55
Oxford University, XIV, 73-79, 108f, 125, 142f

Paget, John, 247 *n* 517
Papacy, see Catholicism, Roman
Paris, 8of, 162
Parker, Alexander, 144
Parnel, James, 112
Pemberton, Phineas, 51
Pemberton MSS., 254 *n* 538, 256 *n* 543, 338 *n* 725
Penington, Isaac, 1of, 32, 70, 112, 138, 309
Penington, Mary Springett, see Springett
Penington, S., 48
Penn, Christian (Forbes), 56f
Penn, Christiana Gulielma, 57
Penn, Dennis, 64
Penn, George, 16
Penn, Giles, 15f
Penn, Granville, 7 *n* 1, 16 *n* 14, 18f, 20 *n* 20, 25, 30 *n* 48 & 49, 64, 88-91 (*n* 190-5, 199-202), 114, 295, 345
Penn, Gulielma Maria Springett, XIII, 11, 13, 32-39, 41, 70, 92, 102f, 112, 120 *n* 243, 121, 123f, 278, 344f
Penn, Gulielma Maria, 39
Penn, Gulielma Maria, 55f
Penn, Hannah Callowhill, XIII, 13f, 44f, 49, 55, 57-63, 105, 283, 290-3
Penn, Hannah, 13, 61

Penn, Hannah (Lardner), 65
Penn, Hannah Margarita, 61f
Penn, John ('The American'), 14, 56, 61ff
Penn, John ('The Proprietor'), 64
Penn, Governor John, 65
Penn, Lady Juliana (Fermor), 63f
Penn, Letitia, 14, 41, 44-49, 58
Penn, Lady Margaret Jasper, 17, 20, 22, 23 *n* 25, 25-31, 36, 85f, 112 *n* 234, 118, 299 *n* 636
Penn (Freame), Margaret, 61f
Penn (Lowther), Margaret, 23 *n* 25, 30f, 49, 92
Penn, Mary, 39
Penn, Mary (Jones), 49, 54f
Penn, Richard, 23 *n* 25, 31, 64
Penn, Proprietor Richard, 48, 64f, 301
Penn, Governor Richard, 65
Penn, Springett, 35, 40-44, 49, 58f
Penn, Springett, 56
Penn, Thomas, XIII, 63f
Penn, Admiral Sir William, XIII, 6-10, 16, 17-24, 27-30, 65, 70f, 73, 78f, 84-92, 107, 114-118, 159, 182f, 185f, 189f, 191, 220f, 256, 295, 299
PENN, WILLIAM
Achievements, 325-39
Aliens and Naturalization, 232f
Ancestry, 15-6, 209
Author, 137-73, 279ff
Biographies, VII, 349-52
Birth and baptism, 6, 65f
Bridewell, 185f, 195
Brother, 31
Character, 128f, 131, 151, 171, 179, 221ff, 248, 266, 309-24, 328
Charles II, 8-9, 114f, 117f
Children and grandchildren, 39-57, 61-5
Colonizer, 80, 121f, 124, 216-23, 247, 253f, 272, 277, 312f, 334ff
'Comprehension', 82, 123
Controversialist, 84, 137-54
Costume, 302-9
Courtier, 241-9, 251-65, 273ff, 284, 314 (*see* Jesuit)
Crime and punishment, 240, 330f
Debater, 96, 100, 132-7
Democracy, 69, 74, 118, 176f, 226-31, 234, 241, 256f, 259f, 290, 314f, 318f, 326, 328, 335
Diplomatist, 254f, 319f
Elm Tree, 37 *n* 66, 67
England, 1f
Equestrian, 98, 109, 314
Era, 2ff
Ethics, 68f, 72ff, 81, 119f, 157-73, 184, 193, 210, 224, 234f, 262
Expelled from home, 34, 114-9

358 Index

Penn, William (*Continued*)
  Father, 17-24, 30 (*see* Penn, Sir William)
  France, 79-82
  Germany, 121ff, 130, 174, 196, 208
  Government (*see* Pennsylvania)
  Grand Tour, The, 78-84
  Greatness, VIIf, 164f, 174, 181, 190f, 213f, 215ff, 223-7, 233, 266, 282, 325, 326f, 333-8 (*see* Achievements and Character)
  'Hat Honour', 117f, 187, 285, 305ff
  'Hat Worship', 174f, 306
  Holland, 26, 29, 98f, 121ff, 130, 174, 196, 204 *n* 442, 208, 219, 239, 254f, 261, 268, 281, 297
  Homes, 6-15
  Imprisonments, 42, 66, 95f, 133, 151, 160f, 181-97, 256, 288f
  Indians, 61, 67, 122 (*see* Pennsylvania)
  Internment, 266-78
  Ireland, 8, 10, 88-105, 181f, 272, 281
  Italy, 82f
  Jacobite and Traitor, 265-72, 274f, 278, 323
  James II, 9, 114f, 117f, 125 (*see* James II)
  Jesuit, 94f, 98, 103, 133, 212, 214, 241f, 249ff, 274f
  Jews, 119, 122f
  Last illness and death, 127, 290-4
  Last Years, 279-94
  Law, 9, 186f
  Letters, 36, 38, 29 *n* 72, 46-58, 62ff, 85f, 89, 102f, 112f, 131, 135f, 142, 149, 168, 176, 178 *n* 408, 185f, 189 *n* 422, 191, 202, 208, 212, 218, 229f, 232ff, 239, 242 *n* 509, 247 *n* 517, 250, 253f, 256f, 270f *n* 576 & 578, 272 *n* 581, 275ff, 282, 288 *n* 610, 289ff, 307, 315 *n* 679, 319, 334, 338
  Marriage (first), 11-12, 31 *n* 52, 32-34 (*see* Penn, Gulielma Maria Springett)
  Marriage (second), 57 (*see* Penn, Hannah Callowhill)
  Missionary, *see* Preacher
  Mother, 25-31 (*see* Penn, Lady Margaret Jasper)
  Newgate, 121, 185-91, 193ff, 203
  New Jersey, 87, 112, 219f
  Oaths, 193, 199, 204f
  Oxford, 9, 69, 73-9, 81, 108f, 125, 155, 218, 257ff
  Paris, 80f
  Parliament, personal appeals to, 144, 205, 209, 253, 281f
  Peace and War, 9, 70, 78, 80f, 94-91, 93, 109, 121, 138 *n* 300, 161-6, 171f, 182, 232f, 236-9, 255, 268f, 272f, 282f, 308, 318, 331f, 336

Penn-Meade Trial, 87, 143, 185-92
Pennsylvania:
  Dutch in, 26, 121f, 219, 222f, 231f
  Geography of, 285f
  Government and Laws, 87, 197f, 203, 206ff, 213, 225-41, 327, 335f (*see* Magna Carta)
  Grant to Penn, 7, 18, 22, 220-5, 227f, 244, 250
  History, 223
  'Holy Experiment', 77, 165, 198, 216f, 220, 224f, 239f, 273, 287, 289, 332, 336ff
  Indians, 220, 231, 313, 315, 321, 327, 329ff
  Irish Quakers in, 99, 105
  Military defence, 53f (*see* Peace and War)
  'Mount Joy', 44
  Name, 9, 15
  Penn's difficulties with, 286f, 289f, 292
  Penn's loss and recovery of, 272f, 278, 283f, 287, 289f
  Penns in, 36f, 45f, 48ff, 52, 54, 60, 62-5, 269f, 271 *n* 578, 272, 276f, 290
  Proprietorship, 55, 60f, 63f
  Quakers in, 122, 174, 177f
  'Williamstadt', 53
Pepys, Samuel, 23 *n* 25, 29 (*see* Pepys, Samuel)
Personal appearance, 66, 80, 83, 129f, 245 *n* 513, 294-309
Peter the Great, 282
Plague, The Great, 87f
'Plain Language', 114f, 117 *n* 241
Plan of Colonial Union, 236-9
Politics, 208-16, 249, 262ff
Portraits, 90, 129, 294-301
  Armour, XIV, 294-7
  Bath, 300
  Bevan, 300, 323
  Heemskerk, 297
  Inman, XIII, 298
  Kames, 300
  Kneller, 299f
  Kuhner, 300
  Le Despenser statue, 299 *n* 633
  Paris miniature, 297
  Philadelphia statue, 298f, 335
  Place, 299, 302 *n* 649
  Richardson, 300
  West, 298, 323
Preacher, 60, 96, 100, 104, 114f, 119-32, 280, 281 *n* 596
Puritanism, 69, 71, 73, 76f, 79, 81f, 119f, 192, 310, 316
Quakerism, 8, 21, 23, 70ff, 76f, 79, 87f, 92-181, 184f, 218, 224, 239ff, 262ff,

Index

273-6, 287, 314, 322, 327-32 (see QUAKERISM)
Religious Sects, 4
Saumur, 81f, 241
Scholarship, 68, 74ff, 81, 106, 130, 138, 155ff, 159, 186, 204ff, 210f, 255, 315, 317
Schools, 67-72
Sermons, 126-9, 131 (see Preacher)
Sister, 31
Slavery, 231f, 290, 328f
Social Reforms, 327 (see Ethics)
Theology, 81f, 166-71
Toleration, 77, 121, 123, 125f, 139f, 144, 154, 166, 177, 182, 196-217, 226, 228f, 251-62, 265f, 281f, 284, 289, 333 (see QUAKERISM, Persecution)
Tower, London, 6, 183f, 192, 203, 321
York, Duke of, see James II

PENN, WILLIAM, *Writings:*
Account of The Blessed End of Gulielma Maria Springett, 35, 38f, 43, 49
Address to Parliament - - - Conventicle Act, 195, 200f, 203
Address to Protestants, 2, 210, 250 n 528, 253, 309
Answer to John Faldo's Challenge, 146
Answer to a Letter (Sir William Popple's), 250f, 262
Apology (Autobiographical fragments), 111, 202f, 207, 243f, 251f
Brief Answer to a False and Foolish Libel, 143, 151 n 342
Brief Examination of Spiritual Liberty, 176
Caution - - - the Bill against Blasphemy, 281
Cautionary Postscript to Truth Exalted, 195
Certain Conditions and Concessions,— Pennsylvania, 225
Charter of Liberties (Fundamental Constitutions), XV, 225, 229
Charter of Privileges, 225
Children of Light, To the, 210
Christian Discipline, 316f
Christian Quaker, The, 148, 169, 177
Concessions and Agreements — New Jersey, 219, 222, 225ff, 335
Considerations — Occasional Conformity, 284
Continued Cry of the Oppressed, 207f, 210
Counterfeit Christian Detected, 148
Defence of the Duke of Buckingham's Book, 262
Defence of Gospel Truth, 105, 166f, 169ff, 280
Description of West Jersey, 219

England's Great Interest, 211 n 460, 212ff, 253
England's Present Interest Considered, 205f
Essay towards the - - - Peace of Europe, XIV, 154, 161-6, 171f, 197, 238f, 271
Excellent Privilege of Liberty & Property, 333 n 714
Fiction found out, 242
Frame of Government (1682 and 1683), XV, 214, 225, 227-31, 337
Fruits of a Father's Love, 50, 130, 161, 172f
Fruits of Solitude (Some and More), or Maxims XIV, 154, 158-161, 171f, 197, 271, 279, 294, 305, 309, 317f
General Rule of Faith and Practice, 170
Good Advice to the Church of England, 251, 257
Gospel Truths, 105, 280
Great Case of Liberty of Conscience, 95, 97, 195f, 203f
Great - - - Objection - - - Repeal of the Penal Laws, 257 n 546
Guide Mistaken, 141
Innocency with her Open Face, 142, 167ff, 183
Invalidity of John Faldo's Vindication, 20 n 19, 145f
Jeremy Ives' Sober Request, 134, 146
Judas and the Jews Combined, 106 n 221, 175f
Just Censure, 177, 280
Just Measures, 176, 271 n 579
Just Rebuke to One and Twenty — Divines, 136, 146, 149
Key opening the Way, 271 n 579
Laws (The Great Law), 225, 229
Letter to Mary Pennyman, 106
Letter to my Wife and Children, 33, 41, 69, 161, 172f
Letter to the Young Convinced, 93
Letter to a Young Person, 119f
Life and Writings of Sir B. Whitlocke, 280
Missive or Warning, 121
More Work for George Keith, 177f, 280
My Irish Journall, 92-103, 307
New Athenians no Noble Bereans, 144, 151 n 342, 271 n 579
New England Firebrand quenched (with Fox and Burrough), 149
New Frame of Government, 225
New Witnesses proved Old Hereticks, 75, 150
No Cross, No Crown, XIV, 22-3, 41, 80, 82 n 176, 92 n 204, 113, 154, 156ff, 171, 184, 192, 196, 250 n 528, 280, 305, 309

Index

Penn, Wm., Writings (*Continued*)
  On Primitive Christianity, 178 n 408
  One Project for . . . England, 214f, 253
  People's Ancient . . . Liberties Asserted, XIV, 186
  Persuasive to Moderation, 255f
  Plain Dealing with a Traducing Anabaptist, 148
  Preface to John Banks's Journal, 128, 280
  Preface to Robert Barclay's Works, 156, 271 n 579
  Prefaces to [Three] Books of Sufferings, 211, 216
  Preface to John Burnyeat's Works, 271 n 579
  Preface to George Fox's Journal, SEE *Rise — Quakers*
  Preface to Vindiciae Veritatis, 145
  Primitive Christianity Revived, 59, 170, 280
  Proposed Comprehension, 123
  Quaker a Christian, 148, 280
  Quakerism a new Nickname for old Christianity, 146f
  Reason against Railing and Truth against Fiction, 148
  Reply to a Brief Discovery, 144
  Reply to a Pretended Answer, 151 n 342
  Return to John Faldo's Reply, 146
  Rise and Progress of the . . . Quakers (A Preface to Fox's *Journal*), 111, 180, 271 n 579, 279f
  Sandy Foundation Shaken, 132f, 141f, 167ff, 182, 184, 203
  Saul Smitten to the Ground, 176
  Seasonable Caveat against Popery, 95, 139, 195, 249 n 524
  Serious Apology for the . . . Quakers, 76, 145, 195
  Sermons, 126-9
  Skirmisher Defeated, 147
  Some Account of Pennsylvania, XV, 222
  Spirit of Alexander the Coppersmith, 175
  Spirit of Truth Vindicated, 144, 148
  Summons, or Call to Christendom, 123
  Tender Counsel and Advice, 123
  Tender Visitation, 123
  Testimony to the Truth of God, 169f, 280
  To all those Professors of Christianity, 123
  To a Roman Catholic, 142, 195, 249f
  To Doctor Tillotson, 166
  To Justice Fleming, 151, 204
  To Justices in Middlesex, 204
  To my Ingenious Friend, 142
  To the Friends in Bristol, 217
  To The . . . Quakers, 273f
  To the Vice-Chancellor of Oxford, 142f
  Travails in Holland and Germany, 1677, XIV, 40 n 73, 58, 70 n 157, 72 n 161, 77 n 169, 79 n 172, 87, 90, 106ff
  Treatise of Oaths, 205
  Trumpet Blown, 121
  Truth Exalted, 73, 76, 140f, 152, 249
  Truth rescued from Imposture, 9 n 3, 86 n 187, 143
  Urim and Thummim, 144
  Vindication of my deceased Father's Reputation, 86 n 187
  Visitation to the Jews, 122f, 281
  Winding-Sheet for Controversie Ended, 148f
  Wisdom Justified of her Children, 148
Penn, William, Junior, 10 n 4, 35, 41, 47, 49-55, 103, 286, 289
Penn, William, 15
Penn, William, 39
Penn, William, 48, 56f
Penn, William, 90
Penn-Forbes MSS., 57 n 125
Penn-Gaskells, 10 n 4, 57
Penn-Logan Correspondence, 46 n 83, 47-56 (n 85-90, 92, 94-111, 116, 118-122), 60-64 (n 131, 134-42, 144-5, 149), 288 n 610, 290 n 614, 307, 314
Penn-Meade Trial, 87, 143, 185-91, 226
Penn Parish, 10, 15
Penn MSS., The, 225 n 482, 274 n 584
Penney, Norman, 112 n 234
Pennsbury, XIII, 14f, 45, 51
Penn's Lodge, 15
Pennsylvania Historical Society Library, XIVf, 295, 300
Pennsylvania Historical Society *MSS.*, 38 n 68, 40 n 74, 63 n 146-7, 92 n 205
Pennsylvania Historical Society *Memoirs*, 38 n 69, 46 n 83 & 84, 55 n 114, 111 n 232, 232f n 498-9, 237 n 503, 246 n 514, 259 n 549, 267f n 562 & 567, 270 n 576, 272 n 580, 277 n 586
Pennsylvania Magazine, 57 n 125, 92 n 205, 102 n 217, 114 n 239, 250 n 525
Pennyman, John, 106 n 221, 176
Pennyman, Mary, 176
Pepys, Samuel, 6, 9, 16, 21, 23 n 25, 25, 27, 29ff, 65 n 151, 74f, 78f, 83ff, 86, 92, 116, 141, 156, 295, 297, 301, 304, 306, 310, 322
Perrot, John, 174f
Persecution, Religious, 76f, 79 (see QUAKERISM)
Peter the Great, 282
Peters, Hugh, 326
Petre (Peters), Father, 242, 261, 265
Petty, Sir William, 100
Philadelphia, XV, 44f, 62, 233ff, 294, 334f

Index

Phillips, Daniel, 145
Picart, Bernard, 268
Pike, Joseph, 94, 95 n 206
Place, Francis, XV, 299
Plague, The Great, 87f, 101, 132 n 285
Plato's *Atlantis*, 218
Plimpton, George A., 68 n 154
Plimpton, John, 136, 148
Powell, Vavasor, 130
Popish Plot, 209-13, 226, 253
Popple, Sir William, 246, 250f, 272
Powlett, Earl, 55
Prayer, 115, 133, 136f
Presbyterians, 5f, 135ff, 141, 145ff
Prison Reform, 195 (*see* PENN, WILLIAM: Imprisonments)
Proud, Robert, 301
Puritanism, 5, 69, 192, 216, 279 (*see* PENN, WILLIAM, and QUAKERISM)
Pym, John, 214

QUAKERISM (*see* PENN, WILLIAM)
  Charges versus, 144f, 147, 150, 153f, 166f, 209f, 215
  Controversies, 137, 174-8
  Excesses, 101ff, 175, 179
  Meeting Records, 39 n 71, 45f, 58f, 181, 309, 317, 324
  Music, 100f
  Peculiarities, 101-104, 198f, 203, 285
  Penn, Sir William, 23
  Persecution, 32, 76f, 88, 93-102, 108, 111, 124, 126, 133f, 142f, 152, 192, 198-217, 251, 266
  Puritanism, 5, 198, 240
  Women's equality, 176f

Raleigh, Sir Walter, 218
Ranelagh, Lord, 276f
Ranfurly, Earls of, 64
Rawlins, Alfred, XV
Read (Logan), Sarah, 47
Reading, 13 n 11, 93, 120, 125, 127, 291f
Recorde, Robert, 68 n 154
Reeve, John, 150
Religious sects, 4, 113f, 154, 198
Reliquiae Baxterianae, 136 n 296
Richardson, Jonathan, 300
Richardson, Richard, 205 n 447
Rickmansworth, XIII, 11f, 31, 35, 39, 106 n 221, 124, 130, 136
Rigg, J. M., 299 n 636, 302 n 646
Robinson, Sir John, 133f, 183f, 186-93, 312, 321f
Rochester, Earl of, 74, 276f, 319
Rodes, Sir John, 130, 173 n 402, 180
Rogers, William, 176
Rome, 83

Romney, Earl of, 268f, 271, 276f
Rooth, Sir Richard, 89, 98
Rotterdam, 25f, 121, 128
Royal Society, The, 76, 317
Rudyard, Thomas, 121
Ruscombe, 14, 291f
Russell, Lord William, 326
Rutty, John, 99 n 212
Rye House Plot, 246f, 256

St. Martin's Church, London, 28
Saltmarsh, John, 71, 113, 273
Salvation, 169
Santo Domingo, 18
Saumur, 81f, 241
Scribner's Magazine, 299 n 637
Sects, *see* Religious Sects
Sermons, *see* WILLIAM PENN, Preacher
Sewel, Willem, 25, 41f, 44, 101f, 125, 174, 175 n 406, 183 n 418, 223 n 477, 250f
Shaftesbury, Earl of, 211f, 326
Shakerley, Geoffrey, 200f
Shakespeare, William, 68, 282
Shangarry, 9f, 21, 56f, 88, 91
Shannon, Lord, 97
Sharp, Anthony, 99
Sharpless, Isaac, 240 n 507, 333 n 712
Shepherd, Fleetwood, 243f
Shippen, Ann, 47
Shippen, Edward, 47, 51, 307
Shippen, Joseph, 46
Shrewsbury, Earl of, 267
Sidney, Algernon, XIV, 12, 83, 211-214, 226, 229f, 246, 253, 263, 320f, 326
Silent Worship, 170
Simpson, James, 308 n 666
Simpson, William, 77
'Slate Roof House, The', XIII, 14, 45
Slavery, 60 n 132, 107(?), 206 n 451, 209 n 455, 231f
Smallpox, 35, 66f, 74, 223, 283
Smith, Aaron, 246
Smith, Captain John, 218
Smith, Joseph, 39 n 70
Smith, Samuel, 143 n 314
Somerton, 125f
Spence MSS., 181 n 414
Spencer, Lady Dorothy, 83 n 178
Spencer, Robert, *see* Sunderland, Earl of
Sphere, The, 300
Springett, Herbert, 288
Springett (Penington), Lady Mary, 32, 35f, 43, 112, 121
Springett, Sir William, 32
Stamper, Francis, 125
Starling, Sir Samuel, 143 n 314, 185-93
Stevenson, Robert Louis, 159f
Stillingfleet, Edward, 183f, 203

Stillingfleet, John, 144f
Stoke Poges, 64
Story, George, 104
Story, John, 176
Story, Thomas, 47, 98 *n* 209, 103ff, 128, 180, 291 *n* 616
Stoughton, John, 19 *n* 18, 69 *n* 155-6, 71 *n* 158, 113 *n* 238, 131, 143 *n* 311, 152 *n* 349, 154f *n* 355 & 365, 162 *n* 377, 168 *n* 387, 257 *n* 547, 264f, 270 *n* 572
Strickland, Agnes, 37f, 265 *n* 559, 278
Stuart, Sir Robert, 245f
Stuart-Dugald Families, 64
Subliminal Self, The, 168f
Sumner, Charles, 338
Sunderland, Earl of, 82f, 262, 266, 284
Swarthmore College, XIVff, 37 *n* 66
Swarthmore MSS., 112 *n* 234
Swift, Dean, 284f, 317
Switzerland, 82

Tablet, The, 258 *n* 548
Tallow, 96
Taylor, Silas, 121
Taylor, Timothy, 145
Teddington, 12
Temple, Sir William, 165
Texel, Battle of the, 18
Thirnbeck MSS., 36 *n* 63
Thomas, Aubrey, 56
Thompson MSS., Sylvanus, 36 *n* 65, 39 *n* 72
Thorpe, F. N., 225 *n* 479-487, 231 *n* 494
Tillotson, Archbishop, 198 *n* 435, 250, 317
Toleration, Religious, 77 (*see* PENN, WILLIAM)
Tower of London, XIIIf, 6ff, 18f
Transubstantiation, 139
Trenchard, Sir John, 246, 277
Trent, William, 54
Trevelyan, George M., 72 *n* 160
Trinity, The, 132, 141f, 167f, 281
'Truth', The, 106, 128, 131, 134, 149, 153, 158, 276
Turner, Robert, 38, 99, 178 *n* 408, 218 *n* 468, 239 *n* 506
Turner, Mrs. Thomas, 6, 9, 27, 92, 116
Twyford, 14

Union, Plan of Colonial, 236-9

Valdes, Juan de, 113
Vanderscure, Nicasius, 26
Vane, Henry, 326
Venables, General Robert, 7f, 18f
Vere, ———, 190
Vickris, Richard, 252
Vincent, Thomas, 132f, 137, 141
'Vredemakers', 239

Vulliamy, C. E., 19 *n* 18, 27 *n* 34, 138 *n* 300, 141 *n* 304, 151 *n* 343-4, 153 *n* 351-2, 155 *n* 363, 183 *n* 418, 221 *n* 472, 245 *n* 513, 263 *n* 554, 265 *n* 558, 267 *n* 563, 273 *n* 583, 293 *n* 618, 302 *n* 647, 314 *n* 678, 317 *n* 681, 319 *n* 687, 322 *n* 694, 323f, 325 *n* 702, 338

Waldenfield, Samuel, 125
Wales, 15
Wallace, Philip B., XVI
Wallis, Colonel, 90ff, 94, 102
Walthamstow, 6f, 10f, 30f, 40
Wanstead, 6ff, 10, 67, 69
Warburton, John, 184
Washington, George, 294, 312, 314
Waterford, 98
Watson, John F., XV, 45 *n* 81, 62 *n* 143
Wealth, 171
Webb, Maria, 29 *n* 45, 33 *n* 56, 36 *n* 63-65, 107 *n* 223, 153 *n* 354, 161, 167f, 303 *n* 654, 344
Weems, Mason L., 30, 71 *n* 157
'Welcome, The', 40, 67, 223
Wells, 125f, 196
Wesley, John, 6, 129f, 174, 297, 323
West, Benjamin, XVf, 298
West Jersey, *see* New Jersey
Wetenhall, Edward, 105, 151 *n* 342, 167, 280
Weymouth, M.P. and Viscount, 26, 86
White, John, 99
Whitefield, George, 130
Whitehead, George, 112, 120f, 132f, 135, 145, 148, 151f, 202, 263 *n* 554, 281f
Whiting, John, 124ff, 136 *n* 297
Whitlocke, Sir Bulstrode, 280
Whitten, Wilfred, 300 *n* 638
Whittier, John G., 206 *n* 451, 247, 324
Wilkinson, John, 176
William III, 21, 98, 180, 196f, 236, 238, 251, 254f, 261, 265-78, 281, 283, 286f, 319
Williams, Elizabeth, 108
Williams, Roger, 149, 218f
Wilson, Thomas, 76 *n* 166, 292
Wilson, Woodrow, 332
Winchester, Marquis of, 277
Winthrop, John, 218
Women's equality, 176f
Wood, Anthony, 73 *n* 162
Woolman, John, 171
Worminghurst, 11ff, 30, 39, 40, 44, 49, 54ff, 59, 149, 270
Wright, ———, 69 *n* 155

York, Duke of, *see* James II
Youghall, 96